Woodrow Wilson
LIFE AND LETTERS

Books on Woodrow Wilson
by Ray Stannard Baker

◇◇◇◇◇◇◇◇◇◇◇◇◇◇◇◇◇◇◇◇◇◇◇◇◇◇◇◇◇

WHAT WILSON DID AT PARIS
WOODROW WILSON AND WORLD SETTLE-
MENT, AN ACCOUNT OF THE PEACE CON-
FERENCE AT PARIS, IN THREE VOLUMES.
WOODROW WILSON, LIFE AND LETTERS
THE PUBLIC PAPERS OF WOODROW WILSON,
AUTHORIZED EDITION, SIX VOLUMES, ED-
ITED, WITH WILLIAM E. DODD

WOODROW WILSON AT HIS DESK IN THE WHITE HOUSE

Woodrow Wilson

LIFE AND LETTERS

Neutrality

1914—1915

BY

RAY STANNARD BAKER

✦

Illustrated

VOLUME FIVE

Garden City, New York
DOUBLEDAY, DORAN & COMPANY, INC.
1935

PRINTED AT THE *Country Life Press*, GARDEN CITY, N. Y., U. S. A.

PREFACE

THIS volume, like those that preceded it, is founded upon the private documents and letters of Woodrow Wilson, entrusted to the author without restriction by Mrs. Wilson. A vast amount of supplementary material furnished by the President's associates and friends has been of the highest service: and the author has profited greatly by the steady flow of memoirs which, through the years, has been illuminating the mighty events connected with the World War.

Especial acknowledgments are due to the scholarly assistance, in the analysis of the material, of the late Dr. Joseph V. Fuller, chief of the Research Section of the Department of State. Katharine E. Brand has been an invaluable associate in the preparation of the copy and the reading of the proofs.

The author is warmly appreciative of suggestions and criticisms by Professor Lawrence B. Packard of Amherst College, Dr. Carlton Savage of the Department of State, Professor A. Howard Meneely of Dartmouth College, and Mr. Harley A. Notter of Leland Stanford University.

Throughout the task Mrs. Woodrow Wilson has been a firm friend and a helpful critic.

CONTENTS

CONTENTS

VOLUME V

LIST OF ILLUSTRATIONS

LIST OF FACSIMILES

Woodrow Wilson
LIFE AND LETTERS

Woodrow Wilson

LIFE AND LETTERS

CHAPTER I

FACING THE WORLD WAR

Three thousand miles of sea . . . roll between us and the elder past of the world. We are isolated here. We cannot see other nations in detail, and looked at in the large they do not seem like ourselves.

Address at Princeton, October 21, 1896.

Absorbed in our own development, we had fallen into a singular ignorance of the rest of the world. The isolation in which we lived was quite without parallel in modern history.

Article in the Atlantic Monthly, *March, 1901.*

While we have worked at our tasks of peace the circumstances of the whole age have been altered by war.

Address to Congress, December 8, 1914.

I. DETERMINED NEUTRALITY

WOODROW WILSON'S first reaction toward the World War, like that of most of his countrymen, was one of incredulity. Even after a major conflict had become a certainty, and conditions had arisen which the President himself regarded as "unparalleled in recent history,"[1] he could still on August 2nd refer to it as "this incredible European catastrophe."

Elements of a panic were not wanting. The New York stock exchange was closed on July 31st, ocean liners were held in their ports, and tens of thousands of Americans, stranded in war-torn Europe, were clamouring for trans-

---

[1] Woodrow Wilson to A. W. Trenholm, August 2, 1914.

portation homeward. "Scare heads" in the newspapers described the blazing events:

"GERMANY DECLARES WAR ON RUSSIA, FIRST SHOTS ARE FIRED; FRANCE IS MOBILIZING AND MAY BE DRAWN IN TOMORROW; PLANS TO RESCUE THE 100,000 AMERICANS NOW IN EUROPE"[1]

On the morning of August 3rd, the day that brought the fateful news that Germany had declared war on France, the President clearly expressed his view of the situation in a statement to newspaper correspondents who had gathered, an unusually silent and expectant group, in the Executive Office.

He came in alert, erect, well-groomed, but to more than one of the men present he looked, however much he might conceal his emotions, anxious and careworn. They could not forget that, in another room of the White House, Mrs. Wilson lay desperately ill. He lost no time in coming to the subject that weighed heavily upon the entire nation:

"Gentlemen . . . I want to say this . . . in the present state of affairs . . . you should be extremely careful not to add in any way to the excitement. . . .

"So far as we are concerned, there is no cause for excitement. There is great inconvenience, for the time being, in the money market and in our exchanges, and, temporarily, in the handling of our crops, but America is absolutely prepared to meet the financial situation and to straighten everything out without any material difficulty."

He came then to the core of his own conviction as to the part that America should play:

"I want to have the pride of feeling that America, if nobody else, has her self-possession and stands ready with

---

[1] New York *Times*, August 2, 1914.

calmness of thought and steadiness of purpose to help the rest of the world. And we can do it and reap a great permanent glory out of doing it, provided we all coöperate to see that nobody loses his head."[1]

There can be no doubt that these assurances, this steadiness, in the White House encouraged a greater calmness of view throughout the country. The "advice was as practical and its appeal as strong for all the people as for the correspondents."[2]

During the day of August 3rd the President was preparing to take his first official step—the issuance of the usual proclamations of neutrality between the United States and the warring nations. He studied two forms forwarded to him by the State Department, finally writing to Secretary Bryan:

"I agree with Mr. Lansing in preferring the longer and more explicit proclamation."

The proclamations, issued on the following days, were at first nowhere criticized. Even Ambassador Page, who came later to detest the policy, remarked in a letter of August 2nd to the President, "How wise our no-alliance policy is!"[3] The British themselves believed for some time that the United States was of more service to their cause as a neutral than as a belligerent.

In issuing the proclamations of neutrality the President had followed the traditional and normal course; but in his own mind a merely inactive position was intolerable. He wanted to "help the rest of the world." He began at once, therefore, to consider the tender of the good offices of the United States in the interest of mediation.

It is interesting to note that the first dispatch dealing

---

[1] New York *Times*, August 4, 1914.

[2] *Ibid.*

[3] From the original document. See also *The Life and Letters of Walter H. Page*, Vol. III, p. 130.

with the problems of the war found among the President's papers was that of July 28th from Mr. Herrick, ambassador to France. The situation was the gravest in history, the ambassador reported; civilization was at stake; and he suggested a strong plea for "delay and moderation."[1] It is one of the easy "ifs" of history whether, had the President acted boldly at that moment, by throwing a disinterested plea for calm consideration into the panicky counsels of flustered European diplomats, some result might not have been accomplished. Who knows? It might have resulted in nothing beyond a further confusion of the issue of responsibility; for there was no method, no organization, in the world capable of meeting such a catastrophe—only a babel of confused and frightened voices. As General Smuts, a clear-eyed observer, has written:

"Through a thick fog of misunderstanding, confusion, suspicion and ill will, they [the diplomats of the Great Powers] were bombarding one another with endless diplomatic notes at long range. I am positive that not one of them knew exactly how matters stood at any stage of these frenzied negotiations."[2]

In one sense the United States government did act upon Herrick's suggestion, by direction, or possibly only with the approval of, the President. On the evening of July 28th, Secretary Bryan cabled to Page in London:

"Is there in your opinion any likelihood that the good offices of the United States if offered under Article 3 of the Hague Convention would be acceptable or serve any high purpose in the present crisis?"[3]

This was a natural thing to do, since England appeared at the moment to be the central factor in all efforts for a

---

[1]*Foreign Relations of the United States*, Supplement, 1914, pp. 18–19.
[2]General Jan Christian Smuts, in an article published October 28, 1928.
[3]*Foreign Relations of the United States*, Supplement, 1914, p. 19.

peaceable settlement, with some of its leaders as anxious to maintain the peace as any American.[1]

The idea had, indeed, already occurred to Page as a natural consequence of his enthusiasm for Anglo-American coöperation. He replied to Bryan, on the 29th, that he had on his own responsibility asked Sir Edward Grey to inform him if the good offices of the United States could be of use, and received an expression of thanks and a promise to let him know.[2] On the 31st, Page telegraphed that he had approached Sir Edward Grey a second time. Again there was an expression of "great gratitude," but nothing positive, only politely evasive questions as to whether the United States had made offers "at Vienna or St. Petersburg or Berlin."

Grey was pinning his faith, as he told Page, on his "proposals looking to the localization of hostilities," and it is plain that he did not want any suggestions at that time from America.[3] There may have been, in this position, something of the timidity of the old-time diplomacy lest amateur bungling precipitate the crisis it aimed to avert. Colonel House's letter to the President on August 1st— written from Prides Crossing, Massachusetts, without knowledge of what Page and Bryan had already done— lends colour to this view:

"Please let me suggest that you do not let Mr. Bryan make any overtures to any of the powers involved. They look upon him as purely visionary and it would lessen the weight of your influence if you desire to use it yourself later."[4]

Certain it is that by August 3rd the President and

---

[1] At this time a considerable part of the British Cabinet was for maintaining British neutrality. (See John Viscount Morley, *Memorandum on Resignation*.)

[2] *Foreign Relations of the United States*, Supplement, 1914, pp. 19–20.

[3] *Ibid.*, pp. 24–25.

[4] From original letter in Mr. Wilson's files. Also in *The Intimate Papers of Colonel House*, Vol. I, p. 279.

Secretary Bryan were being discouraged by the responses from Sir Edward Grey, and by Ambassador Page, who telegraphed on that day:

"My very definite opinion is that there is not the slightest chance of any result if our good offices be offered at any continental capital. This is confirmed by the judgement of the British Foreign Office. We may have a chance after the war has reached a breathing space."[1]

On the same day, the President explained, in a letter to Secretary Lane, who had written to suggest that he tender his good offices:

"As a matter of fact, I had already done so, as far as I thought it prudent or possible, but things went so fast and so far there upon the very first rush that apparently there is at present, at any rate, no opening for us."

But the President, though frustrated, did not give up his hope of pacifying the maddened nations. There were many evidences in the press, and a resolution in the Senate,[2] which indicated the feeling of the country. On August 4th a letter came from Colonel House:

"Our people are deeply shocked at the enormity of this general European war, and I see here and there regret that you did not use your good offices in behalf of peace."[3]

Wilson replied by telegraph:

"Letter of third received. Do you think I could and should act now and if so how?"

[1]*Foreign Relations of the United States*, Supplement, 1914, p. 37. A letter of Sir Edward Grey, written on August 7th, carried the same intimation, and indicated that war must come before mediation:

"I knew that President Wilson wished to mediate, and, whenever there appeared a fair opportunity of stopping the war by mediation, we should, I felt sure, throw our influence on the side of it, and, having taken part in the war, our influence would be stronger than if we had stood outside." (Sir Edward Grey, *Twenty-five Years*, Vol. II, p. 163.)

[2]On August 4th Senator McCumber introduced a resolution calling upon the President to offer the good offices of the United States. *Congressional Record*, Vol. 51, p. 13210.

[3]August 3, 1914. From document in Mr. Wilson's files. Also in *The Life and Letters of Walter H. Page*, Vol. I, p. 317.

House immediately rejoined:

"Telegram received. Would advise doing nothing for the moment. Richard Olney[1] lunches with me here to-morrow and with your permission I will confer with him and get his opinion. I am entirely satisfied of its value in this country."

On the following day, the 5th, House telegraphed that Olney agreed with him that "it would be unwise to tender your good offices at this time." Both urged that the public demand for action, now voiced in a Senate resolution, be met by a press statement "on high authority" as to the efforts made in the past, and that the American ambassadors should merely inform the belligerent governments "that you stand ready to tender your good offices whenever such an offer is desired."[2] In a follow-up letter on the same day, House repeated the caution to keep Bryan out of any statements made.

"I hate to harp upon Mr. Bryan, but you cannot know as I do how he is thought of in this connection. You and I understand better and know that the grossest sort of injustice is done him."[3]

It was not, however, a characteristic of the President to give up easily. He must have been struck by the danger of sparing even a futile gesture that might help rescue a world rushing to destruction before his eyes. He now had before him reports from all the capitals of Europe revealing the extraordinary gravity of the situation. Great Britain, which had discouraged his previous approaches, seemed now to be slipping into the war. Pressure from members of the cabinet, especially Mr. Bryan, was urgent. On

[1] Richard Olney, whose advice the President greatly esteemed, had been Attorney General, and later Secretary of State, in Cleveland's cabinet. Wilson had offered to make him ambassador at the Court of St. James's.

[2] From original letter in Mr. Wilson's files. Also in *The Life and Letters of Walter H. Page*, Vol. I, pp. 318–319.

[3] *The Intimate Papers of Colonel House*, Vol. I, pp. 282–283.

the afternoon of the 4th, even before he had received House's first telegram[1] opposing action, he had reached a decision. After a long cabinet meeting he went at once to the upper room where Mrs. Wilson lay dying and there, sitting by her bedside, wrote out his brief message, in shorthand, offering "good offices" to the nations of Europe:[2]

"As official head of one of the powers signatory to the Hague Convention, I feel it to be my privilege and my duty under article three of that Convention to say to you in a spirit of most earnest friendship that I should welcome an opportunity to act in the interest of European peace, either now or at any other time that might be thought more suitable, as an occasion to serve you and all concerned in a way that would afford me lasting cause for gratitude and happiness."[3]

Telegrams summoning the representatives of belligerent states to come and receive the communication were sent out by Secretary Bryan just before three o'clock, but the document was not delivered until the following day, the 5th.

Wilson wrote to House:

"Events moved so fast yesterday that I came to the conclusion that if you had known what I knew as soon as I knew it, the advice of your telegram would probably have been different.

"At any rate, I took the risk and sent messages to the heads of the several countries. It can, at least, do no harm."[4]

It was, of course, hopeless. Of the replies, some of which

---

[1] It did not arrive until 9:05 p.m. on August 4th.

[2] See *Woodrow Wilson, Life and Letters*, Vol. IV, p. 477. Bryan wrote that the note had his "hearty approval," and complimented its "felicitous wording."

[3] From document in Mr. Wilson's files. Also *Foreign Relations of the United States*, Supplement, 1914, p. 42.

[4] August 5, 1914.

My dear Mr President.

I am close copy of dispatch sent to St. Petersburg Berlin × Vienna & allow me in doing so to express my hearty approval of your act and to compliment you on the felicitous wording of the offer. With assurance etc. yours truly W. J. Bryan

Letter from W. J. Bryan to Woodrow Wilson, expressing "hearty approval" of the President's offer of good offices.

9

were greatly delayed, none was an immediate acceptance. All the governments—the Kaiser at greatest length in a telegram from Ambassador Gerard received on August 15th[1]—argued that they were absolutely in the right. It was apparent, whatever the earlier chances might have been, that the governments intended to seek a decision by force of arms before they would tolerate counsels of conciliation. Modern war, indeed, involves an immediate transfer of power from civil to military leadership. The necessity for initial speed in attack—lest the enemy strike first—makes this inevitable. All prearranged plans hinge upon the element of time: the generals await impatiently even the formalities of a declaration of war. In short, prevention of war must come before power passes out of civilian hands; it must come by civilian organization and leadership. Wilson stood no chance against the military machine of Europe once it was set going.

Both the President and his Secretary of State, in all of these early feverish activities, did their best to maintain a position of friendly service that might enable them, when the time came, to be useful in the cause of peace. Every request that the American diplomatic service represent belligerent countries in the capitals of their enemies was promptly accepted. When Mr. Whitlock, minister to Belgium, in a telegram received on August 5th, expressed reluctance to act for Germany, Bryan at once replied, no doubt after consulting the President:

"In this critical hour it becomes necessary for our government to render every assistance that a neutral can render, not only as an international duty, but that we may be in better position to exert our influence for peace."[2]

When Japan came into the war, Bryan, delighted with

---

[1]*Foreign Relations of the United States*, Supplement, 1914, pp. 60–61.
[2]*Ibid.*, p. 736.

his new sense of usefulness, could write almost exultantly to Wilson:

"Japan wants us to act for her in Germany & Germany wants us to act for her in Japan. We are in demand."

One other official step remained to be taken in these tumultuous early days of the war. The United States government had already proclaimed its neutrality, it had tendered its good offices: it must now establish clearly its intention of upholding the rights of American trade to the limits of international law. The most recent and comprehensive effort to reach a definite policy regarding the rights of neutral trade in time of war had been made five years before, in 1908–1909, at an international naval conference held in London.[1] After laborious discussions by a distinguished group of experts headed by the Earl of Desart, a statement of what were considered "generally recognized principles of international law," called the Declaration of London, had been presented to the nations of the world. It was not, however, formally accepted by any government; in the United States it was ratified by the Senate, but not by the President. The decisive rejection was that made by Great Britain, the world's greatest naval power, whose government finally concluded, under pressure of urgent public opinion, that its delegates had gone too far in placing limits upon the use of its most potent weapon.

Nevertheless, this Declaration, at the outbreak of the war, although not completely meeting all the new problems involved,[2] was the latest summary of the best thought of the world upon the thorny problems of contraband and blockade. It was, indeed, the only authoritative attempt to deal with situations of great danger, where there were few

---

[1] It was an outgrowth of the Hague Conference of 1907.

[2] For example, it was unsatisfactory in that it did not treat of such entirely new instrumentalities as flying machines.

accepted principles to rely upon, and it was commonly looked upon by jurists of repute as constituting the best there was in current theory and practice.

It seemed at the moment, therefore, the wisest course for the United States to press for the general recognition of this Declaration. The dispatch was drafted in the State Department, probably by Mr. Lansing, then Counselor, but we know that the President saw and approved the copy of the message sent to him on August 6th, for it bears his "Okeh." The proposal no doubt seemed too reasonable to be questioned, and it was telegraphed at once to the representatives of belligerent countries.[1]

Germany and Austria-Hungary promptly replied that they would conform to the Declaration if their opponents did so,[2] but the British government asserted its intention to adhere only "subject to certain modifications and additions which they judge indispensable to the efficient conduct of their naval operations."[3] This attitude determined that of Great Britain's allies and, ultimately, that of her enemies.

For more than two months the American government continued to advocate the general acceptance of the Declaration and urge its unqualified recognition upon the British government. It was the beginning of long and often acrimonious controversies upon the subject of contraband and blockade to which, as we shall see later, the President gave the closest attention. Departures from the rules laid down in the Declaration followed thick and fast. In such a crisis any plan that limited the activities of the belligerent nations—whether the British fleet or the German army—was destined to be bitterly resented by partisans of either. Already there had been complaints of

---

[1] For text, see *Foreign Relations of the United States*, Supplement, 1914, p. 216.
[2] *Ibid.*, pp. 217, 218.
[3] *Ibid.*, pp. 218–220.

partiality from German-Americans,[1] and Ambassador Page, who was devoted to the principle of the unity of the English-speaking peoples, considered the pressure for the recognition of the Declaration "the first great mistake the American government made in its relations with Great Britain."[2] "That Declaration they [the British] think would have given the victory to Germany" if the Allies had adopted it, he declared in a later statement.[3]

It would have seemed that these engrossing activities, to say nothing of the crisis in his own personal life, would have absorbed the entire time of the President. But Congress was in session, and the government had to continue to function as in ordinary times. We find, in examining the letters and documents, that Wilson followed with unremitting zeal the domestic legislation upon which he had set his heart. For example, on August 4th and 5th, when he was tendering the nation's good offices, he was also heavily engaged on the home front. He wrote to Congressman Adamson:

"I understand that a vote is set for today on the Trade Commission bill in the Senate. It will, therefore, I suppose, go to conference tomorrow.

"I have been meaning for some days to ask the pleasure of a conference with you about the bill, but these war matters and a score of others have come upon me in such a flood that apparently it is a matter of despair to set aside the half hour, or whatever it may be, that would be necessary. I am, therefore, going to ask you to forgive me if I take the liberty of sending you this note to express my deep interest in the retention in the bill in its integrity of Section V, the section about unfair competition." .

[1]Professor Hugo Münsterberg of Harvard reported to the President great dissatisfaction among German-Americans.

[2]*The Life and Letters of Walter H. Page*, Vol. I, p. 373.

[3]From original memorandum left by Page with the President in August, 1916. Also in *The Life and Letters of Walter H. Page*, Vol. I, pp. 373-375.

Even during the days from August 6th to 12th, which were devoted to sorrowful duties connected with the death of Mrs. Wilson, the tremendous problems of a world on fire could not be wholly excluded. This was no time for the luxury of personal sorrow. The area of the conflict was steadily widening. On the day of the President's return from Georgia, where Mrs. Wilson was buried (August 12th), war was declared between Great Britain and Austria-Hungary. The German army was crashing through Belgium, and the Russians, mobilizing ponderously, were facing westward. There were premonitions of action by Japan which, by involving the Pacific, might confront America with Asiatic as well as European problems. In Washington a distraught Congress gave no guidance to a nation stunned by a situation that seemed as unwarranted as it was unbelievable. No one knew what to say, or to think, or to do.

On the long trip northward from the funeral, the President sat in almost uninterrupted silence.

"Let me alone," he said to Dr. Grayson, "I want to think."

All day he remained on the observation platform of the train. It was country he knew well, had known all his life —the Old South, where he was born and bred, where he had begun his career, where he had married. His earliest memories were of this smiling land torn by another war, his boyhood filled with experiences of the bitter aftermath of that war. He had considered it the "dark chapter of history,"[1] out of which had finally arisen a new America. During all of his mature years he had been thinking and planning, first as an educator deeply interested in political science, then as a statesman, for the progressive development of this "new nation" toward a "new freedom." It

---

[1] "The Reconstruction of the Southern States," in the *Atlantic Monthly*, January, 1901. *The Public Papers of Woodrow Wilson*, Vol. I, p. 388.

was this America that had conferred upon him its highest honour, and he had covenanted solemnly to serve the interests of its people: "God helping me, I will not fail them. . . ."[1]

Wilson's method was that of the scholar who goes down into his own mind. Again and again in his life we have seen the process repeated: in the early years in England, during his more or less solitary vacations, from which he returned with new purpose to the struggles at Princeton; in Bermuda, after his election in 1912, where a month of solitude fired him with a renewed vision of a reconstructed nation. The method has vast advantages as a source of power and self-confidence; it has also grave dangers for the man of action, particularly the political leader called upon to face unexpected practical problems. In later months it was to lead him sometimes into difficulties and mistakes, for the scholar delving in his own mind, consulting his own spirit, may find there the highest ideals, the most determined purposes—but rarely all the facts in any given situation. Nevertheless, from first to last, in every crisis, it was Wilson's sovereign method. It was, moreover, one of the secrets, perhaps the chief secret, of his power with the people—a power that often puzzled more experienced politicians, since the President seemed to know little and see less of the people—for in penetrating the secrets of his own mind, going down into his own deepest thoughts and aspirations, he descended, as Emerson says of the poet, "into the secrets of all minds . . . in utter solitude, remembering his spontaneous thoughts and recording them, he is found to have recorded that which men in crowded cities find true for themselves also."

He returned to Washington plainly more determined than ever before upon the two courses of action which he

[1]Inaugural address, March 4, 1913. *The Public Papers of Woodrow Wilson,* Vol. III, p. 6.

had already outlined: to maintain the neutrality of the United States, and at the same time aid in every possible way to bring peace again to the world. Almost the first thing he did on the morning of August 13th was to urge upon Senator Stone, chairman of the Foreign Relations committee, the ratification of twenty of the Bryan treaties then before the Senate—hoping, however vainly, that the effort in itself would make the "deepest possible impression upon the world."

"Now that the peace treaties are under actual consideration, may I not send just a line to say that I most earnestly hope that it may be possible to secure their ratification without any restriction as to their scope? They are intended to cover all questions in dispute of every character, so that no cause for war will be left uncovered. This is their peculiar characteristic and is what gives them a force and character which other treaties have not had. If we can have investigation of all questions not covered by other treaties, we will hold war at arm's length in such a fashion as I believe to render it practically impossible. This is a time when such action on our part would make the deepest possible impression upon the world and I covet and pray for it on that account."[1]

Each day the situation grew more acute. Problems of the protection of American shipping, problems of the control of radio messages, protests from both Germans and English, an ultimatum by Japan to Germany which presaged the spread of the war into the Far East, crowded upon the President's attention. It was growing more and more difficult for Americans to avoid the contagion of excited controversy which was sweeping the world. There had begun to develop powerful and excited pro-German and pro-Ally groups within our own borders, neither loath

---

[1] The Senate responded immediately, on that very day, by ratifying eighteen of the treaties.

to express their sympathies. Upon the first real test, our romantic dogma of the melting-pot, our faith in the mystic significance of the ritual of naturalization, began to weaken. On the 17th, Wilson, in a letter to Bryan, set up "perfect impartiality" as the basis of handling the controversy over the control of German wireless stations in America, of which the British had complained: and on the very same day he met a protest from the National German Alliance regarding Japanese action in the Far East with a memorandum for his secretary, Mr. Tumulty:

"Please acknowledge this in some gracious way and say that they may rest assured that this government will do everything in its power to serve peace and accommodation."

As a result of all this confusion and growing passion which might, unless resisted, rend the unity of America, the President had been meditating a further appeal to the people. He saw that neutrality might easily degenerate into mechanical and external observances, cynically challenged by partisans of both sides. What he desired was a sincere neutrality, a genuine suspension of judgement, in the hope that the United States might serve as first friend in the interest of peace. The sanctions of international law could not rest with any security upon mere lip service —to *say* that we were neutral—but upon an attitude of the mind. He had a dread, all his life, of "mere legalism." There are some evidences that he had considered, if not actually drafted, a message during his journey homeward from Rome, Georgia. At any rate the document, written in shorthand on four slips of paper—the original is still in his files—was completed on August 17th and given to the press on the following day, probably after some discussion with his cabinet which met that morning. Addressed to "my fellow countrymen," it made an impassioned appeal for steadiness, for a determined attitude of peace. He urged "the sort of speech and conduct which will best safeguard the nation against distress and disaster." He even went on to argue:

"The United States must be neutral in fact as well as in name during these days that are to try men's souls. We must be impartial in thought as well as in action. . . ."

Mindful of the inconclusive nature of the evidence as to responsibility for the horrors let loose upon the world, he expressed his desire that the nation maintain an "undisturbed judgement" and refrain from jumping to conclusions.

He concluded with an appeal for restraint:

"Shall we not resolve to put upon ourselves the restraints which will bring to our people the happiness and the great and lasting influence for peace we covet for them?"[1]

It is clear that he had steadily in mind, as one of the chief reasons for this restraint, this avoidance of "divisions amongst us," the opportunity and the duty of the "one great nation at peace" to "play a part of impartial mediation" and to "speak the counsels of peace and accommodation."[2]

It was an appeal marked by sound sense, true wisdom; if it could have been followed, it would have strengthened and simplified the problem of America. The first reception was indeed highly favourable, both Democratic and Republican newspapers praising it highly. Colonel House wrote effusively on August 22nd:

"Your address on neutrality is one of the finest things you have ever done, and it has met with universal approbation. Every day editorials of the Republican press speak

---

[1] *The Public Papers of Woodrow Wilson*, Vol. III, pp. 157–159.

[2] This general appeal was preceded by somewhat similar action when, on August 6th, Wilson wrote letters to the Secretaries of War and Navy suggesting that they request all officers, active or retired, to refrain from public comments of a military or naval character relating to the war.

of you as if you were of their party instead of being the idol of ours."[1]

At this time several leaders, who were soon to become bitter critics of Wilson, approved his general policy of neutrality. Senator Lodge believed that our duty involved "the observance of strict neutrality as between the belligerents, with all of whom we are at peace," but in the aftermath, when he wrote his book (1925) he criticized the President's demand for neutrality in thought as well as in action:

"The President's demand was, to my thinking, a perfectly unsound as well as utterly impractical position to take."[2]

Colonel Roosevelt, even a month later, was scarcely less vigorous than the President in advocating strict neutrality:

"It is certainly eminently desirable that we should remain entirely neutral, and nothing but urgent need would warrant breaking our neutrality and taking sides one way or the other."

While Roosevelt's emphasis, unlike that of Wilson, was upon the protection of "our own interests," he too, like Wilson, saw in neutrality the conservation of "our influence for helping toward the reëstablishment of general peace when the time comes."[3]

But the President's appeal, whatever the sincerity of its purpose, however conducive to the real interests of America, was too much for those who had already formed their opinions, whether pro-Ally or pro-German, and who wished to win others to them. How could one be neutral in thought?

The message of August 18th may be said to have con-

---

[1] *The Intimate Papers of Colonel House*, Vol. I, p. 284.

[2] Henry Cabot Lodge, *The Senate and the League of Nations*, pp. 26, 30.

[3] Theodore Roosevelt, "The World War; Its Tragedies and Its Lessons," in the *Outlook*, September 23, 1914.

cluded the first phase of Wilson's attempt to meet the problems presented by the war. He had placed himself and his government behind a policy of determined neutrality, he had tendered "good offices" in the interest of mediation, and by advocating the Declaration of London he had firmly indicated his intention of upholding the rights of American trade.

II. WILSON AND THE AMERICAN STATE OF MIND AT THE OUTBREAK OF THE WAR

However thoroughly the world may have been prepared for war in August 1914, it was utterly unprepared for peace. The Hague Court, the arbitration treaties, the Bryan treaties, the American President's offers of mediation, were straws in the wind of traditional fears and jealousies, of new-born economic needs. All that the strongest, richest, most peaceful nation in the world could do was to stand aside while Europe slipped into anarchy, and declare that it would take no part in the tragedy. Not only was there no efficient organization, no trusted method, for meeting the problems involved, but no statesman of any nation could be sure that he knew all the facts upon which he must decide great issues of life and death. No one knew how far each nation was bound by secret treaties, private economic agreements, defensive alliances and ententes. If this was true of Europe, how much more of America! Neither the President nor any of his more important advisers was familiar with the immediate background of the crisis or of the issues involved. They were absorbed with critical domestic reforms, and, in the beginning, regarded foreign complications as unwelcome distractions. Wilson especially, applying the great powers of his "single-track mind" to internal policies in which he was profoundly interested and which he had been elected to solve, had turned his attention somewhat grudgingly, if energetically, to the Mexican imbroglio and other complications in the Caribbean and the Far East. As for the greater problems of foreign relationships involving Europe, he had believed entirely, as he said in his first annual address to Congress in December 1913—eight months before the war broke—that "many happy manifestations multiply about us of a growing cordiality and sense of community of interest among the nations, foreshadowing an age of settled peace and good will."[1]

American opinion, so far as European affairs were concerned, was not only uninformed, but largely uninterested. The impelling motive of diplomacy in Europe, and one of the principal causes of the far more highly developed concern with international politics—that is, fear—was almost, if not wholly, lacking in America. We were strong, we were rich, we were isolated, we were safe. A few slogans readily sufficed us: "avoid entangling alliances," provide for the "open door" for our trade, insist upon the more or less nebulous implications of a sacred Monroe Doctrine. It was difficult for us to believe in the possibility of a general war.

Beyond and above this negative position of the American, which, after all, did not quite content us, we were moved by an earnest, if ill-informed, idealism, a real desire to help other countries, and forward the cause of universal peace—provided it cost us little or nothing. This spirit had been expressed in years past by our interest in the Hague Court, in arbitration treaties, and at the beginning of the Wilson administration, in Bryan's plan for a "cooling-off" diplomacy. It had inspired our attitude, though with canny limitations, in our dealings with Cuba following the Spanish War, our promises to free the Filipinos, our generous treatment of China at the time of the Boxer uprising. Back of it lay a strange compound of many and deep traits of the American character—among them the reli-

[1]*The Public Papers of Woodrow Wilson*, Vol. III, p. 70.

(PEACE).

The country, I am ~~happy~~ *thankful* to say, is at peace with
all the world, and many happy *manifestations* multiply about us
of a growing cordiality and sense of community of
interest among the nations, foreshadowing an age
of settled peace and good-will. More and more
willingly each decade do the nations manifest
their willingness to bind themselves by solemn
treaty to the processes of peace, the processes
of frankness and fair concession. So far the
United States has stood at the front of such
negotiations. She will, I earnestly hope and
confidently believe, give fresh proof of her
sincere ~~earnest~~ adherence to the cause of international
friendship by ratifying the several treaties of
arbitration awaiting renewal by the Senate. In
addition to these, it has been the privilege of the
Department of State, to negotiate with *of*
the leading and most enlightened government s of
the world treaties by which it is agreed that
wh. ~~cannot be resolved by the ordinary processes of~~
whenever differences of interest or of policy a-
rise they shall be publicly analyzed, ~~and~~ discus-
and reported upon sed by a tribunal chosen by the parties, before
either nation determines its course of action.
There is only one possible standard by which to
determine controversies between the United States
and other nations, and that is compounded of
these two elements: our own honour and our obligations to the peace of the world. A test so
compounded ought easily to ~~make~~ *be made* to govern both
the establishment of new treaty obligations and
the interpretation of those already assumed

(diplomacy)

First page of the President's text for his annual address to Congress,
December 2, 1913. Written on the President's own typewriter, with
corrections in his handwriting.

gious enthusiasm that inspired the foreign-missionary movement, pervasive and deep-seated, especially in the South and West. There was also something, perhaps, of the neighbourhood helpfulness of the pioneer life out of which we had grown; something of our traditional attitude of benevolence toward immigration from "downtrodden Europe"; and much of the intense national sense that American institutions, political and economic as well as religious, were not only the best in the world but indiscriminately good for all people of whatever colour, faith, or nationality. It was a benevolence vastly stimulated by a sense of our superior wealth, our unchallenged power, our confident safety. If it was naïve, it was also, in certain aspects, magnificent—and ridiculous. Henry Ford with his Peace Ship was an extreme manifestation of these characteristics of the American spirit; Colonel William B. Thompson, a little later, spending a million dollars to prevent anarchism in Russia, was another.

Mr. Bryan, who was perhaps nearer to the mass mind of America than any other leader of his time, expressed these views in a highly rhetorical, but entirely sincere, statement, which he sent to Mr. Wilson as an indication of his attitude just before he was appointed Secretary of State:

"I can conceive of a national destiny surpassing the glories of the present and the past—a destiny which meets the responsibilities of today and measures up to the possibilities of the future. Behold a republic, resting securely upon the foundation stones quarried by revolutionary patriots from the mountain of eternal truth—a republic applying in practice and proclaiming to the world the self-evident propositions that all men are created equal; that they are endowed by their Creator with inalienable rights; that governments are instituted among men to secure these rights; and that governments derive their just powers from the consent of the governed. . . .

"Behold a republic standing erect while empires all around are bowed beneath the weight of their own armaments—a republic whose flag is loved while other flags are only feared.

"Behold a republic increasing in population, in wealth, in strength, and in influence, solving the problems of civilization and hastening the coming of an universal brotherhood—a republic which shakes thrones and dissolves aristocracies by its silent example and gives light and inspiration to those that sit in darkness.

"Behold a republic gradually but surely becoming the supreme moral factor in the world's progress and the accepted arbiter of the world's disputes. . . ."[1]

Whatever Wilson may have thought of the rhetoric, he could sympathize with the attitude and the intention of the ideals here expressed. Many of his own addresses in the earlier months of the presidency were marked by a similar earnest idealism. He also had dreamed of a government that could be "put at the service of humanity,"[2] just as earlier his inspiration had been to create a university which should serve the nation: "Princeton for the Nation's Service." He believed that "the old order is dead,"[3] and that America, moved by "moral judgement" that was, after all, the "final judgement,"[4] was to be the leader of a new order. There was to be no "selfish aggrandizement"[5]: "No man who thinks first of himself and afterwards of his country can call himself an American"[6]; service is the prime idea.[7] It was the obligation of the

[1]The Memoirs of William Jennings Bryan, pp. 500–501.

[2]Inaugural address, March 4, 1913. The Public Papers of Woodrow Wilson, Vol. III, p. 4.

[3]Interview with Samuel G. Blythe, May 23, 1914. Ibid., p. 112.

[4]Address in Philadelphia, July 4, 1914. Ibid., p. 146.

[5]Address to Congress, April 20, 1914. Ibid., p. 102.

[6]Address at the unveiling of a statue to the memory of Commodore John Barry, at Washington, May 16, 1914. Ibid., p. 110.

[7]Address at Swarthmore College, October 25, 1913. Ibid., p. 57.

strong,[1] the new *noblesse oblige*, to establish the "standards of righteousness and humanity"[2] in the world. "Her flag" —the American flag—"is the flag not only of America but of humanity."[3]

Two other Americans who were to play a large part in the diplomacy of the war were in the beginning wholly sympathetic with these general ideas. Walter Hines Page, the new ambassador at the Court of St. James's, and Colonel House were also dreaming of a new order and a new service, in which American leadership was to play an exalted part. An inspirational tone, a wistful enthusiasm, marked the earlier letters that passed between them or reached the President:

"Nobody can lead in such a new era but the United States."[4]

"We have more people and more capable people and many times more territory than both England and Germany; and we have more *potential* wealth than all Europe."[5]

"The President is entitled to some big work by the rest of us; and surely the international situation is such that the U. S. can do a great job."[6]

As to the methods to be employed, there were, however, considerable divergences of opinion which were later to broaden into chasms. With the idealist, method is everything, or almost everything; many can dream, few know how to make their dreams come true.

From the beginning, Page saw the new era coming as a result of a kind of Anglo-American entente, each party

---

[1]Address to Congress, March 5, 1914. *The Public Papers of Woodrow Wilson*, Vol. III, p. 93.

[2]Address at Gettysburg, July 4, 1913. *Ibid.*, p. 42.

[3]Address in Philadelphia, July 4, 1914. *Ibid.*, p. 147.

[4]Memorandum written in 1913 by Walter H. Page. *The Life and Letters of Walter H. Page*, Vol. I, p. 272.

[5]Walter H. Page to E. M. House, August 28, 1913. *Ibid.*, p. 270.

[6]Walter H. Page to E. M. House, December 26, 1913.

to it helping the other to solve its problems and heal its feuds with other powers. Wilson was to go to England to cement the understanding and dramatize the new relationship.

"What I want . . . is to have the President of the United States and the King of England stand up side by side and let the world take a good look at them!"[1]

House believed that Germany would also help, while suitable opportunities for Japan might presumably be found in China or in regions under British influence.

All these idealistic plans were based upon the unrealistic conception of a more or less disinterested America, supposedly isolated, but so powerful and rich as to be irresistible. As a matter of fact the United States was already deeply immersed in world-trade rivalries; it had distant possessions, such as the Philippine Islands; it was rapidly acquiring new spheres of power and privilege in Central America; its isolation was an unexploded myth; its disinterestedness mainly political. In fact, the entire world was labouring under the fallacy that somehow political stability and international harmony were attainable without meeting and dealing boldly with the economic necessities and jealousies that were chiefly responsible for the friction. Bryan, actuated by political and religious motives, gave no evidence that he ever properly recognized this fatal duality; and Page and House were early engaged upon new political arrangements which would, even though they shifted the balance of power by bringing the United States into the combinations, prolong the "old order."

The President stood apart. He had long before examined the American attitude toward foreign affairs with the detachment of the scholar and the historian. In comment-

---

[1] *The Life and Letters of Walter H. Page*, Vol. I, p. 275.

WALTER HINES PAGE, UNITED STATES AMBASSADOR AT
THE COURT OF ST. JAMES'S

ing upon the Spanish War of 1898, as remarked in a former volume,[1] he had dealt keenly with the essential duality of the American spirit.

"We have become confirmed . . . in the habit of acting under an odd mixture of selfish and altruistic motives . . . we have sympathized with freedom everywhere . . . have pressed handsome principles of equity in international dealings" but, as he remarks, "when issues of our own interest arose, we have not been unselfish. We have shown ourselves kin to all the world, when it came to pushing an advantage."[2]

He calls attention to the fact that "even Mr. Jefferson, philanthropist and champion of peaceable and modest government," also illustrated this "double temper of the people he ruled." His passion for peace, as Wilson observes, "abated when he saw the mouth of the Mississippi about to pass into the hands of France."[3]

Wilson came to the presidency with a clear sense of this "duality," and with a determination to reckon with it. His earliest pronouncements upon foreign affairs, as we have already seen, dealt with disquieting vigour with the economic aspects of foreign problems; for example, his repudiation of "dollar diplomacy" and his attitude toward the "Six Power Loan" to China, which marked the early weeks of his administration.[4]

"Material interests," as he called them, were there: they were realities: but they were not to dominate in foreign affairs any more than in domestic affairs. His foreign policy, indeed, was an extension and enlargement of his formula of domestic liberalism.

---

[1] *Woodrow Wilson, Life and Letters*, Vol. IV, p. 423.

[2] "Democracy and Efficiency," in the *Atlantic Monthly*, March, 1901. *The Public Papers of Woodrow Wilson*, Vol. I, p. 404.

[3] *Ibid.*, p. 405.

[4] See *Woodrow Wilson, Life and Letters*, Vol. IV, p. 55 *ff.*

Other Americans also perceived this duality of interest but from quite a different angle. They were at the opposite pole from Wilson and Bryan; they were mainly merchants and financiers, a small group mostly in the East who were concerned in international economic problems. They were the champions of "dollar diplomacy" in our dealings with backward peoples, and, so far as relations with the stronger nations were concerned, favoured armament against interference, and collaboration on the basis of interest.

Page and House, like Wilson and Bryan, both came from the West and South, where the isolationist-idealistic views chiefly held sway, but they had had a certain contact with the views held in Eastern economic-imperialistic circles, and this had been broadened by their experience in Europe previous to the outbreak of the war. Their conception of a new order involved a kind of sublimation of the "white man's burden" theory of world policy. The rivalries of the Great Powers would be eased by co-operation in world-wide tasks; the danger inherent in their competitive military preparations would be averted by the diversion of these establishments into constructive achievements. As House put it in a conversation with the German ambassador on May 9, 1913:

"They could ensure peace and the proper development of the waste places, besides maintaining an open door and equal opportunity to everyone everywhere."[1]

And Page, in a letter of August 28, 1913, to House:

"We ought to find a way to use them [armies and navies] in cleaning up the tropics under our leadership and under our code of ethics—that everything must be done for the good of the tropical peoples and that nobody may annex a foot of land."[2]

[1] *The Intimate Papers of Colonel House*, Vol. I, p. 240.
[2] *The Life and Letters of Walter H. Page*, Vol. I, p. 271.

The United States should thus hold her place in world politics, not by descending to the level of the imperialistic powers, playing their game of grab and squabble and arm, but by raising them to our level of benevolent treatment of backward peoples through peaceful coöperation, by which, as a consequence, the stronger peoples would also profit. As Page put it, "investments would be safer."[1] The "interests" as well as the "idealists" would thus be won to the support of the programme. Not less important, it would free the United States from the necessity of entering the competition in armament, would in time relieve the European states likewise of the burden, and would avert the danger of a catastrophic conflict.

As a practical first step in this benevolent coöperation, Page sent a memorandum to the President on August 25, 1913, suggesting that England—and perhaps Germany and France—be invited to join us in "cleaning up" Mexico, under a guarantee of territorial integrity. Getting no response to this suggestion, he fell back upon the idea that our conduct in Mexico and the President's utterances on Latin-American relations should serve to educate the British as to the proper way of going about such business, reviving the lesson of Cuba, and should help regenerate British foreign policy.[2] He even believed he was converting Lord Cowdray, the English oil magnate, to the "New Principle"![3]

What Wilson thought of the Page-House conceptions is not easily arrived at. He was absorbed in vast domestic reforms; he had, in the health of Mrs. Wilson, a relentless personal problem: and with rebellious Mexico on his hands, it is scarcely surprising that he could give little attention

---

[1] In a memorandum written by Walter H. Page, and sent to the President, on August 25, 1913. *Ibid.*, p. 195.

[2] Walter H. Page to E. M. House, November 15 and 23, 1913. *The Life and Letters of Walter H. Page*, Vol. I, pp. 210–214.

[3] Walter H. Page to E. M. House, November 26, 1913. *Ibid.*, p. 217.

to Europe. Nor was it his habit to deal with new problems until he could deal with them specifically and thoroughly. His letters, as we shall see, are extraordinarily non-committal. Moreover, he does not appear to have been taken fully into the counsels of his advisers regarding their schemes for developing a world policy. House conversed with the German ambassador, Count Bernstorff, in New York on May 9, 1913,[1] and with Page and Sir Edward Grey in London on July 3rd,[2] apparently without mentioning to Wilson the larger ideas broached during these talks. He was, indeed, given an insight into Page's concept in a letter of July 20th inviting the President's daughter and her future husband, Francis B. Sayre, to visit the Pages after their marriage.

"Later," Page wrote, "when the first big tasks are done, you and Mrs. Wilson must come here—I mean during your presidency. Then you'll smash a precedent to some purpose!

"The whole subject of American-British relations is the most fascinating and important thing imaginable. The peace of the world hangs on it. They have their Germany and we have our Mexico and we both have our Japan. Of course we want no alliance: we need not engage ourselves to their troubles. Perhaps we can do even without treaties: no great matter. . . .

"There is a way, if we can be so fortunate as to find it, to do a great piece of constructive work in the right adjustment of world-forces by using just right this English admiration of our greatness and strength—using it positively, without boast or formal alliance, with no artificial force at work, with perfect naturalness."[3]

---

[1]*The Intimate Papers of Colonel House*, Vol. I, p. 240.

[2]*Ibid.*, p. 241.

[3]Walter H. Page to Woodrow Wilson, July 20, 1913. From original document in Mr. Wilson's files. Also in *The Life and Letters of Walter H. Page*, Vol. III, pp. 95-96.

As the most fitting occasion for such a visit as suggested, Page indicated the acceptance by the President of Sulgrave Manor in the following year as a feature of the celebration of one hundred years of peace between the two nations. In conclusion, he revealed his idea of the influence of the proposed dual entente in averting possible conflicts of its members with other powers.

"I have a feeling that such a visit," he ventured, " . . . might possibly prevent an Anglo-German war, which seems almost certain at some time, and an American-Japanese war which is at least conceivable a decade or so hence. I think the world would take notice to whom it belongs and—be quiet.

"I mentioned this to House when he was here, and his imagination took fire. Talk with him about it."[1]

Here were conceptions based upon the old "balance of power" theory of international politics which Wilson always repudiated and House regarded with suspicion.

Wilson's reply, delayed until September 11th by the young people's indecision about their proposed visit to London, is disappointingly vague on the larger issues raised by Page, but he refers to the project of a presidential visit:

"I greatly enjoyed your delightful letter of July twentieth and have this to say for our young people: They are not only complimented by your desire to have them visit you at the Embassy but they are very much tempted to accept the invitation. . . .

"As for your suggestion that I should, myself, visit England during my term of office, I must say that I agree with all your arguments for it, and yet the case against the President's leaving the country, particularly now that he is expected to exercise a constant leadership in all

---

[1]Walter H. Page to Woodrow Wilson, July 20, 1913. From original document in Mr. Wilson's files.

parts of the business of the government, is very strong and I am afraid overwhelming. It might be the beginning of a practice of visiting foreign countries which would lead Presidents rather far afield.

"It is a most attractive idea, I can assure you, and I turn away from it with the greatest reluctance.

"We hear golden opinions of the impression you are making in England, and I have only to say that it is just what I had expected."

Nor was Wilson's response to House's proposals any more definite. During the summer of 1913, Page and House had talked and corresponded regarding the new conceptions. Page's enthusiasm to do "something constructive" was shared by House.

"He [Page] asks me to aid him in formulating some constructive policy that will make the President's administration and his notable in the annals of this Embassy. . . . I shall try to outline some plan before I leave, for I have some things in mind which I think may redound to the advantage of both countries."[1]

But House did not get around to the formulation of a plan until December 1913, during the visit of Sir William Tyrrell to the United States.

Starting on this occasion with Winston Churchill's recent proposal to Germany for a "naval holiday," he suggested the idea of using America's influence with Germany to bring about an all-around reduction of armaments. Tyrrell encouraged House in attempting a "mission" to Berlin, representing himself as the "'power behind the throne' in the United States." He suggested it would have a salutary effect to let the Kaiser know on what good terms England and America stood, indicating that it would be well for Germany to come into the understand-

---

[1] House's diary entry on June 19, 1913, after dining with Page in London on the previous night. *The Intimate Papers of Colonel House*, Vol. I, p. 188.

ing by calling off her naval programme. He offered House an insight into the British correspondence with Germany on disarmament to show "how entirely right Great Britain had been in her position."[1] House seems to have taken all this in without perceiving the extent to which he was committing the United States to the British side of the case—or not caring, being already convinced that Great Britain was "entirely right."

It is to be noted that in this little talk House did not open the larger aspects of his peace plan; nor, it is to be presumed, did he do so when he broached it to the President on December 12th. He apparently dwelt only on the prospect of checking the race of armaments through friendly advice given to the European governments on behalf of the President, who, as House wrote Page next day, "seemed pleased with the suggestion; in fact, I might say, he was enthusiastic."[2] Wilson even mentioned the possibility of securing authority to reduce the American naval programme if the European states came round.[3] It was decided that in the early summer of 1914, the Colonel should go to Berlin and talk with the Kaiser. We have no documentary expression of Wilson's attitude toward the proposed mission, prior to his farewell letter of May 15, 1914, referring to House as his "spokesman." But it may fairly be inferred that the President had no idea of committing the United States to any intervention in European politics—surely not of threatening Germany, however vaguely, with an Anglo-American entente if she did not stop building warships! House had presented in general terms a plan of persuasion with possibilities of large results. As in the case of Bryan's plan for the

---

[1] *The Intimate Papers of Colonel House*, Vol. I, pp. 242–243; *The Life and Letters of Walter H. Page*, Vol. I, pp. 277–278.

[2] *Ibid.*, p. 277.

[3] *Ibid.*, pp. 277–278.

16/80

"cooling-off" treaties, Wilson probably merely said, "Go ahead and try, my friend: you have my blessing."

Wilson's attitude, indeed, is made entirely clear in his letter of January 6, 1914 to Page, who had questioned the usefulness of his own life in London because of the lack of definite constructive work:

"I have your letter of December twenty-first, which I have greatly enjoyed. . . .

"I long, as you do, for an opportunity to do constructive work all along the line in our foreign relations, particularly with Great Britain and the Latin-American states, but surely, my dear fellow, you are deceiving yourself in supposing that constructive work is not now actually going on, and going on at your hands quite as much as at ours. The change of attitude and the growing ability to understand what we are thinking about and purposing on the part of the official circle in London is directly attributable to what you have been doing, and I feel more and more grateful every day that you are our spokesman and interpreter there. This is the only possible constructive work in foreign affairs, aside from definite acts of policy.

"So far as the policy is concerned, you may be sure I will strive to the utmost to obtain both a repeal of the discrimination in the matter of the tolls and a renewal of the arbitration treaties, and I am not without hope that I can accomplish both at this session. Indeed this is the session in which these things must be done if they are to be done at all.

"You say something of Mr. Phillips in your letter as a man who would be useful in the Department of State. I wish you would cable me on the receipt of this what you know about him and how I could establish my judgement about him. I have been thinking of him for Third Assistant Secretary of State.

"Back of the smile which came to my face when you spoke of the impenetrable silence of the State Department towards its foreign representatives lay thoughts of very serious concern. We must certainly manage to keep our foreign representatives properly informed. The real trouble is to conduct genuinely confidential correspondence except through private letters, but surely the thing can be changed and it will be if I can manage it.

"We are deeply indebted to you for your kindness and generous hospitality to our young folks and we have learned with delight through your letters and theirs of their happy days in England.

"With deep regard and appreciation,
"Cordially and faithfully yours,
"WOODROW WILSON"

There is no evidence here that Wilson had considered, much less accepted, the "world plan" discussed by Page and House. The emphasis of the letter indeed is personal —he reassures the ambassador and expresses his abiding confidence. But he does define what he considers "the only possible constructive work" and makes as clear as day the limitations of his policies relating to Europe as he then envisaged them—the repeal of the Panama Canal tolls, and the passage of the arbitration treaties and the Bryan treaties—which he had adopted as practical matters for Congressional action.

Nor is it possible to find any more definite evidence that Wilson either envisaged or supported House's rapidly expanding views of the "mission" to Europe which he proposed taking in the summer of 1914. The Colonel's plans, indeed, grew like a green bay tree.

"The general idea is to bring about a sympathetic understanding between England, Germany, and America, not only upon the question of disarmament, but upon

other matters of equal importance to themselves and to
the world at large.

"It seems to me that Japan should come into this
pact . . ."[1]

Here was a "world plan" with a vengeance; but it is to
be noted that, while House was thus casually referring to
a "pact" with three or four powers as his goal, Page at the
same time was "thinking out loud" in a letter to House in
favor of narrowing the undertaking to "the tightest sort
of an alliance, offensive and defensive, between all Britain,
colonies and all, and the United States."[2]

Page had already adopted the English view toward
Germany which was to drive him apart from House after
the war began, though he approved House's plan to begin
his mission in Germany.[3]

In April 1914 we find Colonel House getting more and
more boldly into his stride as a world politician—strangely
enough, for an American idealist, discussing zones of
influence in Asia Minor and Persia.

"I went into some detail as to giving Germany a zone
of influence in Asia Minor and Persia, and also lending a
hope that they might be given a freer hand commercially
in the Central and South American republics."[4]

In his letter to Page on May 21, 1914, written en route
to his "great adventure" as he called it, House says confidently:

"The President has done his part in the letter I have
with me . . ."[5]

The inference here is that the President fully understood

---

[1]E. M. House to Walter H. Page, January 4, 1914. *The Life and Letters of Walter H. Page*, Vol. I, p. 281.

[2]January 2, 1914. *Ibid.*, p. 283.

[3]Walter H. Page to E. M. House, April 27, 1914. *Ibid.*, p. 287.

[4]Colonel House's diary entry, referring to a talk with Irwin Laughlin, April 9, 1914. *The Intimate Papers of Colonel House*, Vol. I, p. 246.

[5]E. M. House to Walter H. Page, May 21, 1914. *The Life and Letters of Walter H. Page*, Vol. I, p. 288.

the Colonel's mission; and had clothed him with authority.

But the only document in the record which qualifies as "the letter I have with me,"[1] is the following:

May 15, 1914

MY DEAR FRIEND:

It is hard to say good-bye, but knowing what I do it is delightful to think of what awaits you on the other side, and it is particularly heartening to me to know that I have such a friend and spokesman.

Mrs. Wilson and my daughters join with me in most affectionate messages and in the hope that you will both find your trip refreshing and stimulating in every way.

Your affectionate and grateful friend,

WOODROW WILSON

MR. E. M. HOUSE
New York City

In this letter Wilson seems far more interested in House and his personal friendship than in his ideas and plans. It is, in fact, notable for its tremendous omissions.

III. COLONEL HOUSE'S "MISSION"

It is doubtful if there was ever in American public life a stranger, more interesting, or more perplexing relationship than that between President Wilson and his friend, Colonel House. Much has already been said in this biography regarding the origins of it;[2] its special application to foreign affairs, where it was to have fateful consequences, is illuminated by House's "mission" to Europe in the summer of 1914. In its immediate object of promoting a better understanding between Great Britain and Germany, through American influence, the visit was, of course, a failure; but it has peculiar value to the student of these tremendous events in revealing, first, the extent and depth of the knowledge of foreign affairs gained by one of the

[1] Not mentioned in *The Intimate Papers of Colonel House.*
[2] See *Woodrow Wilson, Life and Letters,* Vol. III, pp. 294–308.

President's closest advisers: and second, the attitude of the President toward the mission itself and the advice and projects of its sponsor.

There can be no doubt, in launching this project, of the sincere good will and the hopeful idealism of Colonel House; nor, in the beginning, of the lack of any realistic knowledge of the facts or the conditions.

After a trip across in a German liner and a few days in Berlin, House was able, in his first report (May 29th), to convey some idea of Germany's position. His general comments, "jingoism run stark mad," the possibility "some day" of "an awful cataclysm," could have added little to the President's knowledge. But one remark, in which he portrayed the situation in terms strikingly similar to those later used by the revisionists of the "war guilt legend," may well have caught the keen perception of the President:

"Whenever England consents, France and Russia will close in on Germany and Austria. England does not want Germany wholly crushed, for she would then have to reckon alone with her ancient enemy, Russia; but if Germany insists upon an ever-increasing navy, then England will have no choice."[1]

House could go even a step further and envisage the problem of America in the terms of the old balance-of-power diplomacy:

"The best chance for peace is an understanding between England and Germany in regard to naval armaments, and yet there is some disadvantage to us by these two getting too close."[2]

The Colonel, at any rate, saw enough of the dynamite in the European situation to avoid giving any assurances

---

[1] E. M. House to Woodrow Wilson, May 29, 1914. From original letter in Mr. Wilson's files. Also in *The Intimate Papers of Colonel House*, Vol. I, p. 249.

[2] *Ibid.*

as to what England or the United States would do to make such an understanding as he desired of material interest to the Germans. He did not after all offer them "a zone of influence in Asia Minor and Persia."[1]

"I am careful always," he reported to the President, "not to involve you"[2]—and by so much as his caution held true, of course, the value of his suggestions in German eyes must have been reduced.

In his historic conversation with the Kaiser on June 1st, in which he told what "the President and I thought,"[3] he ventured a little further, speaking vaguely of an understanding going beyond Germany and England and transcending the question of armaments. He reported to Wilson on June 3rd:

"The Kaiser concurred also in my suggestion that whatever program America, England and Germany agreed to would be successful. I made it plain, however, that it was the policy of our government to have no alliances of any character, but we were more than willing to do our share towards promoting international peace."[4]

Here in one breath he was suggesting the potency of a kind of triple alliance, or at least entente, which should include America, and in another declaring that America would tolerate no alliances.

Wilson responded:

June 16, 1914.

MY DEAR FRIEND:

Your letter from Paris, written just after coming from Berlin, gives me a thrill of deep pleasure. You have, I hope and believe, begun a great thing and I rejoice with all my heart.

---

[1] See p. 36, this volume.

[2] May 29, 1914. *The Intimate Papers of Colonel House*, Vol. I, p. 248.

[3] Colonel House's diary entry, June 1, 1914. *The Intimate Papers of Colonel House*, Vol. I, p. 256.

[4] This passage is not included among the extracts from this letter printed on page 258 of *The Intimate Papers of Colonel House*, Vol. I. It is more explicit than the diary account on pp. 255–256.

You are doing it, too, in just the right way with your character-istic tact and quietness and I wish you Godspeed in what fol-lows. I could not have done the thing nearly so well.

I have had a little glimpse of your movements in a letter from Page and wish very much that our means of following our friends' movements were better than the occasional letter affords, for my thought follows you constantly.

In haste, with sincere affection,

Faithfully yours,
WOODROW WILSON

MR. EDWARD M. HOUSE,
c–o American Embassy,
London, England.

Wilson's tribute in this letter to House's "tact and quietness" was well deserved. It is a fact that House had no rough edges whatsoever. He was likely to convince those he met that he understood them perfectly: he rarely disagreed with anyone openly.

It is to be noted, however, that in this letter, with all his expressions of interest and approval, the President had not one word for the particular matters at issue. His thought followed his friend rather than the questions he was dealing with. One must doubt if Wilson gave them serious independent thought. His "single-track mind" was not easily diverted. House was in immediate contact with the situations he described, and in a position to understand them; his judgement must be trusted as to their true nature. When the "talks" reached the stage of definite and practical proposals, the President could turn his mind to them.

A week later, as showing how completely Wilson as-sumed that House and he thought alike upon all subjects, he wrote:

June 22, 1914

MY DEAR FRIEND:

I have your letter of June eleventh from London about the French proposal for a revision of the commercial treaty between France and the United States. I will take the matter up with Mr. Bryan at once.

I can not tell you how constantly my thoughts follow you and how deeply interested I am and thankful besides to have a friend who so thoroughly understands me to interpret me to those whom it is most important we should inform and enlighten with regard to what we are really seeking to accomplish. It is a great source of strength and relief to me and I thank you from the bottom of my heart.

The mediation is going slowly here and with many variations of aspect, but I think at last we see a reasonable prospect of success, at any rate, of the success that will be incident to making the whole situation thoroughly understood and putting the responsibility where it belongs.

Give my warmest regard to Mrs. House and to the Pages and remember that I always think of you with deep gratitude and affection.

Affectionately yours,
WOODROW WILSON

MR. E. M. HOUSE,
c–o American Embassy,
London, England.

In Paris, House saw no political personages and discussed foreign policy only with Ambassador Herrick. Yet he wrote as confidently as of the German situation, that French statesmen "dream no longer of revenge and the recovery of Alsace and Lorraine"[1]—and this with Raymond Poincaré in the Élysée! That he saw in France's failure to keep up with the German increase of population a reason for her remaining content with things as they were betrays a curious process of reasoning. But, as indicated in his letters, the President was not subjecting these reports to any close examination.

In this same letter, of June 17th, House described briefly his preliminary meeting with Sir Edward Grey, saying he

---

[1] E. M. House to Woodrow Wilson, June 17, 1914. *The Intimate Papers of Colonel House*, Vol. I, p. 262.

found him "a willing listener and very frank and sympathetic." Again without discussing the questions of international policy raised by his correspondent, Wilson replied:

June 26, 1914

DEAR FRIEND:

Your letters give me a peculiar pleasure whenever they come. They bring with them an air of sincere thought and constant endeavor for the right thing, which is just what I need to sustain the energies in me. I thank you with all my heart for your report of your meeting with Sir Edward Grey with regard to the matter we have so much at heart, and your plan to meet Tyrrell and Sir Edward again interests me as deeply as I am sure you knew it would.

I hope you are getting a lot of fun and pleasure out of these things, and all my little circle here join me in the warmest messages to both of you. Take care of yourself, and think of me always as

Your devoted friend,
WOODROW WILSON

MR. E. M. HOUSE,
c–o American Embassy,
London, England.

Here again the President seems to have been thinking of his friend, and of the kind of friendship he himself needed to "sustain the energies" in him. From the last paragraph one might think that he regarded the whole affair as a pleasure trip— "a lot of fun" —for a devoted friend.

On the same date as Wilson's reply, June 26th, House was writing an account of his further conversation with Grey. After two hours, he says, it was agreed to adjourn to a later meeting, and "in the meantime, the general idea was accepted; that is, that a frank and open policy should be pursued between all the parties at interest."[1] In just

---

[1] *The Intimate Papers of Colonel House*, Vol. I, p. 263.

what connection this admirable policy was to be pursued is by no means clear from the remainder of the letter, but it obviously concerned matters beyond the mere question of disarmament. What these were appears in a second letter bearing the same date, June 26th, which plunges immediately into the heart of the matter:

"DEAR GOVERNOR:

"There is another matter which I have taken up, which I hope may have your approval. I have suggested that America, England, France, Germany, and the other money-lending and developing nations, have some sort of tentative understanding among themselves for the purpose of establishing some plan by which investors on the one hand may be encouraged to lend money at reasonable rates and to develop, upon favorable terms, the waste places of the earth, and on the other hand to bring about conditions by which such loans may be reasonably safe."[1]

Here at last was House's underlying positive scheme hitherto "discussed with Page and Bernstorff"[2] but not previously revealed to Wilson as a feature of the Colonel's mission.[3]

The elaboration of the plan referred to took place on July 3rd at a luncheon given by Colonel House to Sir Cecil Spring Rice, Sir William Tyrrell, Walter H. Page,

---

[1] From original letter in Mr. Wilson's files. Also in *The Intimate Papers of Colonel House*, Vol. I, pp. 264–265.

[2] *Ibid.*, p. 264.

[3] The editor of House's *Intimate Papers* would apparently excuse the Colonel for going ahead with negotiations regarding such a really tremendous scheme involving the United States without either the knowledge or the direct approval of his chief. He says that the Colonel was in the habit of taking Wilson's silence for agreement with his suggestions.

"In the present case, receiving no dissenting cable from Wilson, the Colonel proceeded to elaborate his plan." *The Intimate Papers of Colonel House*, Vol. I, p. 265.

As a matter of fact Wilson did not, so far as the records show, send House a single cablegram during his mission from May to July—whether of approval or disapproval.

and Thomas Nelson Page.[1] The interval of seven days between June 26th and July 3rd might possibly have afforded time for the letter to reach Washington, and for a hard-driven President to study the tremendous scheme for an entente between the "money-lending and developing nations" of the earth, which House plumped at him, and to cable his objections or comments, but for the curious fact that House's second letter of June 26th, disclosing his great plan, *had not been sent.*[2]

If, then, the President knew nothing of the plan, how could he have approved it by his silence or otherwise?

In the conference of July 3rd, Tyrrell expressed Grey's interest in the general plan and assured House of the British government's coöperation, although further time would be required to put the matter in final shape. After being worked out to the satisfaction of the British, it was to be submitted for Wilson's approval. But the fact that "England was the first to accept"[3] was not to be made public. Apparently on Tyrrell's suggestion, House wrote to the President:

"You could then, if your judgement approved, take it to the other governments through Jusserand—ostensibly because he is the dean of the diplomatic corps at Washington, but really because the Central and South American republics would feel more kindly towards a proposal coming from a Latin nation."[4]

[1] Ambassador to Italy since June, 1913.

[2] The first paragraph of Colonel House's letter of July 4th, rendering to the President an account of the conference of July 3rd, is omitted from the letter as published (omission duly indicated) in the *Intimate Papers*, p. 266. The omitted paragraph is as follows:

"I am enclosing you a copy of a letter which I wrote you on the 26th by hand, but which I am not altogether sure was not destroyed before mailing. I had made a pencilled memorandum of it and I am afraid I destroyed the original instead of the letter which I find before me."

This important second letter of June 26th was received, then, at the same time as that of July 4th.

[3] E. M. House to Woodrow Wilson, July 4, 1914. *The Intimate Papers of Colonel House*, Vol. I, p. 266.

[4] *Ibid.*

Decision upon further details of this deep-laid scheme for deciding American world policy, to be conducted with such finesse, was to be delayed until "Tyrrell, Spring Rice, and I meet again on Wednesday."[1] House also remarks:

"I touched lightly upon this subject to the Kaiser and I feel sure he, too, will approve."[2]

In both letters discussing the great plan the Colonel was careful to emphasize its disinterestedness, and in that of July 4th, he asserted that it was "based entirely upon your Mobile speech." More than once in later times Wilson was destined to be astonished at some of the practical applications made of his idealistic phrases.

It was, however, a plan blasted in its making. It was a beautiful example of the wholly unrealistic discussion of international problems which even experienced diplomats seemed at the time willing to indulge in. At the very time that House was writing, a shot charged with the sternest realities rang out in distant Sarajevo[3] which was to change the history of the world.

If we are to understand thoroughly the American adventure into the intricacies of European diplomacy, so perfectly typified by Colonel House, some other aspects of it deserve notice. While we are not fully informed regarding the proposed activity of the new alliance, entente, or combination of Great Britain, Germany, and the United States, certain published entries in Colonel House's diary indicate that his excursions into world diplomacy, the "bargains in Asia," as someone has called them, "where men offer to give that which they do not themselves possess," found little encouragement. In the first

---

[1] E. M. House to Woodrow Wilson, July 4, 1914. *The Intimate Papers of Colonel House*, Vol. I, p. 267.

[2] *Ibid.*

[3] June 28, 1914.

meeting with Sir Edward Grey, we are scarcely surprised to learn that House's proposal to "permit Germany to aid in the development of Persia"[1] was not enthusiastically received. Nor was the extraordinary suggestion that Grey and House should meet the Kaiser at the Kiel regatta, "for the purpose," as the Colonel naïvely put it to Wilson, "of the three of us getting together, so there may be no go-betweens or misunderstandings."[2] On July 3rd, Grey invited House to write to the Kaiser his impressions as to the British government's amenability toward an understanding, but "said he did not wish to send anything official or in writing, for fear of offending French and Russian sensibilities in the event it should become known."[3]

Here was indeed the beginning of a promising excursion in secret diplomacy. The Colonel was touching the fringes of the system of alliances and ententes—the realities of European diplomacy—of which he was apparently uninformed and concerning which the British political leaders did not fully enlighten him. His statement in the letter of June 26th that "they told me that there was no written agreement between England, France, and Russia, and their understanding was one merely of sympathy and the determination to conserve the interests of one another" was no great aid toward an understanding of the developments under way a month later. And there is no evidence that he asked for further light on the Anglo-Russian negotiations for a naval agreement which were actually being discussed in the press at the time and concerning which questions had been put in Parliament and disingenuously answered just a few days before House's arrival in London,

[1] *The Intimate Papers of Colonel House*, Vol. I, p. 260.

[2] This portion of Colonel House's letter of June 3, 1914, to the President, is omitted from the published letter in *The Intimate Papers of Colonel House*, Vol. I, p. 258.

[3] E. M. House to Woodrow Wilson, July 3, 1914. From original document in Mr. Wilson's files. Also in *The Intimate Papers of Colonel House*, Vol. I, p. 271.

or on the Anglo-French military and naval agreements which lay behind. But why should Grey be more frank with the American President's friend than with his own Parliament?

In accordance with Grey's wish, House wrote his remarkable letter of July 8th to the "Emperor of Germany,"[1] referring to the "President's purpose" with which Wilhelm previously and now Sir Edward Grey had both expressed their sympathy. But in attempting to get round the obstacles to an Anglo-German understanding, which were interposed by the existence of the Triple Entente, we find him laying his emphasis upon the pacific tendencies of France as the key to hope of an improvement in the international situation. Whatever might have been the effect of this missive under other circumstances, in fact it had none, for it did not reach the Kaiser until his hasty return from the Norwegian cruise to face the crisis precipitated by the Austro-Hungarian note to Serbia.

On the day on which it was sent, House and his confreres in London decided to suspend their conferences on his plan until he could report to the President, Spring Rice again assuring him that the British government would follow the President's lead "in any way which seemed . . . best."[2] This decision can only have been due to an uncomfortable feeling by all parties concerned that they were reckoning too freely without their host—the man upon whom the decision to commit the United States to their rosy schemes in first instance depended. Is it possible that some of these diplomats may have had reported to them the President's speech of a few weeks before—such expressions are closely watched by foreign chancelleries—in which he said: " . . . we need not and we

[1] From copy in Mr. Wilson's files, dated July 8, 1914. Also in *The Intimate Papers of Colonel House*, Vol. I, pp. 272–274, under date of July 7, 1914.

[2] From an unpublished letter, E. M. House to Woodrow Wilson, July 9, 1914.

should not form alliances with any nation in the world"?[1]

Be that as it may, we know that while the President had sent no message of disapproval, neither had he given House one word of definite assurance. His letter, written on the date of this decision by House and his friends, is as noncommittal as ever:

July 9, 1914

MY DEAR FRIEND:

I have just received and read yours of June twenty-sixth and hurry this note off to send you affectionate messages not only but renewed congratulations on the way you are serving the country we love and the peace of the world. It is perfectly delightful to read your letters and to realize what you are accomplishing. I have no comments except praise and self-congratulation that I have such a friend.

We shall very eagerly look for your return to this side of the water. All join me in warmest regards to Mrs. House and yourself.

Affectionately yours,
WOODROW WILSON

MR. E. M. HOUSE,
c–o American Ambassador,
London, England.

Of course, it is to be borne in mind that, when this was written, Wilson had not yet been informed of House's complete proposals. He did not receive the oral explanations House was to bring him until the end of August, when they were presented as a missed solution of the problems of the world which might have averted the struggle by that time in full course.

Reviewing the "great adventure," it is clear that the President, while sympathizing with the general objective of coöperation for peace, never really identified himself with the "mission," the complete objectives of which were

---

[1]From an address delivered at the unveiling of the statue to the memory of Commodore John Barry, Washington, May 16, 1914. *The Public Papers of Woodrow Wilson*, Vol. III, p. 109.

not communicated to him until the end. While calling House his "spokesman" and applauding all the Colonel's reports of progress, his letters reveal him as giving no advice, comment, or criticism so far as the matters at issue are concerned; neither is there any definite commitment to House's proposals on behalf of the United States. There is nothing to show that he ever even mentioned them to any of his advisers in the State Department, a course necessarily followed by him when he was ready to consider any diplomatic proposal seriously. Nor is there any record that he discussed them with party leaders or cabinet members or senators, whom he would certainly have had to consult and conciliate if such a tremendous new scheme, so foreign to American tradition, was to be seriously considered.

This is indeed a strange attitude to have taken toward an affair of such grave potentialities. But it was not uncharacteristic. As observed of Wilson's earlier relationships with Mr. Hibben at Princeton, and others, he considered that friendship involved also a complete harmony of views. No doubt he really considered House his "spokesman," taking no position he himself would not take, exploring possibilities that might ultimately yield important results. Moreover, he plainly considered European relationships as affording no immediate cause for alarm, and that it was unnecessary for him to turn his attention from the engrossing problems of domestic legislation, from Mexico and the Caribbean, until House should place the definite results of his mission before him. It would be time enough then for close analysis and the consideration of what was practical and possible. He may not fully have realized—and here his inexperience with the practices of diplomacy and his failure to consult the experts of the State Department at any stage in the proceedings were a distinct handicap—that House was not only supposed by diplomats to represent him in Europe, but that he himself was supposed to know exactly what House was doing, and to stand ready to carry out what he represented as the purposes of the United States. Certainly, in any court of practical men, the President would not be justified in resting upon the discretion of any individual whatsoever, or upon the worldly wisdom of European statesmen in not taking his agent too seriously.

In short, this is the first demonstration of the working of that strange and unclear relationship which was to becloud American foreign policy and exasperate European diplomats until, in the end, a revelation of the real disparities led to serious difficulties. On Wilson's part it seemed always to have been a relationship of faith without complete understanding, of trust without actual commitment —wholly creditable to neither, and deplorable in some of its results. But it was one of those "necessary friendships" which throughout his life so often influenced, and sometimes warped, Wilson's clear-running judgements.[1]

House sailed for home on July 21st. The diplomatic crisis in Europe entered its acute phase while he was on his way. He settled down on the North Shore in Massachusetts, maintaining contact with the President at long range by letters, the first of which was written on July 31st. And his only advice during the crisis, to delay the offer of "good offices" by the United States, was not followed by the President.

IV. WILSON'S VIEW OF THE ORIGINS OF THE WAR

In spite of the rush of tremendous and unprecedented events, a period of relative retirement followed the death of Mrs. Wilson, and continued, whatever the outward pressure upon the President's time, after his return to Washington on August 12th. All those who were near him

---

[1]See *Woodrow Wilson, Life and Letters*, Vol. III, pp. 154–169.

bear testimony to his "withdrawal into himself." Dr. Grayson refers to the "awful loneliness" of the President; his brother-in-law, Dr. Axson, who remained with him during most of this dark period, has written:

". . . I know that it is no exaggerated use of words to say that he was the loneliest man in all the world."[1]

Friends avoided intrusion upon his sorrow: and while he neglected no necessary duty—indeed, the reckoning of letters written, statements issued, delegations met is prodigious—yet he cut down to the last degree upon visitors and personal conferences.

"I hope," he wrote to J. P. Morgan on August 13th, "that you know that in ordinary circumstances I would be very glad to see you, but I find myself so out of spirits that I have for the moment only strength and initiative enough for the absolutely necessary duties of my official day.

"I know that in view of all that has happened you will understand and excuse."

For some days his daughters remained with him, also the Misses Smith of New Orleans, old friends of the family. Miss Margaret Wilson, his oldest daughter, was to become the lady of the White House, and with Miss Helen Bones, a cousin, was to take up the social duties laid down by Mrs. Wilson. Secretary McAdoo and Mrs. McAdoo[2] were frequent guests at luncheon and dinner. Dr. Grayson was not only a constant visitor but an intimate friend: but both he and Mr. Tumulty had been under great strain during Mrs. Wilson's illness, and the President insisted that they take a vacation.[3]

There were "a few bitter days," as Dr. Axson relates, "when there were only three of us in the family circle."[4]

---

[1] Stockton Axson, *The Private Life of President Wilson.*
[2] The youngest of the President's daughters.
[3] They left on August 14th.
[4] The third was Miss Helen Bones.

"I can see the lonely figure of the President now, walking down the long hallway, the hair so much whitened in the few months."[1]

Outside of the necessary duties of his great office, especially those involving the crisis of the European war, which have been recounted elsewhere, the President devoted much time to responding to the overwhelming correspondence relating to Mrs. Wilson's death. He wrote many hundreds of letters; one entire letter book of some five hundred pages and parts of two others are filled with them. They let us deep into the spirit of the man.

To Edward Elliott, Mrs. Wilson's brother-in-law, he wrote on August 17th:

"It has seemed to me until now that it was absolutely impossible for me to speak of what has happened to those who I know care deeply, as Madge and you do, but now I am regaining some degree of self-control about it all and I want to use this earliest opportunity to send to you both my dearest love and my gratitude for the messages which you have sent. I cannot yet see or understand, but that is not necessary. I can do what I know she would have wished me to do."

Especially to the tried friends of his youth and of the Princeton period, he turned with strong emotion:

"I am sure that you know what your affection and sympathy mean to me, and they never meant more than they do now. I do not know what would become of me if I did not feel the grasp of loving hands like your own. God bless you!"[2]

"How shall I thank you for your letter of sympathy! Somehow a sort of dumb spirit has had possession of me of late whenever I was in the presence of those who really cared and it has been almost impossible for me to speak or

[1]Stockton Axson, *The Private Life of President Wilson.*
[2]Woodrow Wilson to Robert Bridges, August 21, 1914.

even to write with self-possession. But I must not let any longer time go by without telling you how deeply I was touched by your letter of sympathy or how genuinely grateful I am for a friend who so supports me with his generous sympathy."[1]

He welcomed eagerly the offer of Mrs. Wilson's cousins, the Misses Hoyt, to send him their memories of her:

"It would be a great delight to me if you could from time to time, just as you happen to remember them, jot down things that Ellen said that come back to you. I should prize them so highly because she loved you very much and I know spoke to you very intimately indeed about the things that were nearest to her. It is sweet of you to have thought of this.

"It has occurred to me that if you did what I have suggested, namely, made little memoranda from time to time, you could without even copying them send them to me as they accumulated."[2]

Later he wrote to Miss Florence Hoyt, in acknowledging the "little memoranda":

"Thank you with all my heart for your letter with the reports of conversations with Ellen. The whole thing touched me very deeply,—your thoughtfulness and the sweet flavour of my dear one which the quotations so unmistakably carry. How wonderful she was, in her thought, which went to the heart of things, no less than in the whole loveliness of her nature! Every day, it seems to me, I find something new by which to measure my loss, which is yet truly immeasurable, and yet can be in part understood by those who knew her as we did. How empty everything (everything personal to myself) seems without her. My hardest task is to keep my courage and my vigour and go through with the day's work. Please let me

---

[1]Woodrow Wilson to William J. Bryan, August 25, 1914.
[2]Woodrow Wilson to Mary W. Hoyt, August 25, 1914.

have anything else that comes back to you from time to time."[1]

He wrote many letters to the friends in Georgia regarding Mrs. Wilson's grave and the care of it. He did not neglect to thank the mayor of Rome, Georgia, and other officials who had assisted in any way at the funeral.

"It was generous of you to write me your letter of August sixteenth. I cannot send you many words in return because I find that it is still very difficult for me to speak about my loss, but your words gave me a great deal of solemn pleasure. It is delightful to know that the people at her old home should feel as they do about her grave and that you and other friends who knew her personally should have retained so strong a feeling of affection for her. She never lost for a moment her deep feeling about her home and her friends, and her thoughts turned to them with undiminished affection as the years went by.

"If you get a chance will you not say to the men who are watching her grave how deeply I appreciate it? It makes me regard them as my personal friends.

"I wish I could send you a letter worthy of your own in reply, but I am sure that you will read between the lines the things that are unspoken."[2]

Finally, on August 23rd, he wrote to his friend, Mrs. Hulbert:

"I never understood before what a broken heart meant, and did for a man. It just means that he lives by the compulsion of necessity and duty only and has no other motive force. Business, the business of a great country that must be done and cannot wait, the problems that it would be deep unfaithfulness not to give my best powers to because a great people has trusted me, have been my salvation; but, Oh! how hard, how desperately hard, it has been to

---

[1]October 2, 1914.

[2]Woodrow Wilson to Ethel Hillyer Harris, August 20, 1914.

face them, and to face them worthily! Every night finds me exhausted,—dead in heart and body, weighed down with a leaden indifference and despair (so far as everything concerning myself is concerned). I am making a brave fight, the best I know how to make, to work out into the light and see my way. And I am not ungrateful: how could I be when I had her so many happy, happy years. God helping me, I shall regain command of myself and be fit for my duties again. For a little while it must be only a matter of exhausting will power.

"Meanwhile my dear friends count with me more than ever. Their love and sympathy sustains me and gives me all the light and solace I have to work by."

On the long summer evenings, after the darkness fell, he sat often on the open porch of the White House with Dr. Axson, sometimes in the "oval room," pouring out memories of his long life with Ellen Axson, recalling his youth in the South and his struggles at Princeton.

"I cannot help thinking," he said, "that perhaps she was taken so that she might be spared the spectacle of some awful calamity."[1]

He referred more than once to Sir Edward Grey, whom he admired, and of whom he was hearing through the letters of Walter H. Page. He spoke at one time of Sir Edward's loss of his wife, and at another of his interest in nature, in birds, and in fly-fishing—a "deliverance I do not know." A letter of sympathy from Sir Edward pleased him greatly. He responded on August 19th:

"It was very gracious indeed of you to think of me in my great personal sorrow at a time when you are, yourself, so overwhelmed with affairs with which the whole world is concerned, and I wish to express not only my sincere appreciation but my hope that you will regard me as

---

[1]Stockton Axson, *The Private Life of President Wilson.*

your friend. I feel that we are bound together by common principle and purpose."

Often he read aloud from his favourite books, especially poetry from an old anthology, Burton's, which he prized. Several times he slipped out of the White House and visited the Corcoran Art Gallery to see the pictures of which Mrs. Wilson had been particularly fond. He encouraged some of the work in which she was interested, like that for the mountain whites of North Carolina, "because I know that this is what Mrs. Wilson would have done."[1]

"Knowing as I do how glad Mrs. Wilson would have been to continue paying your tuition . . ." he wrote to a girl in whom Mrs. Wilson had been interested, "I take pleasure in enclosing my check for five hundred dollars. There go with it my most earnest good wishes for you and all your family."[2]

There were moments when his own loneliness and the tasks which confronted him seemed unbearable—and he talked of his "release," and of what he should do when he was able to return to private life. Dr. Axson suggested that he might then write the "great work" which he had planned as a scholar, wherein he was to bring together his ripe conclusions on the subject of politics. It was called familiarly between them, "P.o.P."—"The Philosophy of Politics." It was to follow somewhat the model of Montesquieu. Dr. Axson remarked that he would now be better fitted to do it than ever before.

"I thought of it once," remarked the President, "as a great book: I can put all I know now into a very small one."

But these moments, though they must be recorded for the glimpses they give of certain deep aspects of Wilson's

[1]Woodrow Wilson to Mrs. B. I. Hughes, August 25, 1914.
[2]September 9, 1914.

spirit, were of necessity brief: he could not and he did not yield to "dark questionings." ". . . the best thing possible for me," he wrote to Colonel House on August 18th, "is to stick at my task. The matters I have to consider are imperative. They compel my attention and my great safety lies in having my attention absolutely fixed elsewhere than upon myself. I believe that this is good 'doctor' sense, as well as good reasoning about the public welfare."

The matters he had to consider were indeed "imperative": nothing less than a world war in which, inevitably, his own decisions would be of conspicuous, if not determining, importance.

We find him, therefore, sitting for hours alone in his study poring over the documents relating to the war which gathered steadily, in unrelenting piles, upon his desk. All of the important reports that came into the State Department were forwarded by his direction to the White House —not in digests, but in their original form or in verbatim copies. His attitude was that of the thoroughgoing scholar, impatient to see everything that would contribute to the correction of his knowledge.[1]

It is unfortunate that the record was, from the first, so chaotic, so utterly inadequate. If European foreign offices, as General Smuts observed, groped to their conclusions regarding the crisis "through a thick fog of misunderstanding," the American President and his State Department were, at the beginning, in Stygian darkness. There was never a more glaring demonstration of the utter futility, in such a crisis, of the diplomatic system of the

---

[1]"The truth comes to you in a very singular way. The voices and messages that come to you are contradictory, as a rule, but if you wait long enough with regard to any one subject there seems to be a sort of medium result which is obviously the fact." He called the White House "a sort of clearing house for the needs and opinions of all sorts and conditions of men. And there is an exhilaration in that; there is an education that cannot be described. It makes it ridiculous to read the newspapers. I have stopped reading the newspapers . . ." From an address before the Class of '79, Princeton, June 13, 1914.

United States, or the need of some organization, some world clearing house, where the facts regarding world problems and world relationships could be immediately available. For how decide such tremendous questions without complete and accurate knowledge? Mere good will, excellent ideals, in themselves will not do it.

Consider the situation. With the incoming of the new Wilson administration, after the party had been out of office for sixteen years, the diplomatic service had been generally shaken up; new men were in many posts, and in most of the highest ones men without training for or experience in the work suddenly thrust upon them. The custom of sending inexperienced men, however distinguished or able, to foreign capitals was, of course, American, not Democratic, and while some of Wilson's appointees were equal in ability—and two or three superior —to the ordinary run, they did not *know*. Small wonder that the reports of embassies and legations, shocked by the rushing events of late July and early August, afforded the government little light upon what was actually going on. To add to the difficulties of our representatives, their offices were swamped by the business of caring for and sending home again the hordes of American summer tourists caught in the upheaval without money or passports. As for the Department of State—"swamped" is too inadequate a term to describe its condition. Its force could not keep up properly with the immense volume of correspondence pouring into it. Its higher officers could form no adequate picture of the rapidly moving march of events.

It was thus a hodge-podge of fevered cablegrams, reports, letters that was dumped from day to day in wild confusion upon the President's desk. Few of them were accompanied by any explanatory memoranda to make them more intelligible. To make matters worse, a flood of high-keyed and excited admonitions and suggestions poured in from American sources, including a deluge of articles, editorials, books dealing—who could say with what authority?—with complex foreign problems which the oncoming conflict had thrown into high relief. All these the President was urged to peruse immediately. One who looks back years afterwards into this clamorous mass of papers wonders how any human mind could have drawn any dependable conclusions whatsoever from them. And yet the President must have felt the responsibility, indeed the necessity, of coming to certain conclusions as a basis for deciding what the American attitude toward the war should be. He must consider such questions, vital to a consideration of his course, as those relating to the origins of and the responsibility for the war. He must reflect upon the consequences of victory for either side, and finally, he must not fail to venture some vision, however vague, of what the final settlements might involve for America and for the world.

There is clear evidence that the President, in these days of withdrawal, thought deeply upon all these problems.

As to the information that came to him concerning the origins of the war, it is sufficient to say that the meagre flow of early dispatches[1] does not indicate a German-Austrian plot to bring about a general conflict. As a matter of fact none of our representatives knew what was actually going on between the European chancelleries, yet the sum of their outsiders' knowledge comes to something very like the corrections of the war-guilt legend which the Entente governments afterward built up and even incorporated in the treaties of peace. The most warlike reports came from Russia, where Charles S. Wilson was the competent chargé d'affaires; while, from Berlin, Gerard

---

[1] The most important of which have now been published in *Foreign Relations of the United States*, Supplement, 1914.

was giving acknowledgment to "Germany's efforts toward peace."[1]

Nobody at Washington—and least of all the harassed President, until after his return from Georgia—took the trouble to analyze this correspondence; but even a brief and partial survey may have made upon an open mind an impression that "war guilt" was a matter not easily settled and probably not falling conclusively against any party. It was Wilson's open mind on the subject—if without great knowledge, also without prejudice—that led him to conclusions which differed from those of many better-informed men.

Outside of the scattering early reports already mentioned, Colonel House made his contribution concerning the origins of the war in letters to the President dated July 31st and August 1st, but his information is slight and in some respects misleading.[2] He did hint, however, that Russia's was the deciding rôle in the situation, giving at this time a superficial picture of the clash of interests in

---

[1]*Foreign Relations of the United States*, Supplement, 1914, p. 21. Chargé Wilson reported on July 28th that Russian mobilization had been going on "quietly" for several days, a report which Gerard capped on the 31st, after it became formal, with the opinion that "Russia's mobilization makes war inevitable." (*Ibid.*, p. 23.) Herrick, in France, contributed, on the 28th, the estimate that "It is felt that if Germany once mobilizes no backward step will be taken" (*Ibid.*, pp. 18–19)—unconsciously reflecting the essential terms of the Franco-Russian alliance—and, on the 29th, a statement of "the belief" prevalent in Paris "that England will support Russia and France in any eventuality" although, to be sure, he construed this assurance as contributing to a feeling that Germany would, therefore, keep quiet and the conflict remain confined to the "present belligerents." (*Ibid.*, p. 20.) If he understood by this phrase only Austria-Hungary and Serbia, he was miscalculating Russia's intentions, as Chargé Wilson's dispatches show.

[2]How he knew or whether it was true that England was "exercising a restraining hand upon France and, as far as possible, upon Russia" (letter to Woodrow Wilson, July 31, 1914) is not explained by his biographer; nor did his comment indicate whether Germany in this period restrained Austria at all. Others of House's statements respecting European affairs were similarly defective. On June 17th, he wrote to Wilson that French statesmen "dream no longer of revenge and the recovery of Alsace and Lorraine." On June 26th, on the eve of trouble, he reported to Wilson that, out of his recent conferences, "a long stride has been made in the direction of international amity." And in the midst of the turmoil of August 1st, he analyzed the Triple Entente, in a letter to Wilson, as being an agreement that was "purely sympathetic."

the Balkans and stating—conservatively—that Russia
"has evidently been preparing for some decisive action
since . . . two years ago."[1] Regarding England's relations
with France and Russia, he repeated the inadequate statements of his letter of June 26th.[2] "The great danger," he
put it, "is that some overt act may occur which will get
the situation out of control. Germany is exceedingly
nervous and at high tension and she knows that her best
chance of success is to strike quickly and hard, therefore
her very alarm may cause her to precipitate action as a
means of safety."[3]

In his reply to these letters, written on August 3rd,
after the storm had burst, as in other letters to House, the
President characteristically emphasized his need of the
Colonel's friendship:

"The delight and comfort of having such a friend as you
are is to be sure that he understands perfectly, and the
pressure and anxiety of the last week have been the most
nearly overwhelming that I have yet had to carry. I have
not had a thought or a moment except for public business,
but you may be sure that there was constantly in the
front of my private thoughts a contentment that you
should be back in this country and that I should presently
have a chance to see you and confer with you as I am longing to do."

But there is strangely little response to House's reports.

"Your letters are invaluable to me. I know how deep a
sorrow must have come to you out of this dreadful
European conflict in view of what we had hoped the European world was going to turn to, but we must face the

---

[1] *The Intimate Papers of Colonel House*, Vol. I, p. 278.
[2] *Ibid.*, pp. 263–264.
[3] E. M. House to Woodrow Wilson, August 1, 1914. From original letter in Mr. Wilson's files. Also in *The Intimate Papers of Colonel House*, Vol. I, p. 279.

situation in the confidence that Providence has deeper plans than we could possibly have laid ourselves."

But we know from other sources how his mind was tending. His friend Charles R. Crane sent him a letter enclosing an article by Professor Albert Bushnell Hart of Harvard University, published in the New York *Times* of August 2nd. Wilson had long known Hart and respected him as a renowned historian. He therefore read the article, as he wrote Crane, "with genuine interest."

This article, after giving some background of the Balkan troubles, laid the immediate responsibility for the existing crisis on the Austrians, setting forth as their motive a "fear that their empire will be killed by a Serb empire." Hart denied the Austrian charges against the Serbian government of complicity in the assassination of Archduke Francis Ferdinand (afterwards confirmed from Serbian sources), although mentioning suspicious blots in recent Serbian history. He showed something of the close connection between Russian policy and Serbian aspirations and sketched the system of secret alliances and ententes to bring all the powers into any war. He pointed out some of the consequences and ironies of such a tragic general conflict—among them "that the splendid navy of Great Britain, the most liberal of all European countries, should be used to support the most despotic of powers [Russia] in taking provinces away from Austria."

Here the disinterested comments of a trustworthy scholar confirmed the uncertainties of the early dispatches, and we find the President writing to Charles R. Crane on August 4th:

"Thank you for your letter with the article by Professor Hart. I have read it with genuine interest. The more I read about the conflict across the seas, the more open it seems to me to utter condemnation. The outcome no man can even conjecture."

The phrase, "utter condemnation," applied to the conduct of all parties, appears to sum up Wilson's attitude toward the war at its beginning. It was this conviction, no doubt, that lent energy and sincerity to his appeals for American neutrality. How take sides when responsibility was still so uncertain, when the entire conflict was open to "utter condemnation"?[1]

As to the President's "personal feeling for the Allies," can he be suspected of entertaining any high regard for Russia? Is there any evidence whatsoever that he was especially devoted to France? On the other hand we know that he had the greatest respect for German scholarship. He had read and used German works on politics and law; an early essay bespeaks his admiration

---

[1] Several writers have endeavoured to show that from the beginning the President really "sided with the Allies." Robert Lansing, in a forthright article in the *Current History Magazine* (January 1925), meets the charge of the deposed Kaiser of Germany that "there was a 'gentlemen's agreement between Great Britain and the United States' which 'bound America to the chariot of the Entente, without the knowledge or consent of the American people' . . ." He asserts that the sole authority for the false statement that "Woodrow Wilson was responsible for leading us into war in accordance with an agreement of long standing between the government of the United States and the powers of the Entente," was apparently Professor Usher. He goes on to say:

"There is an attempt to support this charge of 'treason' on the part of the former President by a reference to Joseph P. Tumulty, in whose book, it is declared, is revealed the fact that 'Woodrow Wilson was determined from the first to come, if need be, to the rescue of England,' and that 'he did not dare to show his hand until he had succeeded in "educating" public opinion.' In my constant and intimate intercourse with Mr. Wilson, during the years of American neutrality, there was never the slightest indication of such an underlying motive to his policies. On the contrary, he sought in every way to keep his mind free from prejudice and to remain in thought, as well as in word and deed, strictly neutral and impartial. His endeavors to bring the war to an end by acting as the friend of both parties were made with honest purpose and with the high hope that they would be successful."

Mr. Tumulty's book, *Woodrow Wilson As I Know Him*, is a product of a warm and loyal heart, rather than of a cool and accurate mind. Its feeling is impeccable, its facts often highly undependable.

Professor Seymour says in the *Intimate Papers* that "the personal feeling of the President was with the Allies," and implies that from the beginning he adopted a policy of neutrality only as apparently expedient for the good of the country and of the world, and because the people were not prepared to support any other. This is at best a loose statement; at its worst it involves, however high-minded the motives alleged, a charge of dissimulation, and gives a handle to charges that the administration's neutrality was from the first insincere and, if unconsciously, was inequitably put into practice. (See *The Intimate Papers of Colonel House*, Vol. I, p. 293; also Charles Seymour, *American Diplomacy in the World War*, p. 18 ff.)

for Bismarck. But it is entirely true that he did have a strong personal feeling for the English people. His fore-bears, not so far removed, were all Scotch or English, his mother was born in Carlisle. His early heroes, so far as he had any, were mostly English—Burke, Bagehot, John Bright. His poets were English poets—Wordsworth chief amongst them. He was near to Gladstonian liberalism in his general political views. His first and greatest book advocated a reconstruction of the American govern-mental system in the direction of the British parliamentary practice of "responsible government." Above any other spot on earth, probably, he loved best the English lake country—Rydal and Grasmere, the gentle country of Wordsworth.

Colonel House records an interview on August 30th in which Wilson criticized German philosophy and mili-tarism, the violation of Belgian neutrality, the destruction of Louvain, etc.[1] Yet it is to be noted that this denuncia-tion of Germany is accompanied by no exoneration—much less praise—of the conduct of her enemies. In com-mon with John Morley and John Burns in England at the beginning of the war, while he might be critical of Ger-many, he was profoundly suspicious of Russia.[2]

Indeed, Colonel House himself a little later developed the alternatives of a complete victory for either side in terms not at all calculated to shake Wilson's neutrality—rather to confirm him in his verdict that the war was upon all accounts open to "utter condemnation."

"If the Allies win," wrote House, "it means largely the

---

[1]*The Intimate Papers of Colonel House*, Vol. I, p. 293.

[2]Lord Morley argued: "If Germany is beaten and Austria is beaten, it is not England and France who will emerge pre-eminent in Europe. It will be Russia. Will that be good for Western civilisation? I at least don't think so. . . . Germany is unpopular in Eng-land, but Russia is more unpopular still. And people will rub their eyes when they realise that Cossacks are their victorious fellow-champions for Freedom, Justice, Equality of man (especially Jew man), and respect for treaties (in Persia for instance)." (John Viscount Morley, *Memorandum on Resignation*, p. 6.)

domination of Russia on the continent of Europe, and if Germany wins, it means the unspeakable tyranny of militarism for generations to come."[1]

To this letter Wilson replied:

August 25, 1914

MY DEAR FRIEND:

Thank you for your letter of August twenty-second. It expresses in a way that was somewhat poignant to me my feeling about the possible alternative outcomes of the war. I feel the burden of the thing almost intolerably from day to day, I think largely because there is nothing that we can as yet do or even attempt. What a pathetic thing to have this come just as we were so full of hope!

Affectionately yours,

WOODROW WILSON

MR. EDWARD M. HOUSE
Prides Crossing, Mass.

The importance of Russia's participation on the Allies' side in influencing Wilson's opinion of their cause requires some further emphasis. It was put before him early by Chargé Wilson's telegrams, by Hart's article, by House's letter, and by a letter from President Eliot of August 20th —which will be referred to later. Her despotic form of government, her nakedly imperialistic policy, her suspect motives must have filled him with distrust.

There is not anywhere to be found a dependable statement—this biographer has looked diligently—which indicates that at this time, or indeed for long afterwards, the President had come to any conclusions whatsoever as to "war guilt." With a true scholar's instinct, he recognized in his own ignorance what many professed scholars in glib cocksureness denied—that the world's information on these matters was too slight to permit of a final judgement.

---

[1] E. M. House to Woodrow Wilson, August 22, 1914. From original letter in Mr. Wilson's files. Also in *The Intimate Papers of Colonel House*, Vol. I, p. 285.

Wilson's approach to the problems of these tumultuous days was, indeed, so far as he could make it, that of the scholar, "neither justifying nor condemning but only comprehending"—the attitude he had taken with determination years before, in his study of the Civil War which had divided this country, and in which, as a Southerner, his own personal feelings had been deeply engaged.[1] He knew the difference between feeling and thought not only as a scholar but as a judge knows it, or should know it, when a friend appears as a litigant in his court. While the feeling for his friend continues what it was, he can and must control his thought in the sober examination of the facts and in his decision, finally, upon the issues of the case. This it was that Wilson demanded alike of himself and of his countrymen. "We must be impartial in thought . . ." We must not "passionately take sides." We must preserve the "fine poise of undisturbed judgement." It is easy "to excite passion and difficult to allay it."[2] He knew well that undisciplined emotion easily reduces a democracy to a mob or a dictatorship.

To many warm-hearted natures like Walter H. Page and that knight errant, Robert Bacon,[3] whose devotion to France was even more unquestioning and romantic than that of Page to Great Britain, this dispassionate attitude later became irritating if not infuriating.[4] They soon decided which side was right and which was wrong. "A

---

[1]"The Reconstruction of the Southern States." *The Public Papers of Woodrow Wilson*, Vol. I, pp. 368–395. Wilson's own ideal, expressed in his appreciation of General Lee, was "a conscious self-subordination to principles which lay outside of his personal life." *The Public Papers of Woodrow Wilson*, Vol. II, p. 70.

[2]These phrases are from Wilson's special neutrality appeal of August 18th.

[3]Robert Bacon, New York aristocrat, friend of Theodore Roosevelt, had been ambassador to France from December 1909 to January 1912. He was, before that, Assistant Secretary of State and then Secretary of State.

[4]At that time, however, Page was rejoicing in the American policy of aloofness. As he wrote to House on August 28, 1914: "What a *magnificent* spectacle our country presents! We escape murder, we escape brutali ation; we will have to settle it; we gain in every way." *The Intimate Papers of Colonel House*, Vol. I, p. 286.

government can be neutral," Page wrote to his brother, "but no *man* can be."[1]

What Wilson was asking of the nation was that it await the evidence. He was asking that his country be governed by its knowledge and its reason rather than by its impulses, its sentiments. Is there a greater appeal that statesmanship can make?

The President's own record during the period of neutrality can be interpreted as the struggle to "put a curb upon our sentiments," remain "impartial in thought"—with the corrosive tides of emotion and impulse, fed by a flood of lies, stimulated by excited rhetoric, urged by economic interest, and horrified by actual events, rising higher and higher until they became, finally, irresistible. We shall see him struggling manfully with these tides, trying to bring order and reason out of chaos, hampered by his own inadequate knowledge, weakened by the limitations of his own temperament, subject to the most powerful pressure from partisans of both sides, baffled by the demands of avid profit seekers, yet stubbornly doubtful of the rights and wrongs involved, and eager, above everything, to use the nation's power as a peace maker.

Straight through the period of neutrality Wilson was to reject all ex-parte statements of the belligerents, insisting that an accounting be deferred until the end of the struggle.[2] He stated his policy in this regard most definitely in a letter to Secretary Bryan on September 4th:

"I have thought a great deal about the matter of a protest with regard to the dropping of the bombs and my present judgement is that we do not know in sufficient detail the actual facts and that we ought to be very slow to make formal protests, chiefly because we shall no doubt

---

[1] *The Life and Letters of Walter H. Page*, Vol. I, p. 361.

[2] See his replies to the Belgians, to the Kaiser, to the French president, on atrocity charges, this volume, pp. 161-162.

be called upon by every one of the belligerents before the fighting is over to do something of this kind and would be in danger of becoming chronic critics of what was going forward. I think the time for clearing up all these matters will come when the war is over and the nations gather in sober counsel again."

And more than two years after the outbreak of the war he was still stubbornly asking:

"Have you ever heard what started the present war? If you have, I wish you would publish it, because nobody else has, so far as I can gather. Nothing in particular started it, but everything in general. There had been growing up in Europe a mutual suspicion, an interchange of conjecture about what this government and that government was going to do, an interlacing of alliances and understandings, a complex web of intrigue and spying, that presently was sure to entangle the whole of the family of mankind on that side of the water in its meshes."[1]

v. VISION OF A NEW "WORLD ORDER"

On the day that he returned from Mrs. Wilson's funeral, August 12th, the President found upon his desk a letter from former President Eliot of Harvard. It had been written on August 6th and sent on August 8th,[2] and it

---

[1]Address at a luncheon of the Women's City Club, Cincinnati, October 26, 1916. *The Public Papers of Woodrow Wilson*, Vol. IV, p. 381. But with the American entry into the war, as will be fully developed later, the President accepted largely the Allied explanation regarding the origin of the war. On June 14, 1917, he said:

"The war was begun by the military masters of Germany, who proved to be also the masters of Austria-Hungary. . . .

"Their plan was to throw a broad belt of German military power and political control across the very center of Europe . . ." *Ibid.*, Vol. V, pp. 62–63.

[2]In transmitting the letter of August 6th, Dr. Eliot wrote:

"I have hesitated three days to mail the enclosed letter to you, and should still hesitate to forward it while you are overwhelmed with sorrow, did I not recall that under such circumstances there is comfort and relief for the sufferer in resolving that he will thereafter do everything in his power to help other people who are suffering or bereaved.

"At this moment millions of men are apprehending death or agonies for themselves or poverty and desolation for their families, and millions of women are dreading the loss

represented Eliot's first indignant reaction toward the catastrophe in Europe. Wilson had had, as a fellow college president, the opportunity, through many years of acquaintance and association, to test Eliot's qualities of mind and of character, and he looked to his judgement and his advice with the greatest respect. He read his letter immediately. Its contents exactly suited the qualities of his mind; there were specific suggestions upon which to test his policies, and broad general considerations to stimulate his thought. At various times in his career some such incidental letter, or memorandum, or article furnished the President with a starting point for a train of fertile reflection. Professor Hart's article of August 2nd, to which reference has already been made, was an instance in point.

Eliot had evidently decided, in his first indignant reaction toward the invasion of Belgium, that Germany and Austria were "utterly untrustworthy neighbors, and military bullies of the worst sort," and he suggested to the President that he "propose a combination of the British Empire, the United States, France, Japan, Italy, and Russia in offensive and defensive alliance to rebuke and punish Austria-Hungary and Germany for the outrages they are now committing," by a general blockade in which the American navy should participate. A condition of this common enterprise should be "the abandonment by all the European participants of every effort to extend national territory in Europe by force" as the United States had repudiated such extension in America. The immediate use of force was defended as "an effective international

---

of lovers, supporters, and friends; and perhaps you have the power to do something to stop these miseries and prevent their recurrence.

"In such an effort you would find real consolation.

"With deepest sympathy in your affliction, I am

"Sincerely yours
"CHARLES W. ELIOT"

police method, suited to the present crimes, and the probable issues of the future"—replacing, as a method capable of regular application, the outworn and futile "balance of power." Such a course should lead to "the future establishment and maintenance of federal relations and peace among the nations of Europe," with a consequent reduction of the burden of competitive armaments which was stifling social progress. By way of expanding his suggestions, Eliot referred to passages in his report on the Far East entitled *Some Roads Towards Peace*, published by the Carnegie Endowment in January 1914. One of these, on "The Fear of Invasion," advocates elimination of this cause of war by working out other methods than war of settling international disputes. The other, on "The Exemption of Private Property from Capture at Sea," advocates an international agreement to this effect as reducing the need for competitive naval armaments.

We know, not only from the President's response to Eliot on August 14th, but because he talked about it at much length with Dr. Axson, that he gave this "momentous proposal" his "most thoughtful consideration." He also read this letter, and a later one from Dr. Eliot, to several members of his cabinet.

Both of Eliot's specific proposals—for an alliance with certain European nations, and for immediate American intervention in the war—ran wholly contrary to his declared beliefs and policies. He was against alliances: and he had already declared formal American neutrality and was even then considering the further and more determined appeal which he was to issue on August 18th. Moreover, he approached the problem with a far more comprehensive knowledge of all the facts than Eliot could have had at that time; and he had reached no decision, impulsive or otherwise, as to the culpability of the nations involved. But his response to Eliot on August 14th befitted the respect he felt for his correspondent:

"It is a momentous proposal you make in your letter of the sixth of August. I have just had an opportunity to turn to it among the papers awaiting my attention on my return home from Georgia. You may be sure that it will receive my most thoughtful consideration.

"I am afraid that its feasibility at present is very doubtful and it might be that it would add to the burden already put upon mankind by this terrible war if the only neutral nation should withdraw from the position of influence afforded her by her neutrality. But this is only my first thought about the matter. Thank you for your frankness in laying so important a suggestion before me.

"May I not thank you most sincerely for your generous personal sympathy."

Five days later, on August 19th—the day after his appeal for neutrality "in thought as well as in action" was issued—he wrote again to Eliot:

"Your letter of August sixth contained suggestions of so great importance that I have taken some time to turn them over in my mind. I have consulted with my colleagues also and you may be sure that we have given the most careful and deliberate consideration to the momentous thing you suggest.

"On the whole, our judgement does not accept it. I believe that we should not have the support of our own public opinion in it and that lacking that we should lack the momentum to accomplish the object in view, even if the course itself were practicable.

"I do not feel that I can venture upon it."[1]

[1]Several months later in a letter to a friend, he discloses his personal reaction to Eliot's proposal: "Many weeks ago, when the war had but just begun, Mr. Eliot wrote me a long and earnest letter arguing that we should actively join the Allies against Germany. I was amazed and distressed then, because I so sincerely respect Mr. Eliot and had thought that he might so confidently be counted on to serve always as part of the

Curiously enough, this letter crossed one written by Eliot on the 20th in which he frankly confesses to the President that in attempting to elaborate his proposal, he had decided to retract it, primarily for the reason that he had decided that the evidence for Germany's conviction was not sufficient to warrant proceeding against her, while Russia constituted a doubtful factor on the other side. Here Eliot was coming around, after advocating hasty and impulsive action, practically to the position that the President had held all along.

"The extreme rashness of Germany's action," Eliot wrote, "cannot but suggest that elements of the situation, still unknown to the rest of the world, were known to her. I do not feel the confidence I then felt in the information accessible when I wrote my letter to you of August 6th."

He also found undesirable the "secret diplomacy" which would be the necessary preparation for the coöperation with the Allies which he had suggested. While continuing to believe that "the interests of civilization and peace" required the defeat of the Central Powers, he felt that the forces of the Allies would suffice for this, while the existing hostilities would furnish an adequate needed demonstration of the horror and destructiveness of war.[1]

While this letter of August 20th, the product of an honest mind, must have served further to confirm Wilson's doubt concerning the origins of the war, and strengthen him in his policy of neutrality, the real importance of the correspondence lay in the train of "careful and deliberate" thought which the broader considerations in Eliot's letter and his Carnegie report aroused in Wilson's mind.

---

ballast of the nation, and utter what would be its sober second thought; but that shock has passed . . . *Somebody* must keep cool while our people grow hotter with discussing the war and all that it involves!" (Woodrow Wilson to Nancy Toy, December 12, 1914.)

[1] Eliot went further in this same letter and warmly commended Wilson's neutrality address of August 18th.

For many years he had been considering, as we have seen, the duties and obligations of America, with its power and its riches, in the world of the future. There had been, all along in his career, a prophetic sense of national opportunity, not of material expansion but of spiritual leadership. "The idea of America," he had told the graduating class at the Naval Academy in June, only a few weeks before the outbreak of the war, "is to serve humanity."[1] A little later, in his address on July 4th, he had asked:

"What are we going to do with the influence and power of this great nation?"[2]

And he answered his own query with a fervid vision of that service:

"My dream is that as the years go on . . . the world . . . will turn to America for those moral inspirations which lie at the basis of all freedom; that the world will never fear America unless it feels that it is engaged in some enterprise which is inconsistent with the rights of humanity; and that America will come into the full light of the day when all shall know that she puts human rights above all other rights and that her flag is the flag not only of America but of humanity."[3]

The crisis had now appeared. It was not merely a question of immediate action: the President had already been balked in his attempts in that direction: but what could be done in the future? The war could not last forever: what of the settlements? What would the "new world" require? What was America to advise?

Dr. Axson, with whom the President "thought aloud" on this and many other problems, has preserved a record of a conversation in which Wilson clearly set forth his vision of the essential terms of settlement, and first suggested

[1] June 5, 1914. *The Public Papers of Woodrow Wilson*, Vol. III, p. 127.
[2] Address at Independence Hall, Philadelphia. *Ibid.*, p. 142.
[3] *Ibid.*, p. 147.

his interest in the old idea of a league of nations.[1] Axson has no record of the exact date of the conversation, but it was "just after the return from Georgia."[2] It is as follows:

"I am afraid something will happen on the high seas that will make it impossible for us to keep out of the war. I have been thinking recently of one of Napoleon's sayings to the effect that nothing is ever permanently settled by war. It is perfectly obvious that this war will vitally change the relationships of nations. Four things will be essential to the reëstablishment in the world after peace is made.

"1. No nation shall ever again be permitted to acquire an inch of land by conquest.

"2. There must be a recognition of the reality of equal rights between small nations and great.

"3. Munitions of war must hereafter be manufactured entirely by the nations and not by private enterprise.

"4. There must be an association of the nations, all bound together for the protection of the integrity of each, so that any one nation breaking from this bond will bring upon herself war; that is to say, punishment, automatically."

---

[1] Dr. Axson to the author.

[2] Wilson's love for and confidence in Dr. Axson, his wife's brother, were deep-seated. He regarded him not only as a devoted friend but as a trusty confidant. He wrote on September 14, 1914:

"MY DEAR STOCK:

"I do not know when I have been so disappointed as not to find you at Cornish. I had set my heart on seeing you there. You know, my dear fellow, I must depend upon you very much more than I ever did before now. Will you not console me a bit for the disappointment in Cornish by coming down to Washington for the week-end, or as soon thereafter as possible, to stay just as long as it is possible for you to stay? It would not only cheer and benefit me but also help dear little Helen Bones very much indeed.

"Lucie and Mary send a great deal of love. It took us all aback not to find you when we arrived. I am now on my way home, having left Lucie and Mary at Cornish. In the forty-eight hours I was there it was astonishing and delightful to see how Mary picked up.

"Be sure to come soon.   "Affectionately yours,
                                                     "WOODROW WILSON"

WILLIAM J. BRYAN
SECRETARY OF STATE

WILLIAM G. McADOO
SECRETARY OF THE
TREASURY

COLONEL EDWARD M. HOUSE

JAMES W. GERARD
AMBASSADOR TO GERMANY

DR. CHARLES W. ELIOT
PRESIDENT EMERITUS OF
HARVARD UNIVERSITY

WOODROW WILSON'S ADVISERS DURING THE EARLY
PERIOD OF NEUTRALITY

It will be readily observed that the first and fourth of these "essentials" appear to have been suggested by Dr. Eliot's letter, although the fourth is given more definite form—a form, however, which was current enough at that time. Both, however, were ideas that had long been in Wilson's own mind. The first was referred to in the Mobile speech on October 27, 1913, and the fourth had been set forth in an article written for the *Political Science Quarterly* for June 1887—he was then thirty-one years of age and an associate professor at Bryn Mawr—in which he said:

"There is a tendency—is there not?—a tendency as yet dim, but already steadily impulsive and clearly destined to prevail, towards, first the confederation of parts of empires like the British, and finally of great states themselves. Instead of centralization of power, there is to be wide union with tolerated divisions of prerogative. This is a tendency towards the American type—of governments joined with governments for the pursuit of common purposes, in honorary equality and honorable subordination."[1]

The other two points appear neither in Eliot's letter nor in the report to which it refers. The third, the importance of which, with reference to the European war, was not then apparent, must have been suggested to Wilson by his own difficulties in Mexico and other Latin-American states, where revolution and disorder incited to foreign intervention and strife, of which gun-running constituted both a cause and an effect. The second was but a reiteration of the doctrine Wilson had long been preaching in opposition to "dollar diplomacy."

The initial and prophetic remark about the United States being drawn into the war by events on the high seas may have been suggested by Eliot's discussion of the exemption of private property from capture, but it is more

---

[1] *The Public Papers of Woodrow Wilson*, Vol. I, pp. 157-158.

likely that it arose out of a consideration of the state of
affairs which even then existed, involving the serious
embarrassment of American commerce, and out of the
proposal for acceptance of the Declaration of London
which he had lately approved, with the statement that
such acceptance "would prevent grave misunderstandings
which may arise as to the relations between belligerent
and neutral powers."[1] Great Britain's rejection of that
proposal was not yet made, but might be regarded as
probable. In this statement Wilson made no reference to
the doctrine of the "freedom of the seas" upon which he
was later to set such store.

It is noticeable that Axson's record of these remarks
includes no expression of feeling for or against either side
in the war, and no mention of the immediate aspect of
Eliot's plan to "punish Austria-Hungary and Germany
for the outrages they are now committing." Instead,
appears Wilson's melancholy reflection that "nothing is
ever permanently settled by war." As a whole, it shows
the President rising above the actual conflict and casting
his glance ahead toward a fairer vision. It shows him trying
to evolve a settlement on the basis of general principles of
justice—to bring order out of chaos and derive good from
evil. It shows him casting about for means to carry the
world with him in his high endeavour. It also shows him
wrestling with the problem of applying the vision to the
reality—facing the dilemma of keeping himself and his
country above the brutal conflict while yet intervening in
it for the purpose of putting his ideal settlement into effect.

---

[1]*Foreign Relations of the United States*, Supplement, 1914, p. 216.

CHAPTER II

THE HOME FRONT

Democratic institutions are never done—they are, like the living tissue, always a-making. It is a strenuous thing this of living the life of a free people: and we cannot escape the burden of our inheritance.

Address at Middletown, Connecticut, April 30, 1889.

The President can lead only as he can command the ear of both Congress and the country . . .

"The Making of the Nation," in the Atlantic Monthly, *July 1897.*

Our program of legislation with regard to the regulation of business is now virtually complete. It has been put forth, as we intended, as a whole, and leaves no conjecture as to what is to follow. The road at last lies clear and firm before business. It is a road which it can travel without fear or embarrassment. It is the road to ungrudged, unclouded success. In it every honest man, every man who believes that the public interest is part of his own interest, may walk with perfect confidence.

Address to Congress, December 8, 1914.

I. THE CAMPAIGN OF 1914

THE President was keenly aware of the effect that the European war might have upon his cherished programme of domestic reconstruction. As an historian he knew the disruptive possibilities of any foreign war: it was one of the reasons for his policy, so vigorously pursued, of determined neutrality. He told Secretary Daniels:

"Every reform we have won will be lost if we go into this war. We have been making a fight on special privilege. We have got new tariff and currency and trust legislation. We don't know yet how they will work. They are not thoroughly set."[1]

---

[1] Reported to the author by Josephus Daniels.

If he was clear in his perception of the danger, he was strong in his determination to meet it. Nothing must be allowed to divert him and his party until the programme was complete; a breakdown, at that time, of the new banking legislation, the new tariff law, the scheme for trust regulation, with the accompanying loss of confidence in Democratic leadership, might produce such confusion and uncertainty as to endanger American unity and stability.

The mid-term elections, always regarded with anxiety by a new administration, since they furnish the first popular test of its success, were rapidly approaching. Many Democratic senators and congressmen, standing for reëlection, were much concerned. What would be the reaction at home toward the new legislation? Would the people approve the attitude of the administration toward the war? Business had been slowing down even before the outbreak of the conflict, the first economic repercussions of which were also sharply unfavourable, and the opposition did not fail to blame the new tariff law and the "campaign against business."

While it was clear that the President was far stronger with the country than his party, it was equally clear that his own power and prestige would be severely tested. George Harvey, shrewdest of political commentators and no worshipper of Wilson, remarked:

". . . the return of a Democratic majority, however greatly reduced, would signalize the most striking personal triumph of any President since Andrew Jackson overwhelmed the opposition in 1832. Now, as then, the issue is not a party, but a personality, so completely has Mr. Wilson by sheer force of intellectual vigor and unsurpassed power of resolution dominated the political aggregation which even today, after two years of full authority, can hardly be designated, in comparison with the Republican phalanx in the fullness of its strength, as an organization."[1]

The President met the challenge with extraordinary vigour and skill. It stirred within him all of his latent convictions as to the need, in time of crisis, of strong leadership,[2] and the necessity of a vigorous and effective party control. "When party government fails, all definiteness goes out of politics."[3] Confronted by great national danger, "somebody must be trusted."[4]

The President decided at once, however, that he could not "in any ordinary sense take an active part in the approaching campaign."[5]

The people, excited by the events in Europe, would expect their President to remain in Washington.

"My job, I now know, can be done best only if I devote my whole thought and attention to it and think of nothing but the duties of the hour. I am not at liberty and shall not be, so far as I can now see, to turn away from those duties to undertake any kind of political canvas."[6]

But he began a campaign of letter-writing, of endorsements of Democrats who were or thought they were in danger, that was comprehensive and persistent. In two long letters designed for publication, the first on September 4th to Congressman Doremus, chairman of the Democratic Congressional Campaign Committee, and the other on October 17th to Congressman Underwood, he appealed to the people on the basis of the record of the

[1]George Harvey, "Uphold the President," in the *North American Review*, October 1914.

[2]"Leaderless government" he had long believed to be the chief defect of the American system. See his address before the Virginia State Bar Association on August 4, 1897. *The Public Papers of Woodrow Wilson*, Vol. I, pp. 336–359.

[3]*Ibid.*, p. 339.

[4]*Congressional Government*, p. 283 (1885).

[5]Woodrow Wilson to Frank E. Doremus, September 4, 1914. *The Public Papers of Woodrow Wilson*, Vol. III, p. 166.

[6]*Ibid.*

party, which he presented in glowing terms, and the need
of support until the "scheme of peace and honor and disinterested service . . . be brought to its full realization."[1]
He did not, however, rest wholly upon past achievements.
The fight must go on. ". . . a great work of constructive
development remains to be accomplished . . ." While the
new proposals constituted a programme that would have
occupied the entire energies of any ordinary administration—"building up our merchant marine," "a great
program for the conservation of our natural resources,"
"the development of the water power of the country"[2]—
it was excellent fighting psychology. For he was not only
proposing to consolidate the gains already made, but
to advance boldly into new territory. The European war,
no matter how serious, only made it necessary to go forward with greater determination.

Both of these letters, as well as scores of personal
appeals, radiated confidence, courage, optimism. Containing not a word of doubt or uncertainty, they were
designed to put a fighting spirit into every faint-hearted
follower. The session of Congress just closing was " . . . I
venture to say . . . more fruitful in important legislation
of permanent usefulness to the country than any session
of Congress within the memory of the active public men
of our generation."[3]

He contended with campaign optimism that the "questions which plagued business" had been "thoughtfully
settled" and "the apparent antagonism between government and business cleared away and brought to an end."

How had this been done? By "a single purpose, namely,

---

[1]Woodrow Wilson to Oscar W. Underwood, October 17, 1914. *The Public Papers of Woodrow Wilson*, Vol. III, p. 193.

[2]*Ibid.*

[3]Woodrow Wilson to Frank E. Doremus, September 4, 1914. *The Public Papers of Woodrow Wilson*, Vol. III, p. 164.

to destroy private control and set business free."[1] ". . . Monopoly is to be cut off at the roots."[2]

Here indeed lay the core of Wilson's programme: in its essence a formula for coöperation between democracy and capitalism, but with democracy in firm control. The great trusts and financial interests had been brought to heel; but private initiative and competition, within the limits prescribed, were not only to be maintained, but encouraged. Such control might be called "socialistic"; it sought to preserve the benefits of a chastened capitalism.

While the President could assert that "business has already adjusted itself to the new conditions with singular ease and elasticity,"[3] business itself was by no means so sure. There were ominous rumblings of economic unrest, out of which might easily develop political difficulties of the first order. A consequence of the new formula was that the President, who had all along been fighting "big business" and "privilege," must now lead and direct and conciliate these interests. If democracy was to control business, then democracy must boldly accept the responsibilities and the difficulties. It was also clear that the coöperation of these powerful "interests" would become indispensable in facing the crisis due to the European war.

Wilson perceived the situation and accepted the full responsibility. While little was publicly known of his activities in this field, they were of the utmost importance, not only in preventing powerful opposition in the campaign, but in developing a united front to meet the difficulties then confronting the government.

Evidence in plenty indicates that business leaders generally, even the greatest of them, though they might have

---

[1]Woodrow Wilson to Oscar W. Underwood, October 17, 1914. *The Public Papers of Woodrow Wilson*, Vol. III, p. 187.

[2]*Ibid.*, p. 190.

[3]*Ibid.*, p. 188.

been skeptical, were prepared to accept or, at least, to invoke the President's leadership. In time of difficulty the country turns instinctively to the strong man. On September 9th the complicated problems of the railroads were unceremoniously laid upon the President's desk. A committee of railroad presidents[1] waited upon him to set forth the emergency which confronted them, and to urge the support of their credit. On the following day Wilson replied, in a letter to Frank Trumbull, chairman of the board of directors of the Chesapeake & Ohio Railway Company, in which he met the situation with candour and in a spirit of genuine coöperation:

"Since you read it to me yesterday, I have read again the statement you made on behalf of the committee of railroad presidents whom I had the pleasure of meeting and conferring with at my office. It is a lucid statement of plain truth.

"You ask me to call the attention of the country to the imperative need that railway credits be sustained and the railroads helped in every possible way, whether by private coöperative effort or by the action, wherever feasible, of governmental agencies; and I am glad to do so, because I think the need very real. . . .

". . . we must all stand as one to see justice done and all fair assistance rendered, and rendered ungrudgingly."[2]

About the same time, J. P. Morgan, in an urgent letter to the President, said that he was "appalled at the prospect before us." The war by cutting down the trade of other countries furnished a tremendous opportunity for America, but business was fearful, under the new laws,

---

[1]Frank Trumbull; Samuel Rea, president of the Pennsylvania Railroad; Daniel Willard, president of the Baltimore & Ohio Railroad Company; Fairfax Harrison, president of the Southern Railway Company; E. P. Ripley, president of the Atchison, Topeka & Santa Fe Railway Company; Hale Holden, president of the Chicago, Burlington & Quincy Railroad Company.

[2]September 10, 1914. For complete letter, see *The Public Papers of Woodrow Wilson*, Vol. III, pp. 172–173.

for "its own capital invested in its own country."[1] The President replied on September 17th:

"Your letter of September fourth, though unanswered, has by no means been overlooked. I have read it with the closest attention.

"I am sincerely sorry that you should be so blue about the situation. I believe that being blue is just the wrong thing, if you will permit me to say so. It is a situation which requires nothing more, in my judgment, than courage and the kind of intelligence which our bankers and men of affairs have shown themselves equal to applying to any circumstances that have yet arisen, and my judgement differs radically with yours with regard to the pending legislation. Some features of the bills passed will, I hope, be changed in conference, because they seem to me to involve a risk of injustice as well as of disturbance. But, essentially, they attack nothing but practices which it has been generally agreed should be abandoned in the interest of sound and honest business, and my own judgement (which I pray may be verified by experience) is that the clearing of the air and the removal of the doubt as to what legislation is to be passed will be beneficial, not detrimental.

"I may be mistaken in all these things, of course, but I have sought to take as wide a view as possible and to be guided by the net result of my observation and information,—information drawn from many quarters,—and my own confidence in the result is considerable.

"I need not tell you that I value your frank letters, not only for information, but also because I sincerely want to consider the judgement of men in the midst of affairs and whose judgements are based upon actual contact with business."

On September 24th Mr. Morgan replied that the Presi-

[1] September 4, 1914.

dent's letter to Mr. Trumbull had given him and many others "very great encouragement."

The President soon discovered, however, that in so far as economic problems were concerned, it was one thing to accept leadership in a democracy, quite another to get anything done. If the system of "checks and balances" operated with difficulty in the political field, as the President had been arguing all his life, how much more in handling complex economic problems. Raiload rates and railroad regulation, for example, were in the hands of a deliberative independent body, the Interstate Commerce Commission, which the President in theory at least could not direct, or even influence. He had told Congress that the "government and business men are ready to meet each other half way," and that "we shall now be their spokesmen,"[1] yet when it came to acting in a crisis, he had to reckon with the cumbrous, slow-moving, semi-independent agencies of democracy.

Some of the railroad leaders urged the President to use his influence with the Interstate Commerce Commission. He replied in a letter marked "Personal and Confidential," to Henry L. Higginson of Boston[2]:

"I have your letter of October twenty-sixth and agree with its main conclusions almost entirely. I would if I thought it justified make some very plain recommendations to the Interstate Commerce Commission, but they are as jealous of executive suggestion as the Supreme Court would be, and I dare say with justification. I can only hope and believe that they will see the rate case in a new light in the new circumstances."[3]

---

[1]Address to Congress, January 20, 1914. *The Public Papers of Woodrow Wilson*, Vol. III, pp. 82–83.

[2]Henry Lee Higginson was a banker. He was a director of the American Telephone & Telegraph Company, the General Electric Company, the National Shawmut Bank, the Ashburton Mining Company, and others; and a trustee of the Carnegie Institution at Washington.

[3]October 29, 1914.

In spite of his doubt regarding the justification of an appeal, he sent Higginson's letter to W. M. Daniels, his old friend of the Princeton years, whom he had appointed a member of the commission:

"I know how you feel and I am sure you know how I feel, but I am awaiting the decision of the commission in the newly opened rate case with deep and serious anxiety. I believe that a concession to the railroads is absolutely necessary to steady and relieve the present extraordinary difficulties of the financial situation.

"It is for that reason that I am taking the liberty of sending you this letter of Major Higginson's, which I think in the main is true. I wonder if it would make any impression on any of your colleagues to see it."[1]

When the commission did not act favourably, there is evidence that he considered, later, a further and more definite appeal—which he never made:

"I think you know already how strong I feel the case of the railroads to be before the Interstate Commerce Commission.

"The question that I have been debating with myself is this: How far am I at liberty, if at all, to express to that commission my opinion, or, rather, my convictions, in this matter, and if I should think it wise or permissible to act, what form should my action take?

"I see no reason to hope that the attitude of the commission will be changed; it was so fixed and showed itself so inveterate in the former decision."[2]

Trust and tariff legislation were also highly disturbing, and we find the President making every effort to coöperate with and conciliate the interests involved—and yet, in

---

[1] October 29, 1914.

[2] Woodrow Wilson to Charles Francis Adams, November 2, 1914. A month later the commission, on its own initiative, moved by the gathering difficulties of the railroads due to the war, did permit an increase of rates.

every case, holding to his legislative policies with good-humoured inflexibility. He wrote to Henry L. Higginson, who had become in some measure a spokesman for business leadership:

"That was a very kind letter you wrote me yesterday. You must have known that I was feeling a little blue by reaction and strain and needed cheering, and you have cheered me very much.

"I believe with you that the main work of the session is going to work out into things which, when we have tried them, we shall approve, and I believe that all that is needed now is confidence on the part of the business men of the country to embrace great opportunities and achieve great results.

"As I have said always, I am not afraid of big corporations merely because of their size, and I believe that properly managed they can be of great service to the business of the country, but I am afraid of businesses of different sorts interlocked with one another and organizations within the same field of business nominally independent but really under a single direction.

"These things we shall work out with moderation and, I hope, with wisdom, and I am sure that men like yourself will give the heartiest coöperation and the fairest judgement of the result."[1]

That he was not unsuccessful in his efforts is attested by a later letter:

"I am heartily glad that you and your partner feel that we down here have been of real assistance in stiffening the courage and backing the efforts of our business men, and if this cotton loan fund can be put through, I shall feel that we are on the high road to a real recovery and regeneration of our business. I feel that it is absolutely necessary to complete that fund and I was greatly pleased the other

[1]October 23, 1914.

day when Mr. McAdoo told me you had promised to lend your influential aid."[1]

There can be no doubt that the President's activities in the direction of coöperating with business men, many of whom were Republicans, played an important part in the campaign. There was little evidence of that subterranean movement of worried money interests so potent in many campaigns. This is the more surprising because the President never for a moment gave over his programme for a more extended regulation of economic affairs, nor did he cease throughout the campaign to attack the system under which "big business" had been operating.[2] If the reconciliation seemed for the moment effective, it was not, as we shall see, to last long.

Wilson's prestige, during the campaign, seemed to increase steadily. There was "the sudden recognition of the fact that we were facing a crisis and the instant thankfulness that our interests were in the hands of Woodrow Wilson instead of some other. For his bitterest assailants[3] had all along felt his high purposes and his firmness, and when danger confronted the country they were as grateful as anyone else for a combination of high purpose and firmness."[4]

---

[1]Woodrow Wilson to Henry L. Higginson, November 16, 1914.

[2]He referred in his letter to Mr. Underwood, on October 17th, to the "private control" that had "shown its sinister face on every hand in America . . . sometimes very brazenly," and he had even charged "the interests" with fomenting a panic—but "the panic that the friends of privilege had predicted did not follow." *The Public Papers of Woodrow Wilson*, Vol. III, pp. 187 and 188.

[3]Excepting probably Theodore Roosevelt who was attacking Wilson's foreign policies.

[4]Editorial in the New York *Times*, September 5, 1914. A little later the *Times*, speaking of Wilson's "mastery of the situation," said:

". . . Mr. Cleveland never, even in his first administration, had the grasp of it that Mr. Wilson has. His will was iron, but he could not always bend the wills of other men. His second administration was a ceaseless battle with a faction in his own party which, toward the end, became the majority faction. Mr. Wilson has curious resemblances to him, made fleetingly apparent through the more obvious differences. The resemblances come down to the fact that his will is as iron as Cleveland's, though the iron hand is hidden in a velvet glove that Cleveland never wore. The fundamental difference is in the measure of success." (October 12, 1914.)

The Republicans wisely made no attempt to attack the President on his record as a whole; they centred chiefly upon the tariff and the extravagance of Congress.[1]

By the middle of October, the President had not only largely silenced the opposition, but he had secured a high degree of unity in his party.[2] Some even of Wilson's former enemies, among them George Harvey, watching with a shrewd eye Wilson's developing powers of leadership, had become newly favourable. Possibly reflecting the shifting interests of "big business," which had so curiously driven him apart from Wilson in 1911,[3] he was now for the moment highly commendatory,[4] and on October 4th he called upon the President at the White House, the first meeting of the two men since the famous "break." A little later Henry Watterson was received, and the "making up" was complete.[5] It was, however, in Harvey's case,

---

[1] "I deny that there is any need for additional internal revenue taxation at this time. I assert that the government can run along without embarrassment if it will exercise proper economy. The present Democratic administration has been more grossly extravagant than any administration which preceded it. . . .

"If the President will stop the extravagance of the government and practice as well as preach economy, there is no need for increased taxation." Congressman Mann, Republican, in the House of Representatives, September 25, 1914. *Congressional Record*, Vol. 51, pp. 15697–15698.

[2] In an editorial on October 6, 1914, the New York *Times* remarked:

"The Republican party is still divided, but the Democrats are united—a reversal of ancient tradition. That unusual state of affairs is due chiefly to the remarkable personality of the President. He has inspired the nation with confidence in him as a leader; he has inspired the world with confidence in him as a statesman; it is not strange that he has inspired his party with confidence in him as its chief."

[3] See *Woodrow Wilson, Life and Letters*, Vol. III, p. 246 ff.

[4] In the *North American Review* of October 1914; an article widely republished in the newspapers.

[5] Watterson had himself invited the reconciliation in a letter written on September 24th, in which he said:

"I hope that hereafter you and I will better understand one another; in any event that the single disagreeable episode will vanish and never be thought of more. In Paris last winter I went over the whole matter with Mr. McCombs and we quite settled and blotted out our end of it. I very much regret the use of any rude word—too much the characteristic of our rough-and-tumble political combats—and can truly say that I have not only earnestly wished the success of your administration but have sought to find points of agreement, not of disagreement.

"I am writing as an old man—old enough to be your father—who has the claim upon

purely a political reconciliation, for Wilson no doubt thoroughly understood the forces that were at work behind the scenes, nor did he easily forgive or forget, once he had made up his mind regarding a man.

As a politician Wilson had travelled far in two years. It was now no longer "only progressives on guard," nor yet the sovereign "appeal to the people" upon which his earlier successes had been founded. He no longer exhibited contempt for the devices of political mechanism. While he indeed employed vigorously his old method of popular appeal, through scores of letters, public and private, in behalf of Democratic candidates for Congress,[1] he also showed himself an adept in many of the other arts of the politician. We have seen him smoothing the ruffled plumage of the millionaires and meeting George Harvey with a wry smile. He was to go a long step further—to win the support of the old "bosses" of the Democratic party, with some of whom he had fought so bitterly at an earlier time.

In New York, for example, the anti-Tammany faction, backed by the President's friends, had presented Franklin D. Roosevelt and John Hennessy as their candidates in the primaries for United States senator and governor.

---

your consideration that all his life he has pursued the ends you yourself have aimed at, if at times too zealously and exactingly, yet without self-seeking or rancor."

To this the President replied on September 28th:

"Your kind letter has gratified me very deeply. You may be sure that any feeling I may have had has long since disappeared and that I feel only gratified that you should again and again have come to my support in the columns of the *Courier-Journal*. The whole thing was a great misunderstanding."

[1]Here, for example, is a letter to Powell Evans, of Philadelphia, supporting the candidacy of A. Mitchell Palmer for the Senate against that of Senator Boies Penrose:

". . . for a long time to come, legislative questions will be questions of progress, of suiting means to new ends, of facilitating business and using to the utmost the resources of the country in the vast development of our business and our enterprise . . . In such circumstances, what sort of man do you wish to have represent you in the United States Senate? A man who wishes to hark back to the old conditions but cannot? A man who can, possibly, obstruct but who can do nothing more? Or a man with the zest and vision of a new age, a man full of the spirit of Pennsylvania as she is going to be? . . .

"I have seen Mr. Palmer tested. I know his quality. Pennsylvania ought to accept and trust him and through him play her proper part in the constructive policies of a new generation." (October 20, 1914.)

While Wilson had little or nothing to do with the primary campaign, it was most important, in the coming election, that the breach be healed and the Democratic forces united against the common opposition. Although he had been at swords' points with Tammany from the beginning of his political career, although the organization had nearly defeated him at the Baltimore convention, he now wrote letters cordially endorsing both Glynn and Gerard, though both were badly beaten in the primaries. To Glynn, who afterwards became his devoted friend and who made the keynote speech for him in the convention of 1916, he wrote:

"I am very glad to hear of the hopeful prospects of the campaign in New York. I . . . want to give myself the pleasure of expressing to you personally my earnest hope that the voters of the state will return you to your post as governor with an emphatic majority. Your record is open and to be judged for itself. . . . I hope that every man who goes to the polls next month will look upon your candidacy as embodying the cause of progressive legislation and the advancement at every point of the interests of the people."[1]

While both Glynn and Gerard were defeated by the Republicans in the election, Wilson's support had made for party harmony.

The President also took steps to harmonize the Democracy of New Jersey. The Smith-Nugent machine was still smarting from the drubbing it had received at his hands a few years before, but when, in September, Representative Walter I. McCoy, an organization congressman, was made associate justice of the Supreme Court of the District of Columbia, Nugent came over to the President's support.

Similarly he was prepared to make a friendly gesture to

[1]Woodrow Wilson to Martin H. Glynn, October 15, 1914.

the Democratic Old Guard of Illinois, through a letter favouring Roger Sullivan, the state boss, who had become candidate for United States senator.[1] It was written to Congressman Henry T. Rainey:

"I have read with the greatest interest the account you were kind enough to send me of the Illinois Democratic state convention. The whole thing is full of fine promise for the party; for it shows how heartily all the elements of the party are drawing together in Illinois for a successful campaign; and with this union success is sure to come.

"You call my attention to the fact that some gentlemen connected with the recently organized Wilson-Bryan League are urging Democrats in Illinois to vote for the Progressive candidate for the Senate of the United States[2] rather than for the nominee of the Democratic primaries. You ask me if I approve of this. Certainly I do not. I have held myself very strictly to the principle that as a party man I am bound by the free choice of the people at the polls. I have always stood by the result of the primaries; I shall always do so; and I think it the duty of every Democrat to do so who cares for the success and sincerity of his party."[3]

For some reason this letter was never publicly used,[4] but it represented nevertheless the purpose of the President to stand by the party organization.

The President also encouraged members of his cabinet to take part in the campaign, McAdoo and Garrison in New York and New Jersey, Houston in Missouri, and

---

[1] Sullivan had played an important part in the Baltimore convention by swinging the Illinois delegation to Wilson's support on the forty-third ballot. See *The Life and Letters of Woodrow Wilson*, Vol. III, p. 361.

[2] Raymond Robins, a man of the highest character, devoted to the public service.

[3] October 12, 1914.

[4] In an address given later, at Peoria, Postmaster General Burleson announced that the President favoured the election of Sullivan. Congressman Rainey, in a letter to the author, asserts his belief that if the President's letter had been used in the campaign Sullivan would have been elected.

Burleson in Illinois, and he even sought the support of certain newspapers, a course always distasteful to him.[1]

Coming into office originally as a revolter from the old leadership of his party, with slashing appeals to all progressives and independents, party organization and party discipline had begun to seem highly important to him. So often the rebel who comes into power fighting the old organization remains in power by using it: this is one of the arts of politics. The secret of the President's legislative success during the session of Congress just closing had been due largely to the support of the old, tried and experienced party men. He had said to Burleson:

"What you told me about the old standpatters is true. They at least will stand by the party and the administration. I can rely on them better than I can on some of my own crowd."[2]

And Tumulty reports him as saying:

"My head is with the progressives in the Democratic party, but my heart, because of the way they stood by me, is with the so-called Old Guard in the Senate. They stand without hitching."[3]

As a result of all of these extraordinary political activi-

---

[1]On September 19th he wrote to George S. Johns, editor of the St. Louis *Post-Dispatch*:

"I have heard that the *Post-Dispatch* is not friendly to the candidacy of Mr. Collins, the Democratic candidate in the Twelfth District of Missouri. I must frankly say that I do not know Mr. Collins, but the maintenance of a large Democratic majority in the House of Representatives is so absolutely essential to the administration that I am going to ask you to be very sure of your ground before taking a positive stand against the Democratic candidate in your district. . . .

". . . I feel so particularly concerned that nothing should happen to break the course of what we are now trying to do that I thought you would pardon this word of interest in Mr. Collins' candidacy from me."

Mr. Johns replied, explaining the stand taken by the *Post-Dispatch*. To this the President replied, in a letter of October 9th:

". . . I have nothing to say in reply to your letter about Mr. Collins. I wrote merely in my anxiety to leave nothing undone to insure a majority in the next House. I knew all along that I could trust you to follow the right line."

[2]See *Woodrow Wilson, Life and Letters*, Vol. IV, p. 49.

[3]J. P. Tumulty, *Woodrow Wilson As I Know Him*, p. 101.

ties—which were, of course, added to the burden of the war problems which he was carrying—Wilson secured a degree of harmony, a political morale, in the Democratic party that was most unusual.

Some of the letters of the time indicate a warmth of feeling and a depth of confidence quite surprising in a man so often charged, as the President had been, with coldness, aloofness. We find Vice-President Marshall writing to Wilson:

"For all your faith and confidence in me I thank you.

"I am going tonight or tomorrow to Indiana, Missouri and Colorado to tell in my way the story and to help, if I can, heal any dissensions in our ranks.

"I wish you continued health and prosperity. And may He, without Whose approving smile our labors are all in vain, be round about you as the mountains are round about Jerusalem!"[1]

And Wilson replied, not so easily and colloquially, but sincerely:

"I want to send you just these few lines of sincere and genuine and personal appreciation. The pleasure of being associated with you grows as the months pass and I want to send you as the session closes this simple message of congratulation and thanks."[2]

At the same time he wrote to Champ Clark, who had been his sharpest opponent in the Baltimore convention:

"Just one final word of friendship and congratulation upon the closing of the session. I want to say how sincere a pleasure it has been to me to be associated with men like yourself devoted to the interests of the country through the action of the Democratic party. I hope and believe that we can all of us look back always upon the

[1] October 17 (?), 1914.
[2] October 19, 1914.

two sessions of the sixty-third Congress with unalloyed satisfaction."[1]

Wilson himself glowed for the moment in the warmth of good feeling—but not without the characteristic skepticism with which he regarded personal popularity. He wrote to his friend Mrs. Hulbert on September 20th:

"For the moment I am approved of and trusted by the party and the country and am popular. But I am not deceived. I know by what tenure a man holds popularity. It is only a tenancy at will, and may be terminated without notice. Any day I may find it my duty to do something that will make me intensely unpopular, it may be, the object of fierce and passionate criticism. The place has brought me no personal blessing, but only irreparable loss and desperate suffering. I am not complaining; I am only stating the facts, and letting you see the very inside of my mind."

The Democrats did not fail to stress the necessity of giving the President support in view of the European situation, although the war itself played little part in the campaign.

"War in the East! Peace in the West! Thank God for Wilson!"[2]

Throughout the campaign Theodore Roosevelt hurried from place to place to do what he could for the Progressive candidates, but it soon became apparent that his new party was disintegrating. Colonel Harvey remarked with evident glee:

"... our Colonel ... is ... rapidly becoming the rank and file of the Recessive Party."[3]

Former President Taft took no active part in the campaign. While doubtless not in sympathy with some of the

---

[1]October 19, 1914.
[2]Democratic Text Book, 1914.
[3]George Harvey, in the New York *Times*, November 1, 1914.

President's domestic reforms, he publicly commended him for his maintenance of neutrality.

"President Wilson has taken the exact stand and has expressed it with admirable accuracy."[1]

The election took place on November 3rd, the President travelling to Princeton to cast his ballot. While the result was far from being what he and his friends had hoped, the Democrats managed to maintain control of both houses of Congress, which was, after all, their main objective.[2]

The greatest revulsion against the Democrats came in the East, especially in New York and New Jersey, where the collapse of the Roosevelt Progressive movement enabled the regular Republicans to win. The Democratic congressional candidate in Wilson's own district in New Jersey failed of election—a hard blow. But the President comforted himself with the record made in the West. To Mrs. Toy he wrote on November 9th:

". . . after all is said that can be said, there was the very strong reaction, at least in the East, and good reason furnished for raising the question abroad (where alone I care for personal prestige just now) whether I could really be accepted as the spokesman of the United States. What I get solid satisfaction out of is the support the West gave us, the real heart of America, which has hitherto really never manifested its confidence in the Democratic party by *majorities*. That gives me vital comfort and a very lively hope. We have had a change of venue. A different part of America now decides, not the part which has usually arrogated to itself a selfish leadership and patronage of the rest. For the first time it turns to the Democratic

---

[1] New York *Times*, October 16, 1914.

[2] The final returns showed that the new House would be composed of 227 Democrats, 200 Republicans, 7 Progressives, and 1 Socialist. The Democrats had lost 63 seats and the Progressives 11; the Republicans had gained 73 and the Socialists 1. In the Senate the Democrats held their majority of 10, 53 seats as against 42 Republicans and 1 Progressive.

party. A few years ago there were only two lone Democrats in the Senate from any part of the country west of Kansas City (always excepting Texas), but now there are to be seventeen. A party that has been called sectional is becoming unmistakably national. The sweep of its influence and power is immensely broadened. *That* puts tonic in my lungs."[1]

It is plain that many aspects of this kind of political activity, since it involved appealing to elements in the electorate which did not and never would believe in him or in his ideals and purposes, were repugnant to the President and that he entered upon them only because he felt that a defeat at this time, and the loss of control in Congress, would destroy the effectiveness of his leadership during the last two years of his administration. His defeat in the East certainly cooled his *rapprochement* with the "interests," encouraged the opposition then developing in both Senate and House; and the new relationships with the bosses, whether or not they whole-heartedly supported his candidates, proved of doubtful value.

Nevertheless the election cleared the way for the President to meet, without undue opposition in Congress, the crowding new problems occasioned by the war.

II. THE PRESIDENT AND ECONOMIC LEADERSHIP

While the November elections clarified the political atmosphere, few of the real issues that confronted the nation had been submitted to the people, and the result was rather a deed of trust to the President than a mandate to guide his course. As such he accepted it and continued to wrestle with the four tremendous groups of problems either precipitated by the European war or aggravated

---

[1]Taft also found room for a hearty chuckle. While he was undoubtedly pleased at his party's recuperation of strength, he was even more pleased that the Progressive party and its rampant leader had been "relegated to innocuous desuetude." (New York *Times*, November 4, 1914.)

by it. The first of these dealt with principles and measures for meeting the disastrous economic dislocations caused by the sudden and almost complete stoppage of foreign commerce, and the crisis in finance. The second, the struggle to secure an American merchant marine. The third involved the President's hurried, if determined, attempt to round out his programme of domestic reform before the storm had become utterly overwhelming. The fourth was diplomatic; the effort of the President, fearful that the ship of state be engulfed in the tidal wave from Europe, to maintain the neutrality which he had already declared. The first three of these groups of problems will be presented in this and following sections; the fourth will require a more comprehensive treatment in other chapters.

It would be difficult to exaggerate the effects of the economic crisis in America that followed the outbreak of the war. It was not merely the closing of the stock exchanges, which could have been predicted, or even the demoralization of international finance and the threat to the stability of the American banking system, but foreign commerce, endangered by the activities of the belligerents against each other and by their moratoriums and embargoes, had come to a sudden and practically complete stoppage. Merchant vessels of all belligerents, except those converted to naval uses and so removed from trade, scurried for port and hesitated to put to sea—a withdrawal which became permanent so far as German and Austrian ships were concerned. Even neutral vessels had to use caution about what cargo they took and where they took it. This situation bore particularly hard upon the United States. Having few ships in foreign trade under her own flag, the loss of use of the great carrying fleets of England and Germany meant an interruption of her commerce not only with those countries, but with all others as well. Produce of all kinds intended for shipment lay clogged on wharves, in warehouses and freight cars. Even when ships did begin to take to the sea again, new barriers confronted the shippers. Freight rates had suddenly shot up to unheard-of figures; insurance rates were all but prohibitive. To make matters worse, the crisis developed in the autumn just as American crops were being harvested and farmers and planters were looking forward to the customary settlement of their credits. The great staples were all seriously affected. Cotton that had sold for an average price of 13½ cents a pound in 1913 had dropped by the middle of August 1914 to 6 or 6½ cents. Ruin threatened the farmer, the railroads that transported his crops, the merchants that supplied him, and the banks that loaned him money.

Other serious consequences soon developed. Demoralization of trade, by suddenly decreasing the return from tariff and other taxes, created a crisis in government finance. During August 1914 there was a decrease of more than $10,629,000 over the same month in 1913,[1] and McAdoo informed the President on September 2nd that a continuation of this reduction would mean a loss of customs revenues for the fiscal year ending June 30, 1915, of from $75,000,000 to $100,000,000.

It was most fortunate at this time—a fortune that the American people have not yet assessed at its true worth— that the administration in Washington had courage, that it did not fear the full responsibility of economic as well as political leadership. Weak hands, a doubtful or subservient spirit in the White House, during these anxious months might have involved the country in economic and financial confusion of the first magnitude. Wilson's formula for the coöperation of democracy and capitalism, which has been referred to, with democracy in firm control,

---

[1] See Woodrow Wilson's address to Congress on September 4, 1914. *The Public Papers of Woodrow Wilson*, Vol. III, p. 160.

the consequences of which involved a vigorous and fearless leadership in Washington, became in this time of crisis an incomparable asset to the nation. It is truly remarkable that there is nowhere in the letters or documents so much as a shading of doubt or of fear: the President met the most difficult problems and rose to important and far-reaching decisions with firmness and confidence. The statesman, like the field marshal of a great army, who is thus prepared to lead, to accept unlimited responsibility, may make mistakes—Wilson made them—but the value to the nation in a time of crisis of his courage, his self-reliance, his utter confidence in his own course are beyond measure.

The President was fortunate, also, in having, in his Secretary of the Treasury, Mr. McAdoo, a man of action and of courage comparable with his own—and with whom he could work on terms of confidence and understanding. It is significant that at the very onset of the crisis, as we have seen, it was to Wilson and to McAdoo that the great financiers and railroad and industrial managers, as well as the frightened cotton planters of the South, turned immediately and instinctively. The visit of the railroad presidents to the White House has already been recounted. The financiers of Wall Street sought the leadership of Washington even more earnestly. McAdoo relates in his reminiscences:

"About nine-thirty on Friday morning, July 31st, J. P. Morgan, of New York, called me on the telephone. He said that in view of the demoralized condition of the market the Governors of the New York Stock Exchange would meet at ten o'clock that morning to consider the question of closing the Exchange. He went on to say that they would be glad to have my advice as to whether or not this should be done. . . .

"I did not exactly relish the thought of assuming any

part of the responsibility, but after some reflection I said,
'If you really want my judgement, it is to close the Exchange.' He said it would be done, and it was done that
day."[1]

There can be no question that in the following days the
prompt and decisive action of the Treasury, strongly
backed by the President, prevented a disastrous panic in
the money market.

"I discussed the matter with President Wilson; we
concluded that it would be wise for me to go to New
York."[2]

McAdoo met a group of the most powerful bankers in
New York. He promptly offered to supply them with
$50,000,000 of emergency currency then in the Subtreas-
ury in New York, and to seek an immediate amendment
to the Aldrich-Vreeland Act (the Federal Reserve banks
not yet having been opened) which would enable still
greater advances of emergency currency to be made. The
President came unhesitatingly to his support, and on
August 4th the amendment had passed Congress and
Wilson had signed it—a record for emergency legislation
that can scarcely be equalled in our annals. Within
the next three months the Treasury advanced about
$370,000,000 to the banks throughout the nation, all of
which was eventually retired without the loss of a dollar
to the government. The value of such immediate and
effective coöperation with Washington had a steadying
and reassuring effect upon the country that can scarcely be
exaggerated.

During the next few weeks both the President and his
Secretary of the Treasury held many conferences with
groups of business men, bankers, farmers, trade union
leaders, to devise methods for meeting the crisis that

[1]William G. McAdoo, *Crowded Years*, p. 290.
[2]*Ibid.*

confronted them. It is to be commented upon that little or no jealousy was shown by groups of Western farmers and of labour men on account of the assistance given to the great financial interests of the East. This was due, no doubt, to the demonstration already made by the administration of its genuine interest in the welfare of the "little man."

The President, as we have seen, had already won the entire confidence of organized labour. During the Congressional struggles of the previous year, Samuel Gompers and other labour leaders had become his staunch supporters. The administration had also acted to relieve the pressure upon the farmers. In the summer and fall of 1913 —a year before the war began—the situation among the cotton planters of the South had become serious. Money had been "tight." Local banks had found it difficult to secure the usual credits in Wall Street. Demands were therefore made upon the farmer for the immediate marketing of his crops and the settlement of his debts. This meant the sale of his products in a glutted market: with the profits going to the larger dealers and the bankers who could afford to hold his product for higher prices. After advising with the President, Mr. McAdoo had met the situation boldly. First, he had announced that there was a reserve fund in the Treasury of $500,000,000 available to national banks to facilitate circulation. This had at once caused a decrease in interest rates. In July 1913 he called a conference of clearing-house committees from the crop-moving centers of the South and West, and on July 31st he offered to transfer $50,000,000 from the Treasury to national banks in the agricultural regions to help in moving the crops. Assurance was given that more would be forthcoming if necessary.[1]

---

[1]New York *Commercial*, September 29, 1913. A special feature of this arrangement was that the banks could obtain these funds by placing as security high-class com-

The great banks in the East, which had all along controlled the national credit situation with an iron hand, naturally fumed against this governmental action, but it was effective in easing the situation and forcing down interest rates. By the end of September it had been necessary to advance less than $25,000,000 of the total available sum, and in all only $37,386,000 was borrowed from the government.[1] In short, the government here acted to provide that elastic credit which the Federal Reserve law, not then enacted, was designed to provide.

The importance of this bold assumption of leadership lay not merely in the temporary relief of the Southern and Western bankers and farmers, but in the vivid demonstration of the sincerity of the administration in its declaration that it was primarily interested in the "common man," and that its energies would be devoted to "freeing credit," breaking down monopoly, especially banking monopoly, and enlarging individual opportunity.[2]

These activities had the strong backing of the President. As he wrote to John Skelton Williams, then Assistant Secretary of the Treasury, on August 25, 1913:

"I think that the Secretary and you, yourself, are to be warmly congratulated on the assistance the Treasury has

---

mercial paper as well as the usual government, state, municipal, and other bonds. Special safeguards were taken in the case of the commercial paper, and McAdoo himself became the final judge of its acceptance or rejection. The paper was accepted at 65 per cent. of its face value. The government interest rate was 2 per cent.

[1] See Mary Synon, McAdoo, pp. 106–110.

[2] A frank article in the New York Commercial of September 29, 1913, gave full acknowledgment to Mr. McAdoo's activities:

"But the country has seen Secretary of the Treasury McAdoo handle the money situation more successfully and with greater skill than the bankers have ever done. He has been right and they have been wrong this year. Somehow or other, this has removed from the minds of the business community, other than the bankers, the fear of administration control of the banking system through the Federal Reserve Board. In the past Secretaries of the Treasury have not put out Treasury funds before the harm was done, and then they devoted the money to checking panics in Wall Street, while the business of the country came to a standstill. . . . Deep down in the mind of the public rests the suspicion that the banks have not been wise in the past and that government control in the open is something not to be feared."

been rendering the country. It is fine to feel that we are being of real service."

The administration came thus to the crisis, a year later in 1914, with the habit of leadership firmly fixed, and the confidence of both financial and farming interests. This was a tremendous asset: it enabled the President and Secretary McAdoo to dominate the situation. In the case of the cotton crop, now facing difficulties with which the flurry of 1913 was child's play, the administration had only to repeat with assurance the policy of the previous year, depositing government funds in banks throughout the crop-moving regions. Their usefulness to agriculture under the extraordinary conditions existing would be hard to estimate.

It is impossible here, and indeed unnecessary, to enter upon a detailed account of the economic difficulties occasioned by the onset of the war: that task awaits the economic historian: it is rather the office of the biographer, having indicated the problems, to show what policies Woodrow Wilson laid down in each case, and what action he took. Three major difficulties presented themselves: cotton, ships, federal revenue. In reality they were closely bound together: wanting ships, cotton and other products could not be exported: wanting foreign trade, tariff revenues decreased.

At the heart of the entire congeries of problems, and in part the cause of them, was the utter failure of private capital to meet the crisis. In such an emergency, private capital, bold and domineering in times of fat prosperity, shrank from responsibility, shirked leadership, fled for safety to its cool vaults. Ships were needed instantly: private capital, without the bribe of huge subsidies, would not venture to buy or build them. Cotton had to be shipped or held; private capital feared to undertake either. Banks in the farming regions clamoured for money to assist their clients: the supply from Wall Street had dried up. In time of crisis private capital thinks only of itself.

In all of these cases the key of the President's policy was to step in and take the responsibility and assume the leadership. The nation must not be allowed to fail. "America," he said, "cannot properly be served by any man who for a moment measures his interest against her advantage."[1] What was necessary must be done. He expressed the essence of his view in a letter to Oswald G. Villard, then editor of the New York *Evening Post*, who feared the proposal, which Wilson was strongly supporting, of a government-owned merchant marine, because it savoured of socialism. The President wrote:

"I appreciate, I think, almost as keenly as you express them the difficulties and doubts about the ship purchase proposal, and yet sitting here and hearing all sorts and varieties of suggestions it becomes clearer to me day by day that private capital is not going to undertake this thing on an adequate scale or in the most serviceable way without asking for the very kind of government backing and support[2] to which I feel the deepest objection on principle not only, but because of some interests that would be necessarily involved.

"The idea in the proposal is not that the government should permanently embark in these things, but that it should do the immediate and necessary thing.

"At the same time, I realize that all the questions must be asked and, if possible, answered which are propounded in last evening's editorial in the *Post*. I wish I knew more but I am trying to find out all there is to get at.

"With warm regard and sincere thanks for your letter of August twenty-seventh . . ."[3]

In the case of cotton there were the usual more or less

[1]Woodrow Wilson to Frank E. Doremus, September 4, 1914. *The Public Papers of Woodrow Wilson*, Vol. III, p. 167.
[2]He meant the demand for subsidies.
[3]September 4, 1914.

hysterical proposals. A "buy-a-bale" movement was started with considerable furor, and on September 8th we find the President himself buying a number of bales. The perennial effort to persuade the nation to use more cotton[1] and Southern planters to raise less was inaugurated, and we find the President expressing, somewhat doubtfully, his interest in this movement.[2] Suggestions were even made that the government itself purchase the entire cotton crop and hold it.

Throughout the crisis the President's course was marked by a cooling good sense. He told the members of the North Carolina delegation including senators and representatives who came to the White House in a body on October 7th—at a time when cotton was selling on the farms at six cents a pound, two or three cents less than the cost of production—that the problem "must be solved, not with the heart, but with the head." The facts must be faced. The crisis had been caused by the war: and the demand for cotton could not be restored "through any arbitrary process." He was "not in sympathy with any plan to valorize cotton," regarding such proposals as "unwise and dangerous." A sound solution must be found that would not disturb the country's currency system: nevertheless he and the Secretary of the Treasury and the Federal Reserve Board, "within the limitations of economic law and safe finance," would render all the financial assistance in their power.[3]

---

[1] Judges of the Supreme Court of Mississippi were reported on October 26th to be wearing overalls and cotton shirts: with the lawyers appearing before them clad in the same garb.

[2] "I do not feel that I am on very certain ground in endorsing what Mr. Cooper wishes me to endorse, but I am perfectly willing to say that I am in entire sympathy with any effort to reduce the cotton crop of 1916 [1915] which will be consistent with the interests of the farmer and lead to a diversification of his crops, and that I commend as patriotic and in the national interest all disinterested efforts to that end." (Memorandum by the President, attached to a letter of October 17, 1914, from W. G. Cooper of Atlanta, Georgia.)

[3] From the report of the conference in the New York *Times*, October 8, 1914.

His own practical programme comprehended first and foremost the provision by the government of American ships to carry the cotton and other products. Second, a determined effort to prevent cotton from being declared contraband, which would entirely destroy the German and largely the neutral markets.[1] Third, he gave his vigorous support, after making sure of its legality by consulting Attorney General Gregory, to a plan for a "cotton loan fund," to enable the Southern producers to hold their surplus until conditions improved.[2] This helpful plan was superbly engineered by Mr. McAdoo, who secured the coöperation of New York and other bankers in raising a fund of $135,000,000.[3]

In the difficult months that followed, when both cotton growers and bankers were often restless and suspicious, we find the President using his great prestige to disarm criticism and secure coöperation in the application of the extraordinary measures adopted by the government. He wrote to Senator Tillman[4] on December 15th:

"I fear that you are under a misapprehension, my dear

---

[1] After much pressure, cotton was declared non-contraband by the British on October 25th.

[2] What the President feared was that this government-directed effort might form a dangerous precedent for further demands upon the government. He wrote to Mr. Gregory:

"It occurs to me that the 'fund' contemplated stands in a class by itself. It is hardly conceivable that such arrangements should become settled practices or furnish precedents which would be followed in the regular course of business or under ordinary conditions. They are as exceptional in their nature as the circumstances they are meant to deal with and can hardly be looked upon as, by possibility even, dangerous precedents." (November 7, 1914.)

[3] The last few millions came hard. On the final day a tall man of striking appearance stepped into the Secretary's office. McAdoo knew him at that time only slightly.

"Mr. Secretary, I understand that you need subscriptions to complete your Cotton Loan Fund. How much is required?"

Upon learning the amount—some $3,000,000—he said to Mr. McAdoo's astonishment:

"I will subscribe a million dollars of it. I am a Southerner and am deeply interested in helping the cotton growers in their desperate emergency."

This was Bernard M. Baruch of New York.

[4] Benjamin R. Tillman, of the Senate Committee on Naval Affairs.

Senator, in saying that the 'Secretary of the Treasury loaned the New York bankers the government's resources when he formed the gold pool.' As a matter of fact, he merely did the same thing that he has done in connection with the cotton pool, and you will notice that after the conference yesterday, in which the Southern men who had come up to confer began by criticizing the conditions of the cotton pool loans, they ended by endorsing the scheme unanimously and without qualification. I think I can say with entire confidence that no favorites have been played and I hope at the bottom of my heart that things will be worked out as well as it is possible to work them out in the present extraordinary conditions.''

While the situation was temporarily relieved by these various devices, cotton shipments during the following year were constantly delayed by the British, who were seeking to prevent shipments into Germany. In July 1915 the situation had become such as to make shipments that fall "exceedingly hazardous, very costly, and inevitably limited."[1]

On August 20, 1915, the British reversed their earlier decision and cotton was made contraband,[2] adding greatly, as we shall see, to the difficulties of the administration.

Severe as the problems were, both in the South and in the West, they would have been immeasurably greater if the President and his Secretary of the Treasury had not held the situation strongly in hand, providing a firm and steady leadership.

III. THE STRUGGLE FOR SHIPS: A FUNDAMENTAL TEST
OF WILSON'S LEADERSHIP

The President considered that the key to the restoration of American foreign trade, prostrated by the war, was an

---

[1]Senator Morris Sheppard of Texas to Woodrow Wilson, July 22, 1915.
[2]*Foreign Relations of the United States*, Supplement, 1915, p. 174.

immediate and extensive increase in the supply of ships.

The woeful deficiency in its merchant marine was no new problem in the United States; the crisis of August 1914 ruthlessly laid it bare. Masterfully resourceful as producers, we had for years been dependent upon foreign shipping for carrying what we produced. Corrective legislation had again and again been proposed in Congress: the platforms of both Democratic and Republican parties in the campaign of 1912 had contained emphatic planks.

"We believe," said the Republicans, "that one of the country's most urgent needs is a revived merchant marine."

The Democratic platform expressed the same concern, but took the stand that governmental encouragement must not rest upon "bounties or subsidies from the public treasury."

Wilson had thought of the subject especially in connection with tariff problems. He had said in his acceptance speech in August 1912:

"The question of a merchant marine turns back to the tariff again, to which all roads seem to lead, and to our registry laws,[1] which, if coupled with the tariff, might almost be supposed to have been intended to take the American flag off the seas."[2]

He then went on to say:

"Merchants who must depend upon the carriers of rival mercantile nations to carry their goods to market are at a disadvantage in international trade too manifest to need to be pointed out . . ."

He referred to the fact of our building a Panama canal and having "no ships to send through it" as "ridiculous."

"There have been years when not a single ton of freight

---

[1]Ship registry laws had excluded any but American-built ships from registry under the American flag.

[2]August 7, 1912. *The Public Papers of Woodrow Wilson*, Vol. II, p. 471.

passed through the great Suez canal in an American bottom, so empty are the seas of our ships and seamen . . . We must build and buy ships in competition with the world."

In 1912, before Wilson became President, there had been a feeble effort to lift the barriers by allowing foreign ships not more than five years old to be registered under the American flag, but it had provided little relief, and there was a swelling and popular appeal for further action.

At the very first indication of a general conflict in Europe, it seems to have been the vision of a shipless America that most concerned the President. On July 31st he postponed his usual cabinet meeting and called a conference at the White House of two leaders of the Senate, Kern and Clarke, and two leaders of the House, Underwood and Adamson, who was then chairman of the Interstate and Foreign Commerce Committee.

Mr. Adamson wrote a memorandum of the conference[1] in which he quoted the President as having outlined with extraordinary clarity the possibilities that might grow out of a general European conflict.

"Our bountiful crops are ready to harvest. Unless they can be carried to the foreign markets, they will waste in the warehouses, if they do not rot in the fields. . . .

"My object in calling you gentlemen [together] was to lay before you the circumstances and ask you to provide ships [to] . . . carry our commerce to all ports of the world."

An emergency measure, drafted by Mr. Adamson,[2] was immediately introduced into Congress providing that any foreign-built vessel might, under certain restrictions, be transferred to American registry. The President was much pleased with the prompt response, writing to Major Henry L. Higginson on August 3rd:

---

[1] A copy is in the author's hands.

[2] W. C. Adamson to the author.

"I think that the Congress will act today in the matter of the shipping and the very best spirit of coöperation prevails with regard to anything that it may be necessary to do."

Opposition was, however, to develop in quite an unexpected quarter. Both the British and the French at once took alarm. Did it mean that Americans meant to purchase the magnificent ships owned by Germans and tied up in American ports? In such a case the purchase money would not only help their enemy with money, but enable him to secure shipments of American goods in American ships that could not easily be interfered with. There was also, unquestionably, the fear of trade rivalry: while Europe was busy with its war, the Americans would be building up a powerful merchant marine to seize the trade of the world. This was to be prevented if possible.[1] The French chargé d'affaires at once[2] made "all reserves," the first of many protests, and a little later the British also objected. The Solicitor in the Department of State hastily compiled a report[3] maintaining the legality of the transfer of merchant ships from belligerent to neutral flags made in good faith after the commencement of hostilities, but in August Sir Edward Grey was arguing that the Declaration of London forbade "the sale in a neutral port of a ship belonging to a subject of a belligerent and the use of that ship under a neutral flag to escape the consequences of its original belligerent ownership."[4] The issue here

[1]Secretary McAdoo wished to "establish immediately lines to South America and Central America. We have an unusual opportunity for South American trade but without ships we can do nothing. With them we can quickly establish business and political relations that will be of inestimable value to this country—perhaps for all time." (From a memorandum prepared by Secretary McAdoo and read to the President on August 16, 1914. Mary Synon, *McAdoo*, p. 179.)

[2]August 4, 1914. *Foreign Relations of the United States*, Supplement, 1914, p. 485.

[3]August 7, 1914.

[4]Walter H. Page to W. J. Bryan, August 18, 1914. *Foreign Relations of the United States*, Supplement, 1914, p. 482.

joined was later to cause great difficulties for the administration.

Opposition also developed in the Senate: would not the
desired measure involve fraudulent transfers of foreign
ships, and possibly involve our government in serious disputes? Wilson, in a letter to Senator Saulsbury on August
15th, characteristically expressed his willingness to accept
risks, assume leadership, trusting "to wise and prudent
administration" in order to accomplish the purpose he
had in mind:

"It disturbs me to differ with men like yourself and
Senator Pomerene but I must say that I do not see how
the conference report on the Shipping bill differs in principle from the law as it stood already. That made it possible
for ships not more than five years old to be purchased by
American corporations without any stipulation as to the
proportion of the stock held by Americans; and in any
case stock can be temporarily assigned without great
difficulty and whatever requirements we might put in
might be nominally but really complied with.

"It seems to me the whole question comes down to the
proof of *bona fides* in the transaction. There must, of
course, be *bona fides* and we could offer no reasonable
objection to seizures of ships in the ownership of which
bona fides could not be shown.

"I think the whole thing can be divested of its risks
by a wise and prudent administration of the law."

Whatever doubt senators may have felt, the act, under
the President's forceful leadership, was passed by the
Senate on August 17th and signed on August 18th. But
the transfers under it soon proved too few to meet the
tremendous demands for the shipment of even one commodity—cotton. Here again the obstacle was the timidity
of private capital. Shipping interests hung back from the
risks involved, especially those connected with the pur-

chase and operation of the idle German ships. What was to be done? The administration at once assumed the leadership that private interests were refusing. McAdoo, the irrepressible, called a meeting of leaders for August 14th, and it was agreed that one of the chief difficulties— exorbitant, even prohibitive insurance rates for protecting ships at sea—should be met by the government. A measure providing for a Bureau of War Risk Insurance was introduced into Congress on August 19th, promptly passed, and signed by the President on September 2nd; but since this new governmental insurance could apply only to American ships and to goods in American bottoms, assistance to trade was slight so long as the ships themselves were lacking.

In short, the main problem still remained. Since there seemed no likelihood of action by private capital, McAdoo was for attacking the problem directly and boldly. Like the President, he was "opposed to the government owner- ship of business enterprises"[1] but these were extraordinary circumstances involving the welfare if not the safety of the entire nation. He therefore evolved a scheme for a government-owned corporation to buy or build the neces- sary ships. It was not without precedent. While construct- ing the Panama canal, the government during the presi- dency of Theodore Roosevelt had purchased and was still conducting the Panama steamship line. McAdoo knew that the proposal would be attacked as "socialistic," but the President, when he had studied it, merely remarked:

"We'll have to fight for it, won't we?"

"We certainly shall."

"Well, then, let's fight."

"We did," remarks McAdoo in his memoirs. "We fought for it, and, as I look back over the prolonged

---

[1] William G. McAdoo, *Crowded Years*, p. 295.

battle, I recall it as a fantastic nightmare of partisanship and politics."[1]

The President called a conference of leading senators and representatives at the White House on August 19th and set forth the situation that confronted the nation and asked for the prompt support of Congress. A few days later (August 24th) a bill with broad provisions for the purchase or construction of ships was introduced in the House by Mr. Alexander, chairman of the Merchant Marine Committee.[2]

McAdoo was quite right: a tremendous and bitter fight immediately developed. The Congress had indeed just passed the War Risk Insurance Act which was equally open to the charge of being socialistic. It had been approved by everybody, both big and little business, ship owners and ship builders. Why? Because, as McAdoo remarked, "there was a general impression that no money could be made from the business of war risk insurance. That being the case, why not let the government take the loss?"[3]

When the government, however, proposed to supply needed ships, it interfered with a private interest that had, with the outbreak of the war, become enormously profitable. American ship owners, now made safe under government insurance, and with the competition of the British and the Germans entirely removed, could charge any rates they pleased. "Tramp steamers not infrequently cleared their entire cost or value in a single voyage. In the course of a year an ocean-going freighter would bring in a net return—clear profit above all expenses—of three hundred

---

[1] William G. McAdoo, *Crowded Years*, p. 296.

[2] The bill provided for the appropriation of $30,000,000 to buy or build ships, and for the organization of a corporation capitalized for not over $10,000,000, the government to own a controlling share in the stock to conduct the enterprise.

[3] William G. McAdoo, *Crowded Years*, p. 304.

to five hundred per cent on the money invested in the ship."[1]

Is it surprising that a fight developed in Congress? "Prompt action on the part of Congress," Mr. McAdoo observed, "would have blown up this orgy of profiteering." Some of the interests that had so recently appealed all but frantically to the government to save them when threatened by panic were now equally vigorous, even passionate, in trying to prevent any action upon the shipping bill. J. P. Morgan called upon McAdoo at the Treasury to oppose the purchase or construction of any ships by the government.

"He said," reports Mr. McAdoo, "that . . . the government's entrance into the field would be considered a menace."[2]

A few days later Mr. Morgan wrote to the President that he had received from his London firm "which is at the moment in very close touch with the British government" a cablegram asserting that the British "would not hesitate to capture such ships [German ships purchased by Americans] even if sailing under American flag."

The President replied, on August 22nd:

"Thank you sincerely for your letter of August twenty-first and for the important information which it conveys. I shall take the matter up at once with our own legal authorities in the Department of State."

He wrote at once to Mr. Lansing:

"Surely if Mr. Morgan's information is correct as stated in the enclosed letter, the British government is in danger of taking a very unjustifiable and high-handed action. I would very much like your carefully considered opinion on the subject."[3]

---

[1] William G. McAdoo, *Crowded Years*, p. 304.
[2] *Ibid.*, p. 305.
[3] August 22, 1914.

Lobbyists began to swarm at Washington, sharp opposition developed in Congress among Republican leaders. It was like the tariff and Federal Reserve fights all over again. It seems to have disturbed the President greatly, since it came just at the time when he was doing his best to coöperate with big business in other matters—for example, in assistance to railroad interests—on the supposition that the leaders, having been chastened by the struggles of the past eighteen months, were now ready to accept his leadership. It was beginning to appear that they desired coöperation only when they were in trouble.

At any rate, the President hardened, quite characteristically, behind the struggle. "President Wilson had his jaw set hard today when he let it be known that there was no truth in reports that he had decided to abandon the plan to obtain legislation for a government-owned ocean steamship service. On the contrary, said the President, he had not taken a backward step in the matter, and he not only intended to push the legislation, but expected it to be enacted in the next two or three weeks."[1]

At the same time he made it clear that he did not want to have the government embark in the shipping business if it could possibly be avoided. He told reporters that "if private capital was furnished in sufficient amount to organize lines to give adequate ocean transportation facilities to American exporters, the government might not carry out the scheme. But there had been no indication of any such purpose on the part of private parties . . ."[2] The shipping interests were willing to criticize but not create.

During the months that followed, we find the President carrying forward the struggle on two fronts: diplomatically, with the British and French who were determined to prevent American purchase of German ships interned

---

[1]New York *Times,* August 25, 1914.
[2]*Ibid.*

in her ports; and politically, with the opposition in Congress. He clung doggedly to the belief in the necessity and rightfulness of the purchase, but worried over the possibility of trouble with the belligerents. It is curious how both the French and the British, while refusing to accept the Declaration of London without change on such subjects as the definition of contraband, harped on its provisions regarding transfer of flags as against the American desires.[1] On November 8th the President wrote to McAdoo:

" . . . if we bought what are probably the only ships we could buy for the service . . . some very serious and difficult questions would arise. The French government in particular has taken an inflexible position about the transfer of flags in such circumstances, and its position is giving me and the State Department the greatest concern."

A little later, November 23rd, in preparing for his annual message to Congress he sought light from Mr. Lansing on the situation:

"One of the bills I want to urge upon the attention of the Houses is the Shipping bill, which would involve, as you know, in all likelihood, the purchase of a number of ships that have been owned hitherto by subjects of one or other of the belligerents. You will remember that a little while ago the attitude of the English government in this matter of the transfer of flag[s] during hostilities seemed to be very different from the attitude of the French government. I would like very much before writing my message to know just what you think the attitude of those two governments would be toward the purchase by a corporation in which the United States government was interested of such ships as those now belonging to the North German Lloyd and the Hamburg-American Companies, and which are interned in our waters."

[1] See *Foreign Relations of the United States*, Supplement, 1914, pp. 481–482; 490–492.

In his reply Lansing dealt mainly with the opposition of the French to transfer, indicating that the British would be more amenable but for the attitude of their allies.

In his message of December 8th the President avoided discussion of the direct issue of the purchase of the German ships, but this aspect of the problem was to continue to give him much concern: it was, indeed, as we shall see, to furnish the first crisis in international relations in the following year.

In the meantime the struggle in Congress continued stubbornly. The two or three weeks of the President's hope lengthened into months. Although engaged upon many other matters of the first importance—including his activities in the political campaign of 1914—he continued to exert pressure, talk with congressmen, write letters. He even seemed doubtful of some of the members of his own cabinet. On October 3rd he wrote to Secretary Redfield:

"I notice that you presided yesterday over a meeting which discussed the shipping interests. I hope that you were able to guide them away from antagonism to the plans of the administration. I noted how the conference was made up and how the intrenched shipping interests predominated and it must have been a hard task if you were able to accomplish it.

"I regard the Shipping bill as of capital consequence to the administration and I hope that you were able to do something to determine their point of view."[1]

But Congress adjourned on October 24th without having taken any action. It had indeed been overwhelmed with other matters. The President had been pressing relentlessly for action upon the final measures in his rounded programme of domestic reform. He felt that it was now

---

[1]Redfield responded that the President had been misinformed as to the meeting; and he added that, while he was not publicly opposing the Shipping bill, he did not understand its purpose.

or never: for the storm of the European war was likely,
soon, to blot out every other interest. One after another
the measures he sought had been passed. On September
26th he signed the Trade Commission bill, providing a
board of five members with large powers to investigate
business organizations and to advise and guide them.
On October 15th he signed the long-debated and much-
opposed Clayton Anti-Trust Act with its provisions pro-
hibiting interlocking directorates, clarifying the Sherman
law and exempting labour unions from being restrained as
illegal combinations.[1]

On October 20th his plan for the development of Alaska,
begun in March with the provision for a government-
owned railroad, was completed with the signing of the
Alaska Coal Lands Leasing bill which, while providing for
private exploitation, retained government control over
vast and valuable properties in Alaska.[2]

Since all of these measures, in one way or another, struck
at the "interests," and were open to the charge of being
socialistic, it seemed, no doubt, unwise to many of the
hard-driven leaders of the President's own party to ask
for immediate action on such a controversial proposal as
the Shipping bill.

Wilson had also in the closing days of this exhausted
session of Congress to ask for more taxes to meet the de-

---

[1]*Woodrow Wilson, Life and Letters*, Vol. IV, p. 373.

[2]Wilson took a strong position then and later regarding the alienation of public lands,
a problem that was to bring disaster in the administration of Mr. Harding. On December 29, 1914, he wrote to Secretary Bryan on this subject:

"I have so often discussed the subject matter of Senator Shafroth's speech on the
leasing system for the public domain with Senator Shafroth himself that I find I am
familiar with the things that he says in the speech you were kind enough to send me, but
I do not find myself at all convinced by them. The facts are assembled altogether from
the point of view of those who wish the Federal government in effect to turn over these
great properties to the states themselves, and my conviction is that that would be a very
difficult step to justify in any circumstances.

"Senator Shafroth is sincere and impressive, but I must admit he has not convinced
me."

ficiency in revenue caused by the war—a demand that also affected the stricken business of the country. He had gone before Congress with his appeal on September 4th. He asked an additional revenue of $100,000,000, not in loans, but in taxation.

". . . we ought not to borrow. We ought to resort to taxation, however we may regret the necessity of putting additional temporary burdens on our people. . . . The country is able to pay any just and reasonable taxes without distress. And to every other form of borrowing, whether for long periods or for short, there is the same objection. . . . The people of this country are both intelligent and profoundly patriotic. They are ready to meet the present conditions in the right way and to support the government with generous self-denial. They know and understand, and will be intolerant only of those who dodge responsibility or are not frank with them."[1]

Sharp debate followed, but with both Houses in control of the Democrats and the President's prestige at its highest, as it was just before the election, the bill was passed and signed on October 22nd.

It is not to be doubted that the President's steady, implacable, unrelenting pressure in completing his reform programme and in forcing through various emergency measures, including the tax bill, was in part responsible for the revolt on the proposal for government ships which took place in the next session of Congress. The President had become a dictator! The partial defeat of his party in the election in November, especially in the East, in which his own leadership was challenged, may also have been a contributory factor.

It never occurred to the President, however, to give over his fight. He believed in the measure; he had committed himself to it. Congress met on December 7th, and

---

[1] *The Public Papers of Woodrow Wilson*, Vol. III, p. 162.

in his address the next day he left no doubt as to his intentions:

"In my judgement such legislation is imperatively needed and cannot wisely be postponed. The government must open these gates of trade and open them wide; open them before it is altogether profitable to open them, or altogether reasonable to ask private capital to open them at a venture. It is not a question of the government monopolizing the field. It should take action to make it certain that transportation at reasonable rates will be promptly provided . . . and then, when the carriage has become sufficiently profitable to attract and engage private capital, and engage it in abundance, the government ought to withdraw. I very earnestly hope that the Congress will be of this opinion, and that both Houses will adopt this exceedingly important bill."[1]

Two days later he wrote to Speaker Clark of the House:

"Each day additional evidence comes in of one kind or another of the great need for immediate action in this matter. For example, the ocean freight rates have increased, I am told, three fold, and some such action as is proposed by the bill would undoubtedly tend to remove that great impediment to the shipment of our goods." He urged Clark to talk to McAdoo about the matter, for the Secretary was "full of the most interesting and important information concerning it."

The short session which followed, from December 1914 to March 4, 1915, proved to be one of the stormiest Wilson encountered during the entire eight years of his service. The Ship Purchase bill was not only distasteful on many counts to the powerful Republican, conservative leadership of the Senate, but it provided a vulnerable point of attack upon the rising power of the Executive. Moreover, Republican prestige and discipline were being challenged

---

[1] *The Public Papers of Woodrow Wilson*, Vol. III, p. 220.

One page of the President's shorthand notes of the text of his annual address to Congress, December 8, 1914. The pencilled "C" indicates that the notes have been transcribed.

as they had not been before in years by their triumphant opponents under the masterful leadership of the White House. With the outbreak of the European war, they saw, none more clearly, that the Executive, unless checked, would inevitably become still more dominating: for democracy, in time of strain, inevitably tends to the vast enhancement of executive power.

The real struggle did not begin until after the holidays. On January 4th the Senate took up the bill, and sharp attacks were made upon it by Lodge, Root, Gallinger, and others. The government was forsaking the American tradition and proposing to engage in business in competition with private ship owners.

"It means," said Root, "a repudiation more signal than has ever yet been made of the principles of the great leader of the party which 'has the votes' to put this bill through."[1]

Another important objection, in the opinion of the opposition, was that the measure would embroil the United States in foreign complications of the most serious nature.[2] There is no doubt that some of the opposition was due to real anxiety over what was regarded as a radical proposal. Neither can it be doubted that the fight involved a concerted revolt against "executive domination"; for the attack just at this time was begun all along the line. On the 6th Senator Lodge made a lengthy and carefully prepared attack on the President's Mexican policy,[3] although it was not just then a critical issue. By the 7th it was clear that there was a wide divergence of opinion between Congress and the President on the Immigration bill which was later to be vetoed.

---

[1] *Congressional Record*, Vol. 52, p. 909.

[2] Senator Lodge asked: "Have we not enough international complications . . . without encouraging new and perilous questions?" (*Ibid.*, p. 907.)

[3] *Ibid.*, pp. 1016–1021.

It was plain that the Republican leaders, covertly encouraged by certain Democrats in the Senate[1] who had all along been more or less opposed to Wilson's programme of reform, had deliberately embarked upon a campaign to curb his leadership. The President was wholly aware of the purpose, and in an address at Indianapolis on Jackson Day, January 8th, accepted the challenge. No President ever went into a fight that he believed in with more relish than Woodrow Wilson.

In few addresses of his career did he give more complete reign to the emotion of the moment: and few were more criticized. He had come hot from the battleground at Washington; hot and determined. His subject was Andrew Jackson, the most militant and extreme of Democrats. "There was nothing mild," said he, "about Andrew Jackson . . . Andrew Jackson was a forthright man who believed everything he did believe in fighting earnest."[2]

He liked, he said, a fighter: he liked to "breathe the air of Jackson Day," he liked to be "reminded of the old militant hosts of Democracy."[3]

Nor did he forget that he was in the Middle West, among progressives, among friends. In the recent election it was the West that had come again to his support: the East that had held back. He tended always to idealize the spirit of the West as more American than the East. It drew him now into an unaccustomed ardour of partisan attack. The entire address was marked by a tumultuous colloquialism that fired his immediate hearers,[4] but distressed some of his devoted and judicious friends. The

---

[1] The names of the Democratic senators who opposed the President on the Shipping bill are given on p. 128.

[2] *The Public Papers of Woodrow Wilson*, Vol. III, p. 236.

[3] *Ibid.*, p. 237.

[4] A large crowd heard the address, and a passage in which it seemed to be implied that the President would seek a renomination for the presidency in 1916 evoked the wildest enthusiasm.

Republican party had "not had a new idea for thirty years."[1]

"The Republican party is still a covert and refuge for those who are afraid, for those who want to consult their grandfathers about everything."[2]

He attacked hotly the Republicans in the Senate who were blocking the Shipping bill.

"I hear it said in Washington on all hands that the Republicans in the United States Senate mean to talk enough to make the passage of that bill impossible. These self-styled friends of business, these men who say the Democratic party does not know what to do for business, are saying that the Democrats shall do nothing for business. I challenge them to show their right to stand in the way of the release of American products to the rest of the world! . . . You know it is the peculiarity of that great body that it has rules of procedure which make it possible for a minority to defy the nation; and these gentlemen are now seeking to defy the nation and prevent the release of American products to the suffering world which needs them more than it ever needed them before."[3]

He hit at the newspapers in a paragraph that descended as far beneath the natural dignity and power of his addresses as any utterance of the period of his presidency:

"With all due respect to editors of great newspapers, I have to say to them that I seldom take my opinion of the American people from their editorials. So that when some great dailies not very far from where I am temporarily residing thundered with rising scorn at watchful waiting, Woodrow sat back in his chair and chuckled, knowing that he laughs best who laughs last—knowing, in short, what were the temper and principles of the American people.

---

[1]*The Public Papers of Woodrow Wilson*, Vol. III, p. 237.
[2]*Ibid.*
[3]*Ibid.*, pp. 241-242.

If I did not at least think I knew, I would emigrate, because I would not be satisfied to stay where I am."[1]

The comment upon this address was highly significant. The politicians who were always egging him on to strong partisan action were delighted. Even Colonel House wrote:

"That was a splendid, militant, democratic speech that you made at Indianapolis yesterday and it will do great good.

"I have heard many comments upon it already and it has put your followers into a better frame of mind than they have been for a long time."[2]

But the address was sharply criticized not only in the press[3] but by some of the President's most loyal friends, while he himself could admit, in a personal letter to Mrs. Toy, that he had been carried away by the "psychology of the stump." Yet he would abate nothing of his position upon the issues of the struggle, nor indeed, of his opinions of the men who were opposing him. He had said in his address: "You know Jackson used to think that everybody who disagreed with him was an enemy of the country."[4] It was what he himself tended also to do: it was so at

---

[1] *The Public Papers of Woodrow Wilson*, Vol. III, pp. 248-249. In certain reports he was quoted as having said "Woody," not "Woodrow," but the official records do not bear this out, nor do the letters which refer to it. It is one of the strange complexities of Wilson's character that he would undoubtedly have delighted in being hailed by the people as "Woodrow" or even "Woody"—and would have frozen the individual who ventured upon such an informality in his presence. Several times—we have records —we find him delighted by such a shout of feeling from the crowd. David Lawrence relates in his book, *The True Story of Woodrow Wilson*, pp. 56-57, that after having made a speech from the observation platform of his train in a small town, Wilson said:
"'. . . at last I feel that I have arrived in politics.'
"'Why?' a newspaperman asked.
"'Somebody out there in that crowd waved his arms and yelled "Hello, Woody" at me.'"
[2] January 9, 1915.
[3] "The friends of President Wilson will be moved to apology and extenuation by his Indianapolis speech. . . . It is below the very high level of his usual achievement, the level which the country expects him to reach; and he said some things that he might well wish to unsay." (New York *Times*, January 10, 1915.)
[4] *The Public Papers of Woodrow Wilson*, Vol. III, p. 249.

Princeton; it was so at Trenton; it was so later in Washington, and he himself in the flashing white-hot revelations of the platform all but admitted it. "I have never," said he, "got quite that far in my thought, but I have ventured to think that they did not know what they were talking about . . ."[1]

His letter to Mrs. Toy, highly interpretative of the man himself, is here presented in full:

"Of course you did not like the Indianapolis speech (that palpable lapse of taste, 'Woodrow &c.' was only a silliness of the moment; was not in the notes; was produced by the psychology of the stump, no doubt, and admits of no excuse); I instinctively knew that you would not: any more than you would like a real fight, or anything that wore the aspect of partisanship. But there is a real fight on. The Republicans are every day employing the most unscrupulous methods of partisanship and false evidence to destroy this administration and bring back the days of private influence and selfish advantage. I would not, if I could, imitate their tactics; but it is no time for mere manners. The barriers of taste may be overstepped in stating the truth as to what is going on: it must be displayed naked. All that I said was true, to my knowledge, though I did not shade it or trace the lines of it artistically or with literary restraint. The struggle that is on, to bring about reaction and regain privilege is desperate and absolutely without scruple. It cannot be met by gentle speeches or by presidential utterances which smack of no bias of party. A compact and fighting party must be led against them. I think you cannot know to what lengths men like Root and Lodge are going, who I once thought had consciences but now know have none. We must not suffer ourselves to forget or twist the truth as they do, or use their insincere and contemptible meth-

[1] *The Public Papers of Woodrow Wilson*, Vol. III, p. 249.

ods of fighting; but we must hit them and hit them straight in the face, and not mind if the blood comes. It is a blunt business, and lacks a certain kind of refinement, but so does all war; and this is a war to save the country from some of the worst influences that ever debauched it. Please do not read the speeches in which I use a bludgeon. I do not like to offend your taste; but I cannot fight rottenness with rosewater. Lend me your indulgence. At any rate forgive me, if you can do nothing else.

"As for the Shipping bill, it does, as you perceive, permit us to commit blunders, fatal blunders, if we are so stupid or so blind; but it is not a blunder in itself, and, if we use ordinary sense and prudence, it need lead us into no dangers. The only dangers it involves have already been created by the Ship Registry bill and the war risk insurance measure, for which the Republicans hastened to vote, some coming back to Washington to advocate what the shipping interests wanted who had been absent from their seats for weeks. But the shipping interests do not want this bill. They will do nothing themselves without a subsidy, unless, that is, they are given government money out of the taxes to use as they think best for themselves; if they cannot get that, and of course they cannot, they do not mean to let the development take place, because the control of ocean carriage and of ocean rates will pass out of their hands. We are fighting as a matter of fact the most formidable (covert) lobby that has stood against us yet in anything we have attempted; and we shall see the fight to a finish; trying, when we have won, to act like men who know very familiarly the dangers of what they are about to undertake. It pleases me that you should be so generously distressed at the possibility of our doing what will lead to disaster or even danger; but those who speak to you of these risks have a very poor opinion of our practical sense, and are unconsciously misled by what the press represent, for their own purposes, as the main object of the measure when it is not its object at all. One would suppose that this was a bill to authorize the government to buy German ships.[1] There would be just as stiff a fight against it, and from the same quarters, if it merely conferred the power to build ships.

"The path is indeed strewn with difficulties at every turn, in this and in many other matters, and God knows I have no serene confidence in my own judgement and discretion: but of one thing I am resolved, to break the control of special interests over this government and this people. Pardon the seriousness of this letter. These are critical things in which much is wrapped up. All join me in most affectionate messages."[2]

It was, indeed, generally recognized as a struggle between the President and the powerful opposition in the Senate. "Wilson Hits Back at Foes in the Senate."[3]

As indicated in his address, one of the chief causes of the President's exasperation was the tactics of the Senate opposition in filibustering obstinately to prevent the passage of the measure. Unable to defeat it in a direct vote, they had determined to exercise the last resource of a Senate minority and talk it to death. In a session that lasted thirty-seven hours through January 30th, Senator Smoot of Utah talked steadily for eleven and a half hours. A revolt of seven Democrats[4] against the bill brought new difficulties for the administration and increased the bitterness. At a later session Wilson was assailed by Senator

---

[1] "The plan," wrote Lodge to Roosevelt, on January 15th, "is to buy the German ships." (*Selections from the Correspondence of Theodore Roosevelt and Henry Cabot Lodge*, Vol. II, p. 451.) There is no doubt that the purchase of the German ships was then a part of the programme of the administration.

[2] January 31, 1915.

[3] A headline in the New York *Times*, January 9, 1915.

[4] Bankhead, of Alabama; Vardaman, of Mississippi; Hardwick, of Georgia; Clarke, of Arkansas; Hitchcock, of Nebraska; Camden, of Kentucky; and O'Gorman, of New York.

O'Gorman of New York for trying to force legislation: Senator Reed of Missouri defended him. At another time the Senate sat for fifty-five hours on a stretch accomplishing nothing. Senator Burton exceeded the record by talking for thirteen hours: at one time cots were placed in the Senate cloakrooms where senators might sleep during the interminable and exhausting sessions.

There can be no doubt that the opposition had the business interests of the country strongly behind it;[1] but the President met their arguments by a plea of national necessity, by showing that private capital would not undertake the risks, without enormous profits, and by arguing that the government was prepared to step aside the moment private vessel owners could and would do the necessary service at reasonable rates.[2] He found this opposition, which was real, far easier to meet than the fear of foreign complications, which he considered merely a "smoke screen" for frightening the public. Nevertheless many thoughtful critics in the country were greatly disturbed by the diplomatic difficulties: nor were they wholly disarmed by the President's demand that he be trusted to use powers which he himself had said might be dangerous if abused.

---

[1] A committee of the Chamber of Commerce of New York, for example, denied "that a sufficient crisis exists to warrant the enactment of a law which departs from established economic standards and may do grave injustice to those citizens who already own vessel property. It is stated that the people of this country are against taxing themselves in order to provide subsidies for steamship lines and it is suggested that they tax themselves to operate government owned lines admittedly at a loss." (New York Times, January 8, 1915.)

[2] When proposals were made for subsidies to encourage private capital—always ardently supported by the interests concerned—the President was unalterably opposed. He wrote to D. M. Barringer on February 4th:

"They amount to this, that money taken from the taxpayers is given into private hands to be used for private profit without regard to the regulation of the service or the study of the interests of the public in general.

"It is a serious matter to use public money for commercial development at all, but if it is used, it seems to me that it should be used under the direct control of those who are responsible to the people for the taxation."

He wrote on February 1st to Henry L. Higginson, who had protested against the Shipping bill:

"I think it is obvious that the Shipping bill does make it possible to do very foolish things, but I hope that it is true that the country need give itself no concern about the possible consequences, for we are very keenly alive to the difficulties we might get into if ships were purchased from the belligerents and shall be very slow to do anything that involves such dangers as are disclosed.

"As a matter of fact, the Ship Registry bill already passed involves the same dangers and, unfortunately, those dangers may be made realities by the action of individuals over which the government has no control."

Former President Eliot of Harvard, who was at once a vigorous supporter of the President and a candid critic, set forth the objections:

"My dear friend Major Higginson has just sent me a copy of a letter you wrote him on February 1st, about the Shipping bill. It gives me hope that you will promote effective changes in the bill, or cease to support it.

"You recognize that the bill makes it possible for the administration to do foolish things. Is not the passage, under pressure from the administration, of a bill which contains such possibilities a bad precedent? Suppose that another Roosevelt should become President of the United States!

"You think it reasonable that the country should trust your administration not to do foolish things. I submit that the question—'Can you not trust *me?*' is never a satis-factory answer to the man or the party that objects to another's demanding or possessing illegitimate and danger-ous powers. If, however, you continue to feel that the answer—'Cannot the country trust me?' ought to be sufficient in the present case, would not your position before the anxious country be strengthened by your saying

WOODROW WILSON'S SECOND ANNUAL ADDRESS AT THE OPENING OF THE LAST SESSION OF THE 63RD CONGRESS, DECEMBER 8, 1914

publicly—'I know that this bill contains powers for possible mischief; but my administration does not propose to avail itself of those powers.'

"I ought to confess that my interest in your disposition of the Shipping bill is intensified by my belief that your relation to the Shipping bill up to this date seems likely to make a breach in the Democratic party, to contribute to the alienation from you of the great mass of the business men of the country, and to make probable the return of the Republican party to power in 1916. These results all seem to me calamitous."

To this the President responded:

"I have your valued favor of the fifteenth of February and am sincerely obliged to you for its candid advice.

"My difficulty in this whole matter has been this: Our rights as neutrals in the matter of the purchase of ships from citizens of belligerent countries is, I believe, susceptible of clear establishment in any impartial tribunal. Just now the United States stands as the chief custodian of neutral rights and I do not think that any branch of the government should say anything officially that would seem to be equivalent to even a temporary renunciation of those rights. That is the reason why I have thought that the only course open to us was to ask the public to trust us on the principle that no administration that had not lost its head would be likely to do anything that would bring extraordinary risks to the country itself and add to the perplexities and hostilities of a terrible season of war like this.

"I think that you will see the nature of the quandary."[1]

---

[1] February 18, 1915. Eliot, however, was not convinced and wrote a few days later: "I see the nature of the quandary, but I do not see that it was the duty of your administration to put yourself into that quandary. The neutral right to buy ships from citizens of belligerent countries during war may exist; but has it ever been good for anything? Has it ever been a right which a prudent and genuine neutral would want

It was reported at one time that the President, in order to disarm some of the opposition in the Senate, had given assurances that the German ships, if purchased, would be used only in trade with South America, thus releasing other vessels for the European shipments and at the same time avoiding the danger of complications in the war zone, but if such assurances were given—and there is no documentary evidence for it that this biographer can discover —it had no effect whatever upon the struggle in Congress.

The President, upon his part, was as unrelenting as he had been in the tariff and Federal Reserve fights. Toward the middle of February he began to exert a more personal and direct pressure upon the House, where the Democrats were strongest.

"I am tired of this obstruction," he told Adamson. "We need the ships. It is time for Congress to get behind the matter. I want the House, for the moral effect of it, to pass that Shipping bill and send it to the Senate, and I want you to see that it is put through."[1]

A caucus was held, and the Democrats were whipped into line. On February 16th the House passed the bill by a vote of 215 to 121.[2] Wilson was delighted, writing to Adamson on February 17th:

"You are certainly a fine soldier and I am your sincere admirer."

The passage of the bill by the House did not, as the

---

to exercise? You did not propose to exercise that right; because you saw clearly that it was an irritating and, therefore, inexpedient thing to do."

Wilson responded on February 23rd:

"While it is true, as you say, that the right of neutral nations to buy ships from citizens of belligerent countries during war has never proved of much practical value, it would in this case be of very considerable advantage, because we know that it would be quite feasible to buy such ships and put them upon the direct trade between this country and South America. The only complications that would arise would spring out of putting them upon their old trade routes or attempting to operate them between this country and European ports."

[1] W. C. Adamson to the author, quoting Woodrow Wilson.

[2] *Congressional Record*, Vol. 52, p. 3923.

President hoped, influence the Senate. The attacks continued, ridiculous charges that the administration was dealing with German ship owners were made and exploded —and finally Congress adjourned on March 4th with nothing done.

In the heat of his disappointment with this outcome the President prepared a statement attacking the Senate opposition, including the Democratic members who sided with it. It concluded with the following paragraphs:

"Seven Democratic senators united with the Republican senators to defeat the plan, by filibuster when they realized the weakness of debate, and they have achieved their object. The members of that ill-omened coalition must bear the whole responsibility for it, the very grave responsibility for infinite damage to the business of the United States, to farmers, to laborers, to manufacturers, to producers of every class and sort. They have fastened the control of the selfish shipping interests on the country and the prospect is not a little sinister. Their responsibility will be very heavy, heavier and heavier as the months come and go; and it will be very bitter to bear.

"I shall not call an extra session of Congress. . . . Unless circumstances arise which I cannot at present foresee, I cannot in good faith deny the business of the country this time of adjustment in many large matters, even to remedy the perhaps irremediable damage this unnatural and unprecedented alliance has brought upon our business. Their opportunity to rectify their grievous disloyalty has passed."[1]

For some reason he was dissuaded from issuing this statement, which expressed his real views, and an innocuous message was substituted.

---

[1] From a copy in Mr. Wilson's files, with corrections made in his handwriting and on his own typewriter.

A new note had crept into this controversy of the President and the Senate. However warm the earlier contests over tariff and financial legislation, Wilson had sought "common counsel" with his "colleagues": and the differences, though deep, had remained political.

But this struggle over the ships cut uncommonly deep down into the hidden economic issues that underlie American politics. Here were greedy interests determined, at any cost, to hang on to their golden privileges. With a shortage of American ships private profit saw spectacular returns—provided they could prevent government expansion of shipping resources.[1] The fight developed personal animosities and rancours that were never healed. Nothing certainly could have been more childish than the spectacle of grave senators, wholly forsaking argument and reason, sleeping on cots in their cloakrooms, talking nonsense for unnumbered hours, in order to defeat the will of the majority; but if the President was exasperated, such speeches as that at Indianapolis did his cause little good. If the hostility was smothered for the time by the common compulsions of the war, it continued to smoulder sullenly, until in 1919 it was to burst into flame and destroy the President's greatest achievement, if not his life itself.

Though defeated at this time, neither the President nor Secretary McAdoo considered for a moment a cessation of the struggle. They stuck to their position with a tenacity that was Scotch-Irish: and determined to present their measure promptly to the next Congress. McAdoo lost no opportunity of writing letters and making speeches to support his contentions. In the meantime, during the

---

[1]And those spectacular profits were speedily forthcoming.

"Tramp steamers not infrequently cleared their entire cost or value in a single voyage. In the course of a year an ocean-going freighter would bring in a net return—clear profit above all expenses—of three hundred to five hundred per cent on the money invested in the ship." (William G. McAdoo, *Crowded Years*, p. 304.)

year 1915, the country was being convinced by events of
the serious effects of the European war upon American
trade, that there was really a crisis, really a national
necessity. Moreover there had been growing up a demand
for preparedness, which the President utilized by making
government-owned merchant ships a part of the national
security and defense programme. In his message to Congress on December 7, 1915, he said:

"There are other great matters which will be thrust
upon our attention whether we will or not. . . . It is necessary for many weighty reasons of national efficiency and
development that we should have a great merchant
marine."[1]

He announced that new proposals would be made to
Congress similar to those previously offered, "but modified in some essential particulars."[2] He added: "I am not
so much interested in the particulars of the programme as I
am in taking immediate advantage of the great opportunity which awaits us if we will but act in this emergency."[3]

January 31, 1916, a new Shipping bill was introduced by
Representative Alexander, providing for the establishment
of a shipping board "for the purpose of encouraging,
developing, and creating a naval auxiliary and naval
reserve and a merchant marine. . . ."

But progress on the bill, though the President pressed
hard, was slow. On May 20th it passed the House. Senate
Republicans again offered stubborn resistance, but the
administration was now able to hold the Democrats in
line, and the bill passed the Senate on August 18th by a
vote of 38 (all Democrats) to 21 (all Republicans) and
was signed by the President on September 7th.

[1] The Public Papers of Woodrow Wilson, Vol. III, pp. 415–416.
[2] Ibid., p. 418.
[3] Ibid.

Thus a fight that had lasted over two years was brought to a close in a victory for the contention of the President that the only way to meet the crisis was by buying or building ships and operating them by the government. But the delay, as Mr. McAdoo points out, was to cost the government enormous sums of money, for ships that could have been bought in 1914 at forty dollars a ton cost one hundred and fifty to three hundred dollars a ton in 1916.[1]

It is perhaps futile to inquire whether, if the war had not come as it did, the President could have succeeded in the struggle so clearly typified by the events connected with this shipping legislation. All along, deep down, Wilson's purpose was to rehabilitate democracy, reëstablish democratic aspirations and ideals, prove to the nation and to the world that democracy could successfully and efficiently meet the new economic, industrial, and social problems that confronted the world. We have seen him making the fight at Princeton and failing: we have seen him making the fight as Governor of New Jersey and being saved from failure—perhaps—by his sudden translation into the presidency. We have seen him here vigorously asserting the right of democracy to dominate and direct the economic forces of the nation, we have seen him standing for a democratic government in Mexico—even though it had to be forced upon the Mexicans—and, at the outbreak of the war, we find him asserting that the democratic system was capable of meeting every problem presented, and he was dreaming of a peace which should represent the ultimate triumph of democracy. In all these struggles his first irresistible charge, when he had his cohorts securely behind him, was the most successful, carried him furthest. He once told a friend that he expected his "first year" in the presidency to be the year of

[1]William G. McAdoo, *Crowded Years*, p. 315.

his "greatest efficiency and [that] it was now or never."[1]
In each case, when he began to press his programme to
its further, logical conclusions, his triumphs were succeeded by bitter controversies, in which, determined to
make his cause prevail, he fought obstinately against any
and all odds, personal hostilities developed, and Wilson
found himself toiling against entrenched tradition, im-
movable conservatism. The outbreak of the war just at
the moment when the President was completing his
programme of domestic reform obscured the final test.
Would his formula have worked? Were the powerful industrial and financial leaders of the nation tamed to the
point, as he said, in his ardent hopefulness, of accepting
the leadership and control of Washington?

In the light of the events that followed, his confident
prophecies made in November 1914 seem strange enough:

"The future will be . . . a time of healing because a time
of just dealing and coöperation between men made equal
before the law in fact as well as in name. . . .

"A new day has dawned for the beloved country whose
lasting prosperity and happiness we so earnestly desire."[2]

IV. THE PRESIDENT'S PERSONAL LIFE

The dictum of Edward Gibbon, long ago set down in his
memoirs, that "the most essential and important" part of
the biographer's task lies in discovering and presenting the
"private life" of his subject, applies with peculiar force
in the case of Woodrow Wilson. No man could make a more
determined effort to keep his public and private life completely detached: none was ever, after all, more dependent
than he upon certain of the factors, the necessary sympa-

---

[1]Nancy Toy to Woodrow Wilson, October 9, 1914, quoting a remark he had made to
her during the previous winter.

[2]Woodrow Wilson to W. G. McAdoo, November 17, 1914. *The Public Papers of
Woodrow Wilson*, Vol. III, pp. 213–214.

thies, the intimate understanding, which make a man's personal life at all bearable. "Hearts," he had said in one of his early essays, "frequently give trouble . . . They must be schooled before they will become insensible . . ."[1] But the difficulty then and always was to make the mind and will, however powerful, "their schoolmaster and coach." Those who saw only the President knew little of the man: for they could not penetrate the mask his will put on. The present writer recalls vividly a conversation with the President a few weeks after the death of Mrs. Wilson. "He looked very well—clear-eyed, confident, cheerful—a neat gray suit looking as though it were just from the tailor—a black band on his left arm, a dark tie with a gold ornament. His desk was extremely neat, with a bouquet of roses upon it. He was affable and frank."[2]

In an article written a little later, the writer endeavoured to convey the impression of confident power, easy sufficiency, that the President gave:

"At the end of a hot and wearing summer, with scarcely a day of vacation or of rest, with great questions crowding for settlement, with a domestic affliction which in itself might well be overwhelming, the President remains one of the steadiest, clearest, most cheerful men in Washington. He looks well and strong, with good color and a clear eye.

"There has not once been a sign of wavering, or of weakness, nor has Mr. Wilson allowed his personal sorrow to interfere for a moment with his efficiency in doing the work of the nation."[3]

This was the competent outer man vigorously meeting the inevitable problems, performing the necessary daily tasks: but the intimate correspondence of the time gives us an insight into his broken inner life:

---

[1] *Mere Literature*, p. 45.
[2] From the author's diary, of September 17, 1914.
[3] "Wilson After Twenty Months," in the *American Magazine* of December, 1914.

"My loss has made me humble. I know that there is nothing *for me* in what I am doing. And I hope that that will make me more serviceable. I have succeeded so far, I believe, only because I have not sought my own pleasure in the work or in the office, and have . . . devoted my entire time and energy, alike of body and of mind, to the work of administration and of leadership to be done from day to day. And now self is killed more pitilessly than ever—there is *nothing but the work* for me."[1]

A little later he was writing to another old friend:

"It is amazing how one can continue to function in all ordinary, and some extraordinary, matters with a broken heart. I would not have believed it. I deemed it impossible when I began the experiment. But it is possible; and I think the method is this: not to sit and look on,—especially not to sit and look on at oneself,—but to project oneself as far afield as possible, into fields where one's personal feelings count for nothing, or should count for nothing, except enhanced sympathy and quickened insight. Our own skies are so overcast by the influences of the storm raging in Europe that there is a vast deal to do to keep heart in others and that is the best way to keep our own hearts alive."[2]

He "fights to keep going" by maintaining a "sort of routine" which he thus describes:

"Immediately after an eight o'clock breakfast Swem, my stenographer, comes over to the house and I dictate my letters and go over the papers on my desk which are waiting to be read. Then, about a quarter before ten, I go over to the office and until one receive visitors and delegations of all sorts. When lunch is over (and I am often late to it) I receive one or two more formal visits, such as from an ambassador; then I hurry into my playing clothes

---

[1] Woodrow Wilson to Mary A. Hulbert, September 20, 1914.
[2] Woodrow Wilson to Nancy Toy, October 15, 1914.

and go off to one or other of the golf courses and play golf till the sun goes down. By the time I get home and have a bath and dress there are only a few minutes, fifteen or twenty, before dinner in which to go over and sign the papers awaiting my action on the table in the office. After dinner, there are generally other consultations necessary on pending business or foreign affairs, or papers to prepare on questions which only I ought to formulate, since I am ultimately responsible; and I fall into bed so tired I cannot think. And it is best so. But all this makes Sunday, the only day I have for any letters I may write myself, a day when all my faculties seek rest and are in a sort of coma, and I am no good. I generally sleep (or at any rate stay in bed) until it is time to dress for church and ride all afternoon into the far country round about the city, dozing and silent. Dear little Helen[1] goes with me, a perfect companion because glad to think of me and what is best for me and not anxious to talk and have her own way, bless her heart for the unselfishness! But I hate to think how dull it must be for her, and chide myself for accepting such sacrifices. In a few weeks now the dear little daughter at Cornish will be back; and I see my darling Nell[2] every day. She is here watching constantly over her indefatigable but constantly overworked husband, to whom the whole country turns daily in these troubled times for financial counsel and assistance. She sees almost as little of him as Helen sees of me. It may be better when Congress adjourns (or, rather, *if* Congress adjourns), but for the present it is a killing pace for all of us!"[3]

On November 9th he wrote to Mrs. Toy:

"I am sure you will not gauge the welcome your letters command by the length of time it takes me to sit down for

[1]Helen Woodrow Bones, Mr. Wilson's cousin.

[2]Mrs. William G. McAdoo.

[3]Woodrow Wilson to Mary A. Hulbert, October 11, 1914.

an answer. Somehow the day's work seems absolutely to exhaust my initiative. Almost every day there is some interval when I *could* sit down before this little machine and write. If I were to do so as often as the thought comes and as often as I feel the warmth about my heart that comes whenever I recall the generous messages of dear friends, I would be at its keys many times a day. But with the accomplishment of the tasks of duty each day my energies seem to lag; I want to rest even from thinking; I especially shrink from dwelling upon anything personal to myself. My instinct is to seek some occupation that will take my thoughts far afield where there is nothing that can concern me, as to the reading of some far-away, improbable tale that does not seem to be of this world at all, or of any other unintelligible world. In short I want to run away, to escape something. It is selfish; it is puerile; it is, I trust, short-lived; but it is often my master these barren days! After all, the hardest enterprise in the world is to rule one's own spirit! After that to rule a city were pastime!"

It was at this time that one of those who was close to the President wrote to a friend:

"I cannot tell you how terrible this house seems without Cousin Ellen; and it simply grows worse every day . . . no one can offer Cousin Woodrow any word of comfort, for there is no comfort . . ."[1]

He wrote to Mrs. Toy:

"I have not yet learned how to throw off the incubus of my grief and live as I used to live, in thought and spirit, in spite of it. Even books have grown meaningless to me. I read detective stories to forget, as a man would get drunk! . . .

"What I do love to talk about, however, is things and persons very near to me, not as President (for I am merely

[1] Helen W. Bones to Agnes B. Tedcastle, November 16, 1914.

administering the presidency) but as a human being, a traveler between life and death. Human friendship means an infinite deal to me; and I find my thoughts going out to my friends now as never before, trying to make a circle of them close about me no matter how far away in space they may be, and no matter whether they all know one another or not."[1]

At no time, perhaps, during his administration did the President spend so much time visiting relatives or friends: or in entertaining, at the White House, old friends upon whose sympathy he could count. We find him slipping over at various times to Baltimore to visit the cousins, the Misses Hoyt;[2] going to New York to see Colonel House[3] and to Williamstown to spend Thanksgiving with the Sayres. At Christmas he welcomed Dr. Axson to the White House. The McAdoos, the Sayres, the Misses Smith, the Misses Hoyt, Colonel and Mrs. E. T. Brown, Dean Fine of Princeton, Colonel House, and many other friends were guests at the White House. Mrs. Toy in her diary has given vivid glimpses of a visit in January 1915:

"He looked better than I have ever seen him physically and acknowledged later in reply to a question from Helen that he had never felt better in his life. But in his talk and manner the old buoyancy had gone and I missed it during my whole visit. Also there was more formality beneath the unvarying friendliness of voice and manner—was it, as John Hay said about Roosevelt, 'the kingly shadow falling upon him'? Or, what is more likely, the schooling in self-control which Mrs. Wilson's death has forced upon him? . . . The President announced that some man wanted to print his History of the United States serially in a lot of daily papers—should he do it? he asked the family. 'Is

---

[1] December 12, 1914.
[2] October 4, and November 1, 1914.
[3] November 14, 1914.

there any money in it?' This gaily from Margaret. 'Oh yes—but that's the reason why I don't want to do it while I am President.' Then the talk fell on his books and he declared that he had never written but *two real* books in his life, 'Congressional Government' and 'Mere Literature,' with the latter he had a great deal of fun, keeping it for hours of relaxation. 'But your history!' exclaimed Jessie. 'Oh that I wrote merely to learn the history of the United States,' he said, and continued: 'The worst book of history that I have ever read is Sir George Trevelyan's "American Revolution"—how absurd at this day to believe that the English were all wrong and that we were all right.' At dinner the President seemed very sad. Immediately afterwards he took up a book of Essays by A. G. Gardiner and read aloud a delightfully clever rendering of Bryan. Then he turned over the leaves and began an Essay on Morley which was interrupted by Dr. Mitchell who dropped in after a visit to Mrs. Sayre—interrupted for only a minute for the President said, 'I have nearly finished this, and you must hear it whether you want to or not.' After the doctor's departure the President said: 'I already feel as if Morley were dead. He lives absolutely in the past and can't adjust himself to the very changed environment of the present. He was never a man of action at his best: a man of reflection, of theories which he shrank from putting into action when he had the chance."[1]

The following day was Sunday:

"This morning the President went to church accompanied by Margaret and myself. I suggested walking home but the President hates walking and asked if I should enjoy it always followed by four secret service men. In the afternoon Helen and I went with him for a $2\frac{1}{2}$ hours motor ride. He talked much about Mrs. Wilson, about my mother and about religion. This began with a question

[1]January 2, 1915.

from Helen—did I not enjoy Mr. Fitch's sermons very much? I said I had heard him only once and then he aroused my opposition by declaring that in this breakdown of civilization, these hugenesses of suffering, life would not be worth living did we not believe that God was behind everything and working out His own plan. I do not believe that and still I think life is worth living, I added. The President took up my challenge. His views are those of Dr. Fitch's.

"'*My* life would not be worth living,' he declared, 'if it were not for the driving power of religion, for *faith*, pure and simple. I have seen all my life the arguments against it without ever having been moved by them.'

"'Did you never have a religious *Sturm und Drang* period?' I asked.

"'No, never for a moment have I had one doubt about my religious beliefs. There are people who *believe* only so far as they *understand*—that seems to me presumptuous and sets their understanding as the standard of the universe. Why shouldn't Helen's dog, Hamisch here, set up *his* understanding as a standard! I am sorry for such people'[1] . . . After dinner that evening . . . the President fell to talking about Bryan. It began this way: he took down a book of lectures he had made six years ago at Columbia College on 'The Constitution.' He was then president of Princeton. 'Let's read my chapter on the President,' he said. 'I haven't read these lectures since I delivered them.' And thus we had the piquant experience of hearing the President of the United States read what was an ideal Executive written by the president of a college when he had no idea what Fate had in store for him.

---

[1]Wilson's letters give many evidences of the depth of his religious faith, and of his dependence upon it. He wrote to his old friend Dr. Melancthon W. Jacobus on February 8, 1915:

"I certainly need the support of the confidence and the personal prayers of my friends as I never did before."

He closed the book with a sigh, and I asked, 'Does that mean that you are discouraged? *Are* you discouraged?' 'Yes,' he said simply, 'I am discouraged by the eternal talk with senators one by one. The ideal form of leadership in this country (and I am going to write a book about it one of these days) would be the leadership in the Senate. Now I have to talk with senators one by one—what they say on the floor all the country knows—what I say to them nobody hears. The President should be a mere figure-head like the King of England. The leader of the party should be the leader in Congress and should be heard in debate fully.'"[1]

One of the happier incidents of this forlorn period was the birth, in the White House, of the President's first grandchild, a son, to Mrs. Sayre.[2]

"And so," he wrote, "none of us can think straight. I forget where the keys of the typewriter are as I absent-mindedly try to write this ... My own heart is full of the pity that the sweet, sweet mother could not have been here to share her daughter's joy!"[3]

It was intended that the boy should bear the name of his grandfather, but as the President wrote, "I thought he was entitled to a name of his own."[4] He was called Francis, after his father. A deluge of letters and telegrams of congratulation with the strangest of gifts—Mike Donovan sent a pair of boxing gloves—served to occupy the President's spare moments for some days. "Hooray!" wrote Cleveland Dodge. "Welcome to the ranks of grand-fathers."[5]

A letter written to Mrs. Sayre shortly after she left the

---

[1] January 3, 1915.
[2] Over eighty years had passed since the last child had been born in the White House—a grandson of Andrew Jackson.
[3] Woodrow Wilson to Mary A. Hulbert, January 17, 1915.
[4] Woodrow Wilson to Jessie K. Dyer, January 28, 1915.
[5] January 18, 1915.

White House with her baby lets us deep into the heart of the man:

14 March, 1915.

MY DARLING JESSIE,

I am ashamed of myself when I think I have been so long acknowledging the dear letter from you that made me so happy, and touched me so deeply. You cannot know, I fear, what it meant to me to have you say that I had in some sort taken your incomparable mother's place when you were here! Ah! how little I knew how! and how impossible it was to do more than just let you feel as well as I knew how the infinite tenderness I felt and the longing that was at my heart to make up for what can never be made up for either to you, my sweet daughter, nor to me nor to anyone who ever had a chance to know how sweet and loving and infinitely rewarding she was. I cannot yet trust myself to speak much of her, even in writing. My heart has somehow been stricken dumb. I felt so dumb when you were here, dear. I did not know how to *say* the things that were in my heart about you and the baby and all the crowding thoughts that made my heart ache with its fulness. I had to trust you to *see* them; and your dear letter makes me hope that you did. I can talk about most things but I always have been helpless about putting into words the things I feel most deeply, the things that mean most to me; and just now my heart is particularly voiceless. But I do love you and yours, my dear, more than words can say, and there *is* added to my love now the mother tenderness which I know the depths and beauties of in *her* heart. She was beyond comparison the deepest, truest, noblest lover I ever knew or ever heard those who knew the human heart wish for!—It is delightful to hear how well everything goes with you. God bless you. You will have heard of Mac's operation. He has come out of it finely: and is doing as well as anyone could in the circumstances. Nell is here with us, of course, and as steady and brave as usual. Nothing happens to the rest of us except daily crises in foreign affairs.

Love beyond measure from us all to you all.

Your loving
FATHER

WOODROW WILSON AND HIS FIRST GRANDCHILD, SON OF
MRS. FRANCIS B. SAYRE, TAKEN IN THE WHITE HOUSE,
FEBRUARY, 1915

In this connection it may be well to touch upon certain expressions of this deep and sympathetic side of the President's nature in relation to the duties of his office. Even in the rush of events of world importance we find his interest attracted and his heart touched by instances of misfortune, and particularly of injustice.

"Here is a letter from a very old woman who has been dropped from the lists of the Pension Office. It is represented to me that she is in extreme need and I write for information about her. I should like to help the poor lady if it is possible for us to do so."[1]

He became deeply interested in the case of a young army lieutenant:

"I have been going over the papers in the case of First Lieutenant ——, —— Cavalry, sentenced by court-martial to be dismissed from the service for intoxication and other offences. I would like very much to know if there is any precedent or justification in the previous practice of the Executive in such matters for permitting Lieutenant —— to resign or imposing upon him a penalty less than dismissal, such, for example, as reduction to the bottom of the list of first lieutenants.

"I am moved to make this inquiry by sincere interest in the case of this particular man whom I would like to save, if it can be done, without involving consequences too grave to the discipline of the army."[2]

His attention had been called to the miserable remuneration of the "White Wings"—street cleaners—of Washington, and we find him writing to Commissioner Oliver P. Newman:

"This is just a line to ask if you do not think it would be just in making up your estimates to include an increase

---

[1] Woodrow Wilson to G. M. Saltzgaber, Commissioner of Pensions, September 11, 1914.

[2] Woodrow Wilson to Lindley M. Garrison, September 9, 1914.

of twenty-five cents a day for the 'White Wings' who work on the streets of the city. Their present wage seems a pitiful dole."[1]

The President's resources of amusement and relaxation outside of his engrossing labours seem to have been extremely limited. The greatest of these were the delights of his home, to have a group of old and sympathetic friends around him for the evening with lively conversation, good stories, reading aloud. He refused to discuss politics or official business at his table—and this, often enough, to the intense irritation of his visitors. In his home circle he refused to be "the President." Once when a group of friends, among them several ladies, stood aside to give him preference in entering the White House dining room, he said:

"I insist upon being a gentleman in my own house!"

He played golf, indeed, nearly every day, usually with Dr. Grayson, sometimes with Colonel Brown or other old friends, and while he enjoyed it, he seemed to regard it chiefly as a necessary process in keeping him fit for his labours.

"I play golf every day, but only to keep alive and spend and be spent!"[2]

A friend wrote of his playing:

"When he has made a particularly fine drive or accomplished a difficult approach or is complimenting an opponent on a clever putt, you wouldn't think he had a care in the world. He is cheerful and wholesome under any and all circumstances and a delightful companion always."[3]

Nearly every day he took a long drive through country

[1]October 13, 1914.
[2]Woodrow Wilson to Mary A. Hulbert, November 22, 1914.
[3]Colonel E. T. Brown to Mrs. Brown, March 13, 1915.

roads around Washington. Usually there were friends with him, but he himself sat silent and detached. It provided an opportunity not easily found among the distractions of his office to rest or to think out the problems that confronted him.

Most men, whatever their occupation, find their business affairs more or less interesting, if not absolutely absorbing. The amount of time and thought that the average American gives to his finances, whether large or small, is enormous. With Woodrow Wilson, it was almost nil. For years he had known, as a college professor or president, very closely what his yearly income would be, and while there was considerable correspondence at various times relating to business arrangements connected with the publication of his books, it occupied an unimportant part of his life. Indeed, most of the ordinary business matters had been cared for by Mrs. Wilson. When he became President his income, of course, was largely increased, but as he sought only the soundest kind of investments his business affairs required comparatively little of his personal attention.[1]

About the time that the President had completed the first two years of his administration, when the press reviews of his achievements were, for the most part, extraordinarily favourable, he was writing to his friend Mrs. Toy:

"It was generous of you to think of any part of Wordsworth's Happy Warrior as applying to me. I seem to myself so unheroic a figure (just a man who intends right things and looks for them every day with a steady mind, uncommon in nothing except that it is at his command when he wishes, as the result of long discipline) and with none but common tools to work with. If there is anything

---

[1]After the entrance of the United States into the war, the President invested only in Liberty Bonds.

that can infuse the heroic into me it is the trust and confidence of those whom I honour and who know the right from the wrong. Any heroism I may be vouchsafed will come from the outside, not from within."[1]

---

[1] March 7, 1915.

CHAPTER III

THE PRESIDENT AND AMERICAN
DUTIES AS A NEUTRAL

The occasion is not of our own making. We had no part in making it.
But it is here. It affects us as directly and palpably almost as if we
were participants in the circumstances which gave rise to it. . . .
We shall pay the bill, though we did not deliberately incur it.

Address to Congress, September 4, 1914.

We are custodians of the spirit of righteousness, of the spirit of
equal-handed justice . . .

Address at Philadelphia, October 20, 1914.

. . . what a future it is . . . Look abroad upon the troubled world!
Only America at peace! Among all the great powers of the world only
America saving her power for her own people!

Address at Indianapolis, January 8, 1915.

I. FIRST TESTS OF THE AMERICAN POSITION

PRACTICAL problems of the most complicated and
irritating nature arose almost immediately to test
the President's policy of determined neutrality. These fell
naturally into two groups: first, the *duties* of Americans
as set forth in the declaration of neutrality issued by the
President on August 4th; second, the *rights* of Americans
claimed under the Declaration of London, the acceptance
of which by the belligerents the President had asked on
August 6th. Beyond these, its limitations fixed only by
the aspirations of the President and his advisers, was the
obligation of America as peacemaker in a world torn by
war, an obligation first recognized in the offer of good
offices on August 4th. These three groups of problems will
be presented in this and two succeeding chapters.

151

It was one thing to take a correct legal position by the prompt issuance of the declaration of neutrality, quite another to apply even those principles which were generally accepted to immediate and specific problems some of which, owing to the rapid technical changes in world relationships, were quite unprecedented. While organization for possible war had for half a century occupied the best brains of Europe, with every resource of science and invention engaged in preparation for "the Day," little real attention had been given to problems of how to keep the peace, still less to the course which a neutral nation, faced by a general conflagration, should pursue. In the United States practically no neutrality legislation had been enacted since the year 1838: we were trying to function in an age of flying machines with the implements of an age of ox carts. Such projects as the Hague Court, the arbitration treaties, the new Bryan proposals, while in themselves brave beginnings, had been left more or less to visionaries, and at the outbreak of the war had neither the respect of those in power nor the support of any considerable body of public opinion. International law, so called, was merely a feeble and contradictory assemblage of precedents backed by no real sanctions. To start a war it was only necessary to touch the button of a vast and well-ordered machine, which thereafter moved forward of its own terrible volition; but to defend and maintain a shadowy structure of international law, to preserve some semblance of order in a world gone mad, to try to blow the breath of life into feeble projects for international coöperation, was, for neutral statesmanship, a vastly more difficult and complicated matter. If America, in the twenty or fifty years previous to the shot at Sarajevo, had devoted half the intelligence and a ten-thousandth part of the treasure spent by the militarists of Europe, in studying problems of neutrality and in forging the implements of peace and training the people to use them, we could in all probability have prevented the war, and we might have moved forward toward the real leadership in world affairs of which we dreamed. But there had been no such stern antecedent preparation. Good intentions, peace-loving aspirations, even the economic interests of neutrals in that crisis, proved mere straws in the blast. A panicky nation, wholly unprepared, turned helplessly to its President, expecting of him miracles which neither he nor any other human being could have performed.

At the outbreak of the war, Woodrow Wilson was nearly fifty-eight years old: in a sense everything that had gone before was mere preparation for the larger problems, the far more stupendous tasks, which lay ahead of him. The real tests were yet to come: wherein he must not only lead, but build up, during the progress of swift-moving and all but overwhelming events, that knowledge and conviction which must necessarily precede unity of action. The judgement of the future will be founded not so much upon a test of perfection as upon the immensity and intractability of the problems he had to meet—could any man have succeeded?—and upon his handling of his tasks as compared with other contemporary leaders of the world: with Grey and Clemenceau and Lloyd George, with the Kaiser and the Czar. What was the *residue* of his statesmanship? Compared with the others, what did he leave, in ideas, in aspirations, in new laws or organizations, which will be of value to men in future times? A statesman may fail in innumerable details: he may have in his temperamental characteristics what Emerson called "quantities of unavailableness," and he yet may survive by a certain unity of character or purpose which the world needs and will prize. Men are judged by what they strove to do, by the mightiness with which they strove, as well as by what they actually did do.

The President was to have his first illuminating glimpses of the avalanche of difficulties in the way of maintaining American neutrality before the ink was dry on the proclamation of August 4th. While he had chosen the longer form, and the rules laid down were detailed and elaborate, it was immediately apparent that belligerents in a war of 1914 were not easily to be bound by precedents of 1864 or 1898 or even by the codifications of The Hague. The world had moved on, and legal restraints, such as they were, had lagged. Under the old system new precedents required new wars. One of the very first complaints concerned the use of wireless telegraph stations by belligerents —a subject not even mentioned in the neutrality proclamation. The British and French objected that the high-powered station at Sayville, Long Island, operated by a German company, was being used to direct ships at sea. What was the duty of the American government? A rule, or a law, or a precedent had to be created upon the spot.[1]

Not only were new rules required to meet new instrumentalities, but there were immediate and very great differences in the interpretation of old ones. When, at the outbreak of the war, several German ships—notably the *Kronprinz Wilhelm*—scurried out of American ports for conversion into commerce destroyers, the British immediately, on August 4th, reminded the American government that "... His Majesty's government will accordingly

---

[1]On August 5th an executive order was issued, supplementing the proclamation, forbidding all radio stations in America from delivering and transmitting unneutral messages: but it was only the beginning of a long-continued controversy. The complaint that American censorship of wireless news was discriminatory against Germany was easily disposed of by Lansing on December 9, 1914, after it had been specifically voiced by Professor Hugo Münsterberg of Harvard. Germany, wrote the Counselor, had by the fortunes of naval war lost contact with the United States by cable and must rely singly upon wireless which must be censored by this government, as a neutral, since "messages sent out from a wireless station in neutral territory may be received by belligerent warships on the high seas" so as to direct naval action or convey information. A submarine cable manifestly could not be used as a means of direct communication with a warship on the high seas; hence it was unnecessary to censor its use since its use could not make of neutral territory a base for directing naval operations. (See this volume, p. 223).

hold the United States government responsible for any damages to British trade or shipping, or injury to British interests generally, which may be caused by such vessels having been equipped at, or departing from, United States ports."[1] Here was an imputation of negligence on the part of the United States, accompanied by a threat of claims for damages, which aroused great irritation at Washington, since the *Kronprinz Wilhelm* had sailed before there was official knowledge of a state of war. And yet the reminder was based upon a precedent established by the Americans themselves in the famous case of the Confederate raider *Alabama*, fitted out in an English port during the Civil War: for the depredations of which the British government had been obliged ultimately to make amends. But the dignified rejoinder of the American State Department, denying the charge of negligence and disclaiming liability, which the President himself approved —"There is no change I would care to make in the memorandum for his Britannic Majesty's government"[2]—had not been transmitted before the British government had shifted its own ground, because, in arming British merchant vessels to resist German raiders, it had to take care lest the United States treat these as vessels of war and refuse to let them clear from its ports.[3] In all these cases each belligerent was impatient of every restraint, suspicious of every decision.

Many of the problems gave immediate evidence of the utterly baseless legend of American isolation; revealing in what a fool's paradise those had lived who believed that the United States could avoid entanglements with problems in every part of the world. Before the war was a

---

[1] *Foreign Relations of the United States*, Supplement, 1914, p. 594.

[2] Woodrow Wilson to W. J. Bryan, August 14, 1914.

[3] See note of August 9th, *Foreign Relations of the United States*, Supplement, 1914, p. 598.

month old we were involved in the situation in the Far East, with Japan and China; and it was soon clear that if we were to maintain our own neutrality, we would be compelled to assume certain responsibilities based upon our relationships with the Latin-American states, under recent extensions of the Monroe Doctrine, and even in Africa with the tiny republic of Liberia. Since our protection of these states prevented the Allies from dealing with them as they chose, they demanded that we accept the responsibility for seeing that they fulfilled their duties as neutrals. The Allies' principal concern in the beginning was with the operation of German-owned wireless stations in Liberia and Colombia. Our government courteously recommended proper principles to these states and helped disprove some of the allegations against them. All wireless stations in Liberia were closed—the government of that backward state pleading that it could not control them, since the only Liberian who understood wireless was out of the country! The embarrassment of the Latin-American states in maintaining their neutrality possibly had a certain advantage, since it was one of the causes that led to their proposals for common action with the United States in neutralizing the western hemisphere.

If the United States had been a small or weak neutral nation the problems would, of course, have been relatively unimportant, but we were not only powerful, so that our action might at any time determine the fortunes of the war, but we produced immense surpluses of food, cotton, copper, and other commodities which the belligerents not only desired but must obtain. And they needed our money, if they could get it, as much as they needed our goods. From the beginning the President of the United States, by virtue of his position and his power, became to an extraordinary degree the arbiter of the war. His course, not only in going into the war, but for two years and eight months in keeping out of it, had at every point a profound effect upon its fortunes.

All this was recognized by the belligerents on both sides, and every effort was made to win American sympathy or support. Every decision the President made affected in some degree the fortunes of one side or the other and was open to the charges, sometimes by the British or French, sometimes by the Germans—sometimes by both—that he had been unfair, that he did not hold squarely the balance between them. To a degree that is not even yet fully recognized, the fate of the World War was settled at Washington; settled by the President of the United States, who personally dominated, as the head of no other nation, perhaps, dominated, the international relations of the country.

Not the least of the President's difficulties in seeking to guide America justly in the performance of its duties as a neutral was the reaction, from the very beginning, among his own people. Every event in Europe was reflected in the public opinion of America. It was part of the diplomatic technique of the belligerents, by enlisting American sympathy or stirring American anger, to win American assistance. The war had scarcely started before each side was bitterly protesting to the President regarding the military methods of the other.

The matter of aërial bombardment of towns seemed at first sight a sufficiently obvious case of killing and destruction without military objective to warrant discussion with Bryan of the propriety of a protest; yet it turned out not to be so clear (railway junctions or munition factories and depots might be aimed at). On September 4th, Wilson wrote to Bryan:

MY DEAR MR. SECRETARY:
I have thought a great deal about the matter of a protest with regard to the dropping of the bombs and my present judge-

ment is that we do not know in sufficient detail the actual facts
and that we ought to be very slow to make formal protests,
chiefly because we shall no doubt be called upon by every one
of the belligerents before the fighting is over to do something of
this kind and would be in danger of becoming chronic critics
of what was going forward. I think the time for clearing up all
these matters will come when the war is over and the nations
gather in sober counsel again.

Cordially and faithfully yours,
WOODROW WILSON

HON. WILLIAM JENNINGS BRYAN,
Secretary of State.

The note struck in the last sentence set the key for the
public utterances on the subject which Wilson was soon
called on to make.

On September 7th the Kaiser protested to the President
that the Allies were using dum-dum bullets. ". . . this kind
of warfare," he wrote, ". . . has become one of the most
barbarous known in history."[1] Three days later President
Poincaré of France charged that Germany herself was
using dum-dum bullets and was "trying to confuse the
issue and to lay up mendacious pretexts for indulging in
fresh atrocities."[2] These charges capped a tremendous
volume of lurid news reports from the scene of war which
filled every newspaper in the United States. The Germans
were crashing through Belgium: the famous library of
Louvain had been destroyed: ruin, bloodshed, starvation
followed in the wake of the advancing armies. It was
inevitable that the reaction in America should be immediate and profound. It was inevitable that considerable
bodies of our population should begin to take sides, some
because of their love for the homelands in Europe from
which they had come, others because they had already

---

[1] *Foreign Relations of the United States*, Supplement, 1914, p. 794.
[2] *Ibid.*

reached a decision as to which side was right and which was wrong. In years past we had dreamed a roseate dream of the mystic potency of our institutions and our life to make over foreigners who came to our shores. The magic of the melting-pot! But at the first strain of war, the traditional allegiances, the ancient suspicions and hatreds began to reassert themselves. Agencies of organized propaganda fostered these divisions and stimulated militant societies among the various groups. From the beginning, the scales of public opinion in America as a whole showed a tendency to tip away from Germany. The spectacle of a bloody and ruinous invasion of France and Belgium aroused the emotions, and the publication of the documents relating to the onset of the war, the apparently complete Blue Book of the British and the White Book of the Germans, tended among thoughtful Americans to a more favourable impression of the Allied cause than of the German. The New York *Times* presented this reaction exactly:

"Very different from the lucid and complete revelation of England's every thought and act, presented in the White Paper . . . is Germany's statement which we print this morning. The British White Paper is a documentary history; the very documents themselves are made public without comment or coloring. Sir Edward Grey puts all his cards upon the table face upward. . . .

"Germany presents a lawyer's brief, a special pleading in which, with such skill as its authors could command, the attempt is made to present her part in the negotiations that preceded war in a light most favorable to herself. Between these two an impartial world will judge."[1]

---

[1] August 24, 1914.
Professor Sidney B. Fay, in his *Origins of the World War*, writes:
"To the German people, to whom the book was primarily addressed, the argument was convincing. They went through the war, honestly believing that they were fighting

In the midst of such an explosion of violence, hatred, fear in the world, with his country in danger of being divided by embittered partisans and with appeals pouring in upon him to "do something," it is scarcely surprising to find the President writing in a personal letter that "the world itself seems gone mad,"[1] nor that he should, on September 8th, issue a proclamation setting aside October 4th as a day of prayer for peace.[2]

He did not at once reply to the protests of the Kaiser and President Poincaré, but he considered deeply what the attitude of the American government should be. In preparation for the reception of a delegation of Belgians, accredited by King Albert, which had come to this country to protest against the German invasion of Belgium, he worked out in shorthand a general statement of his policy, probably copying it out, as was his custom with papers of the first importance, on his own typewriter.

The Belgians arrived at the White House on the afternoon of September 16th, a distinguished group, accompanied by Secretary Bryan and Secretary McAdoo. Their spokesman, Henry Carton de Wiart, made a moving appeal:

"Peaceful inhabitants were massacred, defenseless

---

a war of self-defense forced upon them by Russia. Outside of Germany, however, the *White Book* made the worst possible impression. . . .

"Compared with the German publication, the British book seemed to be fairly complete, candid and convincing. At first sight it appeared that all documents of any importance were included. They gave the impression that Sir Edward Grey had striven honestly for the preservation of peace, but that he had been thwarted in his efforts by Germany's rejection of all peace proposals, and by Austria's precipitate action against Serbia. Outside Germany, therefore, a host of writers hastily jumped to the conclusion that Germany and Austria had deliberately plotted the war and were solely responsible for it. This conclusion was strengthened by the documentary publications put forth by the other governments in the following months." (Vol. I, pp. 3–5.)

It was not until December 1926 that the British government finally issued a collection of all its diplomatic documents relating to the July crisis of 1914. This collection contained "some 500 new documents and many important passages which were omitted from the British Blue Book of 1914." (*Ibid.*, pp. 14–15.)

[1] Woodrow Wilson to Mary A. Hulbert, September 6, 1914.

[2] See *The Public Papers of Woodrow Wilson*, Vol. III, pp. 170–171.

women and children were outraged, open and undefended towns were destroyed; historical and religious monuments were reduced to dust and the famous Library of the University of Louvain was given to the flames."

In his response, the President expressed his pleasure and pride that "your King should have turned to me in time of distress," and promised that the documents left in his hands should have his "most thoughtful consideration."

"You will, I am sure, not expect me to say more. Presently, I pray God very soon, this war will be over. The day of accounting will then come when, I take it for granted, the nations of Europe will assemble to determine a settlement. Where wrongs have been committed their consequences and the relative responsibility involved will be assessed."

He went on to call attention to the fact that there was already a "plan" for "such a reckoning and settlement," meaning by this the Hague Court, though he did not mention it by name.

"What such a plan cannot compass the opinion of mankind, the final arbiter in all such matters, will supply. It would be unwise, it would be premature for a single government, however fortunately separated from the present struggle, it would even be inconsistent with the neutral position of any nation, which, like this, has no part in the contest, to form or express a final judgement."

There were further gestures of welcome, respect, and sympathy, but the main lines of his policy had been set down with complete clarity. He would take no position as to war guilt or "relative responsibility": this judgement must be left until the close of the struggle: America must maintain its neutral position.

On the same day he replied in nearly the same words to

the protest of the Kaiser, and a little later, to the President of France.[1]

His announcement at the time was well received.[2] Some of the critics who were later to attack him most bitterly for his failure to intervene on behalf of Belgium, at first approved his position. Roosevelt, for example, asserted that we had not the "smallest responsibility for what has befallen" Belgium.

". . . I am sure that the sympathy of this country for the suffering of the men, women, and children of Belgium is very real. Nevertheless, this sympathy is compatible with full acknowledgment of the unwisdom of our uttering a single word of official protest unless we are prepared to make that protest effective; and only the clearest and most urgent national duty would ever justify us in deviating from our rule of neutrality and non-interference."[3]

It is, of course, impossible to say what might have happened had there been time to take up the question of some kind of appeal on Belgium's behalf in advance of the invasion. But that question was swallowed up in the rush of events and, once hostilities between the Belgian and German armies had begun, it became merged, as Wilson saw clearly, in the general problem of our attitude toward the war as a whole. To have allowed our attitude to be determined by the entanglement, however tragic and

---

[1]He revealed again his determination not to pre-judge war guilt in a letter of October 7th to Louis de Sadeleer, Belgian Minister of State, and a member of the Belgian Commission to the United States:

"I am very much moved by your letter from New York bearing date the second of October and beg that you will believe that I refrain from any public expression of any judgement at all in the serious matter you have laid before me only because I think it my duty to withhold all judgement concerning it until everything is made clear with regard to the war and its many distressing incidents. When the time for summing up comes, I feel that we shall be in possession of so many more facts than we now have, and then we shall be upon very much firmer ground in coming to conclusions."

[2]"It is a source of great comfort and satisfaction to feel that in such a time as this we have a President who knows so well how to do and say the right thing." (New York Times, September 18, 1914.)

[3]Theodore Roosevelt, in the Outlook, September 23, 1914.

unmerited, of one small belligerent would have been an unthinkably frivolous decision of a vast and complicated issue. No serious student can now maintain that even England's entrance into the war was solely determined by the violation of Belgium's neutrality—though it formed the proximate occasion—and England had a direct material interest in the matter, while we had not so much as a legal one. However "scornful" Wilson may have been in talking to House of "Germany's disregard of treaty obligations,"[1] it did not occur to him that he was called upon to hold her to them.[2] He took a moral interest in the matter but declined to let it obscure the much larger moral problem of the war as a whole, in which championship of Belgium would have involved him. He saw in the innocence of one victim no cause to change his verdict of "utter condemnation" of the principal actors in the struggle, nor any reason for departing from his general attitude of neutrality. At that time there was no legal wrong in declaring even a war of conquest. Such action did not become illegal until Article 10 was written into the Covenant of the League of Nations.

Not for months afterwards was the question of an American protest raised by any responsible critic—even by Wilson's most determined political opponents. If we are to judge by his published statements of the time, Theodore Roosevelt would have acted, in the beginning, exactly as Wilson did. But as the war progressed and American feeling became stronger, there was a natural tendency to look back and try to assess responsibility for the woes which the world was suffering—to find someone to blame. It was not until November that Robert Bacon,

---

[1] *The Intimate Papers of Colonel House*, Vol. I, p. 293.

[2] His indignation at the destruction of Louvain was natural to any scholar; but his scholarly instinct warned him also against premature decisions based upon purely partisan testimony.

probably "the first American statesman to advocate publicly this protest,"[1] issued a statement criticizing the President on the ground that this nation had not done its duty, that it was obligated under the Hague Conventions of 1907 to protest the violation of Belgium.[2]

As a matter of fact, the United States was bound neither by law nor by treaty.[3] The provision in the Fifth Hague Convention invoked by Robert Bacon and other critics, that the "territory of neutral powers is inviolable," was nullified by another provision[4] which declared that "the provisions of the present Convention do not apply except between contracting Powers, and then only if all the belligerents are parties to the Convention."

Neither Great Britain nor Serbia had ever ratified this Convention.

Nevertheless for months the President was violently assailed for his "poltroonery," chiefly by Roosevelt who later made his course regarding the Belgian invasion and Mexican affairs one of the essential points in his attack.[5] Some of Wilson's friends were much disturbed by these

---

[1] James Brown Scott, *Robert Bacon, Life and Letters*, p. 238.

[2] It was not until two years later, during the heated campaign of 1916, when American public opinion had become highly inflamed, that the issue became of political importance. On February 15, 1916, Elihu Root, then United States senator and a possible presidential nominee, said in an address:

"The American people were entitled not merely to feel but to speak concerning the wrong done to Belgium. . . . The law protecting Belgium which was violated was our law, and the law of every other civilized nation." (New York *Times*, February 16, 1916.)

[3] The original neutralization of Belgium grew out of the treaties of November 15, 1831, and of April 19, 1839. Neither of these treaties was signed by the United States.

[4] Article 20.

[5] As a matter of fact, both Germany and Great Britain invaded neutral territory. If the Germans were in Belgium, the British were in the Greek islands off the mouth of the Dardanelles. There was as much *legal* obligation upon the United States to protest in one case as in the other: but the *feeling* aroused was wholly different. As Arthur Bullard excellently points out in his book, *The Diplomacy of the Great War*, "It was no more 'illegal' for the Germans to enter Belgium than for them to enter Luxembourg. But it was horrible" (p. 297).

At a later time the British lost heavily in our sympathy by policies that seemed illegal and arrogant, but the German methods seemed inhuman, and made us angry.

attacks and wished to answer them, but Wilson's attitude, then and later, was expressed in a letter to Dudley Field Malone:

". . . please don't give yourself any distress or concern about what Mr. Roosevelt is saying. The very extravagance and unrestrained ill feeling of what he is now writing serve to nullify any influence that his utterances could have. He cannot possibly in his present situation or temper cause any embarrassment which need give us a second thought. I am sincerely sorry that he should have so forgotten the dignity and responsibility of a man placed as he is who might exercise so great an influence for good if he only saw and chose the way."[1]

Careful as Wilson was to avoid any expression of opinion as to the truth of the atrocity tales that continually multiplied and to keep down public discussion of such matters, he was unable to refrain entirely from an attempt to mitigate the practice of aërial bombardment of cities by the Germans, which he and Bryan had discussed early in September. On October 19th the President sent to the State Department a telegram for Ambassador Gerard which he had written out on his own typewriter. It directed Gerard to find some roundabout way, through some influential member of the German government, of conveying an intimation that the Germans were injuring their cause in the eyes of the American public by this practice.[2]

This step, which was without effect, does not necessarily indicate that Wilson had come around to the belief that the bombing of towns was done out of pure terrorism and without proper military reasons. It was an attempt to get the Germans to see that the military gains from such operations involving so much destruction of civilian lives

---

[1]December 9, 1914, referring to Roosevelt's article on Mexico.

[2]The original copy of this message, written on the President's own typewriter, is now in the State Department files at Washington.

and property might be outweighed by the loss of moral credit.[1]

From this time onward charges of inhumanity by each side against the other—which there was no dispassionate organization in the world to investigate—were to play a large part in the controversy over neutral rights. The British alleged Germany's inhumane practices as a reason for extraordinary measures of blockade the effects of which would fall upon the civilian population, and which also curtailed the legal rights of American merchants. The Germans in turn alleged Great Britain's illegal measures for the starvation of their people as justification for the submarine blockade, which violated the rights of American persons and property. Our protests against the illegal actions of each side were met by the virtual condition that we get the other to stop its questionable practices. The result was that, in the assertion of neutral rights, the American government finally became entangled in nearly the whole controversy over violations of the laws of war, and the success of its efforts came to depend upon obtaining an agreement between the belligerents that one should cease doing this if the other ceased doing something else. With each distrusting and believing the worst of the other, and each only too anxious to find excuses for hitting below the belt, this became a hopeless undertaking; and the United States was left to drift into war against the party whose measures of extralegal retaliation most seriously injured American lives and property.

---

[1]As the time for Congress to assemble drew near, the State Department had to face the possibility of being questioned by members in regard to its attitude toward violations of the Hague Conventions. Lansing drew up, on November 23, 1914, for submission to the President a statement of the reasons for inaction. These were three: (1) that the evidence was purely *ex parte* and impartial investigation was impracticable; (2) that a neutral government was not bound to interfere in the actions of belligerents which did not affect its own interests or those of its citizens; (3) that the Hague Conventions, while joint instruments, did not bind the parties to joint action in enforcing their observance. Wilson commended these observations, in a note of November 26th, as "sound and wise."

During the weeks that followed the Belgian protest, we find the President struggling, in large matters and in small, to maintain, in fact as well as in form, strict American neutrality. He watched everything—every paper that came from the State Department. We find him, more and more, becoming his own foreign minister. He consulted with Bryan, but day after day he dealt directly with the experts of the Department, chiefly with Mr. Lansing, upon whose knowledge of international law and of diplomatic procedure he seems to have leaned with confidence. We find in the files, on one day, September 17th, eight letters to Mr. Lansing, mostly dealing with problems of neutrality. His promptness and firmness of action in meeting many of the lesser indiscretions, of which little was known at that time, undoubtedly prevented incalculable difficulty and disorganization in later months. He had the schoolmaster's instinct for keeping strict discipline in the classroom by pouncing upon the first signs of disorder. Certain members of the diplomatic corps, among them the German Baron von Schoen, the Turkish ambassador, Rustem Bey, and Sir Lionel Carden, British ambassador to Mexico, had made comments or given interviews which were, to say the least, undiplomatic. The President dealt with them at once and with vigour. Rustem Bey went home, and other cases were followed up with great persistence through the foreign offices.

"Grey promises to investigate Carden interview as soon as Carden arrives.

"He expressed strong disapproval of what Carden is reported to have said, if he said it."[1]

Regarding Baron von Schoen the President wrote to Secretary Lansing:

"I do not feel that we can wisely drop the matter about Baron Schoen. I hope that it will be possible to intimate

[1] Walter H. Page to W. J. Bryan, September 23, 1914.

to Count von Bernstorff that the alleged interview has made so widespread an impression and has been in so many ways called to the attention of the government that it would be an embarrassment for a great many months to come to Baron Schoen himself and it would be certain seriously to impair his usefulness here."[1]

He was not less exacting with himself and with members of his own administration. Numerous letters exhibit his punctilious efforts to safeguard his own position. He wrote to Hall Caine on October 26th:

"It goes without saying, of course, that my warmest sympathy goes out to those who are suffering in Belgium, but I think that in view of my official position it would be very unwise for me to say anything for the book which is being prepared under the auspices of the *Daily Telegraph*. The book will inevitably express a judgement about the war and it is not proper that I should join in the expression of any judgement whatever about the circumstances under which the Belgians have suffered so grievously."

In a fine letter to Ambassador Page, whose sympathies had been deeply engaged by the British cause, while expressing his genuine affection and confidence, there is plainly a warning:

"I was just reading carefully last night your last letter dated the fifteenth of October, written in a way to give me a wonderful impression of the state of mind that prevails among the most thoughtful men connected with the government over there.

"The whole thing is very vivid in my mind, painfully vivid, and has been almost ever since the struggle began. I think my thought and imagination contain the picture and perceive its significance from every point of view. I have to force myself not to dwell upon it to avoid the sort of numbness that comes from deep apprehension and

[1]October 1, 1914.

dwelling upon elements too vast to be yet comprehended or in any way controlled by counsel. You need not doubt, my dear friend, that we comprehend and look into the murky darkness of the whole thing with the same thoughts that you have, though, of course, on this side of the water our own life is, at any rate, still free, and I fancy we can manage a little more perspective than it is conceivable should be obtainable from any point of view on your side the water.

"I have been distressed to have to maintain our recent debate with Sir Edward Grey,[1] but it was absolutely necessary that we should discuss the matters Mr. Lansing presented, because not the least part of the difficulty of this war is going to be the satisfaction of opinion in America and the full performance of our utmost duty as the only powerful neutral. More and more, from day to day, the elements (I mean the several racial elements) of our population seem to grow restless and catch more and more the fever of the contest. We are trying to keep all possible spaces cool, and the only means by which we can do so is to make it demonstrably clear that we are doing everything that it is possible to do to define and defend neutral rights. This is in the interest of all the belligerents no less than in our own interest. I mean that if we are to remain neutral and to afford Europe the legitimate assistance possible in such circumstances, the course we have been pursuing is the absolutely necessary course. Please do not suppose that we are not able to see the thing from the point of view of others, but always remember that it is as necessary for them as it is for us that we should present and emphasize our neutral point of view.

"But these things must be obvious to you. This letter is not a sermon, it is a message of friendship and sympathy and of sincere appreciation for the letters by which you

[1] Regarding the Declaration of London. See this volume, p. 194 *ff*.

enable me to see what is going on about you as you, yourself, see it."[1]

A few weeks later the advice was repeated through
Colonel House, this time with a directness that was blunt
to the last degree:

"The President wishes me to ask you please to be careful not to express any unneutral feeling, either by word of
mouth, or by letter, and not even to the State Department.
He said that both Mr. Bryan and Mr. Lansing had remarked upon your leaning in that direction, and he
thought it would materially lessen your influence.

"He feels very strongly about this, and I am sending the
same message to Gerard."[2]

The President even warned the members of his own
cabinet:

"I am so afraid of getting the delicate and difficult
questions arising in connection with our neutrality confused or mishandled in any way that I am going to ask if
you will not have a conference with Mr. Lansing and with
Secretary Daniels to effect very definite arrangements for
coöperation between the three departments in these
matters. I think we cannot be too careful in these things
and I believe that these three departments ought to keep
in systematic touch with one another.

"I know that you will be willing to do this for me."[3]

This caution was due in part no doubt to the President's
growing perception that the war would probably be long
continued and serious, and that the American attitude
from the beginning must be founded upon correct principles. He seemed never for a moment to have accepted the
easy prophecies of many superficial observers that "six
months would see the end of it"—the "international

[1]October 28, 1914.
[2]December 4, 1914. *The Intimate Papers of Colonel House*, Vol. I, p. 312.
[3]Woodrow Wilson to W. G. McAdoo, November 6, 1914.

bankers will not permit the war to continue." His references in his private correspondence during all of the early months are marked with a singular depression—a sense of immense tragedy, and the impossibility of predicting what would come out of it all. He wrote to his old English friend Yates, in October:

"How terrible the whole thing is! It is like a nightmare. It depresses my spirits more than I can say, and our thoughts go constantly out to you and your dear ones. May God keep you and bring us all into better days!"[1]

And to Mrs. Hulbert in November:

"What will come of all this nightmare who can say, and who will venture, or care, to guess?"[2]

Many of his letters of the time indicate the mystic sense that was as deep in him as in the long succession of his Scotch Presbyterian forebears, of a moving Providence, potent if not comprehensible, that was in command not only of his own life, but of the events of the world, ". . . the sort of faith in God's providence that sustains more than anything else can. I think I should go mad without it! . . ."[3] His appeal for a day of prayer on October 4th—he himself attended the Central Presbyterian Church for the service—was no mere gesture. It went to the roots of his character. All who knew him intimately unite in affirming the seriousness, the sincerity, of his faith. A more skeptical generation does not, perhaps, realize the accession of personal power that such an inner confidence bestows upon a man. It may not always lead him to correct conclusions, it may even warp his judgements, but in Wilson's case it was an abiding aspect of his mind, always to be reckoned with.

The President hated to give over his ambitious plans

---

[1] October 23, 1914.
[2] November 23, 1914.
[3] Woodrow Wilson to Mary A. Hulbert, September 6, 1914.

for domestic reform, but by December he had recognized that foreign problems were destined to swallow up the entire attention of the nation and the world: and he approached the difficulties, the tragedy, of the new situation with profound humility of spirit. As he wrote to Colonel House on December 2nd:

"The Springfield *Republican* is right; the questions of the immediate future are no doubt to be foreign questions, and I am not at all sure that I have the wisdom to meet and solve them, but with the help of counsellors like yourself I hope that it will be possible to guide the old ship in a way that will bring her credit and make her serviceable to the world. These things give me, you may be sure, deep concern and solicitude."

II. THE REAL PROBLEMS OF WAR MATERIALS, COMMODITIES, AND MONEY

The earlier problems of neutrality, of which we have just had glimpses, were child's play compared with those soon to arise. Wilson had met them with promptness and vigour: but they were not the great and vital economic problems of war materials, commodities, and money.

It had been relatively easy for the President and his advisers to act in the case of an armed ship sailing from an American port to engage in hostilities, or of wireless messages directing the actions of a distant warship, for these were specific acts definable in their character and consequences. But what was to be done regarding the shipment to a belligerent country of arms and ammunition, or of motor trucks, blankets, or any of the thousand and one articles useful to its armed forces? And should we loan our money to a belligerent to finance its purchases? And what would happen to us, to our entire economic life, if we did *not* ship our surplus? In the case of a single commodity, cotton, a large percentage of which was ordinarily sold in England and Germany, the total stoppage of trade threatened the ruin of the South.

Of course it would not be permissible for the American *government*, which had declared its neutrality, to sell munitions or lend money to Germany or England or France: but was it the duty of the President to restrain American business men from doing such things? In the past no such duty had ever been admitted by any neutral government, although the President, not without much criticism, had recently, in dealing with disorders in Mexico, declared an embargo on the shipment of war materials across the border. But that action had had reference to civil disturbances rather than to actual war, and the volume of American business affected by it was trivial.

The President's proclamation of August 4th, based upon past theory and practice, drew a clear distinction between the specific unneutral acts, which it forbade, and the general practice of selling war supplies, which it allowed. ". . . while all persons may lawfully . . . manufacture and sell within the United States arms and munitions of war . . . yet . . ." they might not perform such and such definite acts in direct service of a belligerent.

Viscount Grey, in his *Twenty-five Years*, wrote that "the Allies soon became dependent for an adequate supply [of munitions] on the United States."[1] Among the greatest of Germany's problems were those of food, cotton, and copper, which she sought to obtain in America. Every decision of the President therefore which in any wise affected the shipment or supply of these commodities was of fateful importance to one side or the other.

From the beginning, the action of the American government was confused by an enervating duality of opinion and of purpose. Our foreign relations were based politically

[1]Vol. II, p. 107.

upon a theory or tradition of isolation: but economically we were entangled vitally in every part of the world. The *government* could assert its determined neutrality, for it had little politically at stake; but could American industry and finance be kept neutral?

In our domestic affairs the old doctrine of *laissez faire*, so far as it was still operative, was being rapidly undermined: the President himself, as we have seen, had made the government domination of finance (as in the Federal Reserve Act) and of certain large areas of business (as in the Clayton Anti-Trust Act) the essence of his programme of reform. But there had been no such advance, or at least change, of purpose in foreign affairs. The doctrine of *laissez faire* here prevailed in all of its glory. It was the guiding essence of the proclamation of August 4th: the government itself was to be sternly neutral, but private business men were to trade and bankers were to loan as much as they pleased, at their own risk. They could ship to either England or Germany, but they must take the chances of having their ships captured, their goods confiscated, their money lost.

When the war broke, the belligerent nations became at once well-knit economic units with the governments in firm control of all facilities of production and commerce and finance: the United States, driven by no such pressure of necessity and wholly unprepared for the emergency, drifted more or less helplessly between feeble traditional legalities and uncertain moralities on the one hand and powerful economic and emotional compulsions on the other. It was not until the United States itself entered the war that it achieved unity of purpose. From the beginning, and of necessity, decisions at Washington were thus tormented by doubt. What was *legal*, what was *right*, what, after all, was *necessary?*

A perfect example of these difficulties arose soon after

the war broke. Henry P. Davison of the firm of Morgan telephoned to the State Department to inquire what the attitude of the government would be in regard to making loans to belligerents. Secretary Bryan at once consulted with the Counselor, Mr. Lansing, who was the expert upon international law. The precedents, he was told, were all in favour of such loans. They would not violate American neutrality. But Bryan, in a letter to the President on August 10th, argued that "money is the worst of all contrabands because it commands everything else. The question of making loans contraband by international agreement has been discussed, but no action has been taken. . . . We are the one great nation which is not involved and our refusal to loan to any belligerent would naturally tend to hasten a conclusion of the war. We are responsible for the use of our influence through example . . ."

And finally Bryan warned:

"The powerful financial interests which would be connected with these loans would be tempted to use their influence through the newspapers to support the interests of the government to which they had loaned because the value of the security would be directly affected by the result of the war. We would thus find our newspapers violently arrayed on one side or the other, each paper supporting a financial group and pecuniary interest. All of this influence would make it all the more difficult for us to maintain neutrality . . ."[1]

Bryan's view that loans would violate the spirit of neutrality was supported by Lansing:

"He at once endorsed the position as sound in principle, even though not supported by precedent, and later came back to suggest an illustration which appealed to me as a very forcible one, namely, that as the government dis-

[1] From original letter in Mr. Wilson's files.

courages its citizens from enlisting in foreign armies and withdraws the protection of citizenship from them as long as they serve under another flag, it should discourage the money of this country from taking a part in foreign wars."[1]

The President evidently felt that an opportunity was here presented to act upon what seemed a sound principle. He himself "wrote out a sentence stating the government's position very concisely and strongly."[2]

On August 15th the announcement was telegraphed to J. P. Morgan & Company:

"There is no reason why loans should not be made to the governments of neutral nations, but in the judgement of this government, loans by American bankers to any foreign nation which is at war are inconsistent with the true spirit of neutrality."[3]

In consequence of this announcement no loans were made at that time.

From the very beginning, it will be seen, the President and his Secretary recognized that there were principles of neutrality that lay deeper than any legal precedent. Bryan commented in his memoirs:

"This, I believe, is the first time any great nation ever took this position. . . . It may be regarded as setting . . . a new precedent . . ."[4]

But it was a difficult new precedent to follow. It might be supposed that the argument against loans would apply with equal force against sales of military supplies—that it was as unneutral to allow belligerents to enlist our factories, fields, and mines as our money or our citizens, and as unneutral for Americans to become munitions workers

---

[1] *The Memoirs of William Jennings Bryan*, p. 376.
[2] *Ibid.*, p. 375.
[3] *Foreign Relations of the United States*, Supplement, 1914, p. 580.
[4] *The Memoirs of William Jennings Bryan*, pp. 375-376.

as soldiers. But apparently not even Bryan drew this conclusion. We find no correspondence with him or with the President on the subject, and it is not discussed in Bryan's memoirs.

Nevertheless there existed a widespread doubt upon the part of the public as to what American rights and duties really were. Exactly the same sort of inquiries began to come to the State Department from manufacturers, ship owners, even mule breeders, as had come from J. P. Morgan & Company. Was it permissible to sell munitions and other supplies to belligerents? There were also many protests against the sale of war materials on moral grounds: people even petitioned against the cruelty of selling American horses and mules for slaughter on foreign battlefields. So doubtful was the issue that on August 5th the Collector of Customs in New York had been instructed to issue an order against clearing vessels for belligerent ports with munitions of war aboard, but this was speedily rescinded.

One might indulge in one of the easy speculations of the historian as to what might have happened if a pronouncement in August against the sale of military supplies to belligerents similar to that against loans had been issued. It would probably, at first, have been accepted by American business men, but what pandemonium later!—with bankers called upon to meet a huge credit in London which could only be balanced by the shipments of goods, and with American producers suffocating under the accumulation of their unsold surpluses. There was indeed a practical difference at that time between loans and war supplies: we were still a debtor nation with large balances against us in London, and there was no immediate economic necessity for loaning money: but there was an economic necessity, immediate and insistent, to sell our surplus of goods.

It does not appear, however, that the question of interfering with the sale of war supplies was ever seriously
studied in all its aspects by any official, or referred to the
President.[1] Here the administration seemed willing to rest
upon the traditional legal sanctions. The view of the
Department of State was presented in an unpublished
letter from Lansing to the President, December 9, 1914,
in answer to a complaint made by Professor Hugo
Münsterberg.

"There is no power in the Executive," wrote Lansing,
"to prevent the sale of ammunition to the belligerents.

"Trade in munitions of war has never been restricted by
international law or by municipal statute. It has never
been the policy of this government to prevent the shipment of arms or ammunition into belligerent territory,
except in the case of neighboring American republics, and
then only when civil strife prevailed."

Governmental opposition to war loans, as Lansing went
on to explain, did not stand on such legal arguments, however.

". . . a war loan, if offered for popular subscription . . .
would be taken up by those who are in sympathy with the
belligerent seeking the loan. The result would be that great
numbers of our people would become more earnest partisans, having material interest in the success of the belligerent, whose bonds they hold. This . . . would spread
generally throughout our country, so that our people
would be divided into groups of partisans. . . . On the
other hand, contracts for and sales of contraband are

---

[1]But we know he thought about it. He saw clearly the immense difficulties in the way
of establishing new precedents at such a time for controlling private business. In his
conversation with Dr. Axson immediately after the outbreak of the war (see p. 74, this
volume) he had envisioned as one of the essentials of a durable settlement a provision for
government monopolies of the manufacture of munitions. But this was a dream of the
future, and the reflection could have no bearing upon the immediate course of the
government in dealing with the realities of the traffic which set in.

ROBERT LANSING, COUNSELOR OF THE STATE DEPART-
MENT, WHO SUCCEEDED WILLIAM J. BRYAN AS SECRE-
TARY OF STATE

mere matters of trade. . . . No general spirit of partisanship would be aroused . . ."

The protests of pacifists and humanitarians regarding the trade in munitions were ignored or acknowledged perfunctorily. The inquiries of business men were answered by statements to the effect that the federal government had nothing to say as to what its citizens might or might not sell or to whom they might sell it, but that articles listed as contraband of war might be seized, without redress, by the enemy of the belligerent government to which they were consigned. So numerous did these inquiries become that the Solicitor of the Department of State finally published, on August 15th, a printed circular setting forth the rights and duties of neutrality with respect to trade with belligerents.[1] This circular does not appear to have been referred to the President at all.

These two pronouncements, made in August, the first on the basis of "sound principle," establishing, as Bryan thought, a "new precedent," the second on the basis of strict legality, were of fateful importance as a basis for the President's course in the future.

Another exceedingly difficult problem, wherein the President was compelled to explore the shadowy jungles between the legalities of neutrality and the "true spirit" of it, immediately arose. The practice of permitting citizens of neutral countries freely to sell their goods to belligerent nations rested upon the theory that these were transactions of a business nature in an open market in which all belligerents were equally free to participate, while each might interfere with the transit to his enemy of munitions or money as contraband of war. But with the command of the seas falling at once to the Allied Powers, it was clear that the only great neutral market, that of the United States, was closed to the belligerents of the

---

[1]*Foreign Relations of the United States*, Supplement, 1914, pp. 274–278.

other camp. Furthermore, it rapidly became apparent that so inferior was the productive organization of the Allies that they could not maintain their forces without supplies from America. And still further, the prospective quantities of such supplies were so huge that their purchase could not long be financed without obtaining extensive credits in the United States. The United States, therefore, was furnishing supplies—and supplies essential for the continuation of the war—to belligerents of only one side.

A question at once arose as to the moral neutrality of such a situation—even apart from the deeper question as to the morality of selling to belligerents the means of warfare at all. But any attempt to interfere after the war began would raise the issue of real neutrality from the other side. If the existing situation was inequitable as it bore upon the two groups of belligerents, it was so by force of circumstances, and in consequence of the fortunes of war. Any measures to redress it after it had developed would thus appear inequitable.

The historical consequences of this situation, together with the decisions of August, were of the utmost gravity. Besides enabling the Allies to continue the war, in which they might have been overwhelmed without American supplies, the close economic relationships thus established were to have far-reaching consequences both to the nations of Europe and to ourselves.

In these struggles with the problems of neutrality the President and his advisers soon settled down to a reliance upon the strength of the American legal position as a neutral: thinking to make good their position by legal argument alone, as in a court of reasonable men. One of the criticisms of the President was that his "scholarly surroundings" persuaded him to take "too kindly a view of the good intentions of foreign nations."[1] But the

[1]New York *Times*, October 20, 1914.

nations with which he was dealing were under the fiery and unreasoning pressure of war and fought with any weapon that came to hand, be it legal, economic, military, or psychological. We were thus, from the beginning, at a disadvantage. There were two possible extralegal ways of forcing our views of our legal rights—by war, which nearly everyone at that time repudiated, and by economic pressure. Not until the closing days of 1914, and not strongly until the following spring, as we shall see, was the suggestion pushed that the United States by a threat of embargo on war materials might force the British to abandon those drastic interferences with neutral trade which were illegal in the eyes of the American government. Apparently we did not recognize our immense economic power, and we probably could not have used it if we had, since embargoes would have resulted in an economic shock that American business was unprepared to withstand either by knowledge, or vision, or fortitude. Moreover, in the hope that the war would soon end—or yield to the President's efforts to bring about peace—there always lurked an excuse for avoiding drastic measures. For economic pressure in itself might lead to war. Thus by the end of the year 1914 the traffic in war materials with the Allies had become deeply entrenched in America's economic organization, and the possibility of keeping out of the war by the diplomacy of neutrality, no matter how skilfully conducted, had reached the vanishing point. By October, perhaps earlier, our case was lost.

While British diplomacy manœuvred with skill to involve American industry and finance in the munitions traffic, it is certain that American business needed no compulsion to take war orders. Such enterprises not only promised glittering profits but they were practically forced upon our industries as a means of meeting that frightful spectre, the unfavourable balance of trade which then existed. It had been the normal process for years for the balance of imports over exports to develop a heavy balance against us during the first half of each year which we met in the fall and winter by heavy shipments of wheat, cotton, tobacco, and so on. When the war broke in August this balancing outflow, just beginning, was brought to a sudden and complete stoppage—with a short-term American indebtedness in London of some $250,000,000. Unless this debit could be met by reëstablishing a flow of exports before the end of the year, it would have to be settled in cash. With the reorganization of our banking system under the new Federal Reserve Act still incomplete, this prospect inspired panic in American business circles.

The one great alternative lay in finding markets for our surplus cotton, tobacco, and wheat crops. By the end of the year it developed that the loss of cotton exports nearly equalled the amount of American indebtedness in London. But efforts to ship our surpluses, especially to German and neutral ports, were frustrated because we had no ships of our own. The President and his advisers, as we have already seen in another chapter, were making a desperate effort to relieve the situation by providing tonnage to transport such non-contraband goods. They were prevented from taking over the immobilized German ships chiefly by the objections of the Allies; the British commercial fleet had been withdrawn for war purposes; and bitter opposition in Congress balked the President's plan to buy or build American ships. Consequently American business, denied sufficient trade in non-contraband goods which Germany and her allies most needed, had more and more to depend on the shipment of the war materials urgently needed by the Allies.

While the United States hesitated regarding the use of economic pressure to enforce its rights, no such compunctions disturbed either the Allies or the Germans.

The British controlled products, notably wool and alloys of steel, needed by us: Americans were soon given to understand that they would be allowed to receive such raw materials to keep their plants in operation if they would undertake to manufacture articles from them for the Allied armies. The Germans on their side imposed an embargo on the export of certain goods, principally aniline dyes, that were necessary to American industry, but intimated to American business men and to the government that dyes would be released if cotton were brought in exchange.[1]

So the traffic in war materials with the Allies developed apace while at the same time, owing to the fortunes of war, the Germans could not engage in the traffic at all. Realizing that it had no legal ground to stand on, the German government for a long time avoided making an issue of the munitions traffic. It did not in fact need munitions: its own manufacturing plants were adequate. Instead, it concentrated its attention, as we shall see later, upon the support of American efforts to keep open the channels of trade with the Central Powers. For the right to carry on such trade strong legal arguments were available. Protests and arguments were addressed to the American government against British extensions of the contraband list and other measures of interference. If Americans, indeed, could keep open their trade, as neutrals, with Germany—under the provisions of the Declaration of London—it would tend to balance the war-material traffic with England.

Whatever doubts as to the war-munitions traffic may have lurked in the minds of the President or of Mr. Bryan —and protests and inquiries continued to arrive—were finally settled on a basis of strict legality by the issuance on October 15th of a new circular by the Department of

---

[1] *Foreign Relations of the United States*, Supplement, 1914, pp. 410–411.

State on neutrality and trade in contraband.[1] Here it was made wholly clear that American citizens were under no duty not to furnish contraband goods to belligerents and that the government had no obligation or authority to interfere with their sale and transportation. We know that the President saw and approved this document because he wrote to Bryan on October 13th:

"Mr. Lansing was kind enough to submit the enclosed to me. I return it with the assurance that I think it is desirable that such a statement should be issued, and this statement seems to me excellent."

By this time it was clear enough that orders for the Allied armies were proving the salvation of American business and foreign trade; by December it was estimated that 35 per cent. of the production of textile mills was on army contracts. Exports were rapidly increasing, and the rate of exchange was mounting toward the gold point, which it was to reach in mid-November. American bankers were beginning to breathe more easily, although the obligations in London still loomed large. When Sir George Paish, at the invitation of McAdoo, came over in October, representing the British Treasury, he at first made the bankers shudder by talking of payment in gold, but later referred to the increasing exports as a hope of settling accounts without special measures.

For the President to have moved at this time to upset such a comforting trend of trade, which was after all legal, would have produced an instant storm—the more so because at that very time he was asking Congress for a large increase in taxation and the measure passed the Senate[2] only after bitter attacks. Moreover, a congressional mid-term election was then in progress, accompanied by assaults upon the administration for its hostility

---

[1] *Foreign Relations of the United States*, Supplement, 1914, pp. 573-574.
[2] On October 17th.

to business—with the seats of many Democratic senators and congressmen in danger. Even the precarious leadership in domestic economic matters which the President was asserting was in peril: how extend it in such a crisis by attempting to discipline powerful and determined business interests which were now dependent upon war orders to avoid ruin?

While the arms traffic helped the North and the East—and the financiers—it did not help, appreciably, the farmers of the South and West who were in a desperate situation. But here the President was struggling—hopefully at first—to keep open the traffic with Germany, which he regarded as entirely legal under the provisions of the Declaration of London. If he could do that, the South could be relieved and some sort of economic balance preserved between the belligerents. His controversies with the British in this connection will be treated in another section.

It was inevitable that with the shipment of such enormous quantities of war materials to the Allies, the problem of paying for them would again arise. For a considerable time the British could finance their purchases through their large credit balance, but if the war continued, even a quarter-billion dollars would not last long. And when all was said, if the shipment of war materials was unobjectionable, why not loans of money? And if credits were not given, how could the munitions traffic continue? And if shipments were cut off, what would happen to American business?

In October the French were renewing their applications to American bankers for arrangements to finance their purchases by means of Treasury notes. The Russians chimed in with similar approaches, Count Witte intimating that a new commercial treaty, replacing that terminated on January 1, 1913, might be negotiated in return

for a credit loan. Sir George Paish called on the President
on October 19th to present the general economic problems
that confronted both Great Britain and the United States.
But Bryan's announcement of August 15th, issued with
the President's approval, declaring that such loans while
legal were "inconsistent with the true spirit of neutrality,"
stood in the way of governmental action. To clarify the
situation, Mr. Lansing was called upon to prepare a
memorandum for the President, in which he presented in
a nutshell not only the case for credits, but also the case
for the traffic in war supplies which those credits were
required to finance. It is the earliest document found
setting forth the whole matter for Wilson's information.[1]

---

[1]Since this document, entitled "Summary of Information in Regard to Credits of
Foreign Governments in This Country and the Relation to Trade," is not elsewhere
published, the essential points in it are here presented:

"The outbreak of the European war came at a time when this country owed a large
amount to Europe, particularly to England in the form of short time drafts, maturing
between the outbreak of the war and the end of the year. The amount, while large, was
not abnormal, considering the volume of our trade relations and was directly due to the
anticipated shipment of cotton during the autumn.

"War conditions have made cotton bills unavailable for the settlement of this balance
against us and it can only be wiped out by the shipment of the goods, in lieu of the
cotton, that are now needed and desired by the various European countries. This is
true, regardless of any temporary bridging over of the situation, and it has been the
policy of the financial institutions of New York, as far as possible and proper, to stimulate the unprecedented and unusual buying by foreign governments and their nationals
that is now going on in this country. Since the beginning of the war I am informed that
one bank alone has received cabled instructions for the payment of more than $50,000,-
000 for American goods and that the volume of this business is increasing. Owing to war
conditions, this buying is necessarily for cash and it is of such magnitude that the cash
credits of the European governments are being fast depleted. Lately it has been urged
by certain manufacturers and by representatives of some of the foreign governments,
that the banks should provide temporary credits for these purchases. . . .

"The representatives of the banks state that they feel the necessity of aiding the
situation by temporary credits of this sort, otherwise the buying power of these foreign
purchasers will dry up and the business will go to Australia, Canada, Argentine and
elsewhere. They say that it may in the end come back to the United States but that,
in their opinion, the critical time for American finance in our international relations is
during the next three or four months and, if we allow these purchases to go elsewhere,
we will have neglected our foreign trade at the time of our greatest need and greatest
opportunity. . . .

"For the purpose of enabling European governments to make cash payments for
American goods, it is suggested to grant to them short time banking credits, to both
belligerent and neutral governments, and where necessary or desirable replenish their
cash balances on this side by the purchase of short time Treasury warrants. Such pur-

In one sense the arrangement here proposed met Bryan's greatest objection to war loans, which had been the effect of popular appeals for subscriptions in stirring up partisan sentiment throughout the country. If the business could be confined to the banks, this popular reaction would be avoided. Nevertheless the new proposals involved a re-cession from a position based upon "the true spirit of neutrality" to one based upon "strict legality."

Probably the issues raised by Lansing's memorandum were discussed orally by the President and the Counselor: there is no record of a written response. At any rate, before the end of October a credit of $10,000,000 had been extended to the French government by the National City Bank—the beginning of vast commitments by American financiers to the Allied Powers.

As soon as Congress convened in December there was to be sharply critical response to these policies. Congress-man Richard Bartholdt,[1] representing the strongly pro-German district of St. Louis, together with Congressman Vollmer and Senator Hitchcock, introduced bills for an embargo on munitions of war,[2] but the administration was now committed to the approval of the traffic and refused to countenance the proposals. Even Bryan, in reassuring the British embassy to this effect, felt called upon to repudiate the action of Senator Hitchcock.[3]

Whatever the President's earlier doubts had been, he

chases would necessarily be limited to the legal capacity of the particular bank and, as these warrants are bearer warrants without interest, they could not and would not be made the subject of a public issue. These securities could be sold abroad or be readily available as collateral in foreign loans and would be paid at maturity in dollars or equivalent in foreign exchange.

"ROBERT LANSING

"October 23, 1914."

[1] See this volume, p. 235.

[2] *Congressional Record*, Vol. 52, pp. 6 and 12.

[3] "I have explained to Ambassador Spring Rice that Mr. Hitchcock did not consult the President or State Department in regard to his resolution. Though from Nebraska he is not personally friendly to me." (W. J. Bryan to Walter H. Page, December 14, 1914. *Foreign Relations of the United States*, Supplement, 1914, p. 579.)

was now to rest his case upon legal sanctions alone. He was greatly impressed by a telegram of December 8th from Paul Fuller, B. F. Tracey, and F. R. Coudert of New York, in which they argued that "altering the rules of neutrality during warfare . . . aiding the inefficiency of one belligerent to protect its purchases of arms by forbidding all exportation of arms to the other belligerents is an absolute violation of neutrality." This communication was turned over to Lansing, who replied on December 10th:

"I think these gentlemen are entirely right in the general principle asserted."

Wilson's acknowledgment of his letter concluded:

"I now feel fully fortified in the matter."[1]

To Jacob H. Schiff of New York, who urged him to use his influence to prevent the sale of munitions to belligerents, the President replied on December 8th:

"I fear you must have thought me guilty of a discourtesy in not replying sooner to your letter of November nineteenth, but the fact is I wanted to think out very carefully the matter about which you wrote.

"Not that it was the first time that I had tried to think it out, for it is one of the most perplexing things I have had to decide. The law standing as it does, the most I can do is to exercise influence, and in the case of the lending of money I was directly applied to for advice and approval. There my duty was clear. It was my duty to discourage the loans to belligerents. In the matter of sales of goods of all kinds, however, the precedents of international law are so clear, the sales proceed from so many sources, and my lack of power is so evident, that I have felt that I could do nothing else than leave the matter to settle itself. In a single recent case I saw my way clear to act. When it came to the manufacture of constituent parts of submarines and their shipment abroad, complete, to be put

---

[1] December 14, 1914.

together elsewhere, it seemed to me clearly my privilege, acting in the spirit of the *Alabama* case, to say that the government could not allow that, and the Fore River Ship Building Company which is said to have undertaken the contracts has canceled them.

"I am sure that you realize the very great delicacy and difficulty of my task in matters of this sort, and I wanted to make a very frank statement of them to you."

But there continued to be bitter complaints about the "one-sided character of American neutrality." Senator Stone, of Missouri, who was a power in the Senate, sent a letter to Bryan giving a list of twenty grounds of complaint, alleging partiality to the Allies and arguing that the policy of "no interference with the sale to Great Britain and her allies of arms, ammunition, horses, uniforms, and other munitions of war" ought to be condemned because "such sales prolong the war."[1]

The President approved Bryan's reply to Stone of January 20th in which the Secretary argued:

"There is no power in the Executive to prevent the sale of ammunition to the belligerents.

"The duty of a neutral to restrict trade in munitions of war has never been imposed by international law or by municipal statute."[2]

He went even further, in a telegram to Ambassador Page on January 23rd, in which he asserted in answer to complaints of irritation in Great Britain over the course of the United States—for the British were as urgent as the Germans in accusing us of unneutrality—that the criticism in Congress and the demand for an embargo on munitions of war was due to "the protests made by German-Americans and by a portion of the Irish-Americans" and

---

[1] January 8, 1915. *Foreign Relations of the United States,* Supplement, 1914, pp. vi-vii.

[2] See this volume, pp. 236-237.

"while entirely without justification, is not unnatural." He also remarks that "there need be no fear that his proposals [Bartholdt's] will be adopted."[1]

Bryan's letter to Stone also asserts that "the United States has itself taken no part in contraband traffic." This was, in the President's eyes, an important aspect of the duty of neutrality. If he could not legally prevent the trade in munitions by private industry, he could insist that the government itself scrupulously live up to its obligations. When, for example, the British foreign office made "soundings" as to the possibility of acquiring the Krag-Jorgensen rifles[2] just discarded by the American army there was no encouragement at Washington. There followed a series of applications for the arms from agents purporting to be acting for various Latin-American governments. On December 24th, the Secretary of War wrote the President:

"I cannot help but believe that the variety of propositions that are made to me to sell, directly or indirectly, these rifles to governments, are prompted by a desire and intention on their part to re-sell them to some of the European governments. Of course, it would be impossible for us to convince anybody of our entire good faith if these United States rifles got into the hands of any of the belligerents, however much circumlocution might have been indulged in in the meantime."

Wilson answered, January 5, 1915:

"I agree . . . that it would not be wise to sell the Krag rifles now owned by this government to *any* one during the progress of the present war."

Another case arose, regarding the exportation of completed submarines. This was held by our government to

---

[1] *Foreign Relations of the United States*, Supplement, 1915, p. 685.

[2] Ambassador Page, in his letter of October 6th to the President, calls them "Springfield" rifles, but this was, of course, an error. See *The Life and Letters of Walter H. Page*, Vol. III, p. 157.

be a violation of the neutrality proclamation against "fitting out and arming . . . any ship or vessel . . . in the service of either of the said belligerents." But American manufacturers conceived the ingenious device of shipping submarines to England in "knocked down" sections to be assembled only upon arrival. This project, when it reached the attention of the administration in November, caused it a great deal of worry. Bryan and Lansing talked it over on November 12th, and Lansing drafted a letter for the President asserting the legality of shipment in the form proposed. But in forwarding it, Bryan stated that its adoption meant "skating on thin ice," as "we could not convince the average citizen there is any difference"[1] between delivering a war vessel complete or in parts. Informed that Bryan and Wilson doubted the wisdom of following his conclusions, Lansing submitted the matter to the Neutrality Board, which returned an opinion on the 25th confirming his view. The President having in the meantime telephoned his wish that submarines in sections be not exported, Lansing sent him the opinion of the Board on the 28th. But Wilson was not shaken in his attitude and replied as follows:

November 30, 1914

MY DEAR MR. LANSING:

As I intimated to you, I gave the matter very serious thought when the question of the submarines was brought up. I feel that it is really our duty (in the *spirit*, at any rate, of the *Alabama* decision) to prevent submarines being shipped from this country even in parts, and I hope that you will find a way of checking and preventing this if it is contemplated.

Always

Cordially and faithfully yours,
WOODROW WILSON

HON. ROBERT LANSING,
Department of State.[2]

[1] November 12, 1914.

[2] But American manufacturers were still able to get around the order by selling steel plates, fittings, etc. to Canadian plants which built them into submarines. The Ger-

These incidents show that the President was willing to
go out of his way to avoid the appearance of unneutrality
in details where he was guarded by legal sanctions, however feeble; but, of course, decisions such as this, even
where legal sanctions were stretched to their uttermost,
affected an infinitesimal part of the traffic compared with
the immense quantities of supplies shipped by private
industry.

During all of this period letters continued to pour in
upon the President and the State Department, from German sympathizers and Southern agricultural interests,
protesting against the munitions traffic with the Allies
and also demanding that the rights of neutral trade with
Germany and other countries be strongly asserted. There
are also to be found in the record many protests against
loans being made to belligerents. Rear-Admiral Chadwick[1]
wrote to the President arguing the essential unneutrality
of the situation and setting forth the ultimate dangers of
it. On the other hand, business men in large numbers
expressed their fear that any change in policy would be
destructive to the newly reëstablished economic stability
of the country—for example, Andrew Carnegie, for all his
advocacy of peace. We have only vague expressions of
interest in these communications in Wilson's acknowledgments, and no step was taken by the government to interfere with the business, even to the extent of a threat.

However we may repudiate the motive, the intricate
business connections with the Allies developed during
1914, 1915, 1916—until the very economic life of the
country rested upon the munitions traffic—stimulated a

---

mans protested, but the manufacturers categorically denied that they were doing anything more than make sales of ordinary articles in the open market, and the government's inquiries and investigations revealed nothing more.

[1]Rear-Admiral F. E. Chadwick had retired in 1906. He had rendered conspicuous
service to the country in the war with Spain; and he had occupied during his period of
active service a number of important posts, among them President of the Naval War
College and Commander-in-Chief of the South Atlantic Squadron.

powerful interest in the victory of the Allies. On the other hand, German efforts to break up this relationship, with consequent injury to life and property, tended to provoke our government to vindication by force. There was a kind of fatality about it all, due on the one hand to the weakness and futility of the political power in such a crisis, with its inadequate legal sanctions, and on the other to the inexorable implications in the realities of a world-encircling economic system. No human being could, once the crisis arose, do much to change the disastrous course of events. And history since the war indicates in America neither a change in attitude toward this fatal duality nor any effective move to correct it.[1]

---

[1]We are still involved (1935) in world economic and financial relationships which make political isolation an unreal concept, and which will prevent the United States from keeping out of any important conflict of the future.

CHAPTER IV

CONTROVERSIES WITH GREAT BRITAIN

The government of the United States, still relying upon the deep sense of justice of the British nation . . . expresses confidently the hope that His Majesty's government will realize the obstacles and difficulties which their present policy has placed in the way of commerce between the United States and the neutral countries of Europe . . .

Message to the British government, December 26, 1914.

Your Majesty will doubtless rest assured that the administration of the laws of this country in regard to trade will be entirely impartial as between the belligerents; although it must be expected that those who are engaged in the agony of a deadly struggle will readily catch at causes of suspicion or complaint, and although even the most upright neutrality can hardly work in all cases with a perfect equality as between the contending parties.

Mr. Gladstone to Queen Victoria, August 4, 1870. The Queen and Mr. Gladstone, *by Philip Guedalla, p. 290.*

I. THE STRUGGLE OVER THE DECLARATION OF LONDON

BY OCTOBER 1914 President Wilson and his advisers had taken their position finally and firmly, as we have seen, upon the legal right of American citizens to sell munitions and loan money to the Allies; and they had also asserted and supported their legal right, under the Declaration of London, to sell cotton, wheat, and other commodities to the Germans—and anything they pleased, without interference, to the Dutch, Scandinavians, and Italians. But it was the guiding principle of the diplomacy of the British and their allies, while using the United States as an enormous arsenal and supply depot on which they could draw without even paying anything down, since, under the decision of September, American bankers could take over the bills, to see to it that the Central Powers secured as little as possible from American markets.

In seeking to checkmate the Germans by virtue of their control of the sea, however, they had to consider, narrowly, the effect on American trade and American public opinion. Viscount Grey, in his *Twenty-five Years*, discusses this situation with entire candour. Acknowledging the dependence of the Allies upon the United States for an adequate supply of munitions, he says that, as a consequence of this dependence, it would have been a "cardinal mistake" to have brought on "a breach with the United States, not necessarily a rupture, but a state of things that would have provoked American interference with the blockade, or led to an embargo on exports of munitions from the United States."[1]

"If we quarrelled with the United States we could not get that supply [of munitions]."[2]

Grey's summary of his task in directing British diplomacy was "to secure the maximum of blockade [of Germany] that could be enforced without a rupture with the United States."[3]

In short, the British must insist upon the legality of their munitions trade with the United States and, by the immensity of their purchases, knit closer the important economic bonds between the two nations: and they must combat or override the legal right, claimed by the United States, of trading with Germany and with European neutrals, and, at the same time—and this, as Grey himself

[1] Vol. II, p. 160.
[2] *Ibid.*, p. 107.
[3] *Ibid.*

remarks, "was very delicate and uncertain ground"[1]—
they must not irritate the United States to the point of
real interference. It was a neat problem, and Grey handled
it with consummate skill. If the American government,
at that time, had realized the immense strength of its
position, if it could have played the game as cleverly as
the British government, say by threatening embargoes to
enforce what it considered its legal rights, it might possibly
have kept open its trade with Germany and with neutral
nations in non-contraband goods. But the question, easy
enough to pose long afterwards, raises a thousand difficult
considerations, some of which go to the heart of the
President's problem. Unlike the British, whom war had
unified in purpose, American action was weakened by the
necessity on the part of the political government, with its
façade of power, to consider at every turn the stupendous
economic forces, highly organized, ably led, with their
fierce desires and necessities, which really dominated the
situation. The President had also to consider an excited
public opinion which was on the whole sympathetic with
the Allies. If the President had threatened an embargo,
could he have controlled the economic forces in his own
country, faced as they were by utter disaster? At this very
time, as we have seen, he was approaching the doubtful
fall elections, which by returning hostile majorities in
Congress might effectually destroy his leadership. He was
already being balked by Congress in his earliest efforts to
maintain shipments to Europe—that is, in his ship-
purchase proposals. Moreover, might not a course of
economic compulsion have involved us in war with the
Allies? The President, as we shall see a little later, clearly
envisaged and dreaded such a possibility.

On the other hand, had the American government, by
the use of embargoes or the threat of them, been able to

---

[1]Vol. II, p. 107.

break up even in part the Allied efforts at blockade, Germany's course of action, since she would then have hesitated to endanger her economic relationships with the United States, would undoubtedly have been far different—with what ultimate result upon world affairs it is purely speculative now to inquire.

The more one studies the course of President Wilson during the period of neutrality the clearer become the fateful consequences that hung upon his decisions. As a matter of fact the war was decided not so much by American battalions on the French front in 1918 as by the President's decisions during the period of neutrality in 1914 and 1915, which involved the disposition of indispensable supplies of American goods and money.

The first attempt of the American government, as we have seen, to protect its citizens' rights of trade was the inquiry sent to belligerent governments on August 6, 1914 as to whether they would observe the Declaration of London. While the Central Powers expressed a willingness to do so, the British government, anxious to make the utmost use of its command of the sea, inflexibly resisted compliance. On the 22nd it notified the American government of its intention to make "certain modifications and additions" to the rules of the Declaration, the first set of which had already been laid down in an Order in Council of the 20th and the practical effects of which upon American commerce had been felt even earlier.

Having adopted as a matter of high policy the government's stand on the principles of the Declaration of London, the President turned his attention to other crowding affairs and duties and left the legal controversies over details to the Department of State. We find among his papers no evidence that the earlier correspondence was sent to him. The writer, who called on him at the White House on September 17th, found him chiefly absorbed in domestic matters. Quoting from a diary entry of the conversation made on that day:

"Speaking of the record of the administration, he said that he felt that he had nearly reached the end of his economic program as outlined in the campaign and in the Democratic platform. There were some social reforms still to be achieved, but he thought that most of them should be the work of the states. The next two things to be done were:

"1. Improve our machinery of commerce. Our shipping must be built up.

"2. Develop further our conservation policy. 'Conservation for use.' "[1]

It was not, indeed, until the last of September that the President, awakened by the swift accumulation of problems and difficulties, turned his attention sharply to the controversy with Great Britain. American trade had

---

[1] A few weeks previous to this interview the writer had gone to Oyster Bay to call upon Theodore Roosevelt and had found him also discounting the war and devoting himself chiefly to domestic problems. It indicates, perhaps, in the case of Roosevelt as of Wilson, a sense that the country at large was still far more interested in its own problems than in those of Europe, even with the Great War in progress. I venture to reproduce my notes of the visit, since they give a glimpse of Roosevelt, then Wilson's chief critic, as he appeared at that time:

"August 14, 1914. I went this morning to Oyster Bay to see Colonel Roosevelt.... The Colonel did not look as worn and old as I expected from seeing his last published picture. He is still a wonderful physical specimen—clean, strong, white teeth, hair thin but not gray, and his whole figure full of vigor. He wore a gray linen suit with knickerbockers and green woven stockings. He showed me copies of two speeches he will soon deliver in Illinois in the campaign of Raymond Robins for senator, and also a letter he has just written to Mr. Costigan, Progressive candidate for governor of Colorado. The speeches are a reiteration of what he said in 1912—the Progressive platform—with the addition of a series of criticisms of Wilson and attacks on the policies of the present administration. In the face of this thundering European war, how distant seem these discussions....

"Roosevelt's characteristics intensify with age. His speeches are more balanced than ever, less based upon principles and more upon the effort to dispense moral judgments—blame this side, and, to balance it, blame the other side. He seems less to strike the high note, and to be more critical and more on the defensive. Especially he attacks the Bryan-Wilson peace treaties. He said that no treaties were ever effective unless backed by guns. He cited instances of how all the great nations had recently abandoned or broken over solemn treaties. He decries any effort to cut down armaments or to rely upon arbitration."

already been suffering severely. Practically all exchange of goods with Germany had come to a stop, and that with neutrals had shrunk to mere trickles. A conference of representatives of banking and shipping interests at Washington had urged action for the release of cargoes detained by the British and the funds tied up in them. The entire South was irritated if not enraged by the inability to ship its surplus cotton. German-American groups were beginning to complain bitterly of unfair restrictions on trade with the Central Powers.

The early controversies over the British Orders in Council had been conducted on the American side largely by a Texas lawyer, Cone Johnson, who was then Solicitor of the State Department. He had been a member of the Texas legislature and a candidate for governor: and he had played an important part with the doughty Texas delegation in nominating Wilson at the Baltimore convention. He was a Southerner, with the feeling of the cotton country, and he and his assistant, F. K. Nielsen, pounded away at Secretary Bryan and Counselor Lansing with memoranda showing how the British Orders in Council ran counter to recognized international law, setting forth the damage done by action under them to American trade, stating the cases of individual claims for redress, and preparing drafts of instructions to Ambassador Page on all these matters, many of which Lansing felt called upon to tone down.

It was these documents and instructions which so intensely irritated Ambassador Page.

"God deliver us ... from library lawyers," he cried out in a cablegram to Colonel House.[1]

---

[1] *The Intimate Papers of Colonel House*, Vol. I, p. 305. Page's biographer, Mr. Hendrick, is in error in ascribing the ambassador's difficulties to Mr. Lansing. (*The Life and Letters of Walter H. Page*, Vol. I, pp. 369–370.) The records show the Counselor, later Secretary, to have played a rôle of moderation in the controversy with Great Britain. Cone Johnson was the man!

It is to be noted as an important factor in our relationships with Great Britain that the presentation of the
American side both in the general controversy and in
special cases was, as his letters show, intensely distasteful
to the American ambassador. He ordinarily followed his
instructions, but often lacked any conviction as to their
justice.

Page was one of the most lovable of human beings. He
had charm of manner, he had humour, he was the soul of
courtesy. His gifts as a letter writer are well exemplified
in his *Life and Letters*. President Wilson once remarked to
Irwin Laughlin, Counselor of the American Embassy at
London:

"I have known Page for many years and I have never
known anyone more compelling on paper . . . I never could
resist him. I get more information out of his letters than
from any other single source. Tell him to keep it up."[1]

It was the warmth of Page's impulsive feeling, his genius
for friendship, that committed him from the beginning to
a deep sympathy with the British cause. He accepted quite
uncritically the British version of the origin and causes of
the conflict, which laid all the responsibility upon Germany. He eagerly lent his pen to the cause by endeavouring to convince President Wilson and the American government of the correctness of this version. In contrast
with Colonel House, whose relationships with the President rose seldom to a really full or frank opening of his
mind, Page's devotion to the President "was such that he
never hesitated to tell him the truth, however unwelcome
it might prove to be."[2] Holding the view that England was
entirely right and Germany entirely wrong, he believed
that America should help England defeat Germany. His

---

[1]May 4, 1914. (Irwin Laughlin to the author.) Mr. Laughlin was closely associated
with Mr. Page throughout the period of the war: few men knew him more intimately.

[2]Irwin Laughlin to the author.

deep-seated conviction that an Anglo-American entente—based upon common ties of blood, language, traditions, and institutions—was the proper pivot of world policy, headed up in this belief. His ambition to do something big to make this entente a practical reality, thwarted in preventing war, turned now toward winning it for the cause he espoused. He did not yet advocate America's entrance into the war as a belligerent; even the British still felt that we could be of more service to them as a neutral. But he did feel that we should contribute our resources to the Allies and acquiesce in all their measures for preventing the Germans from getting any access to these resources. He seemed to hold the question of the rights of Americans under international law subordinate to the right of the British to beat Germany. If the lawyers of the State Department proved that legal rights were actually violated, the utmost support of their case he believed justified was the filing of claims to be settled by the British government at its leisure—after the war. Bothering that government for immediate settlement while it was so busy he held to be inconsiderate of our higher duty to help it. Calling upon it to stop what it was doing, however illegal, he felt was flying in the very face of that duty.

Naturally such an ambassador was a poor advocate of the policies which the American government, considering its position as a neutral power, was striving to follow.[1]

[1] If Ambassador Page acted only as an unwilling advocate of these rights, they found ardent champions in other quarters—in the Solicitor's office in the State Department, as we have seen, and in the Consulate General in London. Robert P. Skinner—whose appointment, though a Republican, to this plum among consular posts, was an outstanding case of recognition of merit by the Wilson administration—from the beginning appeared little affected by the Page version of the real issues of the war. He was stirred by what he considered the unfair and illegal treatment American merchants were getting from the British government. He took up energetically the cases which Page was disposed to let slide and buzzed so assiduously about the ears of the British authorities that Page was constrained to request the State Department to instruct him that he was not to deal directly with the Foreign Office, but only through the embassy. Skinner usually reported new enactments against neutral trade, as well as new actions under them, before the embassy got round to it, and was quick to point out their detrimental effect

Wilson was often disturbed by the attitude of the ambassador. He remarked to Colonel House that if "Page were to represent the American government, he must see the matters under discussion in the light in which they were seen in the United States." Wilson insisted that Page's advice was of great value, but he expressed the fear that his intense feeling for the British case might prove a danger. He himself was "sometimes disparaging in his remarks about professional diplomats, but he did not enjoy having the work of the State Department, which emphasized the American point of view, referred to as that of 'library lawyers.' "[1]

As a matter of fact, Page seemed often to have blunted the edges of the American case and even to have advised with the British government as to the best ways of meeting it. Viscount Grey says in his memoirs:

". . . Page's advice and suggestion were of the greatest value in warning us when to be careful or encouraging us when we could safely be firm. . . .

"Page came to see me at the Foreign Office one day and produced a long dispatch from Washington contesting our claim to act as we were doing in stopping contraband going to neutral ports. 'I am instructed,' he said, 'to read this dispatch to you.' He read, and I listened. He then said: 'I have now read the dispatch, but I do not agree with it; let us consider how it should be answered.' "[2]

As early as August 25th, the ambassador was warning the President that American insistence upon its neutral rights might involve us even to the extent of war with

---

upon American interests. His reports were filled with denunciations of the delays and circumlocutions he encountered; and when, in 1915, he took to demonstrating by statistics how British trade was profiting by the restrictions placed on American trade, Page at one time reported that the British government was considering a request for his recall.

[1] *The Intimate Papers of Colonel House*, Vol. I, p. 306.

[2] Viscount Grey, *Twenty-five Years*, Vol. II, p. 110.

Great Britain. Officials in the Admiralty Office had asserted that if matters got desperate "the War Office and the Admiralty might take over the management of foreign relations. . . . Then, to prevent Germany from receiving food or other help, they might issue a proclamation that neutrals must not trade with Germany, and they w^d be prepared, if necessary, to go to war with any neutral power, even the U.S., who sh^d disregard such a proclamation. In other words, in extreme need they might practically forbid neutrality."[1]

Page discounted Grey's efforts to reassure him as to Cabinet control of high policy by asserting in his letter to the President that, in the crisis foreseen, "the Cabinet w^d be out of commission." Page probably touched Wilson upon a sensitive spot in suggesting the overthrow of civilian government in the English democracy, but his alarm did not shake the President—at least at that time —in his support of the policy of the State Department, which was to defend what he considered to be American rights.

Wilson's replies to Page, like those to Colonel House during his "mission" in the summer just passed, were at once personally warm and appreciative, and for the most part noncommittal. Moreover they were few in number and mostly brief, as though written by one under great compulsion by other affairs, and possibly, as yet, not turning his full attention to the matters discussed. Between the outbreak of the war in August and January 1, 1915, he wrote only five letters to Page containing references to public affairs.[2] Page's letters of August, indeed, were not answered by the President until September 14th:

[1] Walter H. Page to Woodrow Wilson, August 25, 1914. From original letter in Mr. Wilson's files. See also *The Life and Letters of Walter H. Page*, Vol. III, p. 155.

[2] One or two others were letters of introduction, and one was written in appreciation of Page's fine and sympathetic words regarding the death of Mrs. Wilson.

"I cannot tell you how chagrined both the Secretary of State and I are that the leaks should have occurred of which your distressed cable of the other day spoke. We have for some time been trying to trace them, for they have occurred frequently, and we are now all but convinced that our code is in the possession of persons at intermediary points. We are going to take thoroughgoing measures.

"My thought and sympathy have gone out to you every day along with my genuine admiration for the admirable way in which you have handled an infinitely difficult set of circumstances. I have read your latest group of letters, August ninth and August twenty-fifth, and have made a number of notes with regard to what I shall try to do to make things go easier for you.

"I am writing in haste but with the most genuine concern and appreciation and with gratitude for your letters."

In this letter there is no evidence that the President gave heed to Page's excited warnings, although, as we shall see later, they probably disturbed him. It was of course highly unlikely that even the diplomatic stupidity of army and navy officials would go so far as to turn upon the country which was the chief source of absolutely necessary supplies.

In spite of arguments presented by the State Department, based upon the Declaration of London, the British not only stood upon the alterations and exceptions they had already announced, but on September 21st added a number of raw materials to the list of conditional contraband, chief among them copper, one of Germany's principal needs and an important American export. A number of cargoes on their way to neutral ports were stopped, and a fresh clamour arose among American business men. The situation was daily becoming more difficult; many of the complaints of the cotton, copper, and other producers and exporters were sent directly to the President.

Irritated by the course of the British, the President sent word to the State Department that he wanted a "vigorous protest" prepared—"one with teeth in it."[1] The result was a lengthy letter, ready on September 26th, and forwarded immediately by mail to Ambassador Page. On the following day, the 27th, Colonel House reached Washington, and the President showed him the document. "Someone else"—not Lansing—"prepared it," he wrote Page afterwards.[2] This someone else was, of course, the Solicitor, Cone Johnson. House immediately objected to it, thought it "exceedingly undiplomatic." At the President's suggestion Lansing prepared a briefer cablegram to Page which House also considered "objectionable."[3] On the following day House, at his own suggestion, discussed the entire matter with Spring Rice, the British ambassador, who naturally found the protest too strong. "One paragraph in particular he thought amounted almost to a declaration of war" and would cause a panic if it got out to the public. So the two sought ways of expressing the instruction "to save the *amour-propre* of his government."[4]

While the cablegram[5] was "softened . . . down," both documents were dignified and serious protests against the methods being used by the British.[6] The first was a long dry document—"eighteen pages of fine-spun legal argu-

---

[1] Cone Johnson to the author.

[2] *The Life and Letters of Walter H. Page*, Vol. I, p. 379.

[3] E. M. House to Walter H. Page, October 3, 1914. *The Life and Letters of Walter H. Page*, Vol. I, pp. 378–379.

[4] *The Intimate Papers of Colonel House*, Vol. I, pp. 307–308.

[5] Sent on September 28th.

[6] For a complete copy of the letter, of September 26th, see *Foreign Relations of the United States*, Supplement, 1914, pp. 225–232. For a complete copy of the cablegram, sent September 28th, see *Ibid.*, pp. 232–233. The letter of September 26th was never presented to the British Foreign Office: the controversy centred around the cablegram of September 28th. Both the House and Page books confuse these two dispatches.

ments (not all sound by any means)," the ambassador remarked in disgust, "against the sections of the English proclamations that have been put forth, giving them a strained and unfriendly interpretation"[1]—and it was accompanied by a passage directing Page, in presenting these objections, to remind the British government of the bitterness aroused by its conduct in the past and to inform it of the American government's fear that public discussion of the proposed rules "will awaken memories of controversies, which it is the earnest desire of the United States to forget or to pass over in silence."[2]

The British government was assured in the cablegram of the 28th that "the President earnestly desires to avoid a formal protest" and hoped it would consider the advisability of modifying its announcement of rules; that it was "his earnest wish to avoid every cause of irritation and controversy"; and that the instruction was sent in an "earnest spirit of friendship." But finally:

"The President is anxious that he [Grey] should realize the terms of the Declaration of London represent the limit to which this government could go with the approbation and support of its people."

We do not know how much the effect of the protest may have been diluted by Page's presentation of it to Sir Edward Grey, or by Spring Rice's account of his extraordinary "softening down" conference with Colonel House. At any rate the instruction failed to move the British government from its policy.[3]

---

[1]*The Life and Letters of Walter H. Page*, Vol. I, p. 382.

[2]It is interesting to note that this reference to the War of 1812, which Mr. Hendrick attributes to Lansing and considers a threat, almost certainly came from Wilson himself, as we shall see later, and was an honest expression of anxiety.

[3]Colonel House's biographer, Professor Seymour, comments on the difficulty of finding in all history another instance of diplomacy "so unconventional and so effective" as this conference with Spring Rice.

"Colonel House, a private citizen, spreads all the cards on the table and concerts with the ambassador of a foreign Power the dispatches to be sent the American ambassador

Grey's response to Page when the document was presented was a firm assertion that an unmodified Declaration of London could have no validity so far as his government was concerned. He wished to avoid giving offense or incurring public criticism, but "the British purpose," as Ambassador Page reported, ". . . was to prevent the enemy from receiving food and materials for military use and nothing more."[1] Grey, in his dispatch to Spring Rice, handed to Lansing on October 1st, said:

"We had only two objects in our proclamations: To restrict supplies for [the] German army and to restrict supply to Germany of materials essential for making of munitions of war."[2]

In so far as these statements asserted a right to interfere with supplies which were clearly "for military use," "for the German army," "for making of munitions of war," they were essentially legitimate. Such supplies were acknowledged contraband of war.

But as a matter of practice—and here lay the core of the difficulty—the British were going much further. Under the plea of establishing military destination, they were stopping shipments of food, cotton, and other commodities, taking cargoes into their own ports with costly delays —and thereby, in the view of the United States, infringing on the rights of neutrals to sell ordinary goods to the

---

and the Foreign Minister of that Power." *The Intimate Papers of Colonel House*, Vol. I, p. 308.

If frustration of our own government's purpose, in this case to secure a modification of British policy, be a proper object of diplomacy, then Mr. Seymour is right in his justification of Colonel House's action: "If there is criticism of the method, it is stifled by its success." But how can the result be called a "success" when the protest totally failed of its objective? At that time, whether right or wrong, the policy of the American government was one of "strict neutrality," based upon legal sanctions. It was standing upon that policy: and anything that weakened its position could not, assuredly, be called a "success."

[1] Walter H. Page to W. J. Bryan, telegram, September 29, 1914. *Foreign Relations of the United States*, Supplement, 1914, p. 233.

[2] *Foreign Relations of the United States*, Supplement, 1914, p. 237.

civilian population of belligerent countries. They were also imposing drastic general limitations on the trade of neutrals adjacent to the Central Powers. And both of these activities had a profound effect upon American business and American public opinion.

In vain might Grey explain that his government "wished to attain these objects with the minimum of interference with the United States and other neutral commerce."[1] Great Britain was desperately at war, believing herself absolutely right, and the "minimum" here meant *anything necessary to attain her objectives.*

"We each wish to defend our rights," as the British ambassador, Sir Cecil Spring Rice, wrote to the President on October 20th. "But I am sure you will remember that the rights we are defending are our existence."

Neutral nations had the choice of two courses of meeting such a crisis. They could, like Holland and Denmark, submit to *force majeure*, or they could resist on the basis of principles of public law, or on behalf of the interests of their own citizens. We had taken the second course. We were strong and could take it.

But there were many elements that made it extremely difficult for the United States to hold the legal balance steady. Great Britain, by virtue of her naval strength, controlled the sea. Germany was seriously handicapped geographically so far as American trade was concerned.[2] Moreover, there existed a strong tendency from the beginning in America to sympathize with the Allied cause,

---

[1] *Foreign Relations of the United States*, Supplement, 1914, p. 237.

[2] Neutrality was, of course, based upon a presumptive equality of the belligerents. In a legal argument presented to the President by Counselor Lansing on December 9th, it was argued:

"If one belligerent has by good fortune a superiority in the matter of geographical location or of military or naval power, the rules of neutral conduct cannot be varied so as to favor the less fortunate combatant. To change such rules because of the relative strength of the belligerents and in order to equalize their opportunities would be in itself an unneutral act, of which the stronger might justly complain."

a tendency encouraged by the swift growth of an immense and profitable trade in munitions with Great Britain.

Neutral nations, of course, might consider extralegal sanctions to enforce their rights. But extralegal sanctions for the United States would mean either war or the threat of war, for which we were not prepared, or else economic embargoes, with incalculable results that might be as disastrous as war itself—and might indeed lead to war—as they did in 1812. Moreover, the record of the United States when at war had not been free from criticism; we had often acted, just as the British were doing, according to our conception of "necessity." In short, there was no dependable law or code upon which the nations of the world agreed, or any organization to enforce such a code if one had existed.

It has been said that the art of diplomacy is not to meet difficulties but to avoid them. Diplomacy also nourishes itself upon the hope that the worst will not befall. However distasteful the process, there was plainly, in the conversations which followed the American protest of September 28th, a whittling down of our claim based on legal rights, to trade with Germany and adjacent neutrals. According to Grey's account, Page told him that "there was no desire to press the case of people who traded deliberately and directly with Germany, but there was great feeling against stopping legitimate American trade with Holland which had always been large, and it was difficult to disentangle the two questions."[1] How Page derived from his instructions authority to acquiesce in the stoppage of the debatable trade, either direct or indirect, is hard to see; but he was not rebuked.

In the meantime a parallel discussion had been started

[1]Sir Edward Grey to Sir Cecil Spring Rice, September 28, 1914, handed to Acting Secretary Lansing on October 1st. *Foreign Relations of the United States*, Supplement, 1914, p. 237.

in Washington between Lansing and the British ambassador. On the evening of September 28th, after the instructions to Page were dispatched, the President had sent
Lansing a telegraphic request to see Spring Rice at once
and put the matter before him. We have not this message
to show just how far Wilson authorized him to go in
discussing a settlement of the question, but he went ahead
on much the same lines as Page. His primary argument
against Great Britain's measures was, not that they were
illegal, which was the real strength of our position, but
that they would furnish grounds of criticism to her enemies
in the United States. He agreed with Spring Rice's justification that British interference with foodstuffs bound
for Holland was designed to stop the provisioning by that
route of the German army in Belgium, but added that
"it seemed unfortunate that some other means could not
have been found to accomplish the desired purpose . . . by
getting the Netherlands to place an embargo on foodstuffs
and other conditional contraband."[1]

Spring Rice eagerly agreed that this was a fine way of
handling the problem and went on to put a further suggestion into Lansing's mind: that the difficulty about
applying the continuous-voyage doctrine to conditional
contraband, other than foodstuffs, be cut through by
declaring such things as petroleum and copper absolute
contraband, because "now used almost exclusively for
war purposes." On this point Lansing replied that he
"could not speak for the government but that it seemed
worthy of consideration" as possibly less dangerous to
friendly relations when publicly discussed than the Order
in Council of August 20th.

In the case of both Page and Lansing the policy was
clearly one of avoidance: based not so much upon legal

---

[1] Acting Secretary Lansing's memorandum of his conversation with Ambassador Spring Rice. *Foreign Relations of the United States*, Supplement, 1914, p. 234.

rights as upon public opinion in America. Lansing's proposal actually seemed to involve a suggestion to the British to attain their objectives, without direct offense to us, by coercing other neutrals! And when boiled down, the suggestion that "petroleum and copper" be made absolute contraband, at that time a debatable issue, was a method not of defending our rights but of finding a way to get around them in order to smooth over American opinion. This course may or may not have been expedient or even necessary: but it was a yielding of a legal position which the government had firmly taken.

There is nothing among the President's papers to show that he was aware of the details or the significance of these negotiations. Bryan, though Secretary of State, seems to have had nothing whatever to do with the discussions. He does not appear in the picture at all. If the President knew generally what was being done, as he undoubtedly did, he offered neither approval nor rebuke.[1]

There is no understanding of Wilson's position in this and in many future decisions without emphasizing his dominating purpose. Deep within him, deeper perhaps than any other aspiration, was the desire not only to keep America out of the war, but to be the instrument for making peace in the conflict then in progress, and beyond that,

---

[1] All these incidents reveal how powerful was British influence—sometimes to the point of domination—over American diplomacy. Discussing Spring Rice's service as British ambassador to the United States, Mr. Gwynn, his biographer, writes:
"As to his value in negotiation, it cannot be overlooked that during the period while America was neutral, all the issues in dispute between England and America were decided as England wished. It proved possible for the Allies, and chiefly for Great Britain, to use America as their main source of supply, and at the same time to prevent America from supplying the Central Powers. Loans were raised successfully in America, even while angry controversies were in progress concerning the black list, the blockade and the interference with mails. Even the sale of German shipping to the American government never went through. 'I believe it to be the case,' Lord Reading wrote after Spring Rice's death, 'that the Allied governments were never forced to recede from their position in any important question owing to American opposition, and the result is in itself a sufficient proof of the sagacity with which the negotiations were conducted during the period of American neutrality.'" (Stephen Gwynn, *The Letters and Friendships of Sir Cecil Spring Rice*, Vol. II, pp. 430–431.)

as he told Dr. Axson[1] he had a vision of a "new world order," wherein war should be abolished. Attention has already been called to the antecedents of these profound aspirations—his boyhood in Georgia and South Carolina where the aftermath of the Civil War had been most terrible, his researches as an historian, which had shown him the injustice, the unreason, the futility of war. Read his accounts in his *History of the American People* of the War of 1812, of the Mexican War, of the aftermath of the Civil War.

Especially did he desire to avoid a conflict with the British. At the very time that these controversies were going on, we find the record of a conversation (on September 30th) with Colonel House, during which the President read from a volume of his *History of the American People* an account of Madison's problems at the time of the War of 1812. Colonel House records Wilson's observation that the War of 1812 "was started in exactly the same way as this controversy is opening up."

"Madison and I are the only two Princeton men that have become President. The circumstances of the War of 1812 and now run parallel. I sincerely hope they will not go further."[2]

This incident throws a flood of light upon the President's thinking. It shows his anxiety lest the dispute in progress culminate in a war with England. Page's insistence, in his letter of August 25th, upon the determined attitude of the British Admiralty had possibly impressed Wilson more than at first appeared. The reference to his book also brings into relief his fear lest public opinion, unduly excited, run away with him as it had with Madison. This apprehension probably explains the reiterated note in the American protests pleading with Great Britain to avoid

---

[1]See this volume, p. 74.

[2]*The Intimate Papers of Colonel House*, Vol. I, pp. 303–304.

arousing passions which the American government could not control.

A glance at these significant passages in Wilson's history may also explain why he gave no consideration to the possibility—really the only possibility—of coercing Great Britain by means short of war: that is, by an embargo on munitions. In his account of the origins of the War of 1812, he condemns the Non-Intercourse Act as unsound in itself and makes Madison's attempt to juggle with its enforcement, by distinguishing between the belligerents, responsible for getting him into a situation from which war with England was the only escape. As a matter of fact, while the political similarities which most impressed Wilson were notable, the economic differences were tremendous.

One is probably not unwarranted in pushing further the significance of Wilson's recurrence to his own book in this crisis. It was not yet at all clear that avoidance of a war with England by concessions which whittled down the American contention would entail reprisals by Germany that would cause war with her—but the risk, to Wilson's penetrating mind, must have suggested itself. In 1812, too, there had been as good reasons for war with France as with England, and the one would likely have followed if the other had not. Wilson's conclusion in his book was that Madison's administration had chosen the worse alternative. In condemnation of its "deep impolicy," he wrote:

"Napoleon was the enemy of the civilized world, had been America's own enemy in disguise, and had thrown off the disguise . . . It was a tragical but natural accident that the war should be against England, not against France."[1]

Upon a background of such historical judgement, what

[1] Volume III, pp. 216–217.

must have been the effect of Page's constant and fierce diatribes against Germany:

"It is another case of Napoleon . . ."[1] ". . . Sir John French and Sir John Jellicoe . . . will play the parts of Wellington and Nelson . . . it'll be they who saved Europe and kept England free . . ."[2]

We need not grant that he had been converted, as Page was, to the legend of Germany's sole responsibility for the war—we have seen that he was not—in order to perceive the choice looming in the background of his mind, that if it came to an alternative between war with England or with Germany he would prefer the latter.[3]

Another consideration no doubt played a large part in his thinking. There was still a chance—in his view a large

---

[1] Walter H. Page to Woodrow Wilson, September 6, 1914. *The Life and Letters of Walter H. Page*, Vol. III, p. 139.

[2] Walter H. Page to Woodrow Wilson, September 22, 1914. *Ibid.*, p. 142.

[3] We have an enlightening glimpse of Wilson's thinking in the record of an interview on December 14, 1914, by H. B. Brougham, who had been sent to Washington by C. R. Miller of the New York *Times* in order to secure, not for publication, a clear conception of the President's views. This record, made immediately after the conference, was published years later in *Mr. Miller of "The Times,"* by F. Fraser Bond, pp. 142–143:

"It will be found before long that Germany is not alone responsible for the war, and that some other nations will have to bear a portion of the blame in our eyes. The others will be blamed and it might be well if there were no exemplary triumph and punishment. I believe thoroughly that the settlement should be for the advantage of the European nations regarded as people and not for any nation imposing its governmental will upon alien peoples. Bismarck was longheaded when he urged Germany not to take Alsace and Lorraine.

"It seems to me that the government of Germany must be profoundly changed, and that Austria-Hungary will go to pieces altogether—ought to go to pieces for the welfare of Europe.

"As for Russia, I cannot help sympathizing with its aims to secure natural outlets for its trade with the world, and a proper settlement should permit this.

"If the decision is not to be reached wholly by the forces of reason and justice after the trial at arms is found futile, if the decision by arms should be in favor of the nations that are parties of the Triple Entente; I cannot regard this as the ideal solution, at the same time I cannot see now that it would hurt greatly the interests of the United States if either France or Russia or Great Britain should finally dictate the settlement. England has already extended her empire as far as she wants to—in fact she has got more than she wants—and she now wishes to be let alone in order that she may bend all her energies to the task of consolidating the parts of her empire. Russia's ambitions are legitimate, and when she gets the outlets she needs her development will go on and the world will be benefited."

chance—that a peaceful solution of the conflict would be reached. He was himself, as we shall see elsewhere, doing his best to bring it about, so that embroilment with either side might be avoided. The immediate danger was an involvement with Great Britain; as yet there were no great grievances against Germany. Since the use of economic compulsion—that is, embargoes—seemed as impossible politically as it was dangerous economically, concessions to the point of view of Great Britain appeared the expedient method of avoiding immediate danger. German retaliation, if it was provoked, was a remoter possibility and might be dealt with when it arose.

At all events it is comprehensible that the President, no doubt perceiving clearly all of the alternatives, should have given Lansing and Page a pretty free rein in their efforts to reach an accommodation with the British. The conversations during the first two weeks of October are extremely interesting, but in their minuter details they belong to history rather than to this biography. In their essence they involved an attempt on the part of Lansing to maintain the shadow of the Declaration of London— upon which our government had taken its stand—by sacrificing the substance of certain of our neutral rights. On the part of Page and of Grey it was an impatient and indignant attempt to throw the Declaration entirely overboard.

On October 15th Page sent a heated and eloquent cablegram to the President asserting that "the English will risk a serious quarrel or even war with us rather than yield. This you may regard as final." He set forth vehemently his belief in the unarguable rightness and justice of the British cause:

"This is not a war in the sense we have hitherto used the word. It is a world-clash of systems of government, a struggle to the extermination of English civilization or of

Prussian military autocracy. Precedents have gone to the scrap heap."

He denounced the Declaration of London, called the American contention "academic," "theoretical."

"Here it is a matter of life and death for English-speaking civilization. It is not a happy time to raise controversies that can be avoided or postponed."

He called the controversy a petty matter "compared with the grave danger we incur of shutting ourselves off from a position to be of some service to civilization and to the peace of the world."[1]

Of course the object of Lansing's proposals here so heatedly criticized was not to "admit war materials into Germany." Quite the contrary: Lansing's protests show that he was actually indicating ways of preventing war materials from getting into Germany while retaining the façade of the Declaration of London. But the very name of that instrument had now become anathema to both Page and Grey.

There are evidences of irritation in Wilson's prompt response to Page in a cablegram on October 16th:

"Your October 15, 11 p. m.

"Beg that you will not regard the position of this government as merely academic. Contact with opinion on this side the water would materially alter your view. Lansing has pointed out to you in personal confidential dispatch of this date how completely all the British government seeks can be accomplished without the least friction with this government and without touching opinion on this side the water on an exceedingly tender spot. I must urge you to realize this aspect of the matter and to use your utmost persuasive efforts to effect an understanding, which we earnestly desire, by the method we have gone

---

[1]*Foreign Relations of the United States*, Supplement, 1914, pp. 248–249.

out of our way to suggest, which will put the whole case in unimpeachable form.

"This is private and for your guidance."[1]

In the meantime, on October 15th, the American government had, in its circular giving definite sanction to the munitions traffic,[2] thrown away its best bargaining asset—that of a possible—or impossible!—embargo. It is not surprising, therefore, to find Page telegraphing on October 19th that "all hope of his [Grey's] acceptance of the Declaration entire"[3] was finally ended.

The American position had indeed been wrecked upon the ancient rock of sea power. With Great Britain (or any other nation) in control of the seas, how was a neutral, any neutral, to enforce its rights, or what it considered its rights, without using force?

II. AMERICA WITHDRAWS FROM HER STAND UPON THE DECLARATION OF LONDON

On October 20, 1914, Lansing had arrived at the conclusion that America must surrender her strongly argued stand upon the Declaration of London. He gathered all the correspondence together and sent it over to the President at the White House, with a letter setting forth this new conviction—a letter not before published:

"It seems to me that in view of the rigid attitude of the British government further attempts to obtain an agreement on the Declaration of London would be useless. We must, therefore, stand on the rules of international law which have been generally accepted without regard to the Declaration. In the matter of the transfer of vessels this will be a decided advantage. The great loss is the

---

[1]*Foreign Relations of the United States*, Supplement, 1914, pp. 252–253.
[2]See this volume, pp. 183–184.
[3]*Foreign Relations of the United States*, Supplement, 1914, p. 253.

failure to have a definite code, which will undoubtedly be the source of numerous controversies.

"It is to be regretted that in spite of all that has been done, the purpose of the negotiation has failed."

Wilson approved Lansing's dispatch to Page on October 22nd, formally withdrawing from insistence on the Declaration as the basis of our contentions, but insisting that "the rights and duties of the United States and its citizens in the present war be defined by the existing rules of international law and the treaties of the United States . . . and that this government reserves to itself the right to enter a protest or demand in each case in which those rights and duties so defined are violated, or their free exercise interfered with . . ."[1]

This withdrawal, which, as Lansing observed, involved a "great loss," placed our government in a weaker position than ever to defend our neutral rights. The "existing rules of international law" were uncertain and debatable; the London Conference had been called in 1908 and the Declaration issued because they were so. Now they were all we had left.

Just at this time Page sent his heated cablegram to House excoriating Lansing and declaring against "library lawyers."[2] House forwarded it to Wilson, who replied on October 23rd:

"I am [a] little disturbed by the messages Walter Page is sending recently. It is very necessary that he should see the difficult matters now under discussion between us and the British government in the light in which they are seen on this side of the water, and I am sorry that he should think the argument of them from our point of view the work of mere 'library lawyers.' We are very much

---

[1]Robert Lansing, Acting Secretary of State, to Walter H. Page, October 22, 1914. *Foreign Relations of the United States*, Supplement, 1914, pp. 257–258.

[2]See this volume, p. 199.

helped by his advice, but I hope that he will not get into an unsympathetic attitude. We are handling matters of the greatest difficulty, because they must be handled under the influence of opinion, and it would be very unfortunate if he were to become unsympathetic or were to forget the temper of folks at home, who are exceedingly sensitive about every kind of right."

Both this letter and the letter written a few days later to Page[1] are highly interpretive of Wilson's position—and his intense feeling—at the time.

The delight and relief of both Page and the British over the withdrawal of the demand for the acceptance of the Declaration of London indicate how much of a victory they considered it. Page wrote to Wilson on October 28th:

"In 48 hours after we withdrew the demand for the British acceptance of the Declaration of London without change, every detained American ship and cargo was released but one, and I have no doubt that that one will be released in another 48 hours. I do not mean to imply in the least that these ships and cargoes were held, so to speak, as hostages . . . But so long as we held up their general policy, it was impossible—or surely the more difficult—to get at these concrete cases. . . .

"That insistence on the Declaration of London came near to upsetting the whole kettle of fish. I presented and 'pushed' every insistence—otherwise, I should not have been excusable. But every time I plainly saw matters getting worse & worse . . . For the first time in this stress, my appetite disappeared and my digestion went bad; I didn't know the day of the week nor what month it was —seeing these two governments rushing towards a clash w^h w^d have made my mission a failure and, worse, have left suspicion and bitterness for a generation. . . . I do

---

[1]See this volume, pp. 168–170.

AMERICAN EMBASSY

LONDON. 28. Oct. '14

Dear Mr. President:

In 48 hours after we withdrew the demand
for the British acceptance of the Declaration of London without
change, every detained American ship and cargo was released but one, and I have no doubt that that one
will be released in another 48 hours. I do not mean
to imply in the least that these ships and cargoes were
held, so to speak, as hostages: I do not believe that that
idea entered anybody's mind. But so long as we held
up their general policy, it was impossible — or surely the
more difficult — to get at these concrete cases. They couldn't
issue their revised list of contraband which shippers all
over the neutral world were waiting for, and the ships
of other neutral nations were detained as ours were. Now,
I think, we are going to have the minimum of trouble.

As soon as the insistence on the Declaration was
withdrawn, I was in a position to talk to Sir Ed^w Grey
with the old-time frankness about the whole subject, wh
had become impossible so long as I had to lecture him on
the necessity of accepting a general code that his Parliament and every other European Government had
rejected in peace, when they considered it on its merits.

AMERICAN EMBASSY.

LONDON.

7/ Another similar story was about this Government's improperly influencing insurance rates. I looked everywhere for evidence of that, finding not the slightest. Somebody seems bent on making each Government believe something untrue about the other.

But these mare's nests have no eggs and are, perhaps, not troublesome more than the useless labour they put us to.

Yours heartily — for Mr. Wilmeth can take this, if I stop here),

Walter H. Page

To the President. /

First and last pages of a letter from Walter H. Page to Woodrow Wilson, October 28, 1914.

thank God that we gave up that contention (we had no earthly power to force it on them.)"

As to the attitude of the British, Page wrote:

"Tyrrell met me the day after we withdrew the demand —*greatly* relieved. 'I tell you personally—just between you and me—what an infinite relief it was to us all. We simply couldn't have accepted the Declaration entire and we couldn't see why or by what right you continued to insist that we sh^d. We'd do any reasonable thing to please you —anything but give such an advantage to the enemy as you demanded and demanded and demanded.' "[1]

The Germans on their part were equally stirred, feeling that the case had gone against them. Professor Münsterberg of Harvard University wrote to the President on November 7th complaining that American policy was favouring the Allies at the expense of the Germans and that German-American opinion was sharply in revolt. He spoke of "the submission of the administration to England's wishes," and Germany's suffering by "interpretations and decisions which help the Allies only."

Münsterberg also wrote of the possible political effect of the desertion of the administration by the "German, Swedish, Jewish and Irish vote"—a "very large and influential group." He remarked that he was "fully convinced" that the "strongest factor in the surprises of last Tuesday's elections was the firm will of the friends of Germany to demonstrate against what they call the submission of the administration to England's wishes." He went on to threaten a "regular systematic campaign . . . to take care that the Democratic party becomes tabooed as the one which has made America practically an ally of England."

The challenge of such a political revolt to the President and other leaders of the party at Washington, however

[1]October 28, 1914.

crudely impolitic so bald a threat, was calculated to be highly disturbing. Secretary Bryan, for example, who might have taken a hand in the case, as he had done earlier in the matter of loans, but who was as sensitive as a poplar leaf to every stirring of the political atmosphere, played no part whatever in the negotiations. Mr. Lansing had sent him the Münsterberg letters and his replies. It was so often the misfortune of the German sympathizers to have been impolitic, or offensive, in their methods.

Wilson immediately requested Professor Münsterberg to make his charges specific.

"I have received and read with a great deal of surprise your letter of November seventh. Certainly no administration ever tried more diligently or watchfully to preserve an attitude and pursue a line of conduct absolutely neutral. I would consider it a favor if you would point out to me what are considered the unneutral acts of which this administration is thought to have been guilty. If we have done anything contrary to our professions, I should certainly wish to correct the mistake if it were possible to do so. We have acted in strict accordance with international law, so far as we know."[1]

Münsterberg replied in a long letter on November 19th. He not only criticized the administration for discriminating in favour of the Allies, but he added numerous other complaints:

"Let me emphasize three points to which my correspondents refer most frequently. First, all cables sent by and received by wire pass uncensored, while all wireless news is censored. This reacts against Germany, because England sends all her news by cable, whereas Germany alone uses the wireless. . . . Second, the policy of the administration with regard to the holding up, detaining and searching of Germans and Austrians from neutral and

[1]November 10, 1914.

American vessels is a reversal of the American policy established in 1812. It has excited no end of bitterness. Third, the United States permitted the violation by England of the Hague Convention and international law in connection with conditional and unconditional contraband. The United States, for instance, has not protested against the transference of copper from the conditional to the absolute list, although on former occasions the United States has taken a spirited stand against one-sided interpretations of international agreements. In 1812, in the Russian Japanese war, and in the Boer war, the United States insisted that a neutral nation has the right to send conditional as well as unconditional contraband to neutral nations without permitting an inquiry into its ultimate destination. . . . By permitting this new interpretation the United States practically supports the starving out policy of the Allies. The nation by reversing its own policy thus seriously handicaps Germany and Austria in their fight for existence."

He goes on to say:

"Many of the complaints refer more to the unfriendly spirit than to the actual violation of the law. Here above all belongs the unlimited sale of ammunition to the belligerents. The administration originally advised Mr. Morgan that the making of loans to the nations at war would not be looked upon with favor by the President, and Mr. Morgan cancelled the plans. This attitude has been given up; the State Department has emphasized that money and arms may be sold to the belligerents, while evidently the friends of peace had firmly hoped that the President would denounce the sale of ammunition or any other sale which would be likely to prolong the war. Indeed our friends of peace must regret this encouraging attitude with reference to the sale of agencies of destruction, but the friends of Germany cannot forget that this sympathetic attitude of the State Department under the conditions which objectively exist is not only helpful to the prolongation of the war, but helpful exclusively to the Allies against Central Europe. The favorite interpretation of the Germans is even that the government makes itself a party to the violation of neutrality by giving clearance papers to vessels loaded with war material for England and France. They say, moreover, that the President as Commander-in-Chief of the army and navy could and did restrain the shipment of war material into Mexico. Hence he has the same power to restrain the shipment of such material to Europe."

These charges evidently made a strong impression upon the President, for he transmitted them with the following letter to Counselor Lansing:

"I would be very much obliged if you would read the enclosed letter from Professor Münsterberg and send me a memorandum, if you would be so kind, of the answers and comments that might be made upon his statements. Here at last is a very definite summing up of the matters upon which German anti-administration feeling in this country is being built up, and perhaps it would be wise to take very serious notice of it. The case they make out is *prima facie* very plausible indeed."[1]

A few days later, December 9th, the Counselor replied to the President, much at length. His thoroughgoing explanations and answers to the specific charges of unneutral conduct by the United States government constituted an official, though unpublished, refutation by the Department of State.

"Professor Hugo Münsterberg is a German subject. Dr. Bernhard Dernburg is not only a German subject, but is probably (though the evidence at hand is not conclusive) a paid agent of the German government sent to

[1]December 1, 1914.

the United States to create sentiment in favor of Germany. These two are the principal leaders in arousing antagonism in this country to the policy of the administration in its relations to the belligerent nations.

"These two foreign writers have severely criticized this government's conduct of its foreign affairs, have made charges unfounded in fact or in law, have distorted the truth, and have bitterly assailed the President and the Department of State for alleged injustice to Germany and undue friendliness for the cause of the Allies. In pursuing this campaign of misrepresentation and vilification they have done so by means of addresses and publications which have been widely circulated throughout the country relying upon the freedom of speech and of the press guaranteed to the people by the Constitution."

After this irritated preface on the impropriety of any interference by Münsterberg and Dernburg in the foreign affairs of the United States, Lansing dealt with the legal aspects of American policy, treating each of the complaints in turn. On the important charge that "the United States permitted the violation by England of the Hague Convention and international law in connection with conditional and unconditional contraband," which had appeared to Münsterberg as a reversal of our own policy and as supporting "the starving out policy of the Allies," the Counselor sketched the basic difficulties the United States confronted—we had to argue against ourselves on our claims:

"There is no Hague Convention which deals with absolute or conditional contraband, and, as the Declaration of London is not in force, the rules of international law only apply. As to the articles to be regarded as contraband there is no general agreement. . . .

"The record of the United States in the past is not free from criticism. When neutrals, we have stood for the most restricted lists of . . . contraband. As a belligerent, we have extended the lists . . . according to our conception of the necessities of the case.

"The United States has now under consideration the question of the right of a belligerent to include 'copper unwrought' in its list of absolute contraband instead of in its list of conditional contraband. As the government of the United States has in the past placed 'all articles from which ammunition is manufactured' in its contraband list, and has declared copper to be among such materials, it necessarily finds some embarrassment in dealing with the subject."

We were similarly handicapped when considering "the doctrine of 'ultimate destination' and of 'continuous voyage' " which "is an *American doctrine*." When this government was a belligerent, it not only asserted but extended the rule of "continuous voyage" and enforced it in its tribunals. But so far there had been no instance of a seizure by Great Britain of an American vessel with a belligerent destination. Our protests were being lodged against British seizure or detention of American ships or cargoes destined to neutral ports—and our American doctrines were undermining those protests.

The charge that we had reversed our policy was clearly overthrown; but on the practical issue of restraining belligerent British actions on the seas, in regard to neutral commerce, Lansing was forced to concede that "the right of the neutral, however, seems to be that of protest."

But there were obligations as well as rights involved. Treating them and clarifying the main problems as a whole, he went to the heart of his own conclusions in a short paragraph:

"In the enforcement of the laws of neutrality . . . this government cannot take into account the advantage or disadvantage which may result to any of the belligerents

through the enforcement of neutral duties. If one belligerent has by good fortune a superiority in the matter of
geographical location or of military or naval power, the
rules of neutral conduct cannot be varied so as to favor
the less fortunate combatant. To change such rules because of the relative strength of the belligerents and
in order to equalize their opportunities would be in itself
an unneutral act, of which the stronger might justly
complain."

In his letter to the President transmitting this long
statement, Lansing strongly argued against making a
reply to Münsterberg personally, a German subject and
"an agent of the German government." But he suggested
that the falsity of the charges be proved and made public
in some other way. Lansing's refutation was so strong,
however, that Wilson probably thought it not necessary
to make any public statement; none was made.

Lansing's statement shows how impossible it was to
achieve any real neutrality whatever. Bryan and Wilson
might wish earnestly to be fair alike to both parties in the
conflict. To change the rules of international law would
be legally unneutral; not to change the rules of international law would be morally or practically unneutral.
The position of the fence-sitter in this case was not only
uncomfortable, it was untenable.

III. PROTESTS AGAINST INTERFERENCE WITH AMERICAN SHIPPING

President Wilson's diplomatic retreat from his position
upon the Declaration of London was indeed, as Lansing
said, a "great loss." The Declaration had been the beginning of a real international code: and once rejected
through the insistence of the British, the world slipped
back to the still feebler sanctions of traditional practice.

It was an inevitable retreat, because the Declaration had behind it no sanctions or organization with any power. There was no method of enforcement if any belligerent found it undesirable to accept its restrictions. While it was the British who caused the rejection, any other powerful nation placed in the same position would have done the same thing.

While the first effect of the President's withdrawal was to ease the growing acerbity of the relationships with Great Britain, difficulties were by no means ended. Nations at war are insatiable. On the very day of the withdrawal (October 22nd) the President wrote to Lansing regarding British detention of oil ships:

"I quite agree with you that the only course to take in the matter of the tank steamer *Brindilla* and in other similar cases is to make an immediate and vigorous protest against the action of the British authorities in seizing an American vessel bound to a neutral port."

While the ships in question were released after some delay, difficulties continued to arise. Shipments of copper were constantly interrupted, cargoes of foodstuffs, particularly meat products, were detained and often confiscated. Shippers complained bitterly that their products deteriorated while the cargoes were held up. Even though cotton was still on the free list, shipments were interfered with, the British alleging the necessity of searching the cargoes for concealed contraband such as copper—which in some cases they found. Instead of the immemorial practice of search at sea, they insisted upon delaying ships in British ports, arguing the difficulty of investigating the large cargoes of modern vessels. In short, the trading rights which the British government itself had insisted upon when a neutral in the Russo-Japanese war (and which she had asked the American government to help her maintain) were now denied to Americans and other neutrals.

The State Department, bombarded by angry shippers, made constant complaints which were presented by Page with the best grace he could muster, and received by Grey with weary courtesy. The British Order in Council of October 29th, establishing new rules of absolute contraband—including important commodities such as copper, petroleum, and rubber—further complicated the situation. On November 3rd the British declared the North Sea a military area.[1] Page and Grey tried to devise a "working arrangement,"[2] but the extent and arbitrary character of British interference were so glaringly obvious that tremendous pressure was brought upon the administration by the business interests affected. Letters poured in from excited senators and congressmen, chambers of commerce, trade associations.[3] It was even charged that the government had sold out the rights of neutral trade entirely. To add to the difficulty, German sympathizers continued, with increasing insistence, to charge that the administration was not balancing justly the scales of neutrality.

The President had hoped that Page's "arrangement" with Grey would prove sufficient, and had kept his attention fixed as far as possible upon other great problems, mostly relating to the completion of his programme of domestic reform. But in his second annual address to Congress on December 8th he said:

"While we have worked at our tasks of peace the cir-

---

[1]*Foreign Relations of the United States*, Supplement, 1914, p. 464.

[2]Which Page reported on December 6th. See *Ibid.*, pp. 356–358.

[3]The 1914 volume of the *Foreign Relations of the United States*, Supplement, contains telegraphic interchanges in regard to shipments of wool, hides, meat, rubber, plumbago, chrome ore, etc.—protests and inquiries from the Department of State, replies from the British (p. 417 *ff.*). See also Bryan to Page, December 15, 1914, saying in part: ". . . the business men interested in the cables and shipping are presenting their protests to senators and members of Congress" (p. 526); Bryan to Page, December 16, 1914, transmitting a protest from Senator John Sharp Williams (p. 527); Bryan to Page, December 22, 1914, reporting a protest from the Chamber of Commerce of Manila against cable censorship (p. 529).

cumstances of the whole age have been altered by war."[1]

He was now ready, as he told Congress, to "face new tasks . . ."[2]

It was plain that more drastic protests regarding the actions of the British must be made: even before the address, whether by the President's direction or not cannot be ascertained, Cone Johnson, from his desk in the State Department, had been forging thunderbolts. Both Lansing and Bryan gave their earnest attention to the subject, submitting an early draft to Wilson. He told a friend[3] that Bryan brought him the note "in an entirely rough and unliterary form, threatening, too." "I drew my pen through certain offensive passages, wrote out new statements on the margin and between the lines, handed it back to him and suggested that he should rewrite it."

On December 24th a "second redraft" was sent to the President, initialed "R.L.," and further revisions were made, but only in phraseology. On December 26th the protest was cabled to Page. It was officially given to the press on December 31st,[4] the first public protest against the conduct of Great Britain—or any other belligerent. Previous to its publication, excited rumours had suggested a "crisis," spoken of the note as an "ultimatum," even envisioned war. The feeling thus easily aroused, the President "took pains" to allay at a conference with newspaper correspondents on December 29th, assuring them that there was no threat of reprisal or suggestion of a threat of that character in the American note to Great Britain.[5]

As a matter of fact, while the note "thundered in the

[1] *The Public Papers of Woodrow Wilson,* Vol. III, p. 215.

[2] *Ibid.,* p. 216.

[3] Mrs. Crawford Toy, conversation recorded in her diary, January 3, 1915.

[4] Though it had "leaked" into the papers before this. See New York *Times,* December 29, 1914.

[5] New York *Times,* December 30, 1914.

index," setting forth serious grievances against the British, it was, so far as the actual protest was concerned, a weak affair.[1] It had no teeth at all. It "viewed with growing concern," the "large number of American vessels . . . seized on the high seas," and spoke of the practice of bringing ships into port for the examination of their cargoes as one which "this government cannot without protest permit," but the only right really asserted was that of selling goods to neutrals for their own use. There was no declaration of any right to sell the Germans anything directly or indirectly either for civilian or military use— except for a quotation from Lord Salisbury to the effect that foodstuffs should be seized only upon proof of being destined to armed forces.

But the nub of the American case, its inherent weakness, lay in the acceptance of what was really the British contention that interference by belligerents with neutral trade was justified when "manifestly an imperative necessity." It was also admitted that justification should rest not only upon "the rules of international law," but also "the principle of self-preservation." While this demand on the part of a belligerent is understandable, the admission of it by a neutral robs him of any case whatsoever, for it can be interpreted by the belligerent to cover anything. The Germans were being blamed at this time for so interpreting it. It really leaves the neutral free to criticize only conduct which does not affect the enemy at all, as interference with trade purely between neutrals who were far removed from the theatre of war.

Once the principles of "manifest necessity" and "self-preservation," both to be determined by the belligerent,

---

[1]For text, see *The Public Papers of Woodrow Wilson*, Vol. III, pp. 229–235; also *Foreign Relations of the United States*, Supplement, 1914, pp. 372–375. It seems probable that this was the note referred to by Grey in telling of how Page, after reading it, said: "I have now read the dispatch, but I do not agree with it; let us consider how it should be answered!" (See Viscount Grey, *Twenty-five Years*, Vol. II, p. 110.)

are admitted, the peace of the world, and the rights and even the safety of neutrals, break down.

One may pose the question as to which deserves the more respect in such a crisis, the "rights" of neutrals who are trying to keep the world's peace, or the "necessities" of belligerents who are breaking it? In times of peace most students and even statesmen take the side of the neutrals; but in times of war the belligerents always claim —as we ourselves did during our Civil War—that their safety, their necessities, are superior; and neutrals are helpless to reply except by ceasing to be neutrals. The only alternative to the doctrine of the superior necessity of the belligerent is an international organization that will assert and defend the rights of neutrals.

In the present case, the "protest," in spite of its mildness, aroused great excitement and controversy. At last American reserve had broken down: American patience had been exhausted! But the effect upon the American public was far more pronounced—as it was no doubt intended to be—than upon the diplomats. The British government seemed not at all worried. It perceived at once the weakness of the President's position. Colonel House reported on December 31st that Spring Rice "has gotten in a good humor again"[1] and sent to Wilson a copy of a letter written by him:

". . . the telegram to Page . . . seems to me a very fair, just and courteous and firm presentment of the case to which no objection whatever could be raised on the ground of its form. I am sure it will create a very lasting impression and will remain on the records as an honorable effort to solve, in an amicable manner, the question at issue."

British opinion was well summed up in an editorial in the London *Daily News:*

[1]After his irritation over the premature publicity given to the note in this country.

"The full text of the American note confirms the impression that in phrasing and in temper it is eminently friendly, nor is that all. President Wilson has not, except in one particular, tried to formulate principles of international law different from those adopted by the British government during this war."[1]

If the British so clearly perceived the weakness of the protest and were pleased, the Germans were correspondingly irritated and alarmed. It added fuel also to the flames of discontent and criticism among the German-American population of the United States. In some ways this was more disturbing to the administration, especially to Mr. Bryan, than the direct expostulation from the German government. Senator Stone, who came from a state having a large number of German-American voters, mostly Democrats, and who also occupied the powerful and strategic position of chairman of the Committee on Foreign Relations of the Senate, was much agitated. He hurried to see the President soon after the publication of the British note. Wilson promised to have the charges of unneutrality investigated and refuted through correspondence with Stone himself. Lansing immediately prepared a memorandum which might be employed to meet the "unjustifiable charges of partiality for Great Britain and her allies in the enforcement of neutrality," and the President forwarded it to Senator Stone on January 7th, writing to him:

"Following up our conversation of the other day, I take the liberty of sending you a list of the charges which have been made in various quarters by those who think we have not been dealing fairly with questions of neutrality, charges made chiefly by those who have a very strong sympathy with the cause of Germany and Austria in the existing war."

[1] Quoted in the New York *Times* of January 1, 1915.

On the next day (January 8th) in a letter to Bryan, Stone called upon the administration to justify its neutrality and gave a list of twenty grounds of complaint alleged to indicate partiality shown to the Allies. Five of these related to our "submission" to various aspects of the blockade.[1]

Mr. Bartholdt, also from Missouri, and a leading member of the House, had gone even further and had introduced a resolution demanding that the American government stop selling arms to the Allies. The President wrote to Bryan, who had asked his advice as to what was to be done:

"I hope that when the opportunity offers you will be kind enough to say to the House Committee on Foreign Affairs that I entirely agree with your judgment that 'any action looking to interference with the right of belligerents to buy arms here' taken at the present time 'would be construed as an unneutral act.' My opinion is very clear, as I think the opinion of everyone must be who is fully cognizant of all the implications that would attend such action."[2]

The President was evidently much concerned, for we find him writing to Democratic leaders in several states

---

[1] "4. Submission without protest to English violations of the rules regarding absolute and conditional contraband, as laid down—

"(a) In the Hague Conventions.
"(b) In international law.
"(c) In the Declaration of London.

"5. Submission without protest to inclusion of copper in the list of absolute contraband.

"6. Submission without protest to interference with American trade to neutral countries—

"(a) In conditional contraband.
"(b) In absolute contraband.

"7. Submission without protest to interruption of trade in conditional contraband consigned to private persons in Germany and Austria, thereby supporting the policy of Great Britain to cut off all supplies from Germany and Austria.

"8. Submission to British interruption of trade in petroleum, rubber, leather, wool, etc." *Foreign Relations of the United States*, Supplement, 1914, vi–vii.

[2] Woodrow Wilson to W. J. Bryan, January 7, 1915.

which had large numbers of German-American voters. To George S. Johns, editor of the *Post Dispatch*, of St. Louis, a letter marked "Personal":

"Any advice you can give me as to the best means of handling the sentiment of our fellow-citizens of German extraction would be very welcome."[1]

To Senator Paul O. Husting, of Wisconsin, he wrote:

"I feel to the full what you urge about the mistaken sentiment growing up among German-Americans. I feel it, indeed, so strongly that I have already taken steps which I hope will lead to a public correction of many of the mistaken views which are now prevalent."[2]

Senator Stone's protest, the resolution of Bartholdt, and many excited communications from German-Americans appear to have caused considerable anxiety in the State Department, as it had in the White House. Bryan, realizing that the American position must be clearly stated, had two drafts of responses prepared and sent to the President. The first of these, of which no copy can be found, evidently attacked German-American leaders who were protesting, for the President wrote on January 16th:

MY DEAR MR. SECRETARY,

I think with you that it would be very unwise to use the first of these papers, the one dealing with persons and speaking of the feeling in this country about the interventions of aliens in our affairs. But the other paper is just the right thing, dealing as it does, in a perfectly colourless and impersonal manner with the questions propounded in Senator Stone's letter.

Faithfully Yours,

W.W.

The document used and sent on January 20th to Senator Stone, the result of a great many conferences among the

[1]January 4, 1915.
[2]January 12, 1915.

President, Secretary Bryan and Mr. Lansing,[1] represented the reasoned response of the administration.[2] It eliminated the Declaration of London as a standard of judgement, since it was "not in force."[3] It admitted that the definition of contraband of war was a matter on which "there is no general agreement between nations." References to American practices during the Civil War showed the weaknesses of the American case for contesting the British rules for the treatment of contraband in transit: "As a belligerent, we have contended for a liberal list"; and "the rule of 'continuous voyage' has been not only asserted by American tribunals but extended by them." And, by way of concluding this point: "The government therefore cannot consistently protest against the application of rules which it has followed in the past . . ."

The conclusion of the letter laid all the charges at the door of "partisans of Germany and Austria-Hungary" and stated that the one-sided effect of American neutrality which they attributed to partiality of the government for the Allies "results from the fact that on the high seas the German and Austro-Hungarian naval power is thus far inferior to the British." The proposition that this inferiority should be equalized by an embargo on the export of contraband was condemned as "an unneutral act, an act of partiality."

Regardless of the legal weight of this conclusion, one cannot avoid the impression, after a careful study of this document, that the administration's defense of American policy was in reality a defense of the British blockade, and furnished the British government with a whole arsenal of arguments against our own criticism of that blockade.

---

[1] New York *Times*, January 25, 1915.

[2] For text see *Foreign Relations of the United States*, Supplement, 1914, vii–xiv.

[3] In another place it was stated that "this government is not now interested in the adoption of the Declaration of London by the belligerents."

It exhibits the want in the world of any real machinery, any rules with sanctions for dealing with questions of such profound moment, not only to belligerents but to neutrals. Upon the important problem of contraband of war, "there is," as the document itself states, "no general agreement between nations." It was upon this uncertain, negative, legalistic ground that the President was now forced to rest his policy.

To make matters worse, the British "preliminary observations" regarding the note of December 26th forwarded on January 7, 1915, were by no means as satisfactory as the administration had hoped. Grey had seized eagerly upon the admitted justification of interference with neutral trade when "necessary to protect the belligerent's national safety." The main argument of the note, aimed no doubt at public opinion, was that American business was making money out of the war—the inference being that we ought therefore to be satisfied. With regard to copper, it cited figures showing such an increase in American business with European neutrals as to constitute a strong presumption that it was caused by reëxportation to Germany.[1]

Lansing's comment on this note, in a private letter to the President, sums up his own real views regarding it:

"My general impression of the document is that the tone is conciliatory and that the presentation of the British case is adroit, though transparently illogical in many particulars to one familiar with the facts. It appears to be drafted with the purpose of allaying public irritation in this country without giving any assurance that trade conditions with neutral countries will be relieved."[2]

---

[1] *Foreign Relations of the United States*, Supplement, 1915, pp. 300–301.

[2] January 11, 1915. Lansing suggested a mere acknowledgment of the note, reserving comment until the full British reply was received, but asking that it be hastened "in view of the existing doubt as to British action in the future and the consequent demoralizing effect on American commerce."

We know also Wilson's reaction from a letter to Bryan in which he shows how fully he is committed to the policy of avoiding any real contest with Great Britain:

"I return the English preliminary note with Mr. Lansing's memoranda, and wish to make this suggestion, as I did hurriedly over the telephone the other day:

"The two governments being apparently in substantial agreement about the principles involved, it would seem to me best that the whole argument should be directed to practicable methods of handling the whole matter with the least possible delay, unfairness, or friction, and with a view to bringing the British practices to some basis of uniformity and consistency upon which our merchants could reckon. My feeling is that it is not worth while debating details with them. But this is only a judgement preliminary like the note itself."[1]

In spite of the effort of the administration to explain its position, neither the British nor the Germans were satisfied. Both were irritated and complained of American unneutrality. On January 19th Page cabled regarding the "dangerous mood of public opinion" in England which he said was "exceedingly suspicious and is fast becoming angry."[2]

The situation of the President was, indeed, utterly impossible. In his own country he had at least three noisy groups of opinion to mollify. First and foremost, the immense number of Americans who were suffering economically and financially, as a result of the war—cotton, food, and copper producers and exporters, mostly in the West and South. Second, he had the pro-Ally groups in the industrial East, most of which were beginning to

---

[1]January 14, 1915. It is not necessary here to deal with the full presentation of the British case, delayed for a month (February 10th), (see *Foreign Relations of the United States*, Supplement, 1915, pp. 324–334) since it gave rise to no new development in the President's attitude or policies.

[2]*Foreign Relations of the United States*, Supplement, 1915, p. 7.

profit greatly by war trade with the Allies and feared the interruption of that trade. Third, he had the smaller but vociferous groups of German-Americans and Irish who were pro-German or anti-Ally. Whatever he did was likely to be attacked not only by both sides in Europe, but by all the various groups in America. Well might he cry out:

"Alas, just now my mouth is sealed. There are those among our fellow-citizens who are most ingenious in seeing breach of neutrality in almost anything that I may say or do and the safest way is for me to confine myself to the obvious duties of the day and hour."[1]

Nevertheless the President continued patiently to meet the various difficulties. The note of December 26th, though it was diplomatically weak, had temporarily a good effect on American opinion. He was doing his best to provide better means of shipping non-contraband goods such as cotton. He was carrying forward his strenuous campaign for more American ships. At that very time the fight on the measure in the Senate, already described, was at its hottest. On January 23rd the Democrats were trying desperately to secure unity in favour of the bill.

Although cotton was not yet contraband, the British were seeking to prevent the Germans from getting any. An open attack on the cotton trade, at that time, as the British well knew, might have been dangerous, since the pressure of the entire South upon the Democratic administration might easily have forced some drastic action —such as the use of naval convoys or an embargo on munitions. But on one pretext or another, cargoes were detained. Private shippers attempted test cases by sending out ships—the *Dacia* and the *Wilhelmina*[2]—which were

---

[1] Woodrow Wilson to Isador Singer of the Slavonic Publishing Company of New York, February 1, 1915.

[2] The cases of the two vessels presented marked differences: the *Wilhelmina* testing the sending of foodstuffs to Germany, the *Dacia* testing the use of former German vessels purchased by Americans in trade to Europe.

supposed to observe every rule of neutral trade. Both ships were seized.

While it was contended that the *Dacia* had every legal right to a free passage—the Bureau of War Risk Insurance had underwritten the cargo—Ambassador Page reported that the effect upon British opinion was ominous. The sailing of the *Dacia*, he said, was generally regarded as "proof of our unfriendliness." Feeling in England was like that "just before an earthquake."[1] He said that the idea he found prevailing, even in the mind of Grey, was that the German element in the United States, which had never become assimilated, was gaining the upper hand and making the country "one of the bases from which the Germans carry on the war in spite of our government's neutrality and in spite of the sympathy of most Americans for the Allies."[2]

Wilson was plainly disturbed by Page's stormy letters. He felt that British opinion, which seemed to be shared by the British government, was mistaken, and that a grave injustice was being done to citizens of German and Irish origin in America. Such misunderstandings could lead only to further difficulties. Although at this time under heavy pressure of affairs of great moment, he began drafting in shorthand a message aimed to correct British opinion of the American attitude as reported by Page. He plainly devoted an unusual amount of time and thought to the matter—his stenographic notes remain among his papers —and he sought also advice and information from Mr. Bryan, who responded with suggested corrections quite out of the ordinary. The result was the long telegram of January 23rd to Page—one of the longest Wilson ever wrote—"answering your two telegrams in regard to the

---

[1]Walter H. Page to W. J. Bryan, January 19, 1915. *Foreign Relations of the United States*, Supplement, 1915, pp. 6–7.
[2]Walter H. Page to W. J. Bryan, January 18, 1915. *Ibid.*, p. 683.

irritation and apparent change in public opinion regarding the United States":

"While the English element predominated in the original stock, the immigration in latter years has been largely from other countries. Germany and Ireland, for instance, have contributed very materially during the last half century, and among those who are the children of foreign-born parents the German element now predominates. This element is not only numerous, but it has a strong representation in financial, mercantile life, and agriculture. Congressman Bartholdt is a naturalized American with a long service in Congress. A considerable portion of the voters of his district are naturalized Germans [Americans] or of German descent. There need be no fear that his proposals will be adopted; but they are a sample of our difficulties. There is, of course, not the slightest alteration in the cordial feeling which has always existed between the United States and Great Britain."

In Wilson's draft of the above paragraph he used the words:

"Notwithstanding such influences the vast majority of the American people are genuinely friendly in their attitude towards Great Britain."

Bryan apparently found this too strong an expression of partisan sympathy, and toned it down to "there is, of course, not the slightest alteration in the cordial feeling which has always existed" between the two countries.

But the main object of the telegram was to place the *Dacia* affair in a broader setting than that of mere pro-German efforts of a faction. Wilson argued, with a long exposition of the causes of real irritation against Great Britain's treatment of American trade, that serious issues centred upon the *Dacia* case from the American point of view also. Her transfer and voyage constituted an expression of the urgent demand for shipping, the lack of which was one of the principal obstacles to commerce, especially the cotton trade.[1]

"You may assure Sir Edward that this government will adhere conscientiously to its course of neutrality. It will not intentionally deviate a hair's breadth from the line but it is powerless to prevent the increasing criticism which has been aroused by acts which have, from the American standpoint, seemed unnecessarily severe for the enforcement of belligerent rights."[2]

Page was instructed to transmit these observations to Grey, and he replied that he would do so "when a favourable opportunity occurs."[3] He was not pressed to go ahead, and he pigeonholed the instruction indefinitely.[4]

These events, and the checkered career of the Ship Purchase bill, were developments over a considerable period of time. By the latter days of January, it was clear enough that, however loudly the British might proclaim cotton to be non-contraband, they intended to interfere with its shipment to Germany as far as they could on other grounds, and that they were not disposed to allow what the trade most needed—the development of an American merchant marine through the purchase of German ships.

American and British relationships might have drifted into still greater difficulties and dangers,[5] if an entirely new development had not occurred on February 4th—the announcement of the German blockade of England, the

---

[1]For text, see *Foreign Relations of the United States*, Supplement, 1915, pp. 684–687.
[2]*Ibid.*, p. 686.

[3]January 27, 1915. *Ibid.*, p. 688.

[4]The *Dacia* was captured by a French cruiser on February 27th, transferred to the French flag, and while the case was dragging through the law courts, was torpedoed by the Germans.

[5]Page enclosed in a letter of January 26th an extract from the London *Spectator* in which the possibility of war with the United States was even suggested.

war-zone decree. At once the President's attention, long centred upon the British controversy, was turned toward Germany, and an entirely new series of problems appear. These must be left for orderly treatment to another chapter.

CHAPTER V

CONTROVERSIES WITH GERMANY

The friendship between the people of the United States and the people of Germany is so warm and of such long standing, the ties which bind them to one another in amity are so many and so strong, that this government feels under a special compulsion to speak with perfect frankness when any occasion arises which seems likely to create any misunderstanding, however slight or temporary, between those who represent the governments of the two countries.

W. J. Bryan to Ambassador Bernstorff, April 21, 1915.

. . . the protests made by German-Americans and by a portion of the Irish-Americans, while entirely without justification, are not unnatural. It is difficult for people to think logically when their sympathies are aroused.

Woodrow Wilson to Walter H. Page, January 23, 1915.

. . . American public opinion will never stand for a colorless or timid presentation of a case, in which an American has been killed by an atrocious act of lawlessness.

Robert Lansing to W. J. Bryan, April 5, 1915.

1. "STRICT ACCOUNTABILITY"

WHILE the President was still intensely occupied with controversies with the British over the results of their blockade, endeavouring to maintain American neutrality, and hoping against hope that an opportunity for peace parleys would solve difficulties that were rapidly becoming diplomatically intolerable, the German crisis of February 4, 1915, suddenly developed. On that date the

German Admiralty issued its proclamation declaring the waters surrounding the British Isles a war zone in which, after February 18th, enemy ships would be "destroyed," with the further intimation that neutral ships would not be secure from accidents, owing to the "misuse" of neutral flags by British ships.[1]

Some such action was not wholly unexpected. Late in January, Wilson had received a startling telegram from Gerard, telling of the bitter feeling that had been growing in Germany over what was considered unneutral conduct on the part of the United States.

"I do not think that the people in America realize how excited the Germans have become on the question of selling munitions of war by Americans to the Allies. A veritable campaign of hate has been commenced against America and Americans. . . .

"Zimmermann[2] showed me a long list, evidently obtained by an effective spy system, of orders placed with American concerns by the Allies. He said that perhaps it was as well to have the whole world against Germany, and that in case of trouble there were five hundred thousand trained Germans in America who would join the Irish and start a revolution. I thought at first he was joking, but he was actually serious."[3]

This report Wilson considered "amazing."[4]

We have only irritatingly unsatisfactory glimpses of the reaction upon the President of the news of the German proclamation. The first information came from the newspapers, and we see Lansing—Bryan does not appear in the

---

[1] *Foreign Relations of the United States*, Supplement, 1915, p. 94.

[2] German Undersecretary of State for Foreign Affairs.

[3] January 24, 1915. He refers to it a little later in a dispatch as the "hate campaign . . . against America." February 10, 1915. *Foreign Relations of the United States*, Supplement, 1915, p. 101.

[4] Woodrow Wilson to E. M. House, January 28, 1915.

picture at all[1]—hurriedly writing to Bernstorff and cabling to Gerard, to get official texts of the proclamation and of the explanatory memorandum which accompanied it. He had a conference with Wilson, probably on the 6th (a letter of the 5th remarked that the German action "presents a most delicate situation which will have to be handled with extreme care"), and on the same day he prepared and sent to Wilson the draft for a reply which was quite rightly referred to by him as "sharp." It described the destruction of a merchant vessel without preliminary visit and search as "a wanton act unparalleled in naval warfare," and declared that the destruction of American ships or lives in such manner would be regarded as "a flagrant violation of neutral rights, as one offensive, if not hostile, to the United States." The key statement of determination to hold the German government to a "strict accountability" for the acts of the naval authorities, which Wilson may have suggested in conference the day before, is found in this draft.[2]

The following day—the 7th—upon reading in a newspaper the explanatory memorandum of the German government, Lansing seems to have had a sudden change of heart, for he now wrote—a "confidential" letter in his own hand—to the President:

"The memorandum impresses me as a strong presentation of the German case and removes some of the objectionable features of the declaration, if it is read without explanatory statements. In my opinion it makes the advisability of a sharp protest, or of any protest at all, open to question."[3]

It was not surprising that Lansing should have been

---

[1] Bryan was at this time in the West, making a speaking trip. He had returned by February 8th.

[2] From original document in the Wilson files.

[3] *Ibid.*

impressed by the strength of the German case, since he had himself, in earlier notes, argued that the British blockade was essentially a violation of the rights of neutral trade. In its note of December 26th the United States, as we have seen, had also admitted the principle of "self-preservation," or "manifest necessity," as justifying the conduct of Great Britain in these violations. The Germans were now retaliating, threatening neutral trade, and making the same claim of necessity.

Here was, then, the problem of reconciling Germany's "necessity" with England's. How was this to be done when each belligerent insisted upon determining for itself what its necessities were? When there was nowhere in the world any court of last resort?

Germany's contentions regarding her necessities were clear enough. If her enemies were to cut off her supplies of food and raw material from abroad while themselves receiving not only such articles, but the means of warfare itself as well, she would suffer starvation, privation, depletion of all her resources, while they would be able to equalize her technical superiority. Even more considerable successes in the field than she could now reasonably expect would not save her from eventual defeat. If peace did not come soon, some way must be found of altering the situation. The German navy was not equal to the task of breaking the blockade and opening the way to receive the goods Germany needed, but it offered a means of stopping the Allies from getting what they needed—by means of the submarine, a new weapon, effective only under conditions not foreseen by previous international law. If the flow of munitions could be stopped, the disadvantage of the British blockade might be equalized.

Lansing's letter to Wilson on the 7th indicated that he appreciated much of the logic of the German case; but could he yield to it as he had yielded to the English? It was the horrible dilemma of the legalist faced by situations for which there were no precedents. The difficulties no doubt led to his suggestion that "any protest at all" was "open to question."

Nevertheless, three days later, on February 10th the communication was sent.[1] An incident had occurred which furnished Lansing with the kind of tension-easing compromise that diplomats love. No man was ever more partial to impartial gestures than Lansing. The German statement charging the use of neutral flags by British ships had, just at this crisis, received startling confirmation. Although the German war-zone proclamation was not to go into effect until February 18th, the captain of the *Lusitania* hoisted an American flag upon approaching the Irish coast on February 5th.[2]

Lansing was thus furnished with an opportunity to attenuate the impression made by the protest to Germany against her war-zone proclamation—or make the Germans believe we were being equally strict with Great Britain—by issuing a simultaneous protest to Great Britain against her use of neutral flags.[3]

The President had already worked over Lansing's draft of the note to Germany. We have before us the document itself, bearing his corrections in his pencilled script and in stenographic notes. He had, for example, changed the sentence asserting that he "could not but view" the act of the Germans as "hostile to the United States," to "deliberately unfriendly." On February 8th, with the flag problem in mind, he wrote out a revision on his own typewriter somewhat softening it down and adding new paragraphs denying that the American attitude toward British

---

[1] *Foreign Relations of the United States*, Supplement, 1915, pp. 98–100.

[2] Colonel House, who was aboard the ship, foresaw "many possible complications from this incident," but remarks, "fortunately, I was not an eye-witness to it." (*The Intimate Papers of Colonel House*, Vol. I, p. 361.)

[3] *Foreign Relations of the United States*, Supplement, 1915, pp. 100–101.

Draft Feby 6/15
Robert Lansing

American Ambassador,

Berlin.

Please immediately address a note to the German Government ~~in the sense of~~ the following ~~to~~ effect:

The Department ~~has~~ having had its attention directed to ~~a~~ the
~~report in the press that~~ *proclamation of* the German Admiralty, on February *issued*
fourth ~~issued a declaration~~ that the waters around the
British Isles, including the whole of the English Channel,
considered as comprised within the seat of war;
are to be ~~a war zone after the eighteenth instant;~~ that *all enemy*
merchant vessels ~~every enemy ship~~ found in ~~this war zone~~ *these waters after the eighteenth instant* will be destroyed;
and that neutral ships are in danger, as on account of the
misuse of neutral flags ordered by the British Government on
January thirty-first and the hazards of naval warfare, it
cannot always be avoided that attacks meant for enemy ships
endanger neutral ships. The declaration adds that shipping
around the Shetland Islands in the eastern basin of the
North Sea and in a strip of at least thirty miles in breadth
along the Dutch coast is endangered in the same way.

3/1

If the Imperial German Government should act upon such presumption and destroy on the high seas an American vessel or the lives of American citizens, the Government of the United States could not but view the act as a flagrant violation of neutral rights, ~~as one~~ *seriously* offensive, if not ~~hostile,~~ *deliberately unfriendly* to the United States.

If such a deplorable situation should arise the Government of the United States would be constrained to hold the Imperial German Government to a strict accountability for ~~the~~ *Such an* unwarranted act of their naval authorities and to take ~~the measures~~ *any steps it might be* necessary to *take to* safeguard American lives and property and to secure to American citizens the full enjoyment of their rights on the high seas.

The Government of the United States, in view of these considerations, expresses the confident hope and expectation that the Imperial German Government *can &* will give assurance that ~~the citizens~~ American citizens and their vessels will not be molested by the naval forces of Germany other than by visit and search though the vessels may be traversing the sea area *delimited* ~~prescribed~~ in the declaration of the German Admiralty.

First and last pages of Robert Lansing's draft of February 6, 1915, for the note sent to Germany on February 10, 1915. Corrected in the President's handwriting and shorthand. The last page contains the momentous phrase "strict accountability."

violation of neutral rights was open to any criticism and asserting that we held all governments "responsible in the proper way for any untoward effects upon American shipping which the accepted principles of international law do not justify." The keynote phrase, "strict accountability," was retained. The last brief paragraph of the note as sent contained the important statement that representations were being made to the British government "in respect to the unwarranted use of the American flag for the protection of British ships."[1]

It is not easy to see how the representations to Great Britain could be regarded as a real offset to the note to Germany. If the British agreed not to use the American flag at all, the possibility of trouble over German acts in the war zone would have been little reduced. Moreover the note to the British in attempting to draw the difficult legal distinction between occasional and general use of the flag was pretty indefinite. In an apologetic telegram to House on February 13th, Wilson said:

"I regretted the necessity of sending the note about the unauthorized use of our flag, but it could not be avoided, for sooner or later, the use of the flag plays directly in the hands of Germany in their extraordinary threat to destroy commerce."

As a matter of fact, the flag note was a mere gesture to which the British paid little attention and which we had no real legal grounds for following up. They simply asserted their view of the right to use neutral flags and the Germans' lack of right to sink a ship without verifying its nationality by visit and search.[2]

Whatever may have been the effect of these notes on the crisis itself—which, as events proved, was practically nil—

---

[1]Bryan, who had returned to Washington, signed both notes, although he had had no hand in drafting either.

[2]*Foreign Relations of the United States*, Supplement, 1915, pp. 117–118.

they made, in general, a most favourable impression upon public opinion in the United States—at least upon that dominant public opinion which sympathized with the cause of the Allies. It was felt that the President had got around a dangerous corner. He had avoided "possibilities of the utmost gravity."

"Both notes are a wholesome expression of what should be the firm policy of neutral nations to resist at every point the attempts of belligerents to extend the area of disturbance due to war and to encroach upon the rights of neutrals."[1]

Whatever the approval in America—and his prestige as a leader was a most important element in all of these negotiations—the President was deeply troubled by the gathering difficulties.

"The last two weeks," he wrote on February 14th, "have been like a fever . . . no one who did not sit daily here with me, each anxious twenty-four hours through, could possibly realize the constant strain upon our vigilance and upon our judgement entailed by the rapidly varied conditions both 'on the Hill' (that is, in Congress) and in the war area. Together, England and Germany are likely to drive us crazy, because it looks oftentimes as if they were crazy themselves, the unnecessary provocations they invent. To keep cool heads and handle each matter composedly and without excitement as it arises, seeking to see each thing in the large, in the light of what is likely to happen as well as in the light of what is happening now, involves a nervous expenditure such as I never dreamed of, and drives every private matter into the background to wait for a time of exemption from these things which never comes. I go to bed every night absolutely exhausted, trying not to think about anything, and with all my nerves

---

[1]Editorial in the New York *Times*, headed "Our Diplomacy at Its Best," February 13, 1915.

deadened, my own individuality as it were blotted out. . . .

"I am very well, though worn out. I never knew before that it was possible, when necessary, for a man to lose his own personal existence, seem even to himself to have no individual life apart from his official duties. But it is possible. It has happened . . ."[1]

Wilson's problems and those of the United States were in some ways more difficult than those of the nations actively at war. The belligerents had transcended all law and appealed to the arbitrament of war. But Wilson was still seeking to maintain order and reason in a world gone mad: and that without dependable sanctions either of law or of precedent. It was not only the nations at war that felt themselves dominated by "manifest necessity." America also had its necessities and compulsions—as, for example, the immediate domestic necessity of restoring the trade interrupted by the war, which had led us to accommodations with the Allies who commanded the seas.[2] This immediate necessity had been met; our trade with the Allies promised to offset the loss of trade with Germany. We had thus readjusted our economic position once without great loss, but at the cost of surrendering neutral rights which we had begun by asserting; now we were faced, unless we surrendered more rights, or reversed our policy toward Great Britain, with the practical certainty of a conflict with Germany. The German government had a logical case in asserting that it would "rely on the neutrals who have hitherto tacitly or under protest submitted to the consequences detrimental to themselves of England's war of famine to display not less tolerance toward Germany, even if the German measures constitute

---

[1] Woodrow Wilson to Mary A. Hulbert.

[2] It is doubtful if America can ever in future times remain neutral with any other nation in control of the seas.

new forms of maritime war, as has hitherto been the case with the English measures."[1]

Indeed, if the British pleaded the size and complexity of cargoes and the vulnerability of a stopped warship to submarine attack as reasons for departure from the old rules of visit and search, why should not the Germans similarly plead the vulnerability of a stopped submarine? Was the geographical position of England any better excuse for an irregular kind of blockade than the powerlessness of Germany to get at England by regular methods?

No doubt the President in the beginning—and Bryan and Lansing as well—was led more deeply into the difficulty by a failure to appreciate properly the immense potency of the economic forces involved. The training of both Wilson and Bryan had been political: Wilson's interests, all his life, had been in political adjustments and forms. In the domestic field he had indeed awakened to the importance of economic forces, and the keynote of his policy had been governmental regulation, as of banking, railroads, trusts. When the international crisis, the world war, had leaped at him unawares, his first instinctive reaction, like that of Bryan, was to attempt a similar control of economic forces—as in the note advising against loans to the Allies. But he was soon forced by the threat of economic disaster in America, not less than by the lack of any dependable international rules or sanctions, to fall back upon the policy of maintaining political and legalistic neutrality. It plainly did not satisfy him—but there was always the hope that something might turn up—some peace movement—which would relieve the situation before it became hopeless.

Whatever the political or legalistic correctness of the procedure of the United States government, which the President and Mr. Lansing insisted upon, the *unequal*

---

[1]February 17, 1915. *Foreign Relations of the United States*, Supplement, 1915, p. 113.

effects of our neutrality were brought home in the German reply on February 16th to the note of February 10th.

"Conceded that it is the formal right of neutrals not to protect their legitimate trade with Germany and even to allow themselves knowingly and willingly to be induced by England to restrict such trade, it is on the other hand not less their good right, although unfortunately not exercised, to stop trade in contraband, especially the trade in arms, with Germany's enemies."[1]

The implication here, though this is not insisted upon in view of the lack of legal grounds, is that an embargo on arms would be one consideration inducing Germany to abandon her projected measures for stopping that trade. The other consideration is more clearly stated:

". . . should the American government in particular find a way to bring about the observation of the Declaration of London on the part of the powers at war with Germany and thereby to render possible for Germany the legitimate supply of foodstuffs and industrial raw materials, the German government . . . would gladly draw the necessary conclusions . . ."[2]

But the insistence upon the Declaration of London had, as we have seen, already been abandoned, and with American economic life now deeply involved in the munitions industry, what chance was there for an embargo on arms?

In this crisis both Bryan and Lansing seem to have groped rather wildly for another expedient for relieving the tension. Mention in the German note of the use of mines in the North Sea, which had long been a vexed question, became the basis of a memorandum sent by Lansing to Bryan, suggesting that a vigorous protest be made to all belligerents against their indiscriminate use of

---

[1]Sent February 17th. *Foreign Relations of the United States*, Supplement, 1915, p. 113.
[2]*Ibid.*, p. 115.

mines. It probably struck him as a chance for another excellent gesture of impartial criticism of the methods of warfare of both belligerents. Bryan, who was now as eager to avoid a conflict with Germany as he had been, a little earlier, to avoid a conflict with Great Britain, heartily endorsed Lansing's idea and forwarded it to the President. He was ready to approve almost any step that promised to reduce the growing horror of the war.

But Wilson was skeptical; he answered Bryan on February 19th:

"I need not say that I heartily sympathize with the spirit and purpose of Mr. Lansing's note to you, but these thoughts occur to me:

"1. It is a little late to protest against these things, for they have gone on now for a long time—almost since the beginning of the war;

"2. We have been doing a great deal of protesting, and 'vigorous' protests are apt to be regarded as logically leading to action.

"Would it not be well to ask Mr. Lansing to draw up identical notes setting the matter forth in a very convincing way, from the points of view both of fact and of law, as a strong *argument* and a suggestion as to the best means of removing present grounds of irritation?"

Lansing at once drafted an identical communication to Great Britain and Germany criticizing the use of mines and laying down the lines of a suggested compromise, based upon a telegram from Page on February 17th[1] which Bryan believed furnished a ray of hope.[2] The two countries were to agree on restrictions in the use of mines, submarines, and neutral flags, and for the admission of food into Germany under American supervision. Wilson worked over Lansing's draft with characteristic thoroughness,

---

[1] See *Foreign Relations of the United States*, Supplement, 1915, p. 111.
[2] *Ibid.*, W. J. Bryan to Walter H. Page, telegram, February 19, 1915.

using both his typewriter and his pen. The document indeed gives evidence of the care bestowed upon it by all three men—the President, Bryan, and Lansing. It was sent to both nations on February 20th.[1]

It is probable that Wilson realized the inadequacy of this note, in which Germany was held to a full respect for neutral rights while England was to be held only on one limited point, for he inserted in his own hand the passage expressing "the hope that it may draw forth the views and elicit the suggestions of the British and German governments." In short, it might bring about a discussion of the issues involved, and that, once begun, might even lay the foundations for the active consideration of peace, upon which Wilson had set his hopes.

So keen was the President's interest that he sent a telegram to Colonel House on the same day, in which he not only cautioned House against the dilatory tactics of the British on the subject of peace, but emphasized the importance of the note of the 20th.[2]

A note in Colonel House's diary indicates that but for this direct appeal by the President, Page would have given the proposal no personal support at all. After he and House had solemnly discussed the note from the point of view of whether or not "its acceptance [would be] favourable to the British government," Page agreed reluctantly to take it up personally with Grey, "though one could see he had no stomach for it."[3] His argument was evidently half-hearted and ineffective.

Any hopes of success entertained at Washington were dashed almost at once. On the very evening of the 20th arrived Page's telegram stating that he saw no ray of hope in the proposition, as "it is practically certain that Eng-

---

[1] *Foreign Relations of the United States*, Supplement, 1915, pp. 119–120.
[2] See pp. 312–313 this volume for the entire cablegram.
[3] *The Intimate Papers of Colonel House*, Vol. I, p. 445.

land will prevent everything from entering Germany."[1] Not long afterwards Page's forecast was borne out. The British and French ambassadors on March 1st presented practically identical notifications of the intention of their governments "to prevent commodities of any kind from reaching or leaving Germany."[2]

The replies from both belligerents to the note of February 20th indicated that while the United States might talk about the legalities of neutrality, both Great Britain and Germany, sweating under the burdens and bitterness of the war, were thinking only about the effects of neutrality. The Germans were not inclined to consider the admission of food alone as an adequate compensation for abandoning the submarine campaign, but would expect to get raw materials as well.[3] And the British would not consider any agreement at all.[4] The British alleged atrocities as an excuse for the severities of the blockade and the utter disregard of neutral rights. Bringing these charges into the case gave it a scope precluding any possibility of settlement—certainly beyond the possibility of further intervention by the United States. We might legally discuss the treatment of contraband, the laying of mines, various forms of interference with ships, the use of our flag, and so forth, with the belligerents, since they concerned us; but we could not properly talk with them about actions which affected only each other.

Those actions became steadily more desperate: the debate more bellicose. During late February and nearly all of March 1915 the diplomats of the world, especially our own, seemed to be entangling themselves more and more inextricably in hopeless webs of a legalism that was based

---

[1] *Foreign Relations of the United States*, Supplement, 1915, pp. 118–119.

[2] *Ibid.*, pp. 127–128.

[3] *Foreign Relations of the United States*, Supplement, 1915, pp. 129–130. Note dated February 28, sent March 1st.

[4] March 15, 1915. *Ibid.*, pp. 140–142.

upon little or no reality—while thoughtful men in America looked on with increasing horror lest some disastrous accident, sure sooner or later to befall, might plunge us also into the maelstrom. We have a glimpse of the "poor President" burning the midnight oil over futile cipher dispatches.

"The poor President has had an epidemic of cipher dispatches—one to *make* last night, which took him until nearly midnight, and two to read today which took him every spare moment between Church, & driving and dinner—and when he came to dinner the second was not quite worked out yet."[1]

We find Lansing spinning empty logic based upon the traditions of a world that had utterly vanished—a world that had not known aëroplanes, or the transmission of information by radio, or submarines, or leviathan ships—trying to strait-jacket a war bursting with new devices into the legalisms of 1864 or 1870 or 1898. There was not even agreement among his own associates. We find blunt Garrison, a good lawyer himself, writing in a memorandum for the President:

"What I endeavored to express in cabinet and fear that I failed to do and what I now wish to sum up in as few words as possible is this:

"Great Britain has not in any proper fashion declared a blockade. She has no right to do the things that she orders her own authorities to do in the Order in Council, even if she had declared a blockade. . . . I think that her whole Order in Council contravenes international law and she should be so notified and be told that we will hold her to 'strict accountability,' that being the same phrase which we used to Germany when we informed her of the in-

---

[1]Mrs. E. T. Brown, a guest at the White House, to Mrs. H. S. Mitchell, February 21, 1915.

admissibility of her departure from international law and the consequences therefor."[1]

We find Bryan, with almost no hand in the discussion, befuddled by legalisms, dreaming of peace and anxiously watching the voters of the Middle West. As for the two other men most concerned with the diplomatic controversies of the time, we find Page, our most important representative on the firing line, actually taking the part of our chief diplomatic opponent, playing the game of the British; and Colonel House, wandering anxiously about Europe seeking peace, being used by the Allies as a pawn in their deliberate and most effective policy of delay.

What of the President? During most of March, while each group of belligerents was arguing that its departures from the rules of neutrality were less serious than those of its enemies, Wilson apparently left the debate largely to the lawyers of the State Department. But there is clear evidence that he saw more deeply into the realities of the situation than most of his associates. He could put his finger exactly upon one of the chief difficulties that stood in the way of carrying out his policy of neutrality:

"He said . . . that the conditions of war had radically changed, but the rules had not."[2]

Nor do we find him being driven to the decision, which large numbers of his countrymen were then heatedly making, as to which side was absolutely right and which absolutely wrong.

"Both sides," he wrote on March 7th, "are seeing red on the other side of the sea, and neutral rights are left, for the time being, out of their reckoning altogether. They listen to necessity (and to necessity as they interpret it), not to reason, and there is therefore no way of calculating

---

[1] March 20, 1915.

[2] President Wilson to the newspaper men at the White House, March 2, 1915. Report in the New York *Times*, March 3, 1915.

or preparing for anything. That is what makes the situation such a strain on the nerves, such an exaction on the judgement."[1]

It is terrifying, but what can one do but wait?

"One waits for he does not know what, and must act amidst a scene that shifts without notice, without precedent. In such circumstances it is clearly impossible for me to get away from Washington to go to the Pacific coast, or anywhere else.[2] I must stay where I can, as nearly as may be, keep in touch with all the elements all the time,— a large order!"[3]

Was there nothing that he could do? There were remote possibilities in some peace move. Colonel House's letter of March 9th had enclosed an encouraging statement from Zimmermann:

"You may be sure, as I said before, that Germany's wish for a permanent peace is as sincere as your own. If England would consent to give up her claim to a monopoly on the seas together with her two to one power standard, I think it might be a good beginning."

Wilson had already urged haste upon House and had warned him not to let the British delay him:

". . . you cannot go too far in allowing the English government to determine when it is best to go to Germany because they naturally desire to await some time when they have the advantage because of events in the field or elsewhere."[4]

But both Page and House were being powerfully influenced by the British in behalf of the policy of delay. Page was even declaring that the war, owing to the British

---

[1]Woodrow Wilson to Mary A. Hulbert.

[2]He had thought of attending the Panama-Pacific International Exposition in California.

[3]Woodrow Wilson to Mary A. Hulbert.

[4]February 20, 1915.

reprisals against Germany, was approaching its "final stage"[1] and with great earnestness urged that America make no move, contenting itself with "a friendly inquiry." Even House was critical of Page's "pro-British argument."

"Yesterday, when Page was drawing up his dispatch to the President asking that he do nothing for the moment concerning the proposed blockade of Germany, he had a lot of things in it which I advised eliminating. It was the strongest sort of pro-British argument, and I knew it would weaken his influence both with the State Department and with the President. He reluctantly cut it down to a short statement . . ."[2]

When a note was finally dispatched to the British on March 30th offering very moderate criticisms of the new blockade policy,[3] Grey delayed even a preliminary reply until June 17th[4] and a final reply until July 23rd[5]—nearly four months, at a time when a week was an age. Page explained to Wilson—a remark full of both conscious and unconscious irony:

"The Lord Chancellor said to me, in private conversation: 'We have necessity on our side; you have the law—what is left of it—on your side: we'll not seriously quarrel.' The Prime Minister told a friend of his, who told me, that as a lawyer he greatly admired that document. 'The emphasis was put on the right place exactly.' They are embarrassed in making an answer."[6]

---

[1]Walter H. Page to Woodrow Wilson, telegram, March 3, 1915.

[2]Colonel House's diary entry on March 4, 1915. *The Intimate Papers of Colonel House*, Vol. I, p. 456.

[3]*Foreign Relations of the United States*, Supplement, 1915, pp. 152–156.

[4]Sent June 22nd. *Ibid.*, pp. 443–446.

[5]Sent July 24th. *Foreign Relations of the United States*, Supplement, 1915, pp. 168–171.

[6]Walter H. Page to Woodrow Wilson, April 25, 1915. Viscount Haldane was Lord Chancellor. H. H. Asquith was Prime Minister.

Time was on the side of the Allies! It enabled them to perfect their system for the control of trade: and every added day increased the economic dependence of the United States upon the shipment of war materials to the Allies—thus making our commitment more and more inevitable. Moreover, with German submarines abroad in the seas there might any day occur a catastrophe that would horrify the world and further convince wavering American opinion.

There were indeed feeble stirrings of protest from European neutrals (to add to those of South America). All were protesting against the Allies' blockade orders as they had against the German submarine announcement —much as the United States had done. Further, they dropped broad hints—especially Sweden—of readiness to coöperate with the United States in asserting neutral rights against both groups of belligerents.[1] Some of Wilson's friends saw here another opportunity to put him at the head of a combination of neutral powers for the defense of their common interests. But the same economic processes were at work among these neutrals as in America: the divided forces: and the responses of the United States were dilatory and noncommittal.[2]

In the meantime, whatever political aloofness we might assume, however much the President or America might hate the thought of war, the dreadful possibilities of our own involvement in a world dwarfed into a new intimacy by a century of technical progress were steadily increasing. At any moment, with German submarines abroad in waters crowded with ships, the crisis might occur. Already several ships had been sunk—Wilson concerned himself anxiously about one of them, the *William P. Frye*—and

---

[1]See *Foreign Relations of the United States*, Supplement, 1914, pp. 472–473.

[2]Exchanges of notes between the United States and the Swedish government dragged on through 1915. See *Foreign Relations of the United States*, Supplement, 1915.

on March 28th, when the British ship *Falaba* went down, an American, Leon C. Thrasher, was drowned.

II. AMERICAN LIFE LOST. THE CRISES OF THE "FALABA," THE "CUSHING," AND THE "GULFLIGHT"

The news of the sinking of the British ship *Falaba* flashed across America like an electric shock. Great commotion in the American press: great perturbation at Washington. The necessity of making good the warning that we should hold the Germans to "strict accountability" for the destruction of American lives and property had arrived.

Lansing reacted, as was his habit, sharply. He wanted instant and vigorous action. He considered that we were "dealing with a tragedy," and that there was no "pleasant way" of handling it.

". . . American public opinion will never stand for a colorless or timid presentation of a case, in which an American has been killed by an atrocious act of lawlessness."[1]

Bryan on his part was profoundly disturbed. It might well mean war. He began to fight for time, urging the President in a letter on April 6th to await further information and confessed that he was "very much worried" about the case. He followed this up with vigorous letters on the 7th and 8th, raising the difficult problem of the arming of merchant ships, and whether or not "the fact that the vessel was unarmed was known to the commander of the submarine."

"I feel," he wrote, "that this is the most delicate question we have had to meet—not only because it involves the loss of a human life, but because we are dealing with a nation whose people have been made sensitive by

[1] Robert Lansing to W. J. Bryan, April 5, 1915, forwarded by Bryan to the President.

the course we have pursued in the matter of the export of arms—a course not only entirely consistent with neutrality, but a course compelled by neutrality."

He went on to discuss anxiously the effect of a harsh note upon American opinion:

"We are aware, however, that a large element of our population, influenced by sympathy with the German side, has criticised us violently . . . Whatever we do in this Thrasher case will be viewed with suspicion and we must, therefore, be the more careful to take a position which will be not only defensible but, if possible, so obviously defensible as to appeal to the judgement of the entire country."

And finally, this keen judge of popular opinion argued:

"I am sure that the almost unanimous desire of our country is that we shall not become involved in this war and I cannot help feeling that it would be a sacrifice of the interests of all the people to allow one man, acting purely for himself and his own interests, and without consulting his government, to involve the entire nation in difficulty when he had ample warning of the risks which he assumed."[1]

In his letter of the 8th he urged the President to take the matter up in cabinet meeting "so that we can get the opinions from as many angles as possible."

Here were the elements of Bryan's doctrines which he was to continue to advocate and defend—upon which he was finally to part company with the President and the administration.

In the meantime Lansing was vigorously countering Bryan's doubts and arguments: and on the 10th he sent to the President an opinion of the joint State and Navy Neutrality Board that the procedure of German submarines under the war-zone pronouncement had no justifi-

[1] April 7, 1918.

cation whatever under international law and that the action taken in this case was "not only illegal but revoltingly inhuman."

To complicate the situation, the German ambassador on April 4th sent a memorandum criticizing, rather sharply, American neutrality in general. After pointing out our government's failure to secure observance, by Great Britain, of what we proclaimed to be our rights, from which the German embassy "must . . . assume that the United States government acquiesces in the violations of international law by Great Britain," the memorandum went on to deal with the question of export of munitions of war to the Allies, urging that "in questions of neutrality it is necessary to take into consideration not only the formal aspect of the case, but also the spirit in which the neutrality is carried out," and quoting a statement to this effect by Wilson in connection with the embargo on shipment of arms to Mexico. The memorandum contained no mention of the submarine warfare, but the connection was obvious enough; Germany expected us either to take as strong a stand against Great Britain as against her or to display a like acquiescence in her departures from international law.[1]

But if the Germans were critical of Wilson's neutrality policies, the French and the British were equally so. There was no pleasing anybody!

". . . there is a feeling, which I am sorry to say is almost universal throughout France, that you, personally, are inclined to be pro-German. . . .

"They also believe that it is your purpose to attempt to intervene in order to save Germany."[2]

And the British were complaining:

"When German submarines are sinking merchant ships

---

[1] *Foreign Relations of the United States*, Supplement, 1915, pp. 157-158.
[2] E. M. House to Woodrow Wilson, April 17, 1915.

and drowning non-combatant crews and passengers off our coasts, public opinion is naturally indignant at the idea of goods to and from Germany whether through neutral ports or not passing our doors openly and un-hindered."[1]

In this utter confusion of advice and criticism, Wilson was striving earnestly for calmness and impartiality. In several brief public addresses of this period we find him pouring out his soul to the public with profound sincerity of feeling. More than in any personal letters, as often before, he revealed his own inner ideals and purposes. What he was seeking was steadfastness, self-possession, calmness of view and of action. Before the *Falaba* was sunk he spoke, on March 25th, to the Southern Methodist Conference, referring to those present as "a council of peace," and in solemn earnestness proclaiming "the single supreme plan of peace, the revelation of our Lord and Savior, Jesus Christ, because wars will never have any ending until men cease to hate one another, cease to be jealous of one another, get that feeling of reality in the brotherhood of mankind which is the only bond that can make us think justly of one another and act righteously before God Himself."

He then went on to recommend to hot-heads who were trying to "rock the boat" that they should consider "the great steadfast body of self-possessed Americans not to be hurried into any unconsidered line of action, sure that when you are right you can be calm, sure that when the quarrel is none of yours you can be impartial . . ."

And he concluded with an eloquent appeal for the support and confidence of the American people:

"I need not tell you that the President by himself is absolutely nothing. The President is what the American

---

[1]Sir Edward Grey to E. M. House, a letter which House sent to the President on April 18, 1915.

nation sustains, and if it does not sustain him, then his power is contemptible and insignificant. If I can speak for you and represent you and in some sense hand on the moral forces that you represent, then I am indeed powerful."[1]

In a later address he again emphasized the need of impartiality:

"No man is wise enough to pronounce judgement . . .

". . . no man has the key to this confusion, no man can see the outcome, but every man can keep his own spirit prepared to contribute to the net result when the outcome displays itself."[2]

As the crisis developed he became still more earnest in counselling self-possession, steadiness, and the far look. Addressing the Daughters of the American Revolution on April 19th, he dared to say to those jingoistic, super-patriotic ladies:

"There are many tests by which a nation makes proof of its greatness, but it seems to me the supreme test is self-possession, and the power to resist excitement, to think calmly, to think in moments of difficulty as clearly as it would think in moments of ease . . ."[3]

The next day he told the representatives of the Associated Press in New York:

"The basis of neutrality, gentlemen, is not indifference; it is not self-interest. The basis of neutrality is sympathy for mankind. It is fairness, it is good will, at bottom. It is impartiality of spirit and of judgement."

And, as indicating his hope of the ultimate purpose of America's neutrality, he said:

"We are the mediating nation of the world."

Forecasting his stand at the height of the crisis, fore-

---

[1] *The Public Papers of Woodrow Wilson*, Vol. III, pp. 287–288.
[2] April 8, 1915. *Ibid.*, pp. 297–298.
[3] *The Public Papers of Woodrow Wilson*, Vol. III, pp. 299–300.

shadowing his "too proud to fight" address, he observed:

"My interest in the neutrality of the United States is not the petty desire to keep out of trouble. . . . I am interested in neutrality because there is something so much greater to do than fight; there is a distinction waiting for this nation that no nation has ever yet got. That is the distinction of absolute self-control and self-mastery."

The man to admire, he said, is not the man who fights at the drop of the hat, but "the self-mastered man who watches you with calm eye and comes in only when you have carried the thing so far that you must be disposed of."[1]

Of course, in the last words, he touched upon the difficult point in his own philosophy. When should the self-possessed man or nation, in all calm judgement, decide that the limit of inaction had been reached? Coming down to particular cases, had it been reached, so far as Germany was concerned, with the *Falaba* incident? Would another and still another such incident constitute the limit of endurance? Would the spectacular holocaust of the sinking of a great liner carrying hundreds of Americans warrant the self-possessed nation in proceeding deliberately to action? How many lives, how many ships, should make up the score requiring Germany to be told "you have carried the thing so far that you must be disposed of"? These were the questions which Wilson, however successful his effort at self-mastery, had from now on to face.

Days were passing, full of anxiety for the President:

". . . for two weeks . . . every hour of my time, every bit of my strength has been used, and more than exhausted . . .

"I keep well, keep going, and, I think, with undiminished force, but it is costing all the while, I imagine, just a little more than I have without drawing on reserves."[2]

---

[1] *The Public Papers of Woodrow Wilson*, Vol. III, pp. 303–306.
[2] Woodrow Wilson to Mary A. Hulbert, April 21, 1915.

Bryan was even more disturbed and anxious than the President. On the 19th he wrote a bolder appeal to Wilson than he had yet ventured. He argued that the Germans were "not . . . unreasonable," in asking (1) why Americans should travel on British ships; (2) how we could complain of accidents to American ships while British ships used our flag; and (3) why the drowning of a few people should provoke more irritation than the starvation of a whole nation. He adjured Wilson:

"If we are to prove our neutrality—and unless we do we are likely to be drawn into the conflict by the growing feeling in Germany—it seems to me we must prevent the misuse of our flag and warn Americans not to use British vessels in the war zone unless we can bring pressure on Gt. B. to withdraw [the] threat about making bread or food contraband."

As for the "pressure" to be brought on Great Britain, he made no suggestion; having endorsed the official doctrine regarding the export of munitions,[1] he could not suggest interfering with it, though he observed that it "is likely to get us into trouble." He went on to discuss the prospects for peace, returning to his ideas of 1914. He wrote:

"I doubt if it [is] wise to propose terms but I feel & have felt for some time, that we should urge the Allies to consent to a conference at which terms shall be discussed."

He referred, though not by name, to the activities of Colonel House, then in Europe, trying vainly for some peace opening:

"I doubt if secret proposals will suffice—a *public* appeal strongly worded might have effect, and would it not be justified considering the nature of the contest and our

---

[1] Indeed, he signed the letter to the German ambassador of April 21, 1915, treating the export of munitions as a closed question. *Foreign Relations of the United States,* Supplement, 1915, pp. 160–162.

relation to the nations at war? All the neutral nations I am sure would at once endorse it and it might end the war—I do not see that it could do harm."

Bryan concluded by agreeing with Münsterberg, upon whose letter he had commented, that "*you* are the one to act," and he quoted characteristically from the Scriptures:

"'Who knoweth whether thou art come to the Kingdom for such a time as this!'"

It was hard to move Wilson by any of these pleas. With the feeling what it was in Europe—all the nations, as he had been writing, "seeing red"—he doubted, as we shall see elsewhere, that the time for peace offers had arrived. With such bitter diversities of opinion developing even in America, decisive action might precipitate us also into the universal madness. There was "something so much greater to do than fight." There might be other ways out. He was hoping, though now with considerable impatience, that Colonel House would accomplish something in Europe.

Nevertheless it was plain that something must be done or said, for at any moment there might be new sinkings, more deaths, less excusable tragedies. After much thought the President gave instructions to Lansing to draft a note to Germany on the *Falaba* case much along the lines of the Neutrality Board's opinion—that is, one marked by severity. Bryan had known the drift of the President's thinking and in a letter on April 23rd protested even more vigorously than before:

"As I have not been able to reach the conclusion to which you have arrived in this case I feel it my duty to set forth the situation as I see it."

In this letter he cried out at the contrast between such sharp action with regard to Germany and our conduct toward Great Britain. He recurred to the food-submarine compromise, declaring:

"We suggested the admission of food and the abandonment of torpedo attacks upon merchant vessels; Germany seemed willing to negotiate but Great Britain refused to consider the proposition. I fear that denunciation of one and silence as to the other will be construed by some as partiality. You do not make allowance for the fact that we were notified of the intended use of the submarine, or for the fact that Thrasher knowingly took the risk of travelling on an enemy ship. . . . Our people will, I believe, be slow to admit the right of a citizen to involve his country in war when by ordinary care he could have avoided danger."

Again he pled for some effort to initiate a peace movement:

"Believing that such a note as you propose is, under the conditions that now exist, likely to bring on a crisis, I venture to suggest an alternative, namely, an appeal to the nations at war to consider terms of peace. We can not justify waiting until both sides, or even one side, ask for mediation, and as a neutral we can not have in mind the wishes of one side more than the wishes of the other side. The neutral nations have both rights and duties, and we are the neutral nation looked to to give expression to these."

He summed up eloquently:

"Nearly nine months have passed since the war began and after the expenditure of over ten billion dollars and the sacrifice of several millions of the flower of Europe the war is a draw. Surely the most sanguinary ought to be satisfied with the slaughter. I submit that it is this nation's right and duty to make, not a secret, but an open appeal for the acceptance of mediation. All the neutral nations would support the appeal—several have suggested it. Our own interests justify it—we may be drawn into the conflict if it continues. Our obligation to the neutral nations demands it. Our friendship for the nations at war requires it. They can not reason calmly and neither side is in a position to ask for mediation. As the well-wisher of all we should act: as the leader of the peace propaganda we should act: as the greatest Christian nation we should act—we can not avoid the responsibility. The loss of one American, who might have avoided death, is as nothing compared with the tens of thousands who are dying daily in this 'causeless war.' Is it not better to try to bring peace for the benefit of the whole world than to risk the provoking of war on account of one man?"

It was the beginning of the break between the two men. Bryan grew haggard and lost sleep. He agonized to his wife:

"Mary, what does the President mean! *Why* can't he see that by keeping open the way for mediation and arbitration, he has an opportunity to do the greatest work man can do! I cannot understand his attitude."[1]

Wilson replied to Bryan on April 28th, a letter that may be called decisive in their relationships, foreshadowing the break that was soon to come.

April 28, 1915

MY DEAR MR. SECRETARY,

I have thought a great deal about the contents of the letter you wrote me (the letter written in your own hand) about the Thrasher case. It of course made a deep impression on me.

As I told you yesterday at cabinet, I am not at all confident that we are on the right track in considering such a note as I outlined for Mr. Lansing to work on. I am not sure that my outline really expressed what I would myself say in the note, for, after all, the character of a note is chiefly in the way the thing is said and the points developed. Perhaps it is not necessary to make formal representations in the matter at all.

What I have been thinking about most is your alternative proposition, that we publicly call upon the belligerents to end the war.

---

[1] *The Memoirs of William Jennings Bryan*, pp. 420–421.

I wish I could see it as you do. But in view of what House writes me I cannot. It is known to every government concerned that we believe the war should be ended and that we speak for all neutral nations in that wish. It is known to them that we are seeking to help and that anything they want to say to one another which they are too proud or too prudent to say directly and officially they can say privately through us. They are at present most appreciative and cordial,—ready to accept help when they can accept it. We know their minds and we know their difficulties. They are dependent upon their own public opinion (even Germany) and we know what that opinion is. To insist now would be futile and would probably be offensive. We would lose such influence as we have for peace.

I am afraid, Mr. Secretary, that there is much in this that will seem to you disputable; but I can only state my conviction in the matter, and God knows I have searched my mind and conscience both to get the best, the nearest approach to wisdom, there is in them.

With warmest regard and appreciation,

Faithfully yours,

WOODROW WILSON

Whether America protested, or made peace offers, or merely stood aside in horror, events in Europe pursued their relentless course. It was War, irresistible, irrational, overwhelming. Two days later, the 30th, while the President was toiling over the note regarding the *Falaba* that Lansing had drafted, came the flashing news of an attack on an American steamship, the *Cushing*, by a German aëroplane,[1] and three days later, on May 1st, another American ship, the tanker *Gulflight*, was torpedoed with the loss of several American lives.[2]

Had the moment come when Wilson was to say to the combatants, or to one of them, as he envisioned saying: "You have carried the thing so far that you must be disposed of"?

---

[1] *Foreign Relations of the United States*, Supplement, 1915, p. 378. No lives were lost.

[2] *Ibid.* The news did not reach Washington officially until May 3rd: but press dispatches were shown to the President on the 2nd.

CHAPTER VI

WILSON'S EARLY PEACE EFFORTS

The time has come for great things. These are days big with destiny for the United States, as for the other nations of the world.

Letter to Frank E. Doremus, September 4, 1914.

. . . it is the especial wish and longing of the people of the United States, in prayer and counsel and all friendliness, to serve the cause of peace . . .

Proclamation of October 4, 1914, designating a Day of Prayer.

We are the champions of peace and of concord . . . it is our dearest present hope that this character and reputation may presently, in God's providence, bring us an opportunity such as has seldom been vouchsafed any nation, the opportunity to counsel and obtain peace in the world and reconciliation and a healing settlement of many a matter that has cooled and interrupted the friendship of nations.

Address to Congress, December 8, 1914.

I. FIRST PROPOSALS: THE SITUATION IN SEPTEMBER AND OCTOBER, 1914

DURING all the period of his negotiations with the British and the Germans, regarding neutrality, the President had been steadily seeking a method of settling the terrible conflict in Europe. He regarded peace as "the especial wish and longing of the people of the United States,"[1] as it was his own. More than anything else he coveted for America the office of the peacemaker. Other problems were indeed difficult and dangerous, but he thought of "the great tasks and duties of peace" as the

---

[1]Proclamation designating Sunday, October 4, 1914, a Day of Prayer. *The Public Papers of Woodrow Wilson*, Vol. III, p. 170.

chief "challenge [to] our best powers" demanding "the finest gifts of constructive wisdom we possess." He desired, moreover, no hasty or temporary solution: it was his hope to "build what will last."[1]

It was not only an ideal: it soon appeared that a speedy termination of the conflict afforded the only hope of escape from a steadily increasing American entanglement in the controversies of Europe. It was the only way through the mazes of neutrality which were daily becoming more confusing.

Against the advice of some of his closest associates—Page and House among them—he had, as we have seen, put before the belligerents as early as August 5th his offer to act in the interest of mediation. But there were no acceptances: and the weeks were rolling by. Each side claimed to be fighting in self-defense. The war was nowhere near a decision. The Germans had the best of it on land, although they had failed to overwhelm their enemies entirely; the Allies had the best of it on the sea, but could only render their advantage decisive by the long pressure of blockade.

The President's problem centred not upon the importance of mediation—that was admitted—but upon the proper moment for it. Mediation involved the willingness of both sides to talk peace: if he moved with the approval of one side only, he risked either a failure that would injure his usefulness at some future and more propitious time, or the necessity of assuming the responsibility of forcing peace that might easily involve us, also, in the war.

Nevertheless clamorous individuals and organizations urged that a mere passive gesture of readiness did not liquidate his obligation to his country and to humanity.[2]

[1] Second annual address to Congress, December 8, 1914. *Ibid.*, p. 227.

[2] In a letter of September 14th, the International Woman Suffrage Alliance made a plea for "insistent" and "repeated" demands for peace negotiations, with American mediation. There were many others.

On the other hand, there were still stronger outcries against his doing anything more to hasten peace: these almost wholly from the partisans of the Allies. A speedy peace while the military balance stood in Germany's favour, and before England's untrained man-power, supplemented by the material resources of American munitions and supplies, then beginning to be shipped in enormous quantities, could be thrown into the scale, was the last thing these partisans desired. It was true that the attitude of the United States toward the British blockade was not yet determined. In this there was an element of great danger, since a strong stand by the American government upon its rights as a neutral—as in the war of 1812— or against the sale of munitions to belligerents,[1] might indeed have brought a speedy end to the war. It might also have brought war with Great Britain. In either case it might have meant victory for Germany. These dangers the Allies, however, hoped to avoid by skillful diplomacy, the principal element of which, during the earlier weeks of the war, was delay. Delay meant an increasing dependence of American industry, at enormous profits, upon the business of supplying arms and other supplies to the Allies. And if the delay continued long enough, difficulties between the United States and Germany were almost certain to develop. Delay, then, was the keynote of Grey's diplomacy.[2]

In the absence of any international organization, or any international law with sanctions, there remained only the possibility of exerting a moral pressure for peace. But in

---

[1] A policy of embargo that Wilson had already adopted toward belligerents in Mexico.

[2] ". . . his [Grey's] purpose was to maintain Anglo-American relations on so even a keel that our foodstuffs, our war munitions, our steel, our copper, and other materials would flow uninterruptedly into British ports, while the British Navy, in full command of the seas, was keeping these same materials out of Germany. From the first, however, Lord Kitchener, with the more brutal directness of the practical soldier, was determined to make the United States a military ally." *The Life and Letters of Walter H. Page*, Vol. III, p. 200.

this the President, by training and by conviction, firmly believed. Moral force, the power of the right, the efficacy of reason, were to him the only enduring methods: war really settled nothing.

The first glimmer of an opportunity for mediation came on Sunday, September 6th, and both Wilson and Bryan welcomed it eagerly. Oscar Straus[1] arrived breathlessly in Washington on that day and reported to Bryan a dinner conversation on the previous evening at James Speyer's home[2] at Scarboro, in which Count Bernstorff, the German ambassador, had expressed the opinion that his government would accept an offer of mediation.[3]

Bryan acted immediately, sending for Bernstorff, and asking Straus to call upon the British and French ambassadors.[4] He also reported to Wilson, probably in person, for no documents have been found. Straus records that Wilson "expressed himself as pleased with the possibility of a favourable outcome."[5] The President approved not only Bryan's vigorous and prompt action in sending dispatches to the American ambassadors in Great Britain and France, but, no doubt, the conviction he expressed: ". . . this war is so horrible from every aspect that no one can afford to take the responsibility for continuing it a single hour."[6]

Both were eager for such an opening. Bryan declared: ". . . even a failure to agree will not rob an attempt at mediation of all its advantages because the different

---

[1] A distinguished New Yorker, long active in public life, a former ambassador to Turkey.

[2] James Speyer was a leading New York banker.

[3] See Oscar S. Straus, *Under Four Administrations*, pp. 378–379; also Bernstorff, *My Three Years in America*, pp. 68–69.

[4] Bryan himself also saw Jusserand and Spring Rice. For Spring Rice's account, see *The Letters and Friendships of Sir Cecil Spring Rice*, Vol. II, p. 221 ff.

[5] Oscar S. Straus, *Under Four Administrations*, p. 380.

[6] W. J. Bryan to Walter H. Page and M. T. Herrick, September 8, 1914. *Foreign Relations of the United States*, Supplement, 1914, p. 99.

nations would be able to explain their attitude, the reasons for continuing the war, the end to be hoped for and the terms upon which peace is possible. This would locate responsibility for the continuation of the war and help to mold public opinion."[1]

It may have been, in part at least, the hope awakened by this incident that caused the President, on the very day of Bryan's telegrams to Page and Herrick,[2] to issue his proclamation designating Sunday, October 4th, as "a day of prayer and supplication . . . to Almighty God that, overruling the counsel of men, setting straight the things they cannot govern or alter . . . He vouchsafe His children healing peace again . . ."[3]

But the Straus proposal was met on all sides with tremendous douches of cold water. In the first place it "leaked" to the press, as nearly all the so-called secret communications at that time were doing: and no government would then, publicly, admit a readiness to discuss peace lest it be construed as a sign of weakness. Neither Herrick nor Page ever formally presented the Straus message to the government to which he was accredited.

Herrick gave assurance of "the certainty that a proposal for mediation would be refused by the Entente powers at present." He added:

". . . might it not appear that Germany was making a bid for the aid and sympathy of the neutral powers by espousing a proposition which she knows to be unacceptable to the nations with whom she is at war?"[4]

Page replied on the 10th, saying that he had had an informal conference with Grey, who argued that Germany

---

[1] W. J. Bryan to Walter H. Page and M. T. Herrick, September 8, 1914. *Foreign Relations of the United States*, Supplement, 1914, p. 99.

[2] September 8, 1914.

[3] *The Public Papers of Woodrow Wilson*, Vol. III, p. 170.

[4] September 9, 1914. *Foreign Relations of the United States*, Supplement, 1914, p. 101.

"had deliberately planned" the war and rebuffed all efforts at peace.

"No peace can be concluded that will permit the continuance of or the recurrence of an armed brute power in central Europe which violates treaties to make war and in making war assaults the continuity of civilization. Any terms that England will agree to must provide for an end of militarism forever and for reparation to ruined Belgium."

Like Herrick, Page asserted that "there can be no peace now on any terms that the Emperor will propose, and . . . he knows this and if he proposes anything now he will propose it only to affect public opinion in America."[1]

The statements of both ambassadors clearly meant that the Allies were not ready to make peace on any terms that Germany would accept unless she were completely defeated.

The German Chancellor's reply regarding the Straus message was not less uncompromising:

"Germany did not want war. It was forced upon her."[2]

Any offer of mediation should be based upon proposals from the Allies, though the German government disclaimed soliciting such an offer; the Chancellor declared that "if we accepted America's offer of mediation now, our enemies would interpret it as a sign of weakness and the German people would not understand it." Germany "has a right to demand" guaranties of "rest and security."

Although Page had demanded that his reply be kept "inviolably secret," there were again leaks, which, if there was anything genuine in Bernstorff's suggestion of mediation, made the Germans' position more difficult than before. Their government could hardly suggest any terms after learning that they were sure to be rejected; it could

---

[1] *Foreign Relations of the United States*, Supplement, 1914, pp. 100–101.
[2] September 14, 1914. *Ibid.*, p. 104.

not on its own initiative propose reparation to Belgium when powerful groups at home, convinced of the rightness of Germany's action and of her military supremacy, were even talking of the annexation of that country.

The incident thus ended as a demonstration of the difficulty of peacemaking with nothing to work with but the good will of the peacemaker. Wilson and Bryan decided that nothing more could be done for the moment.[1]

It may be remarked that this eager attempt at mediation was entirely the work of Wilson and Bryan: most of their advisers, particularly Page, but including House and Herrick, were opposed to any such move. Page wrote on September 10th:

". . . such men as Straus . . . may be able to let (by helping) the Germans appear to the peace people as really desiring peace. Of course what they want is to save their mutton.

"And if we begin mediation talk now on that basis, we shall not be wanted when a real chance for mediation comes."[2]

All along, Page had been an ardent and insistent opponent of any sort of mediation. He had, as we have seen, held it to be the duty of America to help the British win, by supplying ammunition and agreeing to the blockade. He believed it wrong for America to suggest peace before the Germans were beaten. He had the President's ear and argued with persistency that "German militarism" was responsible for the war, and that it was a "clash of systems" between this militarism and the principle of democracy represented by Great Britain. (He seldom mentioned Russia.) He had telegraphed to Wilson as

---

[1] W. J. Bryan to Woodrow Wilson, September 16, 1914; Woodrow Wilson to Robert Lansing, September 17, 1914.

[2] Walter H. Page to E. M. House, *The Life and Letters of Walter H. Page*, Vol. I, pp. 410–411.

early as September 3rd that the Kaiser was expected to make a peace offer if his troops took Paris, but that English opinion was, "... if he be let off, then the war will have been in vain," adding:

"The resolve is to give a death blow to the Germans at any cost in time, men and money."[1]

It was the hope of Englishmen, he said, "that neither our government nor American public opinion will regard any proposed peace as worth while that stops short of a final blow to bureaucracy." He himself, in support of this hope, dwelt upon the atrocity stories and the Zeppelin raids.[2]

On the 7th, he telegraphed again that the conclusion of the Pact of London[3] was "England's declaration to the Kaiser that no peace proposals will be entertained till one side or the other is completely exhausted." He concluded:

"They mean to fight till pro-militarism is utterly crushed."[4]

In spite of these warnings, the President and Bryan, as we have seen, had acted on the very first chance, however slim. Page and Grey seem to have been anxious—after Grey's complete rejection of the Straus proposals—lest the President and American opinion be influenced by the feeling that Great Britain was opposed to peace, as Bernstorff was asserting; and on September 19th Wilson received a defensive explanation from Grey, in which the whole argument turned upon the statement that "Germany planned this war, and chose her own time for forcing

---

[1]*Foreign Relations of the United States*, Supplement, 1914, p. 87. Herrick reported utterances to the same effect by Poincaré on September 2nd. *Foreign Relations of the United States*, Supplement, 1914, p. 86.

[2]*Ibid.*, p. 87.

[3]Published September 7, 1914.

[4]*Foreign Relations of the United States*, Supplement, 1914, p. 99. These views and conclusions were repeated with elaborations in Page's letter of the 6th, with a postscript of the 8th.

it on Europe."[1] Grant this, and it naturally followed that
the Allies must have reparation and security against the
menace of repetitions in the future—even to the extent of
crushing Germany entirely.

But Wilson had not yet granted the first premise of this
argument. He was stubbornly withholding judgement as to
war guilt. Just at that time, as we have already seen, he
was responding to Belgian, French, and German charges
of atrocities with his thoroughly considered conclusion
that "we do not know in sufficient detail the actual facts"
and that "it would be premature . . . to form or express a
final judgement."[2] He was not, in fact, prepared to find
Germany solely guilty: and therefore he was eager for
mediation whenever it could be had.

At this point we find a wide and significant divergence
developing among Wilson's principal advisers.

Bryan had left Washington for a brief holiday just after
the receipt of the German Chancellor's note: and in the
quiet atmosphere of Asheville, North Carolina, he evidently gave much thought to the duties and responsibilities of the United States. On September 19th he wrote
a long letter to the President (neatly copied out, probably
by Mrs. Bryan), making the suggestion that the effort
at mediation be vigorously continued.[3]

In this letter Bryan plainly spoke his deep conviction.

"The European situation distresses me. The slaughter
goes on, and each day makes it more apparent that it is
to be a prolonged struggle."

He drew from the Straus incident the lesson that, since
none of the belligerent governments was willing to take the

---

[1] Telegram from Sir Edward Grey to Sir Cecil Spring Rice, sent by Spring Rice to the
President on September 19, 1914.

[2] See p. 16, this volume. He met the Belgian commission on September 16th; his
letter to the Kaiser was of the same date.

[3] This letter, printed in Bryan's memoirs, pp. 388–392, varies somewhat from the
original, quoted here.

initiative toward peace, it should be taken by the United States. He pointed out that they all denied responsibility for the war and professed the desire for a peace that should be enduring.

"Both sides seem to entertain the old idea that fear is the only basis upon which peace can rest. . . . And so, the Kaiser sees peace in a victory which will insure the supremacy of Germany, while the Allies see peace only in a success so signal as to crush the German war machine.

"It is not likely that either side will win so complete a victory as to be able to dictate terms and if either side does win such a victory, it will probably mean preparation for another war. It would seem better to look for a more rational basis for peace."

He went on to suggest some of the possible elements in such a basis:

"Your suggestion, namely, that the manufacture and sale of arms and ammunition shall be a government monopoly, is most excellent.

"It has also been suggested that armaments shall be diminished; that all armies shall be reduced in size with a view to reserving them for internal use in preserving order; that nations shall enter into an agreement to respect present boundaries, etc.

"I believe that a compulsory investigation of disputes before hostilities begin, such as our treaties provide for, would go far toward preventing war, but the most potent of all influences for the promotion of peace is the substitution of friendship for hatred, and your plan of taking away the pecuniary interest which private corporations now have in war, will make it easier to cultivate friendship."

Bryan's idea of the proper first step toward the kind of peace he outlined was that the President should address a new appeal to the belligerents, pointing out:

"... First, that all deny responsibility for the war and that all express a desire for peace and, Second, that responsibility for continuance of such a war is as undesirable as responsibility for beginning it and that such responsibility attaches to this nation, as well as to the participants if, by mediation, we can assist in bringing it to a close."

The belligerents were to be asked only to "meet together and exchange views as to the terms upon which permanent peace can be insured," without being bound to accept any objectionable conditions in advance or even, necessarily, concluding an armistice.

The letter called for no answer, as Bryan stated that he wished to confer with the President about it on his return —and the mention of Wilson's idea for government monopoly of the munitions business[1] indicates that they had discussed the peace problem previously.

Here was broad, sound thought—with constructive ideas which Wilson was afterward to profit by.[2] If Bryan's proposals had been tried at that time—before the capitulations of October, while yet the United States possessed the mighty power of placing an embargo on munitions and of challenging the British blockade—something might possibly have been effected.

But House was at Wilson's elbow urging him to do nothing.

"From the beginning I have thought it was a mistake to push this peace movement too strongly at first. The publicity given to the Bernstorff-Straus conversations has not had a good effect. It is an exceedingly delicate undertaking and any misstep may be fatal to your final influence."[3]

---

[1] See this volume, p. 74, conversation with Axson.

[2] The proposal that "nations shall enter into an agreement to respect present boundaries," found its way into Article X of the Covenant of the League of Nations.

[3] E. M. House to Woodrow Wilson, September 19, 1914.

House proposed that he himself be permitted to "go along with the negotiations."[1] Since the responses from the belligerents had been so unfavourable and the advice of Page, Herrick, and others so discouraging,[2] Wilson was probably convinced that Bryan's suggestion of direct and open proposals was unwise at the moment; but his response to House was by no means hopeful, let alone enthusiastic:

"Think there can be no harm in your going on."[3]

Colonel House at once plunged into a series of secret conversations with the British, German, and Austro-Hungarian ambassadors, lunching with this one, dining with that, and duly reporting to the President.[4] The suggestions on both sides were of the vaguest and most general nature. The "end of militarism"—what did it mean? "General disarmament," "other effective measures," "an indemnity for Belgium." One cannot avoid the impression that the Allied diplomats were playing for time, using House to keep Wilson inactive. Delay was at that time the chief article in their policy.

---

[1]E. M. House to Woodrow Wilson, September 19, 1914.

[2]There was much pressure brought to bear upon the President at this time from weighty pro-Ally sources. Lord Bryce, whom the President had long known and highly regarded, wrote on September 24th:

". . . the wisest friends of peace on this side the Ocean think you were altogether right in not renewing at this moment your offer of mediation in this war. . . .

"The general feeling is . . . that any attempt to patch up a peace now could lead only to a sort of truce rather than peace, an uneasy respite during which preparations for renewing the struggle would go on, armaments growing larger and engines of destruction still more deadly." (From original in Mr. Wilson's files. Published in H. A. L. Fisher's *Lord Bryce*, Vol. II, p. 130.)

Wilson responded on October 9th:

"Thank you sincerely for your letter about mediation. My own judgement accords entirely with yours in the matter. I shall be very careful to suit my action to the developments.

"I need not tell you how deeply concerned we constantly are about the great contest. Our thoughts are upon it constantly and upon our friends whose hearts must be so much distressed."

[3]Woodrow Wilson to E. M. House, telegram, September 19, 1914.

[4]A full account may be found in *The Intimate Papers of Colonel House*, Vol. I, p. 318, *ff.*

Page, on his part, minced no words. He wrote to the President on September 22nd:

". . . peace-talk now is old women's prattle or else it is insincere and is 'springes to catch woodcock'—a part of the German tactics."[1]

Peace meetings, reported from America, he said, "produce the impression here of mutton-headed victims of German special pleaders."[2]

It was evident that House recognized and feared the influence of Bryan and his pressure upon the President. Bryan, once started, might exercise a powerful influence also upon public opinion. On October 3rd House wrote to Page:

"I have always counselled him [the President] to remain quiet for the moment and let matters unfold themselves further. . . . I do not think there is any danger of anyone on the outside injecting himself into it unless Mr. Bryan does something on his own initiative."[3]

Rank outsider—the Secretary of State!

On the following day, October 4th, Bryan confirmed House's worst suspicions. He went to New York to help celebrate the day of prayer which the President had proclaimed, speaking to an immense audience at Broadway Tabernacle.[4] It was an eloquent and powerful appeal for the opening of negotiations.

---

[1] *The Life and Letters of Walter H. Page*, Vol. III, p. 145.

[2] September 22, 1914. *Ibid.*, pp. 146–147.

[3] *The Life and Letters of Walter H. Page*, Vol. I, p. 413. In this letter House went on to indicate some bases for a durable peace, as, for example, "every nation in Europe guaranteeing the territorial integrity of every other nation," which Mr. Hendrick (p. 412) regards as an "astonishing" example of House's foresight, since this idea, embodied in Article X, became the chief point of controversy in the Covenant of the League of Nations. But it had already been presented to the President in Bryan's letter of September 19th which House no doubt had seen, the phrase there being, "that nations shall enter into an agreement to respect present boundaries." (See p. 285, this volume.)

[4] Enthusiastic observation of the day in many churches was reported. "Broadway Tabernacle turned 2000 away, though masses stood two hours hoping to gain admittance and hear Secretary Bryan." (C. W. McMorran to Woodrow Wilson, telegram, October 4, 1914.)

"It is not necessary that we should consider the causes that led up to the conflict or attempt to locate responsibility for the conditions that now exist ... our first duty is to use such influence as we may have to hasten the return of peace ..."

Realizing the extent to which America was becoming entangled in the mêlée, he declared:

"In this age our interests are so entwined with the interests of those who reside in other lands that no nation can live or die unto itself alone. ... Today every neutral nation finds itself greatly embarrassed by the disturbance which the European war has wrought in every department of human activity; and we, therefore, appreciate more fully than ever before how numerous are the ties that bind us together and how far-reaching are the consequences of war."

He decried the ideas that true peace could be based on fear and armaments and that security lay in the crushing of one's enemies:

"And even if one could be completely avenged by the exercise of physical force he could not escape the influence which the use of this force and the winning of a triumph by means of it are likely to exert upon himself."

He extolled America's peace policy, particularly as embodied in the recently signed treaties, as a service to the world—"and with nations, as with individuals, service is the measure of greatness."

This address, and the reception accorded it, plainly made a strong impression upon the President. He wrote congratulating Bryan. Marked by moral enthusiasm and the passion for service, it was a speech he might almost have made himself. It contained, indeed, ideas and even phrases of which he was later to make use.[1]

We know that Bryan's suggestions were immediately

[1] As in the League to Enforce Peace address, May 27, 1916.

engaging the President's thought, for we have the record of a conversation on October 4th at Baltimore made by Miss Mary Hoyt, Mrs. Wilson's cousin and an old friend:

"We discussed the war, and he so obviously felt that all of the wrong was not on one side that even then he was hoping for 'peace without victory'. . . . 'They [the nations of Europe] are all trying to trick and deceive one another, and to get all of the advantage they can; England is safer than the others because she already has all that she can handle and she knows it.'"[1]

Bryan now began to advance still other more immediate and powerful reasons for a prompt and vigorous effort for peace. He reported that other neutral governments, particularly certain Latin-American governments and Spain and Denmark, were appealing to the United States to take an active rôle as a peacemaker, some of them expressing a desire to participate.[2] They were suffering exactly as were Americans from the intolerable conditions of the blockade. Other indications of the desire for peace also came to the President's attention just at this time.[3]

Colonel House reported to the President that Ambassador Dumba, in a conversation, "hardly tried to disguise his eagerness for peace measures to begin."[4]

---

[1]Memorandum made October 1, 1926.

[2]W. J. Bryan to Woodrow Wilson, October 7, 1914.

[3]Judge George Gray, a distinguished jurist and diplomat, sent him a letter of October 5th from Professor Lammasch, one of the most distinguished international lawyers and diplomats of Europe, containing this paragraph:

"I am sure not only in my country but also in other parts of Europe, specially in Belgium and in France, probably also in England, the eyes of all men and women who have not lost entirely their senses, look to your side of the water for words of reason. If the different *governments* in the blindness with which they are struck did not accept at first a mediation proffered by you and some other neutral powers, for instance The Netherlands, Italy, Spain, and one or other of the Scandinavian States, I am quite sure that the *nations*, sick from bloodshed, will constrain them in a very short time to accept the hand of friendship which you tender to them. Therefore I beg you to raise your powerful voice and to solicit your countrymen to do so. It is the greatest service which the United States can do to the cause of humanity."

[4]October 6, 1914.

But the President finally decided—momentously—that the time for active pressure by the United States had not yet arrived: and he disliked, also, to become a part of a movement of neutral nations, which might involve a limitation of American freedom of action without adding any appreciable element of strength. On October 8th he wrote to Mr. Bryan, a letter marked "personal and confidential":

"I have your letter of yesterday about the possible participation of other nations in the mediation which we all hope will soon be possible in connection with the European war.

"My own expectation is that the matter will not lie with us. I do not think we will be called upon to choose which nations shall participate in the mediation or that we shall be at liberty to invite others to participate. I think that when the time comes we shall receive an intimation that our intermediation would be acceptable and I think, speaking confidentially, that it is very desirable that a single nation should act in this capacity rather than several. The difficulties and complications would be many and the outcome much more doubtful if there were several mediators."

The President was undoubtedly much influenced also in delaying action by the prophecies of Page—timely either by accident or design—who reported that there would probably be a "drawn war"[1] by the next summer or autumn. Two emissaries from General French, the British commander in the field, had told him that a decisive victory for either side was an improbability.

"Then," wrote Page, "a great revulsion will come. Not only will the neutral world rise up and say that this slaughter must cease, but the combatants themselves will say so and will at least be receptive to a suggestion. . . . Then the President of the U. S. will be called on to mediate—to

[1]October 29, 1914. From original in Mr. Wilson's files. Also *The Life and Letters of Walter H. Page*, Vol. III, p. 167.

lay down a broad principle or two by which the struggle may be ended."[1]

To Page's letter of October 29th Wilson responded as follows:

November 10, 1914

MY DEAR PAGE:

You may be perfectly sure that you do not weary me with your letters. They give me an intimate view of men and things which I could not obtain without them and are invaluable to me. I cannot have too many.

I only wish that I could return the service in kind by going into the detail of our action and our difficulties and our personalities here. That, unhappily, is out of the question; for one thing, because I have not your gift of presenting these things vividly, but chiefly, because the pressure of a multitude of things throughout the day seems to deprive me of the kind of initiative necessary for writing good letters.

I am glad that the situation has been as much simplified as possible by our no longer insisting on the Declaration of London. Any mistakes that were made then can now easily be forgotten.

I am particularly interested in what you tell me of your conversation with General French's two friends. My only comment at present is that what they suggested seems to me a programme which needs as its premise the practically complete defeat of Germany and not merely a stand-off fight, because it involves to a very considerable degree a dismemberment of the German Empire. But, after all, it is not the details that interest me in these suggestions, but the general judgement as to the prospects of the war and the general principle involved in the outlined settlement. It gives me much to think about. It would indeed be a very great privilege if I could play any part in bringing settled peace to Europe.

Cordially and faithfully yours,
WOODROW WILSON

HON. WALTER H. PAGE,
American Embassy,
London, England.

----

[1] October 29, 1914. From original in Mr. Wilson's files. Also *The Life and Letters of Walter H. Page*, Vol. III, pp. 167-168.

So ended the first and probably the only really hopeful opportunity for a direct and vigorous effort at mediation. It would probably have failed—neither side was ready to be reasonable—but it was not tried. Nearly a year later Colonel House, in a letter to Ambassador Page, admitted the seriousness of the lost opportunity:

"His [the President's] judgement and mine was that last autumn was the time to discuss peace parleys and we both foresaw present possibilities. . . . The wishes of the Allies were heeded with the result that the war has now fastened itself upon the vitals of Europe, and what the end may be is beyond the knowledge of man."[1]

House himself, of course, next to Page, had been the chief and most persistent adviser in urging the President to heed "the wishes of the Allies" by which the British diplomacy of delay was succeeding. On October 22nd, as we have seen, came the surrender of our initial demand for the recognition of the Declaration of London, and our practical acquiescence in the principle of the British blockade of Germany—thus stripping us of our most powerful trading counters in any possible negotiations. More than that, commerce with the Allies (for which we extended credit to them) was becoming the corner stone of our business structure, and any attempt to break it up would have caused a catastrophe at home. We were, in short, at this early stage, being irresistibly drawn toward the side of the Allies.

It is possible that, if Wilson had been able to devote his entire time and energies to these problems, some other course of action might have been discovered. But he was bearing, during these months, burdens taxing his strength to the utmost. He was in the heat of the doubtful mid-term elections which came on November 3rd. He was carrying forward a fierce battle in Congress for his Shipping bill; he

---

[1]August 4, 1915. *The Life and Letters of Walter H. Page*, Vol. I, p. 423.

had a great strike in Colorado on his hands; the railroads were appealing insistently for help, and he was giving much thought to their problems and conferring with their leaders; he was starting the new Federal Reserve system; he was holding hearings on the new Immigration bill, which he was soon to veto. We have seen[1] the studious consideration he was giving to the controversy with the British over the problems of contraband and blockade. In addition to all these things, he was bearing a heavy burden of domestic sorrow.

Another factor also probably played its part. Bryan, the political war horse of the Democratic party, had smelt the air of the approaching campaign of November, and in the excitement and absorption of stump-speaking, temporarily ceased to concern himself about affairs in Europe.

"The wishes of the Allies were heeded"—and those wishes were to prolong the war and get America to help them prolong it until Germany should be on her knees. Of course, they persistently urged that the apparent willingness of Germany to consider peace on terms that might promise durability was insincere—but they offered no proof of it. The favourable moment passed, never to return.

II. WILSON'S ATTITUDE TOWARD PRESSURE FOR PEACE FROM OTHER NEUTRAL NATIONS

For two months, from September 8, 1914, to the middle of November, practically nothing was done in the interest of mediation. On November 17th the President was telling newspaper correspondents that "he had not had the slightest hint, formal or otherwise, from any of the European belligerents that a peace offer would be favorably received."[2]

---

[1]In Chapter IV.
[2]New York *Times*, November 18, 1914.

When the pressure for united action by neutral nations began to appear again about the middle of November—especially long notes and memoranda from South America, couched in sonorous Spanish verbiage—the President wrote to Lansing:

"I should like to coöperate with the South American governments in any way that would be serviceable to them, but I fear that the suggestions here made would lead to more mischief than relief. I think that the wisest course to pursue is perhaps to let the Chilean minister know that we feel that dangerous embarrassments would be involved and that perhaps it is not best to attempt action along the lines suggested."[1]

By December 1st, political matters having calmed down, Bryan again became active in the matter of mediation. He wrote a long letter to the President arguing that our own interests impelled us to act—that the war was disturbing business generally and the cotton trade particularly, that it had tied up transportation even to the extent of embarrassing our railroads, that it was piling up disturbing problems of neutrality. Referring to the constant appeals of other neutral states to our leadership, he put it:

"We owe it to other neutral nations to do everything in our power to bring the war to a close."

We owed it to the belligerents to offer our guidance in finding the way to peace which they were unable to take by themselves—"they cannot consider the question with calmness and their pride will not allow them to ask mediation—the offer must come from us." He advanced anew the consideration that, while responsibility for beginning the war remained a dark issue, responsibility for continuing it could be fixed by calling forth statements from the

---

[1]November 19, 1914. In the ensuing months the opportunity was repeatedly presented to the American government of taking the lead in an organization of neutrals which might have had some such influence upon the European war as Armed Neutrality in 1780 had upon our War of Independence.

belligerents of "the terms upon the acceptance of which they are willing to cease hostilities, leaving responsibility for a continuance of the war to rest upon those who propose unreasonable terms or reject reasonable terms." The possibility of decisive victory for either side, he said, was more remote than ever; while "if either side should win such a victory the peace that would follow would be built upon fear, and history proves that permanent peace cannot be built upon such a foundation." He urged that "it would seem to be this nation's duty, as the leading exponent of Christianity and as the foremost advocate of world-wide peace, to approach the warring nations again and earnestly urge them to consent to a conference with a view to coming to an understanding which will enable them to lay down their arms and begin the work of reconstructing a permanent peace on the basis of justice and friendship."[1]

Again we have from Bryan a fundamentally sound and statesmanlike case based upon ideas which Wilson himself was later to express, as in his message to the belligerent governments on December 18, 1916, when he himself publicly called upon the belligerents for statements of their war aims.[2] But the President was still doubtful, not as to the principles involved, but as to the fit occasion, the appropriate method, upon which sound diplomacy must inevitably rest. The issues were indeed highly con-

---

[1]December 1, 1914.

About this time also Wilson received a letter from Ambassador Morgenthau, dated November 10th, stating that he gathered from his intercourse with the representatives of all the belligerent countries that "all would welcome a demand from the United States and Italy—that this war should stop—Each one thinks the first pressure should be put on the others—and all are looking to you to take the initiative."

Wilson replied on December 9th that he was "not a little impressed by what you say as to the expectations entertained with regard to the possibilities of insisting on peace," and asked Morgenthau, in view of the lack of detailed suggestions on the subject, for his "full thought and information on this great matter in which I should be so deeply interested to move when and as it is possible."

[2]The Public Papers of Woodrow Wilson, Vol. IV, pp. 402–406.

fused. Both sides were clamouring for their "rights": and bitterly accusing their adversaries. On the very day of Bryan's letter Wilson also had in hand Professor Münsterberg's irritating charges, already referred to,[1] of American favouritism to the Allies.

The answer to Bryan's strong appeal, of which we have no record, was probably made orally, but there is evidence that the President was still inclined to listen to House's counsels of delay.

Wilson was, however, beginning to grow impatient. "Pressure is being brought upon him [the President]," House wrote Page on December 4th, "to offer his services again, for this country is suffering, like the rest of the neutral world, from the effects of the war, and our people are becoming restless."

"Something must be done sometime, by somebody," continued House, "to initiate a peace movement. . . ."[2]

The President was evidently irritated by Page's constant and unrestrained defense of the British cause and his criticisms of the American administration. House, as we have seen, conveyed this feeling to Page with a bluntness that it would be difficult to parallel.[3]

There were even rumours, wholly baseless so far as the records reveal, that Wilson was considering the recall of Page; he did not personally write to him again for several months.

During all this time both Bryan and Lansing had been much concerned with the continued pressure of South American neutrals who were now threatening to act upon their own account—which, by virtue of our obligations under a broad interpretation of the Monroe Doctrine,

---

[1]See this volume, p. 223 ff.
[2]The Life and Letters of Walter H. Page, Vol. I, pp. 416–417.
[3]See this volume, p. 170.

might easily involve us, whether we approved or not. Lansing, the legalist, who was against any attempt to alter the rules while the war was in progress, conceived the idea of bringing the matter into discussion by the Pan-American Union. A lively session was held, on December 8th, ending in the reference of the whole subject to a commission under the chairmanship of the Secretary of State of the United States—with the usual result of such procedure. That Wilson approved this shelving of the proposals is indicated by his acknowledgment, on December 10th, of Bryan's report on the meeting:

"I am a little afraid that there may be dynamite in this, but under your chairmanship I dare say it will be possible to direct the action of the commission in a way to avoid serious dangers."

While Bryan and Lansing were struggling with these immediate problems, Colonel House came to Washington on December 16th, and the whole situation was discussed with the President. House had previously proposed that the President take the initiative in welding "North and South America together in closer union."[1]

"It was my idea," he wrote in his diary on December 16th, "to formulate a plan, to be agreed upon by the republics of the two continents, which in itself would serve as a model for the European nations when peace is at last brought about."

He continues:

"My idea was that the republics of the two continents should agree to guarantee each other's territorial integrity and that they should also agree to government ownership of munitions of war."[2]

On House's suggestion, Wilson wrote out the two basic

---

[1]E. M. House to Woodrow Wilson, November 30, 1914. *The Intimate Papers of Colonel House*, Vol. I, p. 208.

[2]*Ibid.*, p. 209.

principles on which such a league of American states might rest, as follows:

"1st. Mutual guaranties of political independence under republican form of government and mutual guaranties of territorial integrity.

"2nd. Mutual agreement that the government of each of the contracting parties acquire complete control within its jurisdiction of the manufacture and sale of munitions of war."[1]

The first of these ideas, as we have seen, had originated with Bryan in his letter to Wilson of September 19th, and the wording of it, in this statement of Wilson's, closely approached that of Article X of the Covenant for which the President was to make such a desperate struggle at a later time; the second idea was Wilson's own, proposed to Dr. Axson in August,[2] and discussed with Bryan in September.

It is to be observed that this project, however admirable, in no way touched the immediate problems that were plaguing the President. Dealing with a far-off world "when peace is at last brought about," its virtues were academic rather than practical. It was the sort of scheme that House loved—vague and great—"the linking of the Western Hemisphere"![3] He began eagerly talking it over with the South American ambassadors and, a little doubtfully, with Bryan, whose "sensibilities" might be hurt[4] by such unofficial negotiations. While House justly observed, "Mr. Bryan is generous and big-minded in matters of this sort," he seemed, according to his own account, somewhat irritated by the Secretary's insistence upon

---

[1] E. M. House to Woodrow Wilson, November 30, 1914. *The Intimate Papers of Colonel House*, Vol. I, pp. 209–210.

[2] See p. 74, this volume.

[3] Colonel House's diary entry, December 17, 1914. *The Intimate Papers of Colonel House*, Vol. I, p. 211.

[4] Colonel House's diary entry, December 16, 1914. *Ibid.*, p. 210.

applying the scheme to the immediate and difficult problems of the moment—"a convention . . . for the purpose of securing the rights of neutrals." It appeared that
House suggested a conference of both neutrals and belligerents, which Bryan forcefully commended in a letter
to the President, hoping that it might open the way to
mediation.[1]

But Wilson's disinclination to tie up with the other neutral states in enterprises in which we should bear the
principal responsibility for any action taken had already
been made manifest enough to require no further assertion,
and nothing came of Bryan's plea.

One of the surprising features of these developments is
the way in which Bryan looms up as the statesman of

---

[1]December 17, 1914. The complete letter follows:
"Mr. House will call your attention to a suggestion which was made to me by one
of the South American representatives and I am inclined to think there is some force in
it. You have not failed to notice the increasing urgency with which the neutral nations
are presenting the idea of mediation or of some form of protection from the burdens
of this war. The sentiment is unanimous among the South [and] Central American
countries that something ought to be done to protect the neutral nations if the war is
to continue. The same idea has been presented by some of the neutral nations of
Europe. A recent dispatch says that the kings of Norway, Sweden and Denmark are to
meet for the purpose of considering what can be done to lessen these burdens. The
Venezuelan minister yesterday handed me a suggestion to the effect that you call a
meeting of *all of the neutral* nations to be held in Washington for the purpose of considering a proposition to be submitted later to a convention in which all the nations,
neutral and belligerent, will be represented. I think, however, that the idea of Mr.
House, which I have mentioned, is the most feasible one, namely, that you invite all
the nations, belligerent and neutral, to send representatives to a conference to be held
in Washington for the purpose of considering ways and means by which the burdens
borne by the neutral nations may be minimized with the consent and agreement of the
belligerent nations. The belligerents could not take exception of [sic] it, were it understood that the changes were to be made through agreement with the belligerents, and I
am sure it would appeal to all the neutral nations. The one who suggested this plan had
in mind the possibility of its opening the way to mediation. He thinks that it would give
you an opportunity to make an address of welcome which might be helpful in advancing
the cause of mediation without directly referring to it. He thinks that the coming
together of these representatives, even for the consideration of questions growing out
of the war and yet not involving the subject of mediation, might lay the foundation
for some coming together of the belligerent nations. I am very much impressed with
the idea and with its possibilities for good. It seemed to commend itself to Mr. House
also, although he only had time to think of it for a moment. It is at his suggestion that
I bring the matter up this evening in order that you may talk with him about it more
fully and let me know your impressions."

largest calibre among Wilson's advisers. His views were not only the broadest and most constructive, but most in accord with the President's own conception of America's rôle in the world. We find Bryan suggesting many of the things that Wilson was to say and do after two years of futile negotiation by House. His plan was simple, yet well conceived. He would have had the American government —with or without the concert of the other neutral governments—make a direct offer of mediation for the opening of peace negotiations at once. The party which refused would incur *ipso facto* the responsibility for continuing the war. He would have accompanied the offer by suggestions as to the general guarantees of a permanent peace—in which the United States would be prepared to play a part—which would offer the security against renewed aggression demanded by all the belligerents. But he would have exacted acceptance of no specific terms in advance. These communications and those to follow might be held as confidential as one pleased, but the American government should exert a constant pressure of moderation to bring the two sets of terms together. The side which held out the more stiffly for the more far-reaching set of terms would still incur the responsibility Bryan aimed to fix—by breaking off the negotiation.

Wilson failed to act, largely, no doubt, because of his intense reluctance to commit the nation to any course that might conceivably involve us in a war "with which we have nothing to do."[1] As we have seen, he remembered acutely, as an historian, the experience of Madison in 1812, and the war that followed. Any interference without the invitation of both belligerents would certainly be

---

[1] Second annual address to Congress, December 8, 1914. *The Public Papers of Woodrow Wilson*, Vol. III, p. 226.

The British ambassador had intimated on October 8th, as House wrote to Wilson the same day, that a direct offer of mediation might be considered by his country as an "unfriendly act."

regarded as favouring the side that desired peace at the moment. The interests and sympathy of his own people, as he felt keenly as a politician, were bitterly divided. He "had gone as far as it was wise to go without some encouragement."[1]

No doubt, also, he was greatly influenced by Page's prediction of a "drawn war" in the summer or autumn when peace efforts would be far more likely to be successful. And both Page and House—to say nothing of Herrick, at Paris, and many other advisers—were earnestly counselling delay. And finally House was at his elbow eagerly suggesting the possibility of secret negotiations to be conducted by himself.

It is significant that after House had travelled about Europe for two years, finger on lips, in an atmosphere of mysterious conferences and secret codes, with no result whatever, Wilson turned back to some of the rejected ideas of Bryan—all except the offer of direct mediation. But it was then too late.

It is not necessary here to go into an account of the preparation for House's mission of 1915, which is fully discussed in his *Intimate Papers*. It will be remembered that when House had first suggested that he be allowed to "go along with the negotiations,"[2] the President had replied: "Think there can be no harm in your going on." In this case, as in connection with House's earlier mission of 1914, the President seemed not to turn the real powers of his mind to the subject at all, but to be willing to trust his friend to see what could be done.

The letter of credentials which he wrote for House on January 29, 1915, was as follows:

"It gives me peculiar pleasure to give you my com-

---

[1] E. M. House to Woodrow Wilson, October 6, 1914, reporting what he had said to the Austrian ambassador, Dumba, as to the President's point of view. *The Intimate Papers of Colonel House*, Vol. I, p. 330.

[2] E. M. House to Woodrow Wilson, September 19, 1914. See this volume, p. 287.

mission to go, as my personal representative, on the mission you are now so generously undertaking, a mission fraught with so many great possibilities, and which may, in the kind providence of God, prove the means of opening a way to peace.

"It is altogether right and fortunate that you are to act only as my private friend and spokesman, without official standing or authority; for that will relieve both you and those with whom you confer of any embarrassment. Your conferences will not represent the effort of any government to urge action upon another government, but only the effort of a disinterested friend whose suggestions and offers of service will not be misunderstood and may be made use of to the advantage of the world.

"The object of this letter is not merely to furnish you with an informal commission but also to supply you with what I know you desire, a definite statement of our attitude with regard to the delicate and important matters you are to discuss and the sort of service we wish to render.

"Please say, therefore, very clearly to all with whom you may confer that we have no thought of suggesting, either now or at any other time, the terms and conditions of peace, except as we may be asked to do so as the spokesman of those whose fortunes are involved in the war. Our single object is to be serviceable, if we may, in bringing about the preliminary willingness to parley which must be the first step towards discussing and determining the conditions of peace. If we can be instrumental in ascertaining for each side in the contest what is the real disposition, the real wish, the real purpose of the other with regard to a settlement, your mission and my whole desire in this matter will have been accomplished.

"I do not know how better to express my conception of your mission than by saying that it is my desire, if they will be so gracious as to permit me to do so, to supply through you a channel of confidential communication through which the nations now at war may make certain that it is right and wise and consistent with their safety and dignity to have a preliminary interchange of views with regard to the terms upon which the present conflict may be brought to an end and future conflicts rendered less likely. There is nothing to which we wish to bind them. It has occurred to us that to ascertain each other's views in this informal way might be less embarrassing to them than to ascertain them in any other way; that they might possibly be glad to avail themselves of our services, offered in this way, rather than run the risk of missing any honorable opportunity to open a way to peace; and that they might be willing to make use of us the more readily because they might be sure that we sought no advantage for ourselves and had no thought or wish to play a part of guidance in their affairs. The allies on both sides have seemed to turn to the United States as to a sort of court of opinion in this great struggle, but we have no wish to be the judges; we desire only to play the part of disinterested friends who have nothing at stake except their interest in the peace of the world."

Quite in line with House's love of secrecy, a second letter of credentials was also prepared—to be shown to those who must be told something, but not informed of the truth. This letter authorized House to make a complete study of the opportunities for relief of particular forms of suffering in Europe, with a view to more effective co-ordination of America's humanitarian efforts.

"I am very grateful to you for consenting to go to Europe at this time to ascertain what our opportunities as neutrals and as disinterested friends of the nations at war are in detail with respect to the assistance that we can render, and how those opportunities can best be made use of; and I beg that you will let this letter serve both as your introduction to those whom it may be necessary for you to consult and as your commission to speak as my personal, though private, representative.

"You know as I do that it is the earnest desire of our fellow-countrymen of all classes to minister to the relief of the suffering in Europe wherever it is possible and legitimate for them to do so; and, more than that, to put themselves and their resources at the service of all the belligerents in whatever way the rules and practices of neutrality permit for the purpose of mitigating the distresses and lessening the friction and the dislocations of a time of war. I would esteem it a very generous service on your part if you would be kind enough to make inquiry in every quarter open to you as to what would in the circumstances be our best course of action in these matters.

"A great many of us feel that our efforts so far have in some degree lacked order and effective coöperation. I would very much like to know if there is any way in which we can effect a better coördination in what we are already doing, whether there are other objects to which it is our duty to turn our attention, and whether I can personally or officially do anything that would helpfully direct or assist such work.

"We cannot answer these questions satisfactorily from this side of the water. They can be answered only by some one person who has made himself familiar with the situation as a whole and in all its parts. I know no one who can do this better than you can. It gives me the greatest satisfaction to be able to commission you thus informally to do it."[1]

The parting of the two men, when House was ready to go, was full of sincere feeling. The President went to the station with him.

[1]January 18, 1915.

"The President's eyes were moist when he said his last words of farewell. He said: 'Your unselfish and intelligent friendship has meant much to me,' and he expressed his gratitude again and again, calling me his 'most trusted friend.' He declared I was the only one in all the world to whom he could open his entire mind.

"I asked if he remembered the first day we met, some three and a half years ago. He replied, 'Yes, but we had known one another always, and merely came in touch then, for our purposes and thoughts were as one.'"[1]

Again, in this mission as in that of 1914, the President's thoughts seemed to follow his friend rather than the problems he was to face. The key sentence to Wilson's whole attitude toward the mission was his reply to House's attempt to discuss what he was going to say:

"There is not much for us to talk over, for the reason we are both of the same mind and it is not necessary to go into details with you."[2]

Here we touch again the fundamental defect of the relationship. In the whole matter of peace efforts, Wilson was trusting House implicitly without any clear-cut understanding as to how House proposed to act or what his reasons were for supposing that it was the right way to act. He felt that House's mind worked just as his own did and that under given circumstances his friend would act exactly as he would wish him to.[3] This was a fatal mistake

---

[1]Colonel House's diary entry, January 25, 1915. *The Intimate Papers of Colonel House*, Vol. I, pp. 357–358.

[2]Colonel House's diary entry, January 24, 1915. *Ibid.*, p. 356.

[3]This had recently been demonstrated to be a false supposition. In the address of December 8, 1914, Wilson had taken a stand on preparedness quite the opposite of that which House had been urging him to assume. But the difference of opinion on this problem had been hurriedly glossed over by House's immediate approval of the address, an approval not mentioned in the *Intimate Papers* (p. 300). "You go far enough to satisfy any reasonable man and your reasons for not going further are, I think, conclusive. It must be patent to all that our protection lies in the navy and must always largely be so." (E. M. House to Woodrow Wilson, December 11, 1914.) Thus Wilson remained blind to the true difference between House's thinking and his own.

House also contributed to this impression by constant and indiscriminate praise of

in Wilson's policy; his trust in House prevented him from seeing things House did not see, but which he might himself have seen if he had looked for himself, without House in the way.

Before leaving, House further built up the structure of secrecy which was to characterize his mission by sending the President a list of code words which was to be used between them. He himself was to be known as "Beverly," Page as "Yucca," Sir Edward Grey as "White," and the Kaiser as "Dante."[1]

Wilson's doings. After the President's address at Indianapolis on January 8th—a speech criticized by some of Wilson's truest friends and about which he himself was apologetic (see p. 126, this volume), House wrote:

"That was a splendid, militant, democratic speech that you made at Indianapolis yesterday and it will do great good." (January 9, 1915.)

Wilson responded:

"Your praise of anything that I do or say is always very sweet to me, and I thank you with all my heart for what you say about the speech at Indianapolis. I would rather have your judgement than that of anybody I know." (January 11, 1915.)

Colonel House, however, always resented the charge that his influence was "based upon his capacity for agreeing with the presidential decisions." "Nothing," remarks his first biographer, A. D. H. Smith in *The Real Colonel House* (p. 276), "galls Colonel House more than this." He quoted Colonel House as follows:

"They say I find out what he wants to hear and then say it to him. . . .

"I never argue with the President when we disagree, any more than with any other man, beyond a certain point. When we have talked a matter over and we find that we are opposed upon it, I drop it—unless and until I come across some new piece of evidence to support my views. A great deal of time is lost in useless argument" (p. 277).

[1]Other words in the code—which an expert could probably have solved in an hour—were as follows:

Allies	Wilmot	Von Bethmann-	
Germany	Zadok	Hollweg	Alto
England	Zenobia	Von Jagow	Othello
France	Warren	Gerard	Youth
Russia	Winter	Sharp	Keen
Greece	Wendell	T. N. Page	Yew
Roumania	Whitney	Penfield	Zebra
Italy	West	Marye	Zenith
Austria	Zeus	Whitlock	Zenda
Bernstorff	Walter	Van Dyke	Zion
Spring Rice	Winkle	Willard	Zeal
Jusserand	Young	Hindenburg	Yonder
Bakhméteff	Wizen	Crown	
Zimmermann	Wolf	Prince	Yammer
Asquith	York	Stovall	Pelham

On January 30th, House sailed away in the fated *Lusitania* in what might be called a blaze of mystery.

III. PEACE EFFORTS OF 1915

House arrived in London on February 6th. It is not necessary here to recount the details of his adventures, since they have already been described in full in his *Intimate Papers*, and referred to by Page and Grey. From February 6th until the sinking of the *Lusitania* on May 7th—three months—House spent most of his time in London, visited Paris, passed nine days in Germany.

About the time of his arrival in London there seems to have been, on the part of Germany, a real desire to discuss peace proposals. A confidential letter from Ambassador Gerard dated February 10th, found among the President's papers, says:

"Our activities should be confined to getting an intimation to the Allies (but in such a way that the Allies can never claim the intention came from Germany) that if certain proposals were made that there was a disposition here to accept them."

A few days later, on February 15th, Gerard was writing to House in London that the Germans would be glad to see him:

"I saw Zimmermann . . . he told me he had written to you saying they would be glad to see you . . .

"Germany will make no peace proposal but I am sure if a reasonable peace is proposed *now* (a matter of days even hours) it would be accepted. . . .

". . . this peace matter is a question *almost of hours.* The submarine blockade once begun a feeling will arise which may make it impossible until after another phase of war.

"If you can get such an intimation from the Allies and

then come here, it will go to the best of my belief. I do not think the Kaiser ever actually wanted war."

There were many reasons why the moment for peace proposals was the most favourable since the beginning of the war. Germany's first great plan to take Paris within six weeks and then turn upon slow-moving Russia had failed. Early in the year 1915 it was plain that Italy would go over to the Allies, but Bulgaria had not yet joined the Central Powers. The sea, wide open to Great Britain, was closed to Germany.

On February 19th Gerard followed up his former appeals with a cablegram to Bryan, again urging haste: "Favourable moment is passing."[1]

The President recognized the opportunity and was eager to act upon it. His first communication to House was on February 13th, in which, after commending him—"You have laid the right foundations of confidence and of comprehension of the nature and spirit of your mission"—he goes on to offer all possible assistance:

"I will do whatever I can to stimulate the interest of Germany from this end through Bernstorff. . . .

"I have learned this afternoon through Wallace[2] that Bernstorff is perfectly confident letter of invitation is on the way to you. He has referred to your contemplated visit repeatedly in his correspondence with his government and feels sure it is expected. He understands the necessity of an actual invitation, and is cabling again today asking what his government has done or will do."

In the meantime House was meeting with Grey and Page. No diplomat in Europe had greater charm, appealed more strongly to Americans, than Grey. He was so reasonable! Grey immediately began to cast doubt upon the

---

[1] *Foreign Relations of the United States*, Supplement, 1915, pp. 15–16.

[2] Hugh C. Wallace, whose letter to the President of February 13th reported his conversation with Bernstorff.

German intimations; reported that the French Minister of Foreign Affairs "does not believe Germany sincere." And House telegraphed:

". . . the Allies have not achieved sufficient military success to insure the acceptance of their demand for permanent peace."[1]

Both he and Page were plainly sympathetic with the Allies. In House's report to Wilson on the 9th, he let slip a comment on the situation of the Allies—it was "not as encouraging as I had hoped"—that indicates his feeling. A few days later he was undertaking to give Grey some military advice:

"I again urged upon him better coördination between the eastern and western fronts."[2]

Strange, in an impartial peacemaker![3]

On February 12th House received the awaited invitation to visit Germany:[4] and there began an adroit series of arguments and efforts on the part of the British to delay his departure. On February 13th House reports lunching alone with Grey:

"We talked of nature, solitude, Wordsworth . . . He told of Roosevelt's visit with him in the New Forest and how it occurred."[5]

Such charm could not be resisted. After luncheon House reports that he showed him Zimmermann's letter—we get the impression, indeed, that House showed Grey everything—and "we discussed it long and carefully."

---

[1] E. M. House to Woodrow Wilson, telegram, February 11, 1915. Transcribed from Mr. Wilson's shorthand notes deciphering Colonel House's message.

[2] Colonel House's diary entry February 18, 1915. *The Intimate Papers of Colonel House*, Vol. I, p. 379.

[3] We find Grey in his book saying that he felt House to have made the same judgement as Page on the merits of the war but to differ from the ambassador on the possibility of bringing the United States into it. Viscount Grey, *Twenty-five Years*, Vol. II, p. 125.

[4] *The Intimate Papers of Colonel House*, Vol. I, p. 370.

[5] *Ibid.*, p. 371.

"I had a feeling that the sooner I went [to Germany], the better . . ."

House saw himself dramatically:

"We sat by the fire in his library, facing one another, discussing every phase of the situation with a single mind and purpose."[1]

Gently and most confidentially Grey told of the British plans: the immense secret military movements under way: "200,000 British troops" to Saloniki: and, at the last, intimated that "he did not think it wise for me to undertake a peace mission to Germany" until after there had been further military developments.

It was a most intimate meeting, House even advising Grey as to his personal plans for retirement, afterwards confiding to his diary:

"He . . . looked at me wide-eyed and serious."[2]

Still under the spell, House went home and wrote to Wilson that his judgement coincided with Grey's advice to "let matters develop somewhat further"[3] before going on to Germany.

On this very day, the 15th, Wilson sent a code cablegram to House which he wrote out—as he did most of his messages to House of this period—first in shorthand, then in code on his own typewriter. He quoted from Gerard's peace message of the 11th:

"It is my belief that if you seize the present opportunity you will be the instrument of bringing about the greatest peace which has ever been signed, but it will be fatal to hesitate or wait a moment; success is dependent on immediate action."[4]

---

[1] *The Intimate Papers of Colonel House*, Vol. I, p. 372.

[2] *Ibid.*, p. 373.

[3] February 15, 1915. This extract is not quoted in *The Intimate Papers of Colonel House*.

[4] For Gerard's entire message see *Foreign Relations of the United States*, Supplement, 1915, pp. 9–10.

Although expressing the opinion that the method proposed by Gerard was "not the right one," Wilson concluded by asking anxiously:

"Have you had any intimation of any kind from Berlin?"[1]

But House was conferring again with Grey and Asquith.

When Gerard's urgent letter came,[2] on the 18th—saying that peace proposals were "a matter of days even hours"—House hurried around to show it to Grey,[3] who called Gerard's prophecies of German victory "absurd" and said England would go on fighting until she attained her ends.[4] House accordingly decided that the trip to Germany should be postponed, at least for a few weeks.[5] He had already cabled to Wilson that he felt "that it is essential to conform to their wishes for they are accepting you as their medium of communication with Germany and it is very important that they continue to do so."[6]

On the 19th House wrote to Gerard that Grey found it "utterly impossible to make any such hasty proposal as you thought the situation required," that he could not get to Berlin soon, and that "we will have to let the matter drift until another period of deadlock ensues."

By this time Wilson was beginning to grow extremely impatient, and on the 20th he sent a cablegram to Colonel House that was decidedly tart, warning him against being influenced by the British policy of delay. It is here printed in full:

---

[1]House received this message on February 16th. He immediately acknowledged receipt of it (in a postscript to his letter to the President of the 15th, which he had not yet sent) but did not indicate that Gerard's message had made any impression upon him.

[2]See this volume, pp. 308–309.

[3]The Intimate Papers of Colonel House, Vol. I, p. 379.

[4]Unpublished postscript to Colonel House's letter to the President of February 18th.

[5]The Intimate Papers of Colonel House, Vol. I, p. 375.

[6]February 17, 1915. Transcribed from Mr. Wilson's shorthand notes deciphering House's code message.

"Your dispatch of the 17th received. It will of course occur to you that you cannot go too far in allowing the English government to determine when it is best to go to Germany because they naturally desire to await some time when they have the advantage because of events in the field or elsewhere.

"If the impression were to be created in Berlin that you were to come only when the British government thought it the opportune time for you to come, you might be regarded when you reached there as their spokesman rather than as mine.

"Do you think we can frankly state this dilemma to Grey? He will doubtless realize how very important it is to learn Germany's mind at the earliest possible moment. No one can be sure what a single day may develop, either in events or in opinion. The whole atmosphere may change at any moment. We are sending today identical notes to the British and German governments.[1] Please say to Page that he cannot emphasize too much in presenting the note to Grey the favorable opinion which would be created in this country if the British government could see its way clear to adopt the suggestions made there.

"Opinion here is still decidedly friendly, but a tone of great uneasiness is distinctly audible now and the events and decisions of the next few days will undoubtedly make a deep impression."

It is clear from this cablegram that the President was growing anxious; his reference to British advantage "elsewhere" indicates that he saw clearly the danger of delay until the submarine controversy became acute. In reply the next day House warned: "We must be patient . . ."

On the 22nd, the President sent another urgent code cablegram to House:

"I learned yesterday . . . that Bernstorff showed great

---

[1] Suggesting an agreement to relieve neutral shipping. See this volume, pp. 257–258.

relief when he learned direct from his government that you would receive 'a most cordial welcome from them any time you chose to go.' [Wallace?] reports Bernstorff as seeming anxious and worried. Do you get it direct from Zimmermann or through Gerard that the terms you suggested as basis for parleys in your letter to Zimmermann would not be considered? I understand the situation but want to be sure of each element in it."[1]

But House was hopelessly involved in a leisurely discussion of details and terms with the British. He wrote to Wilson on the 23rd explaining the delays—"the time was not opportune for peace proposals."[2] He had commented previously[3] on the "usual British slowness" in putting off his conferences and went on to say:

"The psychological time to have ended this war was around the end of November or the first of December when everything looked as if it had gotten into a permanent deadlock. You will remember we tried to impress this upon Sir Cecil and tried to get quicker action, but without success."

Had he forgotten that in November and December he had been equally urging the President to delay?[4]

It was about this time, no doubt largely as a result of House's and Page's letters, that the President seems to have given up the hope of any immediate opening toward peace. Overborne with burdens at home, and attempting to deal with the direct problems of neutrality complicated by the reactions of American public opinion, he seems to have turned his mind aside from House's activities. If nothing could be done—nothing could be done: he reverted

---

[1]Transcribed from Mr. Wilson's shorthand notes.

[2]House was here reporting the ideas of the Russian Minister of Finance and the French Minister of Foreign Affairs.

[3]In his letter of the 18th.

[4]See Section I of this chapter.

to other things. There is an abrupt change in the quality of his letters to House. He no longer advises or urges: his comments, like the comments during House's previous peace venture in Europe, in the summer of 1914,[1] are general and approving. On February 25th he wired:

"Your cables enable me to understand the situation in all its phases. I greatly appreciate them. I am of course content to be guided by your judgement as to each step."

House continued to talk with all sorts of people, even the King, whom he found "the most bellicose Englishman that I have so far met," and who would not talk about peace before the fight was all knocked out of Germany.[2] Balfour he saw, and John Burns and Bryce, and even Curzon, "the worst jingo I have met."[3] He reported regularly to the President, certain he knew the inmost thoughts of the English:

". . . I told him [Grey]," he confides, "that I thought I now knew his mind quite well and also that of practically every member of the Cabinet. In addition I believed I knew what the people of the Empire desired and how far he could go with the Cabinet, the public and with his allies."[4]

As a matter of fact, reading his letters and his diary, one cannot avoid the impression that House was being completely dominated, just as Page was, by British diplomacy, by the sheer persuasiveness and charm of the British statesman at his best—a best that is without equal in this world. A statesmanship that can talk a man's heart away on the subject of "nature, solitude, Wordsworth"!

On March 5th, after having been in England more than a month, House wrote that he had finally persuaded Grey

---

[1] See this volume, Chapter I, section 3.

[2] E. M. House to Woodrow Wilson, March 1, 1915. *The Intimate Papers of Colonel House*, Vol. I, p. 385.

[3] Colonel House's diary entry, March 9, 1915. *Ibid.*, p. 389.

[4] E. M. House to Woodrow Wilson, February 27, 1915.

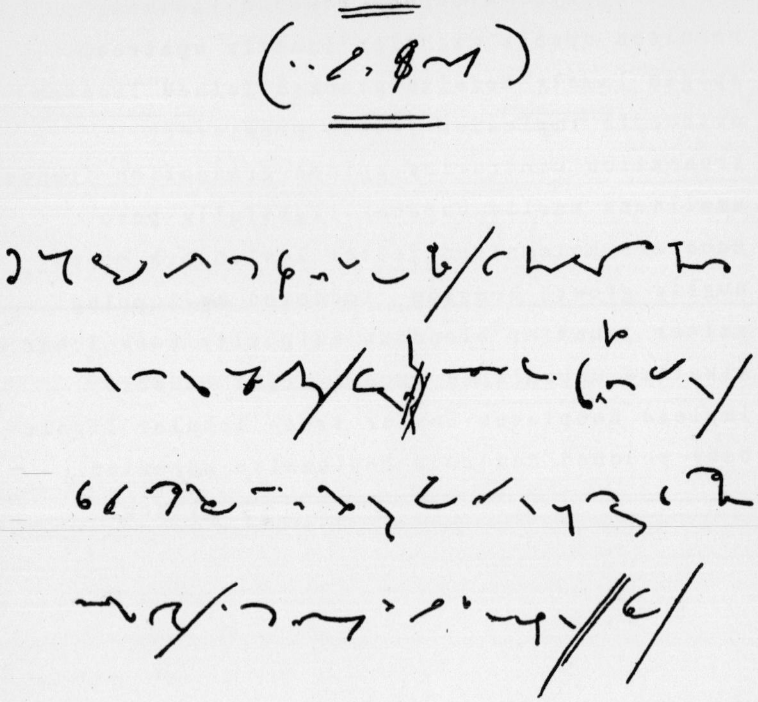

For Beverley. Misspend rosebud Plunkets
repulses upsets mightier innerly upstream
apogee lamely bedsite slacked joined locates
orthoepic impleader jetson presidency
truncation contraries spines graduation francs
smallness snells burdons rightfully pavo
Hoosiers solemnized jetter lowlanders moons
nugify growth bedside foddered ~~tp~~ hopping
smiter jauntier blendous adiposity sunk lobar
alkalize unpunished Tacoma argol bedsore
implead nonpluses Hester truss lobular lignum
baby pouched hundreds Benthamite adhesion.

                                    Wilson.

Amembassy, London.
1-Co. Xa-Pn.
   11:07 p.m.

March 8, 1915.

The President's method of communicating with Colonel House. His
shorthand notes for the telegram to Colonel House of March 8, 1915,
and his transcription into code, done on his own typewriter. The
transcription of the note is given on page 318.

it was time to move on to Germany. He arrived in Berlin more than a month after Gerard had cabled that peace proposals were a question of hours. By that time the German campaign in the East was under way and the submarine zone in effect: he was too late.

Wilson replied on March 8th in general terms, expressing his usual confidence and leaving everything to House.

"There is nothing special to report on this side, and you do not need instructions. Your admirable letters and telegrams keep me posted in just the right way. Your cable of today gives me the feeling that there is at last some real hope. This is just a message of personal greeting and to express the hope that the journey you are about to undertake may be accomplished without untoward adventure and in perfect health. You may manage all the rest. I have no anxiety about it."

Just as during the former trip, the President seems not to have applied his mind to the matter at all. "You may manage all the rest. I have no anxiety about it." And, as formerly, he expressed his personal interest in House.

From that time onward until just before the sinking of the *Lusitania*—two months of important events and great anxiety; three ships were attacked by the Germans and several Americans killed—the President wrote or cabled to House four times, brief communications full of general commendation and personal affection, but with astonishingly little in them that was specific—or that dealt with realities.

On April 1st he cabled:

"Your cable of Monday received and read with great interest and approval. The suggestion you are to carry to London seems to me very promising and may afford the opening we are looking for.

"Page and Willard have obtained leave as requested. I warmly admire the way in which you are conducting your

conferences at each stage. You are laying the indispensable groundwork and sending me just the information I
need.

"In reply to your cable of thirty-first, representations
had already been made by the American ambassador at
St. Petersburg such as Zimmermann suggests. I myself
wrote a personal letter to the Czar at the request of the
Austrian ambassador here. Anything that has not been
done will be done up to the limit of diplomatic privilege."

And on the 15th:

"It is fine how you establish just the right relations and
just the right understanding at each capital, and I am sure
it will bear rich fruit at the right time.

"I am particularly gratified by what you report concerning your conference with the French Minister for
Foreign Affairs. Please express to the Minister and to the
President my feeling of warm gratitude that they are so
generous as to receive our offers of friendship in just
the spirit in which they are offered and with such full
and sympathetic comprehension of the part we wish to
play.

"America will remember these things as she remembers
many another generous attitude of France in her relations
with the United States.

"Has the text of Bernstorff's note about our neutrality
been cabled to France? If so do you think it is possible he
is speaking as the Berlin Foreign Office would speak, or
only in his own voice . . ."

On May 3rd he replied to a three-weeks-old letter from
House:

"Referring to your letter of twelfth April I think the
suggestion you make for starting [correspondence?] between the belligerents is excellent. I shall be glad to play
any part circumstances suggest or permit.

"Your cable of May first gives me some hope that the

first of your alternative suggestions[1] may be about to work.

"I would welcome any advice you may have to give as to the best way of handling the matter of the sinking of the American oil boat in view of all you have learned."

On May 5th, two days before the tragedy of the *Lusitania*, Wilson sent quite another kind of message[2]—sharp and to the point—asking House to protest to Grey against British interference with American cargoes, and citing the irritation of American opinion. A breath of reality!

During all these weeks and months House had been travelling about Europe, accomplishing nothing whatsoever, discussing vague schemes for peace conventions, talking of a freedom of the seas which was a chimera, and writing voluminously to the President. One cannot avoid the impression in reading his letters and extracts from his diary as published in the *Intimate Papers*—describing his meetings and conversations and "luncheons alone" with various celebrities, jumping impulsively at new ideas—that he was enjoying it all enormously. Why not? While his good intentions are undebatable, no real responsibility whatsoever rested upon him: he had no office: his mission was so secret as to be beyond criticism. His letters often contained comments highly flattering to the President:

"I think constantly of the great part I feel sure you are to play, and my desires go no further than to have you preside over the convention composed of all nations.

"I am sure that America would be filled with enthusiastic pride to have you play this part, and there would be

---

[1] First, to start peace parleys by means of a discussion by correspondence on the "Freedom of the Seas" as a basis for peace; second, discuss by correspondence a plan for holding two peace conferences, one by belligerents on war problems, the other by all nations to make terms for permanent peace. (House to Wilson, April 12th. For House's idea of "Freedom of the Seas," see *The Intimate Papers of Colonel House*, Vol. I, pp. 406–407.)

[2] See this volume, pp. 326–327.

no voice raised against your leaving our country for such a purpose."[1]

Quite the most expressive term applied to the peace talk of these two months was that of Sir Edward Grey on April 24th—when it became clear that America might really be embroiled with Germany.

"Fudge!" said Sir Edward Grey.[2]

One thing, certainly, House's mission did accomplish: delay! And delay was another name for the British diplomacy that was seeking to bring America into the war against Germany. It was most unfortunate that America during these crucial months should have had representatives in England who were as completely committed to the Allied cause as Page and House.

And the President's faith in House prevented any attempt on his own part to explore other possible avenues to peace, such for example as those being advocated so urgently by his Secretary of State. Probably everything would have failed, but not everything was tried.[3]

On May 7th every thought of peace was blotted out by the tragedy of the *Lusitania*.

---

[1] March 8, 1915.

[2] Grey to Colonel House, transmitted by House to Wilson on May 7th:
"Your news from Berlin is not encouraging: it reduces Bernstorff's peace talk at Washington to 'Fudge.'"

[3] A month later Colonel House arrived in New York (June 13th) denying that his trip to Europe was in any way connected with a possible mission looking toward peace or that he was the personal emissary of President Wilson.
"I did not talk peace, and that was not my mission abroad," Colonel House declared. (New York *Times*, June 14, 1915.)

CHAPTER VII

THE *LUSITANIA* CRISIS

Long acquainted as this government has been with the character of the imperial German government and with the high principles of equity by which they have in the past been actuated and guided, the government of the United States can not believe that the commanders of the vessels which committed these acts of lawlessness did so except under a misapprehension of the orders issued by the imperial German naval authorities.

First Lusitania *note, May 13, 1915.*

No matter what England does to Germany or Germany to England, our rights are unaltered and we cannot abate them in the least.

W. J. Bryan to J. W. Gerard, May 23, 1915.

The government of the United States is contending for something much greater than mere rights of property or privileges of commerce. It is contending for nothing less high and sacred than the rights of humanity . . .

Second Lusitania *note, June 9, 1915.*

I. CONFRONTING THE OMINOUS SITUATION OF MAY 1915

MAY 1, 1915, was a day of tragedy in the affairs of the world. In the morning newspapers appeared the ominous warning of the German embassy to American passengers against crossing the war zone in ships of Great Britain or her allies.[1] It was made more startling and

---

"NOTICE!

[1]"TRAVELLERS intending to embark on the Atlantic voyage are reminded that a state of war exists between Germany and her allies and Great Britain and her allies; that the zone of war includes the waters adjacent to the British Isles; that in accordance with formal notice given by the Imperial German Government, vessels flying the flag of Great Britain or of any of her allies, are liable to destruction in those waters and that travellers sailing in the war zone on ships of Great Britain or her allies do so at their own risk.

"IMPERIAL GERMAN EMBASSY
"Washington, D. C., April 22, 1915"

(New York *Sun*, May 1, 1915.)

impressive by the news that followed of the sinking of the American tanker *Gulflight* by German submarines and the drowning of several American citizens. Tremendous reverberations in the press testified to the sudden and painful awakening of the American people, not only to the realities of the war in Europe, but to the possibility that the war might actually involve the United States. There had, indeed, been gathering evidence of the spread of the conflagration throughout the whole world. On May 1st had come the announcement of the treaty of London (signed April 26th) which brought Italy into the conflict, and in that very week Japan was presenting her revised demands upon China,[1] indicating that the Far East might also become involved in war. But no one of these vast and distant evidences so touched the American consciousness as the list of dead citizens, men of our own nation, drowned in the zone of war. Even with these proofs, however, the seriousness of the situation was difficult to believe. On this historic first of May the noble ship *Lusitania* eased out of her berth in New York and began her last tragic voyage to Europe. "Sails, Undisturbed by German Warning,"[2] declared the press in a front-page column. The passengers who were aboard her could not credit the extremes of ferocity to which maddened nations could descend. They even commented lightly on the warning as "silly," "tommy-rot."[3]

On this first day of May the President arrived in Williamstown, Massachusetts, where he had gone—a hurried trip, a moment of attention to the common human obligations and personal ties of his life—to attend the christening of his first-born grandchild, Francis Woodrow Sayre. The alarming news of the events of May 1st and

[1] *Foreign Relations of the United States*, 1915, p. 127.
[2] New York *Times*, May 2, 1915.
[3] *Ibid.*

2nd came to him in telegrams upon which he refused to comment. He might well complain of these driven days, as he did in intimate letters, that he was permitted to have no personal life of his own at all, but even he had not yet been wholly swept into and consumed by the events of the war. We shall get no complete picture of his life at this time without glimpses of the problems of domestic policy which he had also daily to meet. To the historian nothing could seem more distant, vaguer, less important at the moment than the tariff question, and yet we find Wilson writing at length on April 29th to the editor of the St. Louis *Republic* regarding Republican attacks on the Underwood tariff.

Though the world might be collapsing, he was bedevilled by the usual appeals for patronage and pardons. Writing to a congressman on the same day, denying a respite that had been asked:

"There are so many applications of this sort that I should be constantly suspending the processes of the courts if I were to do things of this kind."[1]

He had also to consider the Canadian Boundary Commission, writing Bryan on the subject, and railroad policy in Alaska upon which he corresponded with Lane on April 30th.

Wilson returned to Washington on May 3rd to find his desk covered with excited appeals, including two more vigorous memoranda by Lansing forwarded by Bryan: and on that evening Bryan, who was labouring under great apprehension, came to the White House for an extended conference.

Lansing, in his memorandum of May 1st, set forth his belief that the *Cushing* incident was a "more flagrant violation of neutral rights on the high seas [than the *Falaba* case], and indicates that the German naval policy

---

[1]Woodrow Wilson to Joseph Taggart, April 29, 1915.

is one of wanton and indiscriminate destruction of vessels regardless of nationality." He urged that representations regarding Thrasher's death, however, should precede any in this case, lest it "appear that we care less for an American life than we do [for] an American ship," and lest it "might be interpreted as an admission that an American citizen had no right to take passage on a British vessel. . . . An American citizen legally has such a right and in my opinion the government ought to uphold it."

He characterized the German warning as "an impertinent act, which would warrant summary action if it was expedient," concluding that "everything seems to point to a determined effort to affront this government and force it to an open rupture of diplomatic relations."

Here Lansing was challenging his chief's—Bryan's—deepest convictions. Bryan agreed[1] that the *Cushing* case should be taken up with the German government, but he still contested the right of Americans to take the risk of travelling in British ships. He even held the German warning to be a "fortunate thing . . . evidence of a friendly desire to evade anything that might raise a question between Germany and the United States."

The chasm separating the President and his Secretary of State was steadily widening. On May 4th they had a long talk at the White House—"closeted," in the jargon of the press—and a cabinet meeting followed. We do not know exactly what happened, but it is plain, from Bryan's letter of the following day referring to the conversations, that Wilson sought a compromise course—to make strong representations to Germany, but if these failed to bring results, to postpone the final reckoning until after the war.

In this move Wilson was trying earnestly to rise above the passions of the moment: and seems to have attained

---

[1] In a note of May 1st, enclosing Lansing's memorandum to the President.

at least the temporary approval of Bryan, whose letter expressed great relief:

"Since hearing your statement at cabinet meeting indicating an intention to postpone final settlements until after the war, in case present efforts fail, I am not so much afraid of representations—it is the *possibility* of *war* from which I shrink & I think we have a good excuse for asking that the disputes be settled when reason reigns. It occurs to me that the effect might be softened on both if we make a protest against the holding up of our trade with neutrals at the same time we protest against the submarines."[1]

Upon this latter suggestion of another protest to Great Britain which seems also to have been raised in the cabinet meeting,[2] Wilson acted at once—that very day—sending an unusually sharp message to Colonel House:

"There is something I think ought to be said to Sir Edward Grey which I wish you specially to [emphasize?] . . . A very serious change is coming over the public sentiment in this country because of the needless delays and many willful interferences in dealing with our neutral cargoes."

He goes on to say:

"The country is listening with more and more acquies-

---

[1] May 5, 1915.

[2] The general attitude of the cabinet at this time is excellently set forth in a letter from Secretary Lane to Colonel House:

"You would be interested, I think, in hearing some of the discussion around the cabinet table. There isn't a man in the cabinet who has a drop of German blood in his veins, I guess. Two of us were born under the British flag. . . . The most of us are Scotch in our ancestry, and yet each day that we meet we boil over somewhat, at the foolish manner in which England acts. Can it be that she is trying to take advantage of the war to hamper our trade? . . .

"If Congress were in session, we would be actively debating an embargo resolution to-day. . . .

"After all, our one great asset is the confidence of the people in the President. They do not love him, because he appears to them as a man of the cloister. But they respect him as a wise, sane leader who will keep them out of trouble. . . ." (May 5, 1915.) *The Intimate Papers of Colonel House*, Vol. I, pp. 458–459.

cence, just because of this intense irritation, to the suggestion that an embargo be placed upon the shipment of
arms and war supplies, and if this grows much more
before the Congress assembles in December it may be
very difficult if not impossible for me to prevent action
to that end. Please present to Sir Edward Grey very
earnestly the wisdom and necessity of giving utmost
freedom to our commerce in neutral goods to neutral
ports, and the permanent settlement of all questions concerning cargoes seized or detained."[1]

It cannot be doubted that it was about this time, and
in view of the series of events narrated, that there began
to be a sharp intensification of American opinion. The
German warning, the ruthless sinking of ships by submarines, the loss of non-combatant American lives, not
only brought the war home to us, but it angered us—and
perhaps also alarmed us. We had been irritated by both
sides: both were acting, we considered, illegally and un-
justifiably. But if the British irritated us by interfering
with our trade, the Germans shocked and angered us by
spilling our blood. If the British method was lawless, the
German seemed inhuman. And there was a tactless arro-
gance in such acts as the published warning of May 1st
that Americans resented deeply and angrily. Although
Wilson was making every effort himself to maintain the
complete self-possession which he was urging upon his
audiences, there is evidence that it was about this time
that there began to be a real change also in his feeling,
if not in his policies or in his outward attitude, toward
the belligerents. It was probably about this time that
Mr. Tumulty, the President's secretary, as he relates,
"broached the subject of the British blockade and laid
before the President the use our enemies were making of
his patient attitude toward England." Mr. Tumulty's

---

[1] Transcribed from Mr. Wilson's shorthand notes.

sympathies with the cause of Ireland no doubt sharpened his comments. Wilson attributed this criticism entirely to unworthy motives of vote-getting and said:

"I have gone to the very limit in pressing our claims upon England and urging the British Foreign Office to modify the blockade."

Then he referred to a letter from Page quoting Grey's remark that "America must remember that we are fighting her fight, as well as our own, to save the civilization of the world." Wilson said, according to Tumulty:

"He was right. England is fighting our fight and you may well understand that I shall not, in the present state of the world's affairs, place obstacles in her way."[1]

If this statement is authentically reported, the President's fundamental conception of the war must have altered since the submarine warfare began to affect Americans. It is a tenable thesis, then, that we have here the point—about May 1st—at which Wilson ceased to be "neutral in thought" and began to be more and more swayed by the theory of the war that Page and, less strongly, House were so constantly and vigorously urging upon him. Nor could he have been oblivious of the opinion of Lord Bryce and other leaders whom he respected. It does not follow that Wilson's subsequent efforts to maintain neutrality as the best possible course for the United States, the course that promised most in keeping us out of the conflict, were not entirely sincere. It was possible conscientiously to reconcile a change of feeling with consistency of action, to subordinate personal convictions to official responsibilities, and we can discover, indeed, no outward change in his effort to be neutral.

He was even making progress during these early days in May in reconciling the sharp conflict of opinion that existed among his own advisers—between Bryan and

---

[1] Joseph P. Tumulty, *Woodrow Wilson As I Know Him*, pp. 230–231.

Lansing. His own conclusions were closer to those of Lansing and were probably the opinions of other cabinet members. If he was moved by Bryan, and it is plain that he was, it was less because he was convinced by Bryan's reasoning than because he was impressed by the strength and earnestness of Bryan's convictions. Wilson knew well that the Commoner instinctively and formidably represented much that lay deep in the feeling and thought of the people. He had, indeed, a real and deep admiration for Bryan. In a birthday greeting, written on March 18, 1915, he had expressed himself:

"I have learned not only to value you as a friend and counsellor, but, if you will let me say so, I have found a very strong affection for you growing in my heart. Your high motives and constant thought of the public interest have been an example and stimulation to me throughout these years."

Some of the cabinet (though not Garrison) felt much the same. Lane had written, on May 5th:

"I am growing more and more in my admiration for Bryan each day. He is too good a Christian to run a naughty world and he doesn't hate hard enough, but he certainly is a noble and high-minded man, and loyal to the President to the last hair. . . ."[1]

So an arrangement was in process of being made which would be acceptable to Bryan and the great public he represented. The right of Americans to travel on any ships they chose was to be maintained, but presumably the German warning was to stand unrebuked to have its influence. Wilson was to continue his protests against British interference with American trade: in his cablegram to House of May 5th, already quoted, he even came near using the threat of an interruption to the munitions

---

[1]Franklin K. Lane to Colonel House, May 5, 1915. *The Intimate Papers of Colonel House*, Vol. I, p. 459.

traffic by hinting that he might not be able to prevent action of Congress to that end. The illegality of the submarine blockade and of all particular actions under it resulting in loss of American lives or property would be asserted in language firm but not provocative, and a way would be left open for postponing a settlement of the accounting to which Germany was to be held. In the meantime there was always the chance—which Wilson seemed to have counted upon too much—that something would happen, some reaction in Europe, which would stay the progress of the war and bring peace parleys in which he felt that America could be of service to the world. Colonel House was abroad seeking some such opening— and the President was listening—too closely—to his urgent demands for more time.

From Wilson's point of view—the policy of neutrality and avoidance of war—there was much to be said for this programme. It might work as long as only minor incidents arose out of the submarine warfare. The loss of two or three ships and even of two or three lives might be passed over for future settlement.

But the *Lusitania* was on the high seas, loaded with American passengers. On May 7th she was sunk without warning, with the loss of over a hundred precious American lives: a horror that shook the nation to its depths: a catastrophe too overwhelming to be held within the bounds of the President's new formula of action.

Not peace, more terrible war!

II. THE SINKING OF THE "LUSITANIA"

At the close of a busy cabinet meeting, about one o'clock on May 7, 1915, a secretary[1] hurried into the President's room with a cablegram in his hand. It contained the startling news that the great ship *Lusitania*

[1] Rudolph Forster.

had been sunk by a German submarine. Two hours later came the first official report, from Ambassador Page:

"The *Lusitania* was torpedoed off the Irish coast and sunk in half an hour. No news yet of passengers."[1]

It was not until late in the evening that the President knew the worst, that more than one thousand lives, including many Americans, had been lost.

The reaction in the United States was one of horror. Newspapers blazed with it: six solid pages in the New York *Times*. Press comments bristled with such phrases as "wholesale murder," "piracy," "slaughter."

The President's response was one of deep emotion. "Tears stood in his eyes," as the heart-rending reports came in.[2] Nevertheless, he met the flood of passionate comment that filled the press, the demands for immediate and drastic action, pouring in upon him in hundreds of telegrams and letters, with the self-mastery and the calmness of judgement he had been so earnestly commending to the nation.

"If I pondered over those tragic items . . . I should see red in everything, and I am afraid that when I am called upon to act . . . I could not be just to anyone."

Utter condemnation marked most of the comments. "An act of piracy," shrilled Theodore Roosevelt.[3] Colonel House, dining that night in London with Ambassador Page, said, "We shall be at war with Germany within a month."[4] He cabled Wilson, "We can no longer remain neutral spectators."[5] Page looked eagerly, now, to American participation in the war:

". . . we live in hope that the United States will come

---

[1] *Foreign Relations of the United States*, Supplement, 1915, p. 384.
[2] Joseph P. Tumulty, *Woodrow Wilson As I Know Him*, p. 232.
[3] Statement in the New York *Times*, May 8, 1915.
[4] *The Life and Letters of Walter H. Page*, Vol. II, p. 2.
[5] May 9, 1915. *The Intimate Papers of Colonel House*, Vol. I, p. 434.

in, as the only chance to give us standing and influence when the reorganization of the world must begin."[1]

He expressed the same opinion in a lengthy telegram to Bryan:

"The freely expressed unofficial feeling is that the United States must declare war or forfeit European respect."[2]

In returning this telegram to Bryan, Wilson commented on the fact that it expressed not Page's but British opinion, and observed:

"It is a very serious thing to have such things thought, because everything that affects the opinion of the world regarding us affects our influence for good."[3]

He was deeply concerned about it, but, unlike Page, he did not believe that English opinion concerning us was the most important thing in the world. If he resisted allowing his own action to be guided by his emotions, he was not going to permit it to be determined by the feelings and desires of the British.

As for Bryan, he began at once to seek mitigations, for he shuddered at the thought of war. If the *Lusitania* carried contraband, then "England has been using our citizens to protect her ammunition."[4]

He asked Lansing to investigate and found that practically the entire cargo consisted of military supplies of one kind and another,[5] though the only item of ammuni-

---

[1]To Arthur W. Page. *The Life and Letters of Walter H. Page*, Vol. II, p. 5.

[2]May 8, 1915. *Foreign Relations of the United States*, Supplement, 1915, pp. 385–386. It is interesting to note that this telegram contains one of the earliest pieces of definite information sent the State Department about the secret treaties—a reference to the treaty which promised "very large parts of Austrian territory, some of which has a Slavic population," to Italy if she "comes into the war within a month." This probably got scant attention under the circumstances.

[3]May 10, 1915. *The Life and Letters of Walter H. Page*, Vol. III, p. 242.

[4]W. J. Bryan to his wife, on the evening of the sinking of the *Lusitania*. *The Memoirs of William Jennings Bryan*, p. 421.

[5]Based on the report of Dudley Field Malone, Collector of the Port of New York, June 4, 1915, and on a summary of the *Lusitania's* manifest, filed with it; Lansing to Wilson, June 15, 1915.

tion was 4200 cases of cartridges. He wrote to the President, arguing:

"Germany has a right to prevent contraband going to the Allies and a ship carrying contraband should not rely upon passengers to protect her from attack . . ."[1]

Wilson began at once to work upon a note of protest to Germany. He appears to have consulted no one, not even the experts of the State Department. The essential problems had been under intensive discussion since the sinking of the *Falaba*, more than a month before. He even refrained from calling his cabinet together: he could obtain from its members nothing new except their emotional reactions to the appalling catastrophe—which were precisely what he wanted to avoid. He told his secretary, Mr. Tumulty:

"I am bound to consider beforehand all the facts and circumstances surrounding the sinking of the *Lusitania* and to calculate the effect upon the country of every incautious or unwise move."

He would not be carried into "radical action . . . based upon the present emotionalism of the people."

He felt that Congress would support him at the moment if he advocated war, but if war finally came with "all of its horrors and bloody aftermath," would not the people as they pored over the casualty lists say: "Why did Wilson move so fast in this matter? Why didn't he try peaceably to settle this question with Germany? Why could he not have waited a little longer?"[2]

While he was toiling upon his reply—"I had never seen him more serious or careworn"[3]—he was called to Philadelphia[4] to make a promised address to several thousand

---

[1] May 9, 1915.
[2] Joseph P. Tumulty, *Woodrow Wilson As I Know Him*, pp. 233-234.
[3] *Ibid.*, p. 232.
[4] May 10th.

foreign-born citizens who had just become naturalized Americans. He was greeted by tremendous cheering crowds. When Mayor Blankenburg, himself of German origin, in introducing the President thanked God that "we have at Washington a man who knows what is right and just,"[1] the enthusiasm was unrestrained.

It was inevitable that he should make some reference to the crisis which then confronted the nation, and to which he was devoting his entire mind. He poured out, indeed, as often before in public addresses, the deep inner spirit with which he was approaching his problem, appealing passionately for greatness of view, sublimity of action:

"The example of America must be a special example. The example of America must be the example not merely of peace because it will not fight, but of peace because peace is the healing and elevating influence of the world and strife is not. There is such a thing as a man being too proud to fight. There is such a thing as a nation being so right that it does not need to convince others by force that it is right."[2]

To grasp the moral grandeur of this statement it is necessary to read and ponder it in full. Certainly it is most unfair to place by itself the phrase "too proud to fight" upon which the newspapers, particularly the disillusioned English press, at once fastened. It was, of course, inevitable that they should do so; the phrase was so striking, and it rang so mockingly in the ears of those who saw themselves disappointed in their high hopes that America was about to intervene on the side of the hard-pressed Allies.

It was, indeed, only repeating, in a sharper-cut phrase, what the President had said before, what lay, indeed, at the core of his policy. As he had put it in an address delivered in April:

---

[1]New York *Times*, May 11, 1915.
[2]*The Public Papers of Woodrow Wilson*, Vol. III, p. 321.

"My interest in the neutrality of the United States is not the petty desire to keep out of trouble. . . . But I am interested in neutrality because there is something so much greater to do than fight; there is a distinction waiting for this nation that no nation has ever yet got. That is the distinction of absolute self-control and self-mastery."[1]

The President himself recognized afterwards, when the words were caught up everywhere by his critics, that he should perhaps have avoided using the phrase, or developed it further.[2] Nevertheless the truth expressed was of the fundamentals of his mind.

The Philadelphia speech showed that the President had set himself against rushing the country into war, that he felt the limit of forbearance had not yet been reached, that he had decided Germany must have all the chance possible to make amends for what she had done and give assurances against its repetition.[3]

On the morning of the 11th Wilson had the draft of his proposed note ready to submit to the cabinet. In the meantime Germany had taken three steps in the situation: 1. The government had issued a statement, on the 9th, declaring that attacks on neutral ships were contrary to orders and that it would at once tender regrets and compensation for such incidents if the facts clearly warranted such action.[4] 2. It offered preliminary explanations in the

---

[1] April 20, 1915. *The Public Papers of Woodrow Wilson*, Vol. III, p. 305.

[2] Frank Parker Stockbridge to the author. Stockbridge had heard the address—and the next morning, in Washington, had asked the President how he came to use the phrase.

[3] It is significant that among those favouring such a course was ex-President Taft, who wrote, on May 10th, to express his doubt that we had yet reached the point of being obliged to go into the war against Germany and to urge that "if it can now be avoided, in a manner consistent with the dignity and honor of our country, we should make every effort to this end." He thought that, in the probable event of refusal of satisfaction by Germany, diplomatic relations might be broken without war following; but he also commented favourably on a suggestion that the questions of violation of international law be submitted to arbitration. Wilson, on the 13th, expressed his appreciation of the letter and said the suggestions would "have great weight with me."

[4] *Foreign Relations of the United States*, Supplement, 1915, pp. 387–388.

In re Lusitania.

[RECITAL of the facts of the death of Thrasher,
the attacks on the Cushing and Gulflight, and
the loss of American lives by the sinking of
the Lusitania.]

The Government of the Unted States has observed
this series of events with growing concern and
amazement. Knowing, as it did, the humane and
enlightened spirit of the Imperial German Government hitherto in all matters of international
right and particularly with regard to the freedom of the seas; having learned to recognize the
German views and the German influence in the
field of international obligation as always engaged upon the side of justice and humanity; and
having understood the instructions of the Imperial German Government to its naval commanders to
be upon the same plane of humane action prescribed by the naval codes of other nations, it was
loath to believe, it cannot now bring itself to
believe, that these acts, so absolutely contrary
to the rules, the practices, and the spirit of
modern warfare, could have the countenance or
sanction of that great Government. It feels it
to be its duty, therefore, to address the Imperial German Government concerning them with the
utmost frankness and in the earnest hope that it
is not mistaken in expecting action on the part

First page of one of the President's early drafts of the note which
was sent to Germany on May 13, 1915—the first *Lusitania* note.
Written by the President on his own typewriter and corrected in his
handwriting.

Gulflight case indicating a mistake of the kind covered by this statement.[1] 3. Ambassador Bernstorff called at the Department of State on the 10th, and expressed his government's "deep regret" that "the events of the war had led to the loss of so many American lives."[2]

These steps, while they proved the unreality of Lansing's supposition that Germany was deliberately provoking a rupture, apparently led to no changes in Wilson's draft note, which he now read aloud to the assembled cabinet.

The tone of the paper was one of firm forbearance. Reiterating the American declaration of February 10th that the destruction of unarmed merchant ships without visit and search was without legal justification and again using the phrase "strict accountability," the note went on to assert the practical impossibility of observance of the elementary principles of international law by submarines, and the inadequacy of a general warning, such as that issued by the German embassy on May 1st, as a substitute for compliance with the law in each particular case. Accepting the German government's assurances that it desired to respect neutral rights, Wilson declared that the American government "confidently expects, therefore, that the imperial German government will disavow the acts of which the government of the United States complains, that they will make reparation as far as reparation is possible for injuries which are without measure, and that they will take immediate steps to prevent the recurrence of anything so obviously subversive of the principles of warfare for which the imperial German government have in the past so wisely and so firmly contended."

The President read the note with great feeling, and

---

[1] *Foreign Relations of the United States*, Supplement, 1915, pp. 387–388.
[2] Lansing's memorandum of Bernstorff's call. *Ibid.*, p. 387.

considerable discussion followed—the meeting lasting three hours. The chief point raised did not directly concern the note itself, the logic of which was so impressive that the cabinet accepted it as a whole; but dealt with possible eventualities. What if Germany refused the demands made upon her? Garrison expressed the opinion that war would inevitably follow, whereupon Bryan and Burleson suggested that some other course of action be sought for. Wilson argued that relations between countries had been repeatedly broken without hostilities resulting.[1]

On the following day, the 12th, Bryan wrote a long letter to the President, setting forth his suggestions. He admitted that the draft was a clear statement of the American position and agreed that "it is well to act without delay in order to give direction to public opinion." After making a few minor suggestions he went on:

"But, my dear Mr. President, I join in this document with a heavy heart. . . . I cannot bring myself to the belief that it is wise to relinquish the hope of playing the part of a friend to both sides in the role of peacemaker, and I fear this note will result in such a relinquishment . . ."

He held that it had a one-sided bearing as being so much sharper than the remonstrances directed to Great Britain, and as inflaming anti-German sentiment. He regretted that there was no intimation of postponing settlement until after the war (to which Wilson had inclined early in May). He pointed out that the illegal actions we were condemning were taken in retaliation for illegal British actions which we tolerated. He again emphasized the fact that American passengers were being carried by the British in ships laden with contraband. He referred to the misuse of the American flag.

---

[1] This account of the meeting of May 11th is based upon a report in the Washington Post enclosed by Bryan in a letter of May 12th, with a comment attached which intimates that he found it accurate.

"The only way, as I see it," he concluded, "to prevent irreparable injury being done by the statement is to issue simultaneously a protest against the objectionable conduct of the Allies which will keep them from rejoicing and show Germany that we are defending our rights from aggression from both sides."

The more Bryan considered the matter, the more worried he became. Later on in the same day an idea occurred to him which he hastened to embody in a second letter. Fearing the possibility that the President's note would result in too rapid a development of the crisis, he suggested that it be accompanied by some kind of public statement to the effect that "strict accountability" need not be construed as immediate accountability and that a final settlement might be postponed until peace was restored, adding that the United States would extend to Germany the principle embodied in the "cooling-off" treaties with the Allies.[1]

It was this suggestion which was to give rise to the famous supplementary statement, or "postscript," of heated controversy. The next morning Wilson wrote to Bryan:

"After sleeping over your suggestion, I have this to propose: It would not be wise, I think, to give out a direct statement; but I think the same purpose would be served by such a 'tip' as the enclosed, accompanying the publication of the note. And it would be best that this tip should be given out from the Executive Office, while the note was given out by the Department of State. What do you think?

"If you will return the paper in the course of the morning, I will make the necessary arrangements."[2]

The enclosed "tip" was written on the President's typewriter:

[1] *The Memoirs of William Jennings Bryan*, pp. 399–400.
[2] *Ibid.*, p. 400.

"There is a good deal of confidence in administration circles that Germany will respond to this note in a spirit of accommodation. It is pointed out that, while Germany is not one of the many nations which have recently signed treaties of deliberation and inquiry with the United States upon all points of serious difficulty, as a means of supplementing ordinary diplomatic methods and preventing, so far as feasible, the possibility of conflict, she has assented to the principle of such a treaty; and it is believed that she will act in this instance in the spirit of that assent. A frank issue is now made, and it is expected that it will be met in good temper and with a desire to reach an agreement, despite the passions of the hour,—passions in which the United States does not share,—or else submit the whole matter to such processes of discussion as will result in a permanent settlement."[1]

Bryan, much relieved, prepared to have the "postscript" sent out with the note. In the meantime, Lansing, having discovered what was in the wind, consulted with Garrison. Burleson, who was also brought in, called on the President with Tumulty. Wilson endeavoured to calm them, arguing that Bryan was a wise politician, and that the postscript was designed merely to allay American public feeling which was hostile to war. Whether owing to these remonstrances, or to his own reconsideration of the subject while driving alone during the morning, Wilson wrote Bryan a second letter:

"Since I expressed my approval of the statement you suggested for the press, I have heard something, indirectly, from the German embassy, which convinces me that we would lose all chance of bringing Germany to reason if we in any way or degree indicated to them, or to our own public, that this note was merely the first word in a pro-

---

[1] From original document in the President's files.

longed debate. I will tell you what I have in mind when I do not have to write it.

"In the meantime, I beg that you will pardon me for changing my mind thus. I am sure that it is the safer course, the one more likely to produce the results we are all praying for. Please withdraw the message (the supplementary statement) altogether. If we say anything of the kind it must be a little later, after the note has had its first effect."[1]

So it was that on May 13th the note, practically as drafted by the President, was transmitted to Germany.[2] It was signed by Bryan and went out unaccompanied by the supplementary statement on which he had counted to modify it. It appears in a letter written to Wilson on the next day that Bryan now relied for mitigation upon a compensatory protest against Great Britain's blockade measures and some action to restrain Americans from travelling on British ships. Lansing was set at once to drafting notes upon these subjects. Wilson wrote to Bryan concerning the latter on May 14th:

"As to the request to Americans not to take passage on belligerent ships (for I agree with Mr. Lansing that it could be nothing more than a request), my feeling is this: the request is unnecessary, if the object is to save lives,

---

[1]*The Memoirs of William Jennings Bryan*, pp. 401–402.

During the campaign of 1916, Senator Lodge made this so-called "postscript" an election issue. The President met it with an explanation (October 30th) in a letter to Walter Lippmann:

"No postscript or amendment of the *Lusitania* note was ever written or contemplated by me except such changes as I myself inserted which strengthened and emphasized the protest. It was suggested, after the note was ready for transmission, that an intimation be conveyed to the German government that a proposal for arbitration would be acceptable, and one member of the cabinet spoke to me about it, but it was never discussed in the cabinet meeting, and no threat of any resignation was ever made, for the very good reason that I rejected the suggestion after giving it such consideration as I thought every proposal deserved which touched so grave a matter. It was inconsistent with the purpose of the note. The public is in possession of everything that was said to the German government." (See *The Public Papers of Woodrow Wilson*, Vol. IV, p. 383.)

[2]*Foreign Relations of the United States*, Supplement, 1915, pp. 393–396.

because the danger is already fully known and those who do not refrain because of the danger will not, in all probability, refrain because we request them to do so; and this is not the time to make it, not only for the reason Mr. Lansing suggests, but also because, as I urged this morning, it weakens the effect of our saying to Germany that we mean to support our citizens in the exercise of their right to travel both on our ships and on belligerent. If I thought the notice necessary, or effective, to save lives, the second objection might be waived, but since I do not, I think the second objection ought to prevail."[1]

Two of Bryan's cherished plans for modifying American action had now been rejected—postponing the accounting with Germany as we were doing with England, and getting our citizens out of the way of the retaliatory processes. One chance now remained—that of trying again to exact from the British the same degree of strict respect for our rights as we demanded from the Germans. To this Wilson had agreed, and to this hope Bryan now clung.

On the evening of the 14th, after a week of tremendous anxiety and pressure, Wilson was glad enough to escape in the Presidential yacht, the *Mayflower*, for a leisurely trip to New York, where he was to deliver an address and review the Atlantic fleet of the American navy. He was tired and showed it.[2] It was only by going to sea that he could escape even momentarily the exhausting requirements of his great office. Since boyhood he had loved the sea. He was a good sailor, never seasick, and even a short voyage rested and restored him.

The welcome in New York was tumultuous—a "great testimonial of trust and confidence"—assuring him of "having the people solidly with him." As he was driven to the official stand from which he was to review the land

---

[1] *The Memoirs of William Jennings Bryan*, p. 403.
[2] New York *Times*, May 15, 1915.

parade, dense crowds packed the sidewalks; the top of his automobile had been thrown back, and he stood up, bowing and smiling at the crowds.[1] A distinguished group met him at luncheon at the Biltmore Hotel, where he delivered a brief address expressing again and with deep earnestness and fervour his ideal of the mission of America:

"These quiet ships lying in the river have no suggestion of bluster about them. . . .

"We want no nation's property."[2]

He concluded with a solemn declaration that "the force of America is the force of moral principle . . . there is nothing else that she loves, and . . . there is nothing else for which she will contend."[3]

In the afternoon the President, standing on the bridge of the *Mayflower*, received the salute of twenty-one guns and reviewed the fleet, a magnificent spectacle of American power.

At this time there were the most convincing evidences not only of Wilson's personal popularity, but of the general approval of his note to Germany regarding the sinking of the *Lusitania*. Whatever may have been the differences among his advisers, he seems to have satisfied, in a remarkable degree, the great mass of American opinion.[4] He was flooded with messages of approval. President Eliot wrote:

"Your message to Germany is adequate and altogether admirable. Come peace, come war, you will have the American people at your back."[5]

The Lake Mohonk Conference of advocates of peace passed a resolution of appreciation: his action was publicly

---

[1] New York *Times*, May 18, 1915.

[2] May 17, 1915. *The Public Papers of Woodrow Wilson*, Vol. III, p. 330.

[3] *Ibid.*, p. 332.

[4] Comments from the press and from governors, senators, and other public men, published in the New York newspapers, were overwhelmingly favourable.

[5] May 14, 1915.

approved by ex-President Taft. While some of the elements that Bryan represented were probably not enthusiastic, they were not vocal. Bryan himself had signed the note.

But Bryan was then hoping for a makeweight protest to England. While Wilson was in New York, Bryan sent him Lansing's draft of an immediate reply to Great Britain—"along the line suggested by you." Bryan wrote:

"Aside from its being deserved I think it will serve as a counter irritant. Personally I would rather deal with the matter of carrying passengers on belligerent ships but knowing your views on that I turn to this as the only immediate remedy."[1]

At the same time the President, encouraged by a message from House, was eagerly trying to get a voluntary concession from Great Britain that would relieve the tension with Germany. He cabled to House on May 16th:

"Deeply interested in your intimation that Sir Edward Grey would be favorable to lifting embargo on food to Germany, because that would afford a solution of a situation as trying and difficult for England as it is for us.

"Almost the same thing might be accomplished by action on the part of the British government which would assure our practically unmolested access to neutral ports with non-contraband goods, food being regarded as non-contraband goods.

"It would be well to ascertain as soon as you can, how far Sir Edward would be supported by his colleagues in such action, for things are likely to move rapidly now."

House could make no progress—he sent a "discouraging cable" on the 18th; Page was pessimistic; and Wilson cabled again, urgently, showing his determination to go forward with the protest to Great Britain that Bryan had been urging:

---

[1] May 16, 1915.

"It becomes more and more evident that it will presently become necessary, for the sake of diplomatic consistency and to satisfy our public, to address a note to Great Britain about the unnecessary and unwarranted interruption of our legitimate trade with neutral ports.

"It would be a great stroke on England's part if she would of her own accord relieve this situation, and so put Germany wholly in the wrong and leave her without excuse that the opinion of the world could tolerate. It would be a small price to pay for cessation of submarine outrages."[1]

House began at once to dicker with Grey, reporting a series of possible bargains or reciprocal concessions.[2]

It was folly on House's part to suppose that these schemes, as framed by Grey, had any chance of acceptance, even if supported by the rest of the British cabinet. In February, Germany had clearly stated that raw materials of manufacture would have to be admitted in addition to food as compensation for abandoning the submarine blockade just beginning; now that the campaign was proving its effectiveness the British not only still withheld that addition, but exacted from Germany the abandonment of gas warfare besides. Moreover, the freeing of foodstuffs and the other minor concessions offered were inadequate to satisfy the American complaints. Wilson perceived these difficulties, and, following his telegram to House of May 20th, dealing with the danger of seeming to admit a connection between our disputes with one government and those with the other,[3] he sent a forthright mes-

---

[1] May 18, 1915.

[2] See Colonel House to Woodrow Wilson, May 20, 1918. *The Intimate Papers of Colonel House*, Vol. I, pp. 446–448.

[3] "It seems to me very important indeed that we should not even seem to be setting off one government against the other, or try by any means resembling a bargain to obtain from either of them a concession of our undoubted rights on the high seas.

"Each government should understand that the rights we claim from it have no

sage on the 23rd, pointing out the entire insufficiency of the concessions proposed by the British:

"In your conversations with Sir Edward, please make it plain that it is not food-stuffs only in which we are interested, but all non-contraband shipments to neutral ports, and that the purchase of our cotton illegally intercepted does not help matters because it is the principle and not the money we must insist on.

"We feel that the blockade recently proclaimed has not been made in fact effective and the impression prevails here that Sir Edward Grey has not been able to fulfill his assurances given us at the time of the Order in Council that the order would be carried out in such a way as not to affect our essential rights.

"There is an accumulating public opinion here upon our matters of which I think the Ministers there should know, and the recent explanations do not touch the essence or meet the opinion."

There is a touch of asperity in this note: was House being used again in promoting the British policy of delay? Despite his lack of confidence in the proposed compromise, however, Wilson took it up with Gerard[1] with the not unexpected reply from Von Jagow[2] that Germany would accept if raw materials were included in addition to food, which House declared the Allies would not agree to.[3]

While these entirely fruitless negotiations were under way, time was passing. Any day the German reply to Wilson's note might come in, raising new and even more

---

connection which we can recognize with what we claim from the other, but that we must insist on our rights from each without regard to what the other does or does not do.

"I should like to accomplish what you suggest in your message to Gerard, but think it will have to be managed so as to be entirely free from the danger I have suggested. Can Gerard handle it in that way?"

[1] W. J. Bryan to J. W. Gerard, May 23, 1915. *Foreign Relations of the United States,* Supplement, 1915, p. 406.

[2] German Secretary of State for Foreign Affairs.

[3] *Foreign Relations of the United States,* Supplement, 1915, p. 415.

serious problems. Conditions, as Wilson cabled to Gerard, were "rapidly becoming intolerable to the whole world."[1] Italy was declaring war on Austria, Roumania was trembling on the brink, and Mexican affairs were again so uneasy that Wilson was considering issuing a statement.[2]

". . . we are dealing with passion . . . not with reason," Wilson wrote in a personal letter. "Nothing is calculable. One never knows what the next dispatch will contain, or what a day or an hour will bring forth."[3]

While he had indeed been greatly reassured by the public support so necessary to the statesman confronted with such problems—". . . I am deeply touched and rewarded above my desert by the extraordinary and generous support the whole country has given me in this German matter . . ."[4]—such confidence increased his "sense of overwhelming responsibility."

"I know, moreover, that I may have to sacrifice it all any day, if my conscience leads one way and the popular verdict the other."[5]

One bright star on the horizon—the generally favourable attitude of Latin America—served somewhat to comfort him.[6]

Wilson had been urgently seeking, as he cabled House on May 26th, "to influence the matter unofficially and avoid the strong note which must otherwise be sent." He continued to urge action upon Page:

"Will you not explain this to Page and ask him for me whether he will not also present to Sir Edward Grey the

[1]May 27, 1915. *Ibid.*, p. 418.

[2]Made public on June 2, 1915. See *The Public Papers of Woodrow Wilson*, Vol. III, pp. 339–340.

[3]Woodrow Wilson to Mary A. Hulbert, May 23, 1915.

[4]Woodrow Wilson to Nancy Toy, May 23, 1915.

[5]*Ibid.*

[6]On May 24th he delivered an address before the Pan-American Financial Conference at Washington, commenting on this general good feeling. *The Public Papers of Woodrow Wilson*, Vol. III, pp. 333–335.

many arguments for respecting our rights on the high seas and avoiding the perhaps serious friction between the two governments which it is daily becoming more and more evident cannot much longer be avoided if our access to neutral ports with neutral cargoes continues to be interfered with contrary to the assurances given us in note accompanying the Order in Council."

But House continued to urge delay. On May 28th came his telegram containing Page's hopeful predictions of improved English conduct with House's own advice that no new note be sent until the British government had answered the last one, and until the German answer to our note of May 13th was in. Thus the last of Bryan's hopes of a "counter-balancing" protest was frustrated; for only three days later (May 31st) the German reply to the American note reached Washington. From that moment onward the break with Bryan became inevitable.

Throughout these anxious negotiations Wilson's policy appears to have turned upon his consuming desire to keep out of the war. This was the keynote of his action—then and later. As between him and Bryan it was a difference of judgement as to what course would be most likely to keep America at peace. Again and again in these troubled months he expressed his central aim in his letters:

". . . I shall school myself to such a course of action as will keep the country out of war if it is humanly possible to maintain our rights without it."[1]

To Frank I. Cobb he wrote of his discouraging efforts to find a peace opening:

"I have tried to enter every door that was opened even by a mere crack but have always found that somebody had his back against it on the other side."[2]

---

[1] Woodrow Wilson to Senator Robert L. Owen, May 20, 1915.
[2] June 3, 1915.

III. THE BREAK WITH BRYAN

"Bryan's Position Is Rapidly Becoming Painful . . ."

Thus the heading in a New York newspaper on May 30th. It was true, though the reasons given at the time were not. It was no petty irritation on Bryan's part because the President was himself writing the notes that his Secretary signed, nor even because the advice of House, and at times of Lansing, seemed more persuasive than his own. Not a shadow of such resentment appears in any of his papers. The disagreement was based upon different conceptions of policy between two earnest men equally desirous of keeping out of the war.

Bryan, fearful of the effect of the first *Lusitania* protest, as we have seen, wanted a supplementary note sent out that would mitigate its force. He had gone even further than that; he had received the Austro-Hungarian ambassador, Dr. Dumba, who sought a possible means of softening the American attitude toward Germany. While his answers, as his own later report clearly showed, were scrupulously in accord with the policy adopted by the administration, the intent was plainly to mitigate the President's reply. He told Dumba to say to the German government that "he [Dumba] felt sure there was no desire for war in this country and that we expected Germany to answer the note in the same spirit of friendship that prompted ours."[1] In his agonizing solicitude he no doubt betrayed, less by what he said than by the way he said it, his lack of sympathy with the note of May 13th.

In any event the reaction in Europe was most unfortunate. Zimmermann, German Undersecretary of State for Foreign Affairs, said that the note "was not meant in

---

[1] W. J. Bryan to Woodrow Wilson, May 17, 1915, reporting his interview with Dumba. *The Memoirs of William Jennings Bryan*, p. 380.

earnest" and was only sent as a "sop to public opinion,"[1] and the news, of course, spread swiftly in diplomatic circles. While Bryan was able to clear himself immediately by producing the telegrams and the record of the conversation, the incident contributed to the lack of confidence, the uncertainty, regarding Bryan's fitness for the great office he occupied—however undeserved—which had persisted from the beginning. It was charged afterwards that the "Dumba incident" was the real cause of Bryan's resignation. It had nothing, directly, to do with it. As Wilson wrote to Bryan long afterwards:

"My attention has been called to a book in which the author states by very clear implication that I demanded your resignation as Secretary of State because of language used by you in an interview with Ambassador Dumba soon after the first *Lusitania* note. You may quote me as saying that I did not ask for your resignation or desire it, as anyone can learn from my note accepting your resignation. And this statement ought also to be a sufficient answer to the criticism of you based upon the Dumba interview ..."[2]

When the German reply to the President's note came in on May 31st, Bryan's anxiety greatly increased. It seemed to him that, unless drastic changes were made in American policy, war, and possibly immediate war, could not be avoided. The note itself[3] was argumentative, and certainly unsatisfactory in the sense that it did not directly meet the American contentions and demands. It implied that the policy of the submarine blockade would be continued and that cases involving neutrals arising under it would be dealt with individually. Finally, it ventured to contest the American assertion that the sinking of the

---

[1] James W. Gerard, ambassador to Germany, to W. J. Bryan, telegram of May 22, 1915. *Foreign Relations of the United States*, Supplement, 1915, p. 407.

[2] December 17, 1917.

[3] Dated May 28, 1915, sent by Gerard on May 29th. *Foreign Relations of the United States*, Supplement, 1915, pp. 419-421.

Lusitania was absolutely inexcusable and attempted to discuss the matter.

Wilson began at once to draft a reply—working entirely alone. His careful notes, both in shorthand and those written on his own typewriter, remain among his papers. It seems to have been completed in one evening, May 31st, after ten o'clock, with possible corrections early in the morning of June 1st.

It is almost impossible to exaggerate the strain under which the President was toiling at this time. His activities on a single day—this very Tuesday, June 1st, for example —demonstrate the load he was carrying. At ten o'clock he met the Washington correspondents, always a trying ordeal. He was "calm in his bearing,"[1] but refused to discuss the German note. At eleven the cabinet met.

"Bryan was a few minutes late. He seemed to be labouring under a great strain and sat back in his chair most of the time with his eyes closed."[2]

The President read aloud a proposed warning to be sent to factions in Mexico, and there was extended discussion— a highly difficult problem in itself. He then turned to the European situation, presenting the draft of his reply to Germany. There was little discussion of the note itself but heated argument over the demand for a simultaneous protest to Great Britain, which Bryan still hoped to have sent before the final German reply. When other members contested the idea of placing the two controversies on the same plane, Bryan went so far as to call them pro-Ally. Wilson rebuked him for the charge[3] and now came out definitely against the proposition of a new note to Great Britain on interference with neutral trade, which he had

---

[1]New York *Times*, June 2, 1915.

[2]David F. Houston, *Eight Years With Wilson's Cabinet*, Vol. I, pp. 132–133.

[3]This incident is incorrectly placed in the cabinet meeting of May 11th before the sending of the first *Lusitania* note, in *The Intimate Papers of Colonel House*, Vol. II, pp. 5–6.

earlier approved, saying it was "a singularly inappropriate time to take up such a matter with her."[1]

At the close of the meeting the President found himself confronted with a possible first break in his official family —and one that might have a sharp, even dangerous, reaction in the country. Bryan told him he thought it unfair to all concerned for him to remain in the cabinet. Up to this time the President's leadership among his close associates had been marked by extraordinary loyalty and approval.[2]

Most anxious to avert an open break, Wilson asked Bryan to submit new suggestions as to a course of action.

Later in the day Wilson met various visitors, wrote out important cable messages on his own typewriter, and took care of his always heavy correspondence. Yet he found time for his indispensable daily exercise—golf with Dr. Grayson.

The President's proposed note to Germany insisted again upon the principles embodied in acknowledged international law—however that law might apply, or fail to apply, to the new conditions and instrumentalities of warfare.

"Nothing but actual forcible resistance or continued efforts to escape by flight when ordered to stop for the purpose of visit on the part of the merchantman has ever been held to forfeit the lives of her passengers or crew."

---

[1] David F. Houston, *Eight Years With Wilson's Cabinet*, Vol. I, p. 137.

[2] On this very day, June 1st, Secretary Lane wrote to a friend:

"I feel that at last the country has come to a consciousness of the President's magnitude. They see him as we do who are in close touch with him. . . . My own ability to help him is very limited, for he is one of those men made by nature to tread the wine-press alone. The opportunity comes now and then to give a suggestion or to utter a word of warning, but on the whole I feel that he probably is less dependent upon others than any President of our time. He is conscious of public sentiment—surprisingly so— for a man who sees comparatively few people, and yet he never takes public sentiment as offering a solution for a difficulty; if he can think the thing through and arrive at the point where public sentiment supports him, so much the better. He will loom very large in the historian's mind two or three decades from now." (*The Letters of Franklin K. Lane*, p. 175.)

It went even further, asserting that there were also "principles of humanity" involved "which throw into the background any special circumstances of detail that may be thought to affect the cases."

The President went on to say with sober eloquence:

"Whatever be the other facts regarding the *Lusitania*, the principal fact is that a great steamer, primarily and chiefly a conveyance for passengers, and carrying more than a thousand souls who had no part or lot in the conduct of the war, was torpedoed and sunk without so much as a challenge or a warning, and that men, women, and children were sent to their death in circumstances unparalleled in modern warfare. The fact that more than one hundred American citizens were among those who perished made it the duty of the government of the United States to speak of these things and once more, with solemn emphasis, to call the attention of the imperial German government to the grave responsibility which the government of the United States conceives that it has incurred in this tragic occurrence, and to the indisputable principle upon which that responsibility rests. The government of the United States is contending for something much greater than mere rights of property or privileges of commerce. It is contending for nothing less high and sacred than the rights of humanity, which every government honors itself in respecting and which no government is justified in resigning on behalf of those under its care and authority."

Bryan had given sleepless hours to the consideration of the note as the President had drafted it.

"More than once he came home with bloodshot eyes and weary steps . . . He would lie awake three and four hours at a time, tossing, jotting down memoranda . . ."[1]

On the following day he sent a long letter to Wilson

[1] *The Memoirs of William Jennings Bryan*, pp. 420-421.

pleading for delay in sending the reply, arguing that ample time should be taken for deliberation in accordance with the spirit of his "cooling-off" treaties. He also favoured judicial consideration of the allegations of fact brought by the Germans, arguing that the preliminary requirement of acceptance of principles was contrary to customary procedure. He disagreed with Lansing on the rights of passengers in armed ships, arguing "the character of the vessel is determined, not by whether she resists or not, but by whether she is armed or not . . . the fact that she is armed raises the presumption that she will use her arms . . ."[1]

On June 3rd, so exercised had Bryan become that he wrote two long letters to the President, one in the forenoon and the other in the afternoon. In both he reviewed again, rather footlessly, all of his former arguments, treating especially of the fact that the *Lusitania* carried ammunition, and disagreeing with Lansing's proposals. Some of his suggestions for future action did not meet the present crisis at all: he was never good at concrete, detailed reasoning. Fearful that the dispatch of the note "could only be followed by a withdrawal of representatives, which was perilously near war,"[2] he was still casting about for ways of alleviating the dangerous effect of our notes.

The whole matter was delayed until the cabinet meeting on June 4th. A "somewhat tiresome discussion" took place that "tried the President's patience greatly."[3]

---

[1]June 2, 1915. It was on June 2nd, too, that Wilson personally received the German ambassador to discuss means of overcoming the crisis. Bernstorff reports that he found the President determined upon two principal things: 1. To secure the cessation of submarine warfare; 2. To avoid war. He informed Bernstorff that he was principally concerned with the humanitarian aspect of the matter and that this would be emphasized in the forthcoming note which would be sharp. He also gave the ambassador to understand that diplomatic relations would be broken if a satisfactory reply were not received. But he made it clear that he desired a peaceable solution and agreed that all possible time and opportunities should be afforded for reaching one. (See Bernstorff, *My Three Years in America*, pp. 152–154.)

[2]*The Memoirs of William Jennings Bryan*, p. 422.

[3]David F. Houston, *Eight Years With Wilson's Cabinet*, Vol. I, p. 139.

Bryan's letters and the discussion seem only to have hardened him behind his purpose.

"I hope," he wrote to Bryan the next morning, "that you realize how hard it goes with me to differ with you in judgement about such grave matters as we are now handling. You always have such weight of reason, as well as such high motives, behind what you urge that it is with deep misgiving that I turn from what you press upon me.

"I am inclined to think that we ought to take steps, as you suggest, to prevent our citizens from travelling on ships carrying munitions of war, and I shall seek to find the legal way to do it. I fear that, whatever it may be best to do about that, it is clearly impossible to act before the new note goes to Germany.

"I am sorry to say that, study as I may the way to do it without hopelessly weakening our protest, I cannot find a way to embody in our note the principle of long discussion of a very simple state of facts; and I think that our object with England can be gained better by not sending a note in connection with this one than by sending it; and, after all, it is our object and the relief of our trade that we wish to accomplish.

"I recast the note last night. I hope you will think a little better of it.

"I would be very much obliged if you would go over it for substance, making any suggestions that may occur to you, and that you will ask Mr. Lansing to go over it for form and validity of statement and claim.

"With the warmest regard, and with a very solemn and by no means self-confident sense of deep responsibility . . ."[1]

Bryan made one last desperate appeal, expressing again his fear that the note "might rush us into war":

"If the initiative were with us, I would not fear war for

[1] June 5, 1915.

I am sure you do not want it, but when the note is sent it will be Germany's next move. . . . This may be our last chance to speak for peace. . . ."

He was speaking here not only as a pacifist, but as a politician, for he believed deeply that the country was overwhelmingly opposed to war. He said in his letter, "the sober judgement of the people will not sustain any word or act that *provokes* war . . ."[1] He had told his wife:

"If I resign now, I believe it will be possible to bring the real sentiments of the people to the surface."[2]

Various members of the cabinet discussed the crisis with both Wilson and Bryan. Wilson said he was sorry personally, for he had a real affection and admiration for Bryan, but he thought him wrong in his contentions. He discussed also a successor, eliminating House, on account of his health, and Lansing as not a big enough man.[3]

At noon on Monday the 7th, Bryan spent an hour with the President, passionately pleading against a course he felt certain would mean war: the President doing his best to dissuade him from resigning, arguing that his fears were exaggerated and that his course would only increase the difficulties and dangers of the situation. Bryan's agitation and anxiety were painful. Sending out for a glass of water, his "hand was so unsteady that he upset a part of it as he raised it to his lips."[4]

---

[1]June 5, 1915.

[2]*The Memoirs of William Jennings Bryan*, p. 423.

[3]David F. Houston, *Eight Years With Wilson's Cabinet*, Vol. I, p. 141. In the end, Wilson called in Lansing on June 23rd. When Lansing objected that he had little political prestige, Wilson said to him:

"By experience and training you are especially equipped to conduct the foreign affairs of the United States. This, under present conditions, is far more important than political influence." (Lansing's notes, published in the *Saturday Evening Post*, April 18, 1931.)

He was the best material at hand, he could put diplomatic notes in proper form and advise on international law, and the President had determined for the future to be practically his own Secretary of State. (W. G. McAdoo, *Crowded Years*, p. 338 ff.)

[4]Article in the Springfield *Republican*, July 27, 1925.

Bryan toiled painfully over his letter of resignation which was presented the next morning:

June 9th [8th] 1915

MY DEAR MR. PRESIDENT:

It is with sincere regret that I have reached the conclusion that I should return to you the commission of Secretary of State with which you honored me at the beginning of your administration.

Obedient to your sense of duty, and actuated by the highest motives, you have prepared for transmission to the German government a note in which I cannot join without violating what I deem to be an obligation to my country, and the issue involved is of such moment that to remain a member of the cabinet would be as unfair to you as it would be to the cause which is nearest my heart, namely, the prevention of war.

I, therefore, respectfully tender my resignation, to take effect when the note is sent unless you prefer an earlier hour. Alike desirous of reaching a peaceful solution of the problems arising out of the use of submarines against merchantmen, we find ourselves differing irreconcilably as to the methods which should be employed.

It falls to your lot to speak officially for the nation; I consider it to be none the less my duty to endeavor as a private citizen to promote the end which you have in view by means which you do not feel at liberty to use.

In severing the intimate and pleasant relations which have existed between us during the past two years permit me to acknowledge the profound satisfaction which it has given me to be associated with you in the important work which has come before the State Department, and to thank you for the courtesies extended. With the heartiest good wishes for your personal welfare and for the success of your administration, I am, my dear Mr. President,

Very truly yours,

W. J. BRYAN.

Wilson at once replied:

June 8, 1915

MY DEAR MR. BRYAN:

I accept your resignation only because you insist upon its acceptance; and I accept it with much more than deep regret,

with a feeling of personal sorrow. Our two years of close association have been very delightful to me. Our judgements have accorded in practically every matter of official duty and of public
policy until now; your support of the work and purposes of the
administration has been generous and loyal beyond praise;
your devotion to the duties of your great office and your eagerness to take advantage of every great opportunity for service it
offered have been an example to the rest of us; you have earned
our affectionate admiration and friendship. Even now we are
not separated in the object we seek but only in the method by
which we seek it.

It is for these reasons that my feeling about your retirement
from the Secretaryship of State goes so much deeper than regret.
I sincerely deplore it. Our objects are the same and we ought to
pursue them together. I yield to your desire only because I
must and wish to bid you Godspeed in the parting. We shall
continue to work for the same causes even when we do not work
in the same way.

With affectionate regard,

Sincerely yours,
WOODROW WILSON

HON. WILLIAM JENNINGS BRYAN,
Secretary of State.

Bryan attended the cabinet meeting that day but took
no part in the discussion. When he came in, "all the members stood up; there was no evidence of embarrassment in
any direction; the President greeted Bryan very graciously
... Bryan, looking exhausted and appearing to be under
a great emotional strain, leaned back in his chair with his
eyes closed."[1] The next morning, June 9th, Wilson wrote
to him:

"The note is now finished and will go forward probably
this afternoon ... I need not tell you again how sincerely
I deplore what is to accompany its dispatch."[2]

[1]David F. Houston, *Eight Years With Wilson's Cabinet*, Vol. I, p. 142.

[2]It was dispatched on June 9th and bore the signature of Robert Lansing, Secretary
of State *ad interim*. *Foreign Relations of the United States*, Supplement, 1915, pp. 436–
438.

While Bryan's resignation caused a tremendous pother in the press and much speculation as to the "real reasons," it did not result in the uprising of popular support that he apparently expected. Nor was the reaction to the note what he feared: it caused no immediate crisis. As a matter of fact, the note was as warmly received in America as the first protest—with many congratulatory letters and much favourable comment in the press.[1] It was Wilson, not Bryan, who held the country.

Several statements which Bryan issued to the press explaining his course attracted little attention, and he himself gradually subsided into a more or less unquestioning support of the administration. It is to be noted that, although they disagreed to the point of an open break on policies, neither Wilson nor Bryan ever doubted the sincerity of the other, or failed in personal admiration and respect. Long afterwards Bryan wrote to a correspondent:

"I notice you say that the more important affairs of my department were handled by the President. Here, again, you have evidently been misled by the misrepresentations of the Eastern press. No two officials ever got along more amicably. I was in charge of the department and the President and I never differed on a matter of policy until the controversy over American citizens riding on belligerent ships. He did not take a matter out of my hands; he consulted me on every proposition and our correspondence will show that he gave weight to my views. When I found that we differed on an important matter of policy in connection with the German note, I resigned. . . . You will

---

[1]Hearty approval came from a young man named Franklin D. Roosevelt, then Assistant Secretary of the Navy, to whom Wilson wrote, on June 14th:

"Your letter of June ninth touched me very much and I thank you for it with all my heart. Such messages make the performance of duty worth while, because, after all, the people who are nearest are those whose judgement we most value and most need to be supported by."

find my reasons stated in my resignation and they were accepted as the real reasons in his reply."[1]

One of Wilson's oldest friends tells of a discussion as to Bryan's sincerity with several cabinet officers. He reports the President's response when he heard of it:

"I can see W. W. now, looking up from his plate and piercing me with that sharp look which he sometimes had, and saying, 'He is *absolutely* sincere.' Then turning back to his breakfast, he added grimly, 'That is what makes him dangerous.'"[2]

---

[1] W. J. Bryan to George Denby, August 1, 1924.

[2] Stockton Axson to the author. In a speech at Colorado Springs, on October 7, 1912, Mr. Wilson said: ". . . I am more afraid of a sincere man who is mistaken than of a scoundrel who is trying to mislead us."

CHAPTER VIII

WILSON'S LOSING STRUGGLE FOR NEUTRALITY

It is hard with so many passionate forces abroad in the world to keep anything to a definite course of principle.

Woodrow Wilson to Lawrence C. Woods, September 7, 1915.

My chief puzzle is to determine where patience ceases to be a virtue.

Woodrow Wilson to E. M. House, September 20, 1915.

I am sorry to say that the gravest threats against our national peace and safety have been uttered within our own borders. There are citizens of the United States ... born under other flags but welcomed under our generous naturalization laws to the full freedom and opportunity of America, who have poured the poison of disloyalty into the very arteries of our national life ...

Annual Address to Congress, December 7, 1915.

Nations fighting for their lives cannot always pause to observe punctilios. Their every action is an act of war, and their attitude to neutrals is governed, not by the conventions of peace, but by the exigencies of a deadly strife.

The War Memoirs of David Lloyd George, Vol. II, p. 111.

I. TORN BETWEEN GREAT BRITAIN AND GERMANY

WILSON'S second *Lusitania* note, dispatched on June 9th, in spite of the fears that led to Bryan's resignation, caused surprisingly little reverberation. It was in no sense an ultimatum, unless the Germans chose to treat it as such: and this, it was plain, they had no desire to do. Indeed, they took a leaf out of Great Britain's book and postponed any reply whatever for a month. The result was actually a slump in the controversy with Germany, rather than a crisis: and at the same time, renewed irritation with Great Britain.

During the entire summer of 1915—indeed, until the end of the year—there was no shattering crisis comparable with the sinking of the *Lusitania:* but there were steadily gathering clouds, black with portents of the rising storm. Several lesser events, the sinking of the *Armenian* in June, the *Arabic* in August, the *Hesperian* in September, the *Ancona* in November, the cotton controversy with Great Britain during the late summer, all added to the difficulties and complications which the President had to meet. It was a period of interminable note-writing, protests, secret negotiations—with gradually increasing asperity on all sides.

American policy was reduced to futility. Lansing sought vainly to strait-jacket the controversies into the neat traditions of an outworn international legalism—while Europe was dealing terribly with instrumentalities, submarines, aëroplanes, poison gas, and the like, which were beyond law. In the note to Germany of June 9th Lansing had asserted that questions as to the carriage of contraband ammunition were "irrelevant to the question of the legality of the methods used by the German naval authorities in sinking the vessel."[1] At the same time he was arguing with the British that their blockade, in its effects on American commerce, was utterly illegal. To nations at one another's throats, fighting for their lives, seizing any and every weapon at hand, such wordy fleabites made little impression. Yet we continued to make demands upon both combatants, complied with by neither. There was no way then to remain truly neutral, there will be no way in future world wars unless we are prepared for the self-

---

[1] *Foreign Relations of the United States*, Supplement, 1915, p. 437.

WINSTON CHURCHILL'S HOUSE AT CORNISH, N. H., WHERE
WOODROW WILSON SPENT BRIEF VACATIONS FOR THREE
SUMMERS

GOLF LINKS AT CORNISH, N. H., WHERE WOODROW
WILSON PLAYED DURING BRIEF VACATIONS

discipline and the economic losses resulting from embargoes and other restrictions.

Conscious of this futility, Wilson was continuing, during all this period, as we shall see later, to explore every possibility of peace. He was also having to consider the growing anxiety in America, the partisanships now being fanned by widespread and partly secret propaganda, that were dividing our people into hostile groups. Congress would meet in December, and no one could tell when and how popular feeling might there express itself—it might even force the hand of the administration. Two powerful movements were springing up among the people themselves—a demand at one extreme for military preparedness, at the other for voluntary peace organizations. The first great meeting of the League to Enforce Peace was held at Philadelphia on June 17th, and on June 19th Bryan, sponsored by organized labour, was addressing a large peace meeting at Carnegie Hall in New York. Both of these movements must be closely watched and kept in hand.

During all of this time, from June until December 1915, the war itself was growing steadily more desperate, the combatants more reckless, the chance of any sort of accommodation less hopeful. It is not the intent here to enter into a complete account of the complicated developments of the period—that is the province of the historian rather than the biographer—but to make clear President Wilson's part in it, describe his difficulties, and above all, chronicle the gradual changes in his attitude of mind.

It is to be said that during all this period, although the President's personal sympathy with the Allied cause was steadily increasing, the controversies with Great Britain grew more irritating, caused him more anxiety, involved more thought than those with Germany. It is easy to see why this should be so. While many Americans were shocked emotionally or morally by what the Germans did, others were intensely irritated and indeed seriously endangered economically and financially—hurt in the pocketbook—by what the British did. The exactions of the British blockade disrupted American business and industry. Trade with Central Europe was destroyed: a loss not completely recompensed—and not recompensed according to the former proportions of foreign trade—by the increased business with the Allied nations. While trade in munitions was enormously prosperous and profitable, sales of cotton, wheat, and other commodities were languishing, with producers and dealers threatened with bankruptcy. Here again, as in former wars, everything turned upon the control of the seas. Great Britain had it, and, by virtue of it, was gradually involving America. It seems inevitable in any future world conflict that America, with its vast trade, cannot permanently remain neutral with Great Britain or any other belligerent in control of the sea. This was the problem that Wilson had to meet: and this, statesmen of the future whether they like it or not must also meet.

Wilson saw the problem with singular clarity. He had a gift of penetrating to the essence of a confused situation, and of setting it forth in a single brief paragraph or sentence. In a letter written on July 20th to his old friend of the Princeton years, Dr. Melancthon W. Jacobus, he analyzed the dilemma he was confronting—the dualism of the American position:

"The opinion of the country," he wrote, "seems to demand two inconsistent things, firmness and the avoidance of war, but I am hoping that perhaps they are not in necessary contradiction and that firmness may bring peace."

Peace here, as always, was his ultimate. When it became clear that the note to Germany of June 9th had not been regarded as an ultimatum, Wilson went out of his way to ease the strain still further. On July 8th we find him instructing Gerard, through Lansing, to let the Germans know of "the hearty willingness of this government to exercise its good offices with the object of effecting any arrangement which will lessen the dangers to non-belligerents in traversing the high seas," and that "this government is willing to consider and discuss any proposal or suggestion which is reasonable and practicable to discuss unless its purpose is to curtail the clear and established rights of the United States or of its citizens."[1] Even the news on June 30th of the sinking of the liner *Armenian* by a German submarine, with the loss of several Americans,[2] did not serve to sharpen the crisis with the Germans.

The British were plainly disappointed that the German crisis was passing without American involvement. Letters from Sir Edward Grey revealed how much hope he had based upon Colonel House's confident prediction, before leaving London, that the United States and Germany would soon be at war.

". . . the dilemma I foresee is that the desire of the people of the United States to keep out of war with Germany may lead to burying the *Lusitania* issue inconclusively, in which case Germany will disregard and the other belligerents will hope little from American influence in future and the tendency will be to discount it."[3]

At the same time British methods of enforcing their blockade were becoming more onerous to American traders. Their notes (such as the memorandum of June 17th[4]) were much like those of the Germans in evading the main

---

[1] *Foreign Relations of the United States*, Supplement, 1915, p. 462.

[2] *Ibid.*, p. 457.

[3] Sir Edward Grey to E. M. House, June 6, 1915. *The Intimate Papers of Colonel House*, Vol. II, p. 54.

[4] Forwarded by Walter H. Page on June 22nd. *Foreign Relations of the United States*, Supplement, 1915, pp. 443–446.

issue, while they continued with policies—which they no doubt considered absolutely necessary to the prosecution of the war—that caused constant friction. They were even then threatening the shipment of cotton, the most important American export, which had all along been on the "free list." In July these irritations became more provoking than usual, possibly because the British—owing to the fact that Grey, being temporarily incapacitated by his failing eyesight, took a month's vacation—displayed less than their usual sureness of touch in managing us.

At any rate a small tempest of protest broke out in America. A mass meeting at Madison Square Garden, on June 24th, under the auspices mainly of German and Irish societies and with Bryan on the programme, endorsed a resolution calling for an embargo to coerce Great Britain into respecting our rights and to redress the balance of our neutrality. About the same time the President received a petition adopted at a meeting of over four hundred representative American importers, protesting against the practical destruction of their business by Great Britain's tactics.[1] There were red-hot protests from many points in the South, where the condition of the cotton market was causing great alarm—some of them from sources powerful politically:

"I am writing you simply to say that I think the feeling against the flagrant violation of our rights upon the high seas by Great Britain is growing very strong and as soon as you should deem the time opportune a vigorous note of assertion and protest would, I think, meet the hearty approval of the people."[2]

To this Wilson replied:

"I think I feel to the full the force of what you say, but I feel, also, that it would be nothing less than folly to

---

[1] Petition dated June 22, 1915.
[2] Senator F. M. Simmons to Woodrow Wilson, July 3, 1915

press our neutral claims both against Germany and against Great Britain at one and the same time and so make our situation more nearly impossible.

"We are, as a matter of fact constantly in communication with the British government, pressing upon them our rights and the correction of their wrongs, and I think their position is slowly but steadily altering."[1]

The German reply on July 8th to the second *Lusitania* note played upon this growing feeling in America by dwelling forcibly on the case for retaliation against the illegal and inhumane methods of the British blockade.[2]

This note reached Wilson at Cornish, New Hampshire, where he had gone for a vacation, which lasted from June 25th (except for a few days) to August 12th. While he gave considerable thought to a possible reply, he seemed to feel that the controversy had lost its edge and might be allowed to drift.

"Apparently the Germans *are* modifying their methods; they must be made to feel that they must continue in their new way unless they deliberately wish to prove to us that they are unfriendly and wish war."[3]

He seems to have accepted the idea of the Springfield *Republican* that the United States might well accept the Germans' assurances in regard to future conduct and let them know that we stood by our principles, expecting them to be observed, and would shape our future attitude by their actions.[4]

---

[1] July 8, 1915.

[2] *Foreign Relations of the United States*, Supplement, 1915, pp. 463–466.

[3] Woodrow Wilson to E. M. House, July 14, 1915.

[4] The reply to the Germans, sent July 21st, worked out by the President and Mr. Lansing mostly by correspondence, cleverly met the situation. It was firm to the point of being an ultimatum: but it required no other answer than the future conduct of Germany, thus dispelling the fear of any immediate crisis. While the advocates of "direct action," like Page, were disappointed, they had to acknowledge the President's mastery and bide their time. (See *The Life and Letters of Walter H. Page*, Vol. II, p. 16; for the note itself, see *Foreign Relations of the United States*, Supplement, 1915, pp. 480–482.)

Easing of the strain with Germany enabled the President to obtain the rest he needed, as well as to find great enjoyment among the New Hampshire hills.

"I am well and profiting immensely by my delightful vacation, the first real one I have had since I went into politics."[1]

A few days later he wrote to Secretary McAdoo, his son-in-law, a warm personal letter:

"It was delightful to hear from you. We think of you all every day with deepest love. It is fine that the place is everything you hoped and expected and that you are yourself getting at least a little whiff of freedom and rest. I am faring famously. I have not had such a period of comparative rest and freedom for four years. We are all well and happy, and all unite in warmest love to precious Nell, the dear baby, yourself, and all."[2]

One of the things that no doubt contributed largely to the President's pleasure during these weeks of freedom was the visit to Cornish of Mrs. Galt and the presence of his daughters Margaret and Jessie and Eleanor. As he wrote to his old friend Fred Yates, on August 4th:

"We are spending the summer here in New Hampshire, in the same house we had last summer and the summer before, and become more and more attached to the place every year. Jessie and her husband, Frank Sayre, and their little boy are with me; so is Margaret; and my sister and her daughter are here. Nell ran over from Maine the other day for a few hours by motor to see us, and the glimpse we had of her refreshed and delighted us very much. She and her little daughter are getting on famously."

It was during these visits that the President told his daughters of his engagement to marry Mrs. Galt; but the public announcement was not made until October.

---

[1] Woodrow Wilson to E. M. House, July 7, 1915.
[2] July 8, 1915.

In the meantime British relationships were steadily growing more difficult. On July 19th Wilson telegraphed to House:

"Confidential message from Page informs us of very serious movement in England to force the government of the United States to make cotton contraband.

"You of course realize fatal effect that would have upon opinion here, probably changing attitude of this country towards the Allies and leading to action by Congress cutting off munitions.

"Would it not be well to get your press influence to work in England immediately."

On the following day he wrote again, anxiously, remarking that Sir Edward Grey's explanation to Page about the necessity of the British blockade "is perhaps true, but it will not satisfy the United States." He concluded:

"I should like to press for the utmost and yet I should wish to be sensible and practical."

And again, on the 27th:

"I feel very keenly the difficulties of dealing with Great Britain in regard to her present treatment of neutral trade . . . I wonder if you and Lansing discussed, in your talk the other day, a line of action at once practicable and effective that would escape the consequences you (and I) would dread and deplore? I would deeply appreciate any suggestions you may have thought out on this infinitely difficult matter. We cannot long delay action. Our public opinion clearly demands it."

He was here meeting the same old problem of method which had beset him before Bryan's resignation: should he protest openly and vigorously as Bryan had urged; or should he seek concessions by private negotiations, through diplomatic conversations, as House was urging?

There is no doubt that Wilson was finding the British situation far more difficult at the moment than the German controversy because he was more anxious to avoid dangerous consequences. Secretary Lane wrote:

"I saw him last night for a couple of hours, and the responsibility of the situation weighs terribly upon him. How to keep us out of war and at the same time maintain our dignity—this is a task certainly large enough for the largest of men."[1]

At the same time Page in England was so little in sympathy with his chief or with American opinion that he was almost hoping for another *Lusitania* outrage in order to force America into the war. He wrote to House on July 21st:

"It's a curious thing to say. But the only solution that I see is another *Lusitania* outrage, which would force war."[2]

When it became clear that Great Britain intended to proclaim cotton absolute contraband, Lansing, on July 26th, pointed out to Spring Rice that such action amounted to a confession that the blockade itself was not effective, since otherwise it would suffice to keep cotton out of Germany.

"I added that if cotton was made contraband, we would have to assume that the British theory of blockade, so far as neutral ports were concerned had been abandoned, and we would proceed on that assumption, which would create a very difficult situation."

He also dwelt upon the resentment sure to be caused in the United States by the proposed action.[3] But the British government could be moved by no such reasoning.

Wilson grew more and more worried. When Senator

---

[1] Franklin K. Lane to Frederic J. Lane, July 21, 1915. *The Letters of Franklin K. Lane*, p. 177.

[2] *The Life and Letters of Walter H. Page*, Vol. II, p. 26.

[3] See Robert Lansing to Walter H. Page, telegram, July 28, 1915, reporting his conversation with Spring Rice. *Foreign Relations of the United States*, Supplement, 1915, p. 490.

WOODROW WILSON AND MRS. WILSON, THEN MRS. NORMAN
GALT, WITH MAYOR RUDOLPH BLANKENBURG OF PHILA-
DELPHIA, ATTENDING THE WORLD SERIES BASEBALL
GAME BETWEEN THE PHILADELPHIA NATIONAL LEAGUE
AND THE BOSTON AMERICAN LEAGUE TEAMS AT THE
PHILADELPHIA NATIONAL LEAGUE PARK,
OCTOBER 9, 1915

Sheppard of Texas wrote him regarding the seriousness of the problem in the South, he replied:

"The whole subject is surrounded with complexities and difficulties . . . It does not seem as if we ought to go the length of involving the country in war and so cut off the market for cotton altogether, and yet there are many serious offenses being committed on the other side of the water."[1]

On August 4th House wrote to the President:

"Page is in a blue funk. . . . To read Page's letters one would think the Germans were just outside London and moving rapidly westward upon New York."[2]

By this time House had been long enough in America— he had returned from England on June 13th—to understand, somewhat more clearly, the real meaning of American public opinion, and he suggested a similar experience for Page:

"As soon as our affairs with Great Britain become less acute, I think it would be well to send for Page and let him have thirty or forty days in this country. The war has gotten on his nerves and he has no idea what the sentiment of the people in this country is in regard to it."[3]

To this Wilson replied on August 21st:

"With regard to Walter Page, I have this feeling: He is undoubtedly too much affected by the English view of things and needs a bath in American opinion; but is it wise to send for him just now, and is it not, after all, rather useful to have him give us the English view so straight?"

But it was also clear that House himself entirely sympathized with the Allies:

"Our hopes, our aspirations and our sympathies are closely woven with the democracies of France and Eng-

---

[1] July 28, 1915.
[2] *The Intimate Papers of Colonel House*, Vol. II, p. 62.
[3] *Ibid.*

land, and it is this that causes our hearts and potential economic help to go out to them and not the fear of what may follow for us in their defeat."[1]

II. THE GROWTH OF "INTENSE SYMPATHIES";
PROBLEMS OF PROPAGANDA

Midsummer, 1915, proved a trying time for the President. If the German submarine crisis was less acute, there were increasing evidences of the effort of Germany to arouse public opinion in the United States by widespread propaganda. Wilson wrote to House on August 4th:

". . . I am sure that the country is honeycombed with German intrigue and infested with German spies. The evidences of these things are multiplying every day . . ."

McAdoo was bombarding the President regarding the extent and virulence of this propaganda: and suggesting that the only way to meet it was to send Bernstorff home. Wilson himself had begun to doubt Bernstorff. As he wrote to House on July 29th:

"I feel as fully as you do the various difficulties of the situation, and the acute difficulty of our own public opinion, which is being deliberately framed against us. I do not feel that Bernstorff is dealing frankly with us, somehow, and, if you have the opportunity you might see what you can do to make him feel that it is up to him to do more than he has done to make his government realize facts as they are."

But he was not convinced that it was time to act. He wrote to McAdoo on August 21st:

"That was a terribly confident opinion you fired at me the other day about what I ought to do to Bernstorff. I wish the matter looked as simple as that to me."

His growing feeling in these matters was accentuated by the torpedoing, without warning, of the British liner

---

[1]E. M. House to Walter H. Page, August 4, 1915.

Arabic on August 19th, in which more Americans were lost, and by the storm of bitter comment in America that followed it.[1]

While Wilson confessed how disturbed he was[2] he was nevertheless unshaken in maintaining his attitude toward the problems involved:

"Two things are plain to me:

"1. The people of this country count on me to keep them out of the war;

"2. It would be a calamity to the world at large if we should be drawn actively into the conflict and so deprived of all disinterested influence over the settlement."[3]

But he was growing more and more irritated with the Germans. He wrote House on August 25th:

"I do not know what impression you have got from Bernstorff's request that we suspend judgement until we hear the German side of the sinking of the *Arabic*. I am suspicious enough to think that they are merely sparring for time in order that any action we might take may not affect the unstable equilibrium in the Balkans. Do you think that is too far fetched a suspicion? And how long do you think we should wait? When we *asked* for their version of the sinking of the *Orduna* they pigeon-holed the request and we have not heard yet!"

---

[1]Theodore Roosevelt represented one extreme of this highly heated opinion. On August 21st, he issued a statement:

"The time for words on the part of this nation has long passed, and it is inconceivable to American citizens, who claim to be inheritors of the traditions of Washington and Lincoln, that our governmental representatives shall not see that the time for deeds has come.

"What has just occurred is a fresh and lamentable proof of the unwisdom of our people in not having insisted upon the beginning of active military preparedness thirteen months ago." (New York *Times*, August 22, 1915.)

At the other extreme Bryan was declaring in a signed statement that the sinking of the *Arabic* was no cause for war, and reviving his arguments in favour of warning Americans off the danger zone, and of the postponement of final settlement. (New York *Times*, August 23, 1915.)

[2]In a letter to John Sharp Williams, August 21, 1915.

[3]Woodrow Wilson to E. M. House, August 21, 1915.

A little later, after the sinking of the *Hesperian* on September 4th:

"Shall we ever get out of the labyrinth made for us all by this German 'frightfulness'?"[1]

In spite, however, of the advice of his nearest advisers, both Lansing and House, urging drastic action, and the constant criticism of Page,[2] he did not lose patience.

"I must admit that I have at no time recently had any feeling of confidence that the German government would sufficiently yield to our demands to clear the situation, but you may be sure I have not lost patience and that I shall give the matter abundant time for proof."[3]

A few days later, however, on September 20th, irritated by the lack of progress of the negotiations with Bernstorff, whose government was "moving with intentional, and most exasperating slowness in the whole matter," he questioned sharply:

"The country is undoubtedly back of me in the whole matter, and I feel myself under bonds to it to show

---

[1] To E. M. House, on September 7, 1915.

[2] About this time Page's dispatches were particularly bitter. On September 8th he wrote to House that the American government was being laughed at in England for "seeming to jump at Bernstorff's unfrank assurances" (*The Life and Letters of Walter H. Page*, Vol. II, p. 32); and on the same day he cabled Lansing that the "feeling even of conservative men here seems hardening into the conviction that the United States is losing the fear and therefore the respect of foreign governments and of foreign opinion." (*Foreign Relations of the United States*, Supplement, 1915, pp. 537–538.)

Wilson's general attitude toward Page was expressed in his letter of August 21st to Colonel House already quoted (this volume, p. 371).

To Page himself he wrote on September 10th, showing how little he was disturbed by the criticisms:

"I do not often acknowledge your interesting letters, but that is not because they are not of vital interest to me but only because I have nothing to write in return which compares in interest with what you write to me. . . .

"Your letters are of real service to me. They give me what it would not be possible for me to get in any other way, and if it is not too great a tax upon you to write them as often as you do, I hope that you will not leave out a single line or item which is interesting your own thought. It is only in this way that I can get the atmosphere, which, after all, is quite as important as the event because it is out of the atmosphere that the event arises."

[3] Woodrow Wilson to O. G. Villard, September 16, 1915.

patience to the utmost. My chief puzzle is to determine where patience ceases to be a virtue."[1]

Nevertheless the crisis passed with the note of the German ambassador on October 5th that instructions to submarine commanders had been made so stringent as to render repetitions of the *Arabic* incident impossible.[2]

During these weeks of strain, in the late summer and early fall of 1915, it is clear, from the letters, that the President's attitude of mind was steadily changing. While his purpose remained the same, to keep America out of the war, his sympathies were more and more engaged by the Allied cause: it was more and more difficult to be neutral either in thought or in action. His letters show that he was beginning to distrust everything that the Germans did:

"Apparently they [the Germans] do not know how to keep faith with anybody, and we are walking on quicksand."[3]

In an address on October 11, 1915, at Washington, this change became apparent in a revision of the strict rule of neutrality which he had laid down in August 1914—to be "neutral in thought":

"Neutrality is a negative word. It is a word that does not express what America ought to feel. America has a heart and that heart throbs with all sorts of intense sympathies . . ."

But if America had these intense sympathies, she must still control them in the interest of her own ideals. He says:

". . . America has schooled its heart to love the things

[1] Woodrow Wilson to E. M. House, September 20, 1915.

[2] *Foreign Relations of the United States*, Supplement, 1915, p. 560. Wilson's effort to be fair, no matter what his feeling might be, is expressed in a comment to House on October 4th:

"It is hardly fair to ask submarine commanders to give warning by summons if, when they approach as near as they must for that purpose they are to be fired upon. It is a question of many sides and is giving Lansing and me some perplexed moments."

[3] Woodrow Wilson to Lucy M. Smith, September 15, 1915.

that America believes in and it ought to devote itself only to the things that America believes in; and, believing that America stands apart in its ideals, it ought not to allow itself to be drawn, so far as its heart is concerned, into anybody's quarrel."

Again he rose to an expression of his own deepest purpose: to keep the peace:

"We are not trying to keep out of trouble; we are trying to preserve the foundations upon which peace can be rebuilt."[1]

By the end of the year he was saying to Brand Whitlock, ambassador to Belgium, who visited him at the White House and who declared that he was "heart and soul for the Allies":

"So am I. No decent man, knowing the situation and Germany, could be anything else. But that is only my own personal opinion and there are many others in this country who do not hold that opinion. In the West and Middle West frequently there is no opinion at all. I am not justified in forcing my opinion upon the people of the United States and bringing them into a war which they do not understand."[2]

In spite, however, of changing feeling he continued to struggle to be neutral in action. Both sides were impossible! If the Germans had sunk the *Arabic* on August 19th, the British had declared cotton absolute contraband on August 20th. While the President was trying to decide what to do in view of the destruction of the *Arabic*, he was writing to House:

"We must write to England, and in very definite terms. Do you think that there is any chance of our getting them to rescind the Order in Council . . ."[3]

---

[1] *The Public Papers of Woodrow Wilson*, Vol. III, p. 378.
[2] *The Intimate Papers of Colonel House*, Vol. II, p. 50.
[3] August 21, 1915.

He was also having to face the persistent American criticism of the British blockade policy, supported by the reports of Consul General Skinner, that it operated to the advantage of British trade with neutral countries at the expense of American trade, hampered by so many interferences. There was undoubtedly some foundation for the charge, although the intent of the British government was another question.[1]

Demands for some action against the British and threats of an embargo on munitions by Congress grew more pressing—especially as the time for the winter session approached.

House, having a summer residence at Manchester, Massachusetts, near the summer residence of the British ambassador, was working for some means of mitigating the full effect of the announcement that cotton was to be made contraband. Spring Rice emphasized his government's reluctance to have trouble with the United States, but gave House to understand that "they would never forgive us if we pressed them to a point beyond what they considered fair, and took advantage of their unfortunate position."[2] He could count on House's sympathy!

Spring Rice finally suggested that the South might be relieved, at least in part, by an agreement under which the British would purchase large quantities of cotton at ten cents a pound—thus making up to America for the lost markets of central Europe.[3] When rumours of this pending arrangement reached the ears of the German ambassador, Bernstorff, he immediately wrote to Secretary Lansing,

---

[1] On August 13th the Foreign Office took advantage of the opportunity afforded by an inquiry from Skinner, made in June concerning British exports of cocoa, to present a long note denying that British trade with neutrals had profited by the blockade and maintaining that American trade with those neutrals had increased in greater proportion since the closing of German ports. *Foreign Relations of the United States,* Supplement, 1915, pp. 511-515.

[2] *The Intimate Papers of Colonel House,* Vol. II, p. 59.

[3] *Ibid.,* p. 60.

saying that his government stood ready to purchase a larger quantity of cotton than the British and at the full market price, if we could get it through to Germany.[1]

Wilson wrote to Lansing:

"Bernstorff's letter to you about the purchase of cotton is, indeed, amazing. What crude blunderers they are! The idea of offering us a palpable bribe,—or, rather, offering it to the Southern planters. How little they understand us!"[2]

These exchanges indicate clearly how difficult neutrality, at least in feeling, had become. We were quite willing to discuss proposals with the British which became reprehensible when suggested by the Germans. The intense and bitter feeling engendered by the war, inflamed by propaganda, was spreading in America.

Schemes for easing the effect of the cotton proclamation went still further. The hard-driven Allies were short of money. How could they purchase cotton and thus relieve the frightened Southerners? The old suggestion was immediately advanced that American credit should be extended; we should loan the British money to buy our own cotton. This was hotly opposed by certain members of the Federal. Reserve Board, chiefly A. C. Miller and Paul M. Warburg, the latter holding that our government should maintain entire control of the cotton situation by a valorization scheme, instead of allowing the British to control the price-determining surplus. The upshot was that no special purchase scheme was ready when the text of the British proclamation reached Washington on August 24th.

But the situation had to be met: the South was thoroughly aroused. Always, in its efforts to maintain neutrality, the administration was under compulsion from

---

[1] August 6, 1915.

[2] August 9, 1915. Letter written on the President's own typewriter.

immense economic interests at home. Among large numbers of Americans it mattered little—at least at this time—which side was right or wrong, or indeed which side was favoured by American diplomacy, so long as their own daily bread and butter were not endangered. Secretary McAdoo met the situation by issuing a statement to the press to the effect that the Treasury would deposit, if it should become necessary, $30,000,000 or more in Southern Federal Reserve banks for loans on cotton warehouse certificates.[1] Wilson followed it up immediately with a letter to W. P. G. Harding, of the Federal Reserve Board:

"What interests me most is this: It is evident from what you tell me that the country banks with whom the farmer and other producers directly deal can get money at from four to four-and-a-half per cent. and that the question whether the benefit of this advantageous rate is to be extended to the farmer is in their hands. It is inconceivable to me that those who are responsible for dealing directly with the producers of the country should be willing to jeopard the prosperity of the country itself by refusing to share with the producer the beneficial rates now obtainable for money loans. I think that we can confidently expect that the banks in the cotton states and in the agricultural regions generally will content themselves with a rate not more than one or two per cent. above the rate which they themselves pay. I hope that the facts which you have stated to me will become generally known among the producers of the country so that they may feel themselves free to exact of the banks with which they deal what they undoubtedly have a right to expect."[2]

This letter, read before the Alabama Merchants' Association at Birmingham, Alabama, on August 25th, with

[1]August 23, 1915.
[2]August 23, 1915.

McAdoo's announcement, went far toward reassuring the South, but it did not, after all, meet the real and great difficulty, that the Allied governments were running out of money. This not only threatened our cotton industry: it interfered with the whole Allied programme of supplying their war needs from the United States. The balance of trade, which had been against us the year before, was now running heavily in our favour. Foreign exchange, in spite of gold shipments and the sale of American securities by the British and French, was falling steadily. McAdoo, who was the closest to these difficulties, wrote a long, vigorous, and anxious letter to the President on August 21st pointing out that unless large American credits were forthcoming, British and French purchases would have to be curtailed and the prosperity of American industry would be checked.[1]

It is to be noted that the emphasis was no longer, as it was a year before, upon the recovery of a reasonable balance, but upon *expansion* to meet the war requirements of the Allies. Instead of seeking means to meet payments owed by us abroad, we must now finance payments owed by the Allies here, thus becoming a creditor nation on a large scale.

McAdoo used strong language: it was "imperative" that England establish at once large credits in this country —"at least $500,000,000." An appalling sum—exactly double the amount by which we stood indebted in London in August 1914. The trade balance against Europe at the end of the year would be approximately two and a half billions. It was indeed a huge financial stake we were coming to have in the cause of the Allies!

---

[1] "Great Britain is, and always has been, our best customer. Since the war began, her purchases and those of her allies, France, Russia, and Italy, have enormously increased. Food products constitute the greater part of these purchases, but war munitions, which as you know embrace not only arms and ammunition, but saddles, horses and mules and a variety of things, are a big item."

But a serious obstacle stood in the way. This was the bold and unprecedented statement made by Bryan, with the approval of Wilson, in August 1914, that "in the judgement of this government, loans by American bankers to any foreign nation which is at war are inconsistent with the true spirit of neutrality."[1]

McAdoo argued in his letter that this position, which had been reaffirmed during 1915, was "most illogical and inconsistent. We approve and encourage sales of supplies . . . but we disapprove the creation of . . . credit balances here to finance . . . purchases." The prohibition should rightly and logically be modified. Furthermore, it had broken down already. The German government had floated in Philadelphia and New York $10,000,000 short time bonds during the last spring.[2]

"To maintain our prosperity, we must finance it. . . . I haven't the slightest fear. . . . Our credit resources are simply marvelous now."

Wilson made no immediate reply to McAdoo. He had not only adopted the original policy as "sound in principle," but it was plain that such loans, at the very time when he was struggling to secure a modification of the British blockade, would drive us still further into the Allied camp. He therefore delayed a decision at a time when days were weeks, and weeks, months.

McAdoo, who was under urgent pressure from banking and business interests, finally sought the help of Lansing. Both would train their guns on the President. More than two weeks after McAdoo's plea the Secretary of State (on September 6th) was ready with a carefully prepared

---

[1] See for full discussion of this action, this volume p. 175 ff.

[2] The French had also managed to borrow $10,000,000. These were "credit" loans. As early as October 1914 Wilson acknowledged a difference, as Lansing put it, between "general loans" and "credit loans." Over credit loans, as over sales of contraband, the government had no authority to act. What McAdoo and Lansing wanted was consent for general loans.

letter. His argument was based not merely, as McAdoo's had been, on the risk to our prosperity, but on the threat of positive disaster to our economic system, if not to that of Europe.

"To withdraw any considerable amount [of the gold in the vaults of the European nations] would disastrously affect the credit of the European nations, and the consequence would be a general state of bankruptcy."

The result of a stoppage of our trade in Europe would be "industrial depression . . . numerous failures, financial demoralization, and general unrest and suffering among the labor classes."

By this time Wilson had become plainly disturbed. An Anglo-French Financial Commission, headed by Lord Reading, Lord Chief Justice of England, was even then on the Atlantic bound for New York to discuss the situation with American bankers. A decision had to be reached.

On September 7th Wilson conferred with both McAdoo and Lansing at the White House. Of this most important meeting there remains no account, but the result was plain enough. Wilson's earlier policy went down before the relentless pressure of circumstance and necessity. McAdoo had said in his letter that the problem had now become so huge for England that she must "go whole hog." Having become equally involved in the economic maze, it was true also for Wilson and for America. These problems could have been met only at the beginning of the war, and Wilson had at that time no legal sanctions either in accepted international law or in adequate neutrality legislation in the United States; and American public opinion, at that time, had neither the knowledge of foreign relationships to form far-seeing judgements, nor the imagination and the fortitude to bear the strain of a neutrality that would have been economic as well as legal.

Three days later the British Commission arrived in New York. Conversations with American financiers, headed by Morgan, were at once begun in regard to a loan of half a billion, although an amount double that was occasionally mentioned. There were vehement protests, one from Senator Chamberlain, of Oregon, which the President forwarded to McAdoo with the suggestion that it was "important that his misapprehensions should be corrected, or, rather, that he should be shown the real significance of this loan, namely, the maintenance of international exchanges whose breakdown would be absolutely disastrous to the United States. I wonder if you could not get the information conveyed to him without its seeming like an administration announcement in this matter with which we really have nothing to do."[1]

Conferences on the loan did not proceed quite smoothly. Some American bankers objected to its being used to cover purchases of munitions, and this aspect of it was suppressed, emphasis being laid upon the purchase of American wheat. The contract was signed on October 15th.[2]

It is a comment upon the essential unneutrality of these developments—however necessary to avoid disaster in the United States—that Germany's agreement to moderate her submarine policy was accompanied by new developments, financial and economic, of crucial advantage to the Allies. The situation was perfectly clear to Colonel House.

"We have given the Allies our sympathy and we have given them, too, the more substantial help that we could not offer Germany even were we so disposed—and that is an unrestricted amount of munitions of war and money.

---

[1] September 17, 1915.

[2] This action did not pass without sharp criticism. Bryan spoke to Lane (Lane letter to Wilson, September 16th) in strong opposition to any English and French war loan which, he said, was "furnishing money to the Allies with which to buy munitions to destroy their enemies."

In addition to that, we have forced Germany to discontinue her submarine warfare."[1]

In the face of all these difficulties, these evidences of changing feeling, the President continued to pursue his great objective: to keep America out of the war. He continued to hope and indeed to work, as we shall see presently, for some opening toward mediation. So it was that the correspondence and the conversations dragged on from day to day, with the war in Europe steadily growing more implacable. On October 21st, the note on the British blockade—a formidable document amounting to an indictment of the entire British policy[2]—which had been so often threatened, was sent. Wilson himself had little to do with it: he wrote a friend on November 17th:

"I had very little hand indeed in the preparation of the note. I merely touched up its phraseology here and there. Lansing wrote it, and it seems to me an unanswerable paper."[3]

It was probably unanswerable as a legal document: but how far was this from being a legal war!

The note of October 21st did something to create an impression of impartial dealing with the belligerents—an

---

[1] *The Intimate Papers of Colonel House*, Vol. II, p. 72, letter to Page, October 6th. House evidently regretted Wilson's patience. He thought we "had lost our opportunity to break with Germany, and it looked as if she had a better chance than ever of winning, and if she did win our turn would come next . . ." (House's diary account of a conversation with the President about this time. *Ibid.*, p. 85.)

[2] *Foreign Relations of the United States*, Supplement, 1915, pp. 578–601. Colonel House had recommended that the note should not be too categorical in its insistence upon effective blockade, saying that he had conversed with Lord Reading attempting to win an amicable adjustment (E. M. House to Woodrow Wilson, October 17, 1915, and October 19, 1915). Also he had written to Sir Edward Grey a letter which he told Wilson would "minimize all chance of trouble, for he will sense the big things in your mind, and nothing in the note will unduly disturb him." (E. M. House to Woodrow Wilson, October 19, 1915.) Such confidential suggestions no doubt smoothed over our relations with the British government, but they severely weakened the effectiveness of our formal note by methods familiarly used by Page.

[3] Woodrow Wilson to Lucy M. Smith.

impression greatly resented by the British and their sympathizers, as Page reported.[1]

But there was, in fact, no sign of relaxation of the blockade. Rather, it grew more drastic—and the diplomatic correspondence more irritating, so that resolutions directed against both British and German conduct were offered in Congress when it met in December. During the latter months of the year, Wilson seemed to have had little personal part in the controversies. His hands were full of other matters.

He was annoyed by the increasing and often utterly wild reports of propaganda on the part of all the belligerents, but chiefly Germany.[2] It was impossible to check it up or decide where it might be at work; sabotage was suspected, and there were even wild rumours of secret preparations for outbreaks. In that atmosphere, tense with emotion and suspicion, almost any report was credible. On August 25th we find Wilson writing to House:

"I note what you say about being prepared for a possible outbreak in this country; but *where* and *how?* I have thought of that, of course, and with the greatest solicitude; but, though we have followed up every clue, even the most vague, when reports reached us of alleged preparations for outbreak, we have found nothing definite enough to form the basis of even so much as guessing *where* we ought to be ready. What had you in mind? Does your own thought fix the danger definitely enough at any one point in the country to make it possible to suggest any particular concentration of force, or precautionary vigilance?"

Documents stolen from Councillor Albert of the German embassy on an elevated train in New York by an American secret service man gave glimpses of what was going on

---

[1]In his letter to the President of November 19, 1915.

[2]A fact which seems to have escaped attention at this time, and for long afterwards, is that equal if not better propaganda work was being done by the British.

behind the scenes, and caused McAdoo, as we have already
seen, to suggest the recall of the German ambassador.
More specific evidence was furnished in August and
September through the seizure by the British of correspondence carried for Dr. Dumba, the Austrian ambassador, by the American newspaper correspondent,
Archibald. This concerned mainly the promotion of plots to
interfere with the production of munitions for the Allies.
Wilson wrote of the matter to House, on September 7th:

"I see no escape from asking the Austrian government
to replace Dumba with someone who will know better
what he is privileged and what he is not privileged to do.
Do you? And yet, if Dumba, why not Bernstorff also?
Is there any essential difference? And the request that
both of them be withdrawn would have to be managed
mighty well if the implication of a diplomatic breach is to
be avoided."

Dumba, and later Von Papen and Boy-Ed, military and
naval attachés of the German embassy staff, were sent
home, and without resulting in a breach of relations with
the Central Powers. Even the sinking of the *Ancona*, with
Americans on board, by the Austrians on November 7th
was finally negotiated, not without a serious consideration
of the breaking of relations, into an eddy of diplomatic
delay.

But these disclosures of the extent of the secret propaganda in the country, avidly reported in the press, com-
bined with the news of the sinking, one after another, of
ships by German submarines with the loss of American
lives—the execution of the British nurse, Edith Cavell, on
October 13th, played its part—were steadily building up a
nervous, critical, hostile feeling in America. There were
sharp charges that after six months there had been no
settlement even of the *Lusitania* case. What would Congress say?

"Something must be done," wrote Lansing to Wilson on November 24th, "before Congress assembles or else I am afraid we will have some embarrassing requests for the correspondence."

Wilson was able to report in his address to Congress on December 7th the still unbroken circle of our relationships with all the belligerents, and that our position of influence for peace was not impaired.

But the situation all around had become as dangerous as it could well be. Besides the repercussions of the turmoil in Europe, public opinion in America was steadily growing more nervous, anxious, excited, with powerful demands for military preparation.

From this point onward, the emphasis of interest and effort, so far as the President was concerned, shifted from problems of neutrality to a vigorous and difficult campaign for American military and naval preparedness, which will be fully presented in a following volume.

INDEX

DETERMINED NEUTRALITY

His first reaction to the World War one of incredulity, 1; says to newspapermen on August 3, 1914, after Germany has declared war on France: ". . . So far as we are concerned, there is no cause for excitement," 2; his statement to the newspapermen encouraged a greater calmness of view throughout the country, 3; prepares to issue proclamations of neutrality between the United States and the warring nations, and considers the tender of "good offices" of the United States in the interest of mediation, 3; discouraged by responses from Sir Edward Grey and Ambassador Page on the subject of the suggested offer of the "good offices" of the United States in the European crisis, August 3, 1914, 5–6; frustrated, but does not give up his hope of pacifying the maddened nations, 6; on August 5th offers his "good offices" to the nations of Europe, but none of them accepts, 8–10; does his best, in the early days of the war, to maintain a position of friendly service to the warring nations, 10; approves the State Department's dispatch urging recognition of the Declaration of London by the warring nations, 12; despite the war, follows with

the Declaration of London would be useless, 217–218; approves Lansing's dispatch to Page, October 22, 1914, formally withdrawing from insistence on the Declaration as the basis of our contentions, 218; disturbed by Page's messages and his reference to "library lawyers," 218–219; Page in a letter to him, October 28th, is delighted over the withdrawal of the demand for the acceptance of the Declaration, without change, 219; Professor Hugo Münsterberg complains to him that American policy favours the Allies at the expense of the Germans, 222–225; Lansing's statement to him refutes the Münsterberg charges—and shows how impossible it is to achieve any real neutrality, 225–228.

PROTESTS AGAINST INTERFERENCE WITH AMERICAN SHIPPING

Agrees with Lansing about protesting the action of the British authorities in seizing the tank steamer *Brindilla*, 229; revises the first public protest of the American government against the conduct of Great Britain in interfering with American shipping, 231; the inherent weakness of the protest to Great Britain pleases the British and irritates the Germans and German-Americans, and Senator Stone hurries to see him, with charges of unneutrality, 234; opposes the resolution of Congressman Bartholdt demanding that the American government stop selling arms to the Allies, 235; confers with Bryan and Lansing over the response to charges of unneutrality, 236–237; the administration's defense of American policy is a defense of the British blockade, 237; his reaction to the British reply to the American protest shows him fully committed to the policy of avoiding any real contest with Great Britain, 239; with both the British and the Germans irritated and complaining of American unneutrality, his situation is utterly impossible, 239–240; disturbed by Page's stormy letters, in a long telegram to him he defends the German and Irish elements in the United States, 241–242; the announcement of the German blockade of England turns his attention toward Germany, 243–244.

"STRICT ACCOUNTABILITY"

Amazed by Ambassador Gerard's report of an anti-American campaign of hate in Germany, 246; Lansing sends him a draft of a sharp reply to the German proclamation, of February 4, 1915, of a blockade of the British Isles, and the following day Lan-

sing seems to have a change of heart, 247; corrects Lansing's draft of the protest of February 10th to Germany against the proclamation of blockade, and revises and adds to Lansing's simultaneous protest to Great Britain against the use of neutral flags on British ships, 248–252; tells Colonel House he regretted "the necessity of sending the note [to Great Britain] about the unauthorized use of our flag," 252; ". . . England and Germany are likely to drive us crazy, because it looks oftentimes as if they were crazy themselves . . .", 253; skeptical of the usefulness of a vigorous protest to all belligerents against their indiscriminate use of mines, suggested by Lansing, 256–257; at his suggestion Lansing drafts an identical note to Great Britain and Germany criticizing the use of mines and laying down the lines of a suggested compromise, and the note is sent on February 20th, 257–258; cautions Colonel House (in London) against the dilatory tactics of the British on the subject of peace and emphasizes the importance of the note of February 20th, 258, 262; the note of February 20th is unsuccessful, 258–259; says that the conditions of war have changed but the rules have not, 261; still (March 7th) has not been driven to the decision as to which side in the war is absolutely right and which absolutely wrong, 261–262.

THE CRISES OF THE "FALABA," THE "CUSHING," AND THE "GULFLIGHT"

Urged by Lansing to take instant and vigorous action when the British ship *Falaba* is sunk (March 28th) and an American life is lost, 265; Bryan, profoundly disturbed by the *Falaba* sinking, urges him to await further information, 265–266; Lansing sends him an opinion of the joint State and Navy Neutrality Board that the sinking of the *Falaba* was "not only illegal but revoltingly inhuman," 266–267; Germans, French, and British are critical of his neutrality policies, 267–268; in the utter confusion of advice and criticism, strives earnestly for calmness and impartiality, 268–270; Bryan argues that the Germans are not unreasonable and suggests that he make a public appeal for peace, 271–272; instructs Lansing to draft a note to Germany marked by severity, and Bryan protests and again pleads that he make an open appeal for the acceptance of mediation, 272–273; his reply to Bryan states that an appeal for peace would be futile and probably offensive, his letter foreshadowing the break between them soon to come, 274–275.